BLOOMSBURY SEMIOTICS

VOLUME 3

Bloomsbury Semiotics
General Editor: Jamin Pelkey

Volume 1: History and Semiosis
Edited by Jamin Pelkey

Volume 2: Semiotics in the Natural and Technical Sciences
Edited by Jamin Pelkey and Stéphanie Walsh Matthews

Volume 3: Semiotics in the Arts and Social Sciences
Edited by Jamin Pelkey, Susan Petrilli and Sophia Melanson Ricciardone

Volume 4: Semiotic Movements
Edited by Jamin Pelkey and Paul Cobley

BLOOMSBURY SEMIOTICS

SEMIOTICS IN THE ARTS AND SOCIAL SCIENCES

VOLUME 3

*Edited by Jamin Pelkey, Susan Petrilli and
Sophia Melanson Ricciardone*

BLOOMSBURY ACADEMIC
LONDON • NEW YORK • OXFORD • NEW DELHI • SYDNEY

BLOOMSBURY ACADEMIC
Bloomsbury Publishing Plc
50 Bedford Square, London, WC1B 3DP, UK
1385 Broadway, New York, NY 10018, USA
29 Earlsfort Terrace, Dublin 2, Ireland

BLOOMSBURY, BLOOMSBURY ACADEMIC and the Diana logo are trademarks
of Bloomsbury Publishing Plc

First published in Great Britain 2022

Copyright © Bloomsbury Publishing Plc, 2022

Jamin Pelkey, Susan Petrilli and Sophia Melanson Ricciardone have asserted their right under the
Copyright, Designs and Patents Act, 1988, to be identified as Editors of this work.

For legal purposes the Acknowledgements on p. xv constitute an extension of this copyright page.

Cover design: Tjaša Krivec
Cover illustration by Rebecca Heselton

All rights reserved. No part of this publication may be reproduced or transmitted in
any form or by any means, electronic or mechanical, including photocopying, recording, or any
information storage or retrieval system, without prior permission in writing from the publishers.

Bloomsbury Publishing Plc does not have any control over, or responsibility for, any third-party
websites referred to or in this book. All internet addresses given in this book were correct at the
time of going to press. The author and publisher regret any inconvenience caused if addresses have
changed or sites have ceased to exist, but can accept no responsibility for any such changes.

A catalogue record for this book is available from the British Library.

A catalog record for this book is available from the Library of Congress.

ISBN:	HB:	978-1-3501-3936-7
	ePDF:	978-1-3501-3938-1
	eBook:	978-1-3501-3937-4
	Set:	978-1-3501-3944-2

Series: Bloomsbury Semiotics

Typeset by Integra Software Services Pvt. Ltd.
Printed and bound in Great Britain

To find out more about our authors and books visit www.bloomsbury.com
and sign up for our newsletters.

CONTENTS

LIST OF FIGURES	vii
LIST OF TABLES	viii
LIST OF CONTRIBUTORS	ix
ACKNOWLEDGEMENTS	xv
LIST OF ABBREVIATIONS	xvi

Introduction   1
Susan Petrilli and Sophia Melanson Ricciardone

1 Semiotics in Philosophy and Critical Theory   17
   Vincent Colapietro

2 Semiotics in Anthropology and Ethnography   35
   Sally Ann Ness and Steve Coleman

3 Semiotics in History and Archaeology   49
   Marek Tamm and Robert W. Preucel

4 Semiotics in Theology and Religious Studies   69
   Massimo Leone

5 Semiotics in Ethics and Caring   81
   Susan Petrilli

6 Semiotics in Sociology and Political Science   109
   Risto Heiskala and Peeter Selg

7 Semiotics in Learning and Education   129
   Andrew Stables and Alin Olteanu

8 Semiotics in Picture and Image Studies   149
   Sara Lenninger and Göran Sonesson

9 Semiotics in Film and Video Studies   169
   Piero Polidoro and Adriano D'Aloia

10 Semiotics in Music and Musicology   187
    William P. Dougherty and Esti Sheinberg

11 Semiotics in Performance and Dance *Nicoleta Popa Blanariu*	207
12 Semiotics in Rhetoric and Poetics *Per Aage Brandt and Todd Oakley*	227
13 Semiotics in Literature and Narratology *Stéphanie Walsh Matthews and Paul Perron*	245
14 Semiotics in Structural Linguistics *Anne-Gaëlle Toutain and Ekaterina Velmezova*	261
INDEX	285

LIST OF FIGURES

6.1	Front cover of the *Paris Match* magazine that Barthes analyses	111
6.2	The field and subfields of neostructuralist semiotic sociology	121
10.1	Ruwet's analysis of a *Geisslerliede*	189
10.2	Topical analysis (after Allanbrook) of Mozart, Piano Sonata in F Major, K 332; I: 1–24	193
10.3	Beethoven, Piano Sonata No. 6 in F Major, op. 10, no. 2. I: 1–4	199
10.4	Tarasti's Zemic model	200
10.5	The Zemic Process in Mozart, Piano Sonata in C Major, K 545	200
12.1	Lovers, scholars and cats	229
12.2	Elementary narrative enunciation	232
12.3	A semiotic square of story structure	234
12.4	The contractual network of the legend	235
12.5	Diegesis of the legend	236
12.6	The semiotic cascade of theatre, opera and song	237
12.7	A prehistorical rock engraving of collective dancing	238

LIST OF TABLES

8.1 Indexicality of footsteps and photographs　　　　　　　　　162

LIST OF CONTRIBUTORS

Per Aage Brandt is Full Professor in the Department of Cognitive Science at Case Western Reserve University, Cleveland, Ohio, USA. He is the author of a dozen books and more than 150 published papers on cognitive and semiotic theory of language, grammar, aesthetics, art and music. As a scholar trained in Romance Philology (French and Spanish), he has worked his way through structural linguistics and structural semantics, and elaborated a series of models – in particular related to the technical and formal representations of textual phenomena such as enunciation, diegesis and modal schematisms – for describing patterns of meaning in the framework of a discourse-oriented (Greimas) and later a formalized phenomenological (Thom, Petitot) and cognitively (Talmy) oriented semiotics. In 2002, he was awarded the Grand Prix de Philosophie by l'Académie française and was made Officier de l'Ordre des Arts et des Lettres by the French Ministry of Culture.

Vincent Colapietro is Liberal Arts Research Professor Emeritus in the Departments of Philosophy and African American Studies at Pennsylvania State University (USA), presently also affiliated with the Center for the Humanities at the University of Rhode Island. One of his main areas of research is pragmatism, with emphasis on Peirce. He is the author of *Peirce's Approach to the Self* (1989), *A Glossary of Semiotics* (1993), *Fateful Shapes of Human Freedom* (2003) and *Acción, sociabilidad y drama: Un retrato pragmatista del animal humano* (2020) as well as numerous essays. He has written on a wide range of topics, from music (especially jazz) and cinema to psychoanalysis and deconstruction, from art and literature to ontology and phenomenology. He has served as President of the Charles S. Peirce Society, the Metaphysical Society of America, and the Semiotic Society of America.

Steve Coleman is Lecturer in the Department of Anthropology at the National University of Ireland, Maynooth, Ireland. He is a past president of the Anthropological Association of Ireland and a past editor of the *Irish Journal of Anthropology*. His research looks at linguistic anthropology, Irish language discourse and literature, verbal art, music and performance, minority languages and the nation-state, C.S. Peirce's semeiotic political movements, and ethnographic approaches to literature.

Adriano D'Aloia is Associate Professor of Visual Culture at the Università degli Studi di Bergamo, Italy. His research focuses on the interdisciplinary nature of film theories and aims at constructing a new ecological aesthetics of contemporary media experience. He is the author of *Neurofilmology of the Moving Image. Gravity and Vertigo in Contemporary Cinema* (2021) and co-editor of journal special issues on *Neurofimology* (*Cinéma&Cie* 2014), *Snapshot Culture* (*Comunicazioni Sociali* 2016), *Fashionating Images* (*Comunicazioni Sociali* 2017), *Narrative Architectures* (*Imago* 2020) and

VR Storytelling (*Cinergie* 2021). He is a member of the editorial board of *Cinéma&Cie. Film and Media Studies Journal*. He is the founder of E/Me/R/G – Enactive Media Research Group. More at www.adrianodaloia.net.

William P. Dougherty is Emeritus Professor in the Department of Music at Drake University, Des Moines, Iowa, USA. His research is directed towards developing a semiotic approach to the art song, and he has published numerous articles on music and text relationships and on musical semiotics in books and journals (including *Music Theory Spectrum* and *Semiotica*). He is co-editor (with Esti Sheinberg) of *The Routledge Handbook of Music Signification* (2020). In his work as a composer, he has been commissioned by the Polaris Wind Quintet, the Brass Band of Columbus, the Drake University Fine Arts Trio, the Pioneer String Quartet, the Sheboygan Symphony Orchestra, the New Hampshire Music Festival Orchestra, the New England Symphony Orchestra, the New England Wind Ensemble and numerous chamber groups and soloists.

Risto Heiskala is Full Professor of Sociology at Tampere University, EU Finland. He is the author of *Semiotic Sociology* (2021) and *Society as Semiosis* (2003) as well as co-editor of *Policy Design in the European Union* (2018) and *Social Innovations, Institutional Change and Economic Performance* (2007). He is a member of the Finnish Academy of Science and Letters and Vice-Chair of the Society for the Study of Power Relations (SSPR). He has been the Director of the Institute for Advanced Social Research (IASR) at the University of Tampere and a member of the executive committee of the European Sociological Association (ESA) as well as a founding member of its Social Theory Research Network.

Sara Lenninger is Senior Lecturer and Researcher in the Department of Education and the Environment at Kristianstad University, Sweden. Her research in semiotics is focused on the use of visual meanings in communication, especially via pictures. She also researches children's understanding of pictures in adult-child communication from a cognitive semiotic point of view.

Massimo Leone is Full Professor ('Professore Ordinario') of Philosophy of Communication, Cultural Semiotics, and Visual Semiotics at the Department of Philosophy and Educational Sciences, University of Turin, Italy, and part-time Professor of Semiotics in the Department of Chinese Language and Literature, University of Shanghai, China. He has been visiting professor at several universities in the five continents. He has single-authored 15 books, edited more than 50 collective volumes and published more than 500 articles in semiotics, religious studies and visual studies. He is the winner of a 2018 ERC Consolidator Grant, the most prestigious research grant in Europe. He is editor-in-chief of *Lexia*, the Semiotic Journal of the Center for Interdisciplinary Research on Communication, University of Turin, Italy, co-editor-in-chief of *Semiotica* (De Gruyter), and co-editor of the book series 'I Saggi di Lexia' (Rome: Aracne), 'Semiotics of Religion' (Berlin and Boston: Walter de Gruyter) and 'Advances in Face Studies' (London and New York: Routledge).

Sophia Melanson Ricciardone is PhD candidate (ABD) with the joint program of Communication and Culture with York and Ryerson Universities in Toronto, Ontario,

Canada. She is a PhD Research Assistant with Ryerson University's *Meaning Lab*, which is dedicated to research into various facets of Language, Culture. Broadly, her work examines the ways in which we offload facets of cognition to digital technology, which invariably affects how we collectively use language, reason through complex ideas about the world, and how patterns of thought (mental schemas) are altered in the process. She is currently working on a research project empirically evaluating the impact of Twitter-bots on intersubjective discourse. More specifically, she is exploring whether and to what extent bot-generated contributions to political Twitter discourse stimulates the circulation of affectively charged content and what consequences such arrangements impart on minds and bodies.

Sally Ann Ness is Full Professor in the Department of Anthropology at the University of California Riverside, USA. She has written on the semiotics of cultural performance in the contexts of tourism, festival life, the performing and medicinal arts, and sport, in the Philippines, Indonesia, and in Yosemite and Joshua Tree National Parks, California. Her books include *Choreographies of Landscape; Signs of Performance in Yosemite National Park* (2016), *Where Asia Smiles; an Ethnography of Philippine Tourism* (2002), and *Body, Movement, and Culture; Kinesthetic and Visual Symbolism in a Philippine Community* (1992). She is guest editor of the special double issue, *Recherches Anthropologiques/Anthropological Inquiries,* of *Recherches Sémiotiques/Semiotic Inquiry* (2012) and is co-editor, with Patrick Alcedo and Hendrik Maier, of *Religious Festivals in Contemporary Southeast Asia* (2016) and, with Carrie Noland, of *Migrations of Gesture* (2008).

Todd Oakley is Full Professor and Chair of the Department of Cognitive Science at Case Western Reserve University, Cleveland, Ohio, USA. His research and teaching interests include cognitive linguistics, semiotics and rhetorical theory, each of which is represented in his most recent book, *Rhetorical Minds: Meditations on the Cognitive Science of Persuasion* (2020). He is also author of *From Attention to Meaning* (2009) and co-editor of *Mental Spaces in Discourse and Interaction* (2008). He is the past president of the International Association for Cognitive Semiotics, and an associate editor of the journal *Cognitive Semiotics*.

Alin Olteanu is Postdoctoral Researcher and Publications Coordinator at the *Käte Hamburger Kolleg Cultures of Research* of RWTH Aachen University, Germany. Having worked on the dialogue between semiotic theories and educational philosophy, Alin Olteanu is currently interested in the potential of biosemiotics to contribute to society and technology studies, with a focus on digitalization and sustainability.

Paul Perron is Full Professor in the Munk School of Global Affairs and Public Policy, at the University of Toronto, Canada, where he serves as Director of the *Centre des Études de la France et du Monde Francophone*. He has published many works on narratology, semiotics, New France, Québécois, and nineteenth- and twentieth century French literature. His recent books include *Narratology and Text: Subjectivity and Identity in New France and Québécois Literature*; *Classic Readings in Semiotics*; *Lectures de Pierre Torreilles*; *Quête identitaire et subjectivité dans la prose québécoise du 19ième siècle*; *Vladimir Propp: On the Comic and Laughter*; *Edgard Pisani: A Personal View of the World*; and *Edgard Pisani: An Old Man and the Land*. Among other honours, he is Past

President of the Semiotic Society of America, a *Commandeur dans l'Ordre des Palmes Académiques* awardee, a *Chevalier de la Légion d'Honneur* awardee, and a Fellow of the Royal Society of Canada.

Susan Petrilli is Full Professor of Philosophy and Theory of Languages, University of Bari Aldo Moro, Italy, where she teaches Semiotics, Semiotics of Translation, Philosophy of Language, and Semiotics of Law and Intercultural Translation. She has authored, edited and translated many books and articles, contributing to spreading the works of Thomas Sebeok, Victoria Welby, Charles Ogden, Giorgio Fano, among many others. Her recent books include *Sign Studies and Semioethics* (2014); *The Global World and Its Manifold Faces* (2016); *Signs, Language and Listening* (2019). Among her edited volumes are *Challenges to Living Together* (2017), *The Level-Headed Revolutionary* (2021), *Exploring the Translatability of Emotions* (2022), *Intersemiotic Approaches to Emotions* (2022). She is the seventh Thomas A. Sebeok Fellow of the Semiotic Society of America, Fellow of the International Communicology Institute, past Vice-President of the International Association for Semiotic Studies and International Visiting Research Professor at Adelaide University, Australia. She and A. Ponzio have introduced the internationally acclaimed notion of semioethics.

Piero Polidoro is Associate Professor in Semiotics and Chair of the Master's degree program in Communication, Innovation and Experience design at LUMSA University in Rome. He has a PhD in Semiotics (University of Bologna 2005), with Umberto Eco e Patrizia Violi as supervisors. From 2006 to 2008 he had a postdoctoral fellowship at Istituto Italiano di Scienze Umane (now part of Scuola Normale Superiore), supervised by Omar Calabrese. His main research interests are in General Semiotics, Visual Semiotics, Communication Strategy, Web design. His approach is based on interpretative and structural Semiotics. He has published several books, among which *Che cos'è la semiotica visiva*, 2008 (translated in Spanish as *¿Qué es la semiótica visual?*, 2016) and *Umberto Eco e il dibattito sull'iconismo*, 2012. He has recently edited an issue of the journal Versus (n. 127, 2018) about *Fake News, Misinformation/ Disinformation, Post-Truth*.

Nicoleta Popa Blanariu is Associate Professor in the Faculty of Letters at the University Vasile Alecsandri, Romania. Her interests in research include world literature, comparative media, semiotics of performance and dance. She is a member of the editorial board of 'Studii și cercetări științifice – seria filologie' (http://studiisicercetari.ub.ro/). Among her most recent papers: 'Prolegomena to a Semiotic Approach to Dancing' (*Open Semiotics*, Paris: L'Harmattan, 2021); 'A Mythological Approach to Transmedia Storytelling' (*The Routledge Companion to Transmedia Studies*, New York, London: Routledge, 2019), with Dan Popa; 'Towards a Pragma-Semiotics of Ritual(ized) Gesture and Performance' (*Arte, Individuo y Sociedad*, 2019); «Le signe agissant. D'une sémiologie de la *mimesis* vers une pragmatique de la *performance*» (*SIGNA*, 2017); 'Transmedial Prometheus' (*Icono 14*, 2017); 'Paradigms of Communication in Performance and Dance Studies' (*CLCweb: Comparative Literature and Culture*, 2015); 'Towards a Framework of a Semiotics of Dance' (*CLCweb: Comparative Literature and Culture*, 2013).

Robert W. Preucel is Full Professor in the Department of Anthropology and Director of the Haffenreffer Museum of Anthropology at Brown University, Providence, Rhode Island, USA. His research interests include Peircian semiotics, Indigenous knowledge, repatriation and museum studies. He has authored numerous papers on archaeological method and theory for journals such as *Cambridge Archaeological Journal*, *Current Anthropology*, *Historical Archaeology*, *Journal of Archaeological Research*, *Semiotic Review* and *World Archaeology*. He is the author of *Archaeological Semiotics* (1996), an inquiry into the semiotic nature of archaeology. He is co-editor (with Ian Hodder) of *Contemporary Archaeology in Theory: A Reader* (1996), and the co-editor (with Stephen Morzowski) of *Contemporary Archaeology in Theory: The New Pragmatism* (2010).

Esti Sheinberg is a musicologist, and retired professor of Practice in Music History at the Glenn Korff School of Music, University of Nebraska, Lincoln, USA. She is the author of *Irony in Shostakovich* (2000) and the editor of *Music Semiotics* (2012), *Rethinking J.S. Bach's The Art of Fugue* (2016), and *The Routledge Handbook of Music Signification* (with William P. Dougherty).

Peeter Selg is Full Professor of Political Theory in the School of Governance, Law and Society at Tallinn University, Tallinn Estonia. His main research interests include relational sociology, political semiotics, power, governance and wicked problems. His work has been published among other outlets in *Sociological Theory, PS: Political Science & Politics, Journal of Political Power, International Relations, International Review of Sociology, Journal of Language and Politics, Semiotica*, and *Sign Systems Studies*. His recent book (with Andreas Ventsel) is titled *Introducing Relational Political Analysis: Political Semiotics as a Theory and Method* (2020). He is the editor (with Nick Crossley) of the book series 'Palgrave Studies in Relational Sociology'.

Göran Sonesson is Professor Emeritus at the Division of cognitive semiotics, Lund University, Sweden. He holds doctorates in general linguistics from Lund and in semiotics from Paris. He has published numerous papers, both theoretical and experimental, on pictorial, cultural and cognitive semiotics, as well as on the semiotics of communication and translation and the evolutionary foundations of semiosis. Apart from anthologies, his papers have appeared in journals such as *Semiotica, Cognitive Semiotics, Cognitive Development, Sign System Studies, Degrés, Signa, Signata, Sign and Society* and *Frontier of Psychology*. His main book-length works are *Pictorial Concepts* (1989), which is a critique of the critique of iconicity, and *Human Lifeworlds* (2016), which is a study in cultural evolution. His new book, *The Pictorial Extensions of Mind*, will be published next year by de Gruyter.

Andrew Stables is Professor Emeritus in the School of Education, at University of Roehampton, London, UK, and Visiting Professor at the University of Bath, UK. He has written widely on semiotic theory and practice (particularly with respect to education), having produced a number of single-author books. Recent collaborations include with Inna Semetsky on *Edusemiotics* (2014) and with Winfried Noth, Alin Olteanu, Sebastien Pesce and Eetu Pikkarainen on *Semiotic Theory of Learning* (2018). He has had articles in numerous philosophical, educational and semiotic journals, including *Sign System Studies* and *Semiotica*.

Marek Tamm is Full Professor of Cultural History in the School of Humanities at Tallinn University, Estonia. His primary research fields are cultural history of medieval Europe, theory and history of historiography, and cultural memory studies. He has recently published *The Companion to Juri Lotman: A Semiotic Theory of Culture* (co-edited with Peeter Torop, Bloomsbury 2022), *A Cultural History of Memory in the Early Modern Age* (co-edited with Alessandro Arcangeli, Bloomsbury 2020), *Juri Lotman – Culture, Memory and History: Essays in Cultural Semiotics* (2019), *Rethinking Historical Time: New Approaches to Presentism* (co-edited with Laurent Olivier, Bloomsbury 2019) and *Debating New Approaches to History* (co-edited with Peter Burke, Bloomsbury 2018).

Anne-Gaëlle Toutain is Associate professor in diachronic and synchronic French linguistics in the Institut de langue et de littérature françaises, at Université de Berne, Switzerland. Her first research field is history and epistemology of linguistics, especially Saussure, structuralism, and relationships between linguistics and psychoanalysis. She has in particular published three books in this field: *La rupture saussurienne. L'espace du langage* (2014), *La problématique phonologique. Du structuralisme linguistique comme idéologie scientifique* (2015) and *Entre langues et logos. Une analyse épistémologique de la linguistique benvenistienne* (2016). This early research led her to work in the field of neurolinguistics, from both an epistemological and theoretical point of view.

Ekaterina Velmezova is Full Professor of Slavistics and of the History and Epistemology of Language Sciences in Eastern and Central Europe and Vice Dean of Research and PhD Studies at the Faculty of Arts of the University of Lausanne (Switzerland); also Visiting Professor in Slavic Studies at the University of Tartu (Estonia). Her work has focused on Czech and Russian ethnolinguistics, on the history of linguistics as reflected in the history of literature, on the history of structuralism, Russian semantics and semiotics. She is the editor-in-chief of *Epistemologica et historiographica linguistica Lausannensia*, co-editor of *Slavica Helvetica* and associate editor of *Historiographia Linguistica*.

Stéphanie Walsh Matthews is Associate Professor in the Department of Languages, Literatures & Cultures, Toronto, Ontario, Canada and one of the Editors in Chief for the International Association of Semiotic Studies' flagship journal, *Semiotica*. She is currently editing a section of Springer's *Handbook of Cognitive Mathematics*, under Professor Marcel Danesi's editing leadership. She is the co-director of the Meaning Lab at Ryerson University and leads a research group using humanoid robots to investigate the language practices of children with Autism Spectrum Disorder. Along with her publications in semiotics, language and culture, her research also includes post-colonial and magical realism in literature. She supervises students in the joint graduate program of Communication and Culture.

ACKNOWLEDGEMENTS

Out of all the hundreds of individuals involved in this project, we owe a big thank you up front to Andrew Wardell, Senior Commissioning Editor of Linguistics at Bloomsbury from 2017–20. Without Andrew's invitation and his ensuing vision, enthusiasm and patient support for this project, it would never have gotten off the ground; and it certainly wouldn't have grown from a single volume 'companion' into a four-volume 'major reference work'. Andrew issued the invitation for this project while still serving as Editorial Assistant to Gurdeep Mattu. Many thanks are also due to Becky Holland, Editorial Assistant to Andrew from 2018–21; to Morwenna Scott, Senior Commissioning Editor of Linguistics since 2020; and to Laura Gallon, Editorial Assistant to Morwenna since the end of 2021 – each of whom played key roles in shepherding the project along to publication against the bottomless backdrop of tragedy, uncertainty and delay that marked the Covid-19 pandemic. Additional vital support from Bloomsbury during the project's final stages came from Production Editor, Elizabeth Holmes, and from Dharanivel Baskar, Team Lead for project management at Integra Software Services, both of whom engaged untold support from their own dedicated teams. It has been a pleasure to work with all of you: thank you once again.

During the final two years of intensive work, this project benefitted financially from a number of research grants, including a 2020–21 collaborative publishing grant from the Faculty of Arts and Creative Industries, Middlesex University, London (via Paul Cobley) and three grants from Toronto Metropolitan University – including a 2020–21 Faculty Research Grant from the Faculty of Arts (via Jamin Pelkey), a 2021 graduate research assistant grant from the TMU-York Graduate Program in Communication and Culture (via Stéphanie Walsh Matthews) and a 2021–22 Work Study Research Assistant Grant from the Office of the Vice President of Research and Innovation (via Jamin Pelkey). These funds paid for logistical and copy editing support involving seven student researchers: three PhD researchers (Sophia Melanson Ricciardone, Richard Rosenbaum and Jan Vykydal) and four undergraduate researchers (Sari Park, Irene Storozhuk, Leonard Pamulaklakin and Kai Maurin-Jones). Many thanks to all.

Appreciation is also due to nine anonymous peer reviewers for their invaluable guidance and feedback, including a converging series of recommendations that ultimately led to the expansion of the project from one volume to four. The project also benefited from countless consultations, conversations and inspirations afforded by connections with semioticians around the world. Let us say thank you in this regard to colleagues in the Semiotic Society of America, the International Association for Cognitive Semiotics, the International Cognitive Linguistics Association, the International Society for Biosemiotic Studies, and the International Association for Semiotic Studies, many of whom have played a formative role, suggesting in the process the need for additional complementary volumes of this nature to offer expanded scope, depth and range, in terms of topics, angles of coverage, and qualified participants. Semiotics, after all, is still only just getting started; and if these volumes serve the enterprise en route to its next milestone, it is thanks to everyone involved.

LIST OF ABBREVIATIONS

Guide to Critical Peirce Editions

Charles S. Peirce: Primary Sources

CD Peirce, C. S. (1889–91), entries in *The Century Dictionary: An Encyclopedic Lexicon of the English Language*, W. D.Whitney (ed.), New York: Century Co. Cited as CD followed by page number.

CN Peirce, C. S. ([1901–8] 1975–9), *Charles Sanders Peirce: Contributions to 'The Nation'*, 3 vols., K. L. Ketner and J.E. Cook (eds), Lubbock: Texas Tech University Press, 1979. Cited as CN followed by volume number and page number.

CP Peirce, C. S. ([1866–1913] 1931–58) *The Collected Papers of Charles Sanders Peirce*, vols. 1–6, C. Hartshorne and P. Weiss (eds), vols. 7–8, A. Burks (ed.), Cambridge: Harvard University Press. Cited as CP, followed by volume number and section number.

EP 1 Peirce, C. S. ([1867–93] 1992), *The Essential Peirce: Selected Philosophical Writings*, vol. 1, in N. Houser and C. Kloesel (eds), Bloomington: Indiana University Press. Cited as EP 1, followed by page number.

EP 2 Peirce, C. S. ([1893–1913] 1998), *The Essential Peirce: Selected Philosophical Writings*, vol. 2, Peirce Edition Project (eds), Bloomington: Indiana University Press. Cited as EP 2, followed by page number.

LoF Peirce, C. S. ([1895–1910] 2019–2021), *Logic of the Future: Writings on Existential Graphs*. A.-V.Pietarinen (ed.), vol. 1: *History and Applications*; vol. 2/1: *The Logical Tracts*; vol. 2/2: *The 1903 Lowell Lectures*; vol. 3/1: *Pragmaticism*; vol. 3/2: *Correspondence*, Berlin: De Gruyter. Cited as LoF followed by volume number and page number.

LI Peirce, C. S. ([1891–1910] 2009), *The Logic of Interdisciplinarity: The Monist Series*, E. Bisanz (ed.), Berlin: Mouton de Gruyter. Cited as LI followed by page number.

MS Peirce, C. S. ([1857–1914] 1787–1951), The Charles S. Peirce Papers Harvard University, Houghton Library, MS Am 1632. Individual papers are referenced by manuscript number in R. Robin (ed.), *Annotated Catalogue of the Papers of Charles S. Peirce*, Amherst: University of Massachusetts Press, 1967, and in Robin, 'The Peirce Papers: A Supplementary Catalogue', *Transactions of the Charles S. Peirce Society* 7, 1971: 37–57. Cited as MS, followed by manuscript number and page number.

Note: Houghton Library catalogue available online: https://hollisarchives.lib.harvard.edu/repositories/24/resources/6437.

Many of Peirce's papers and letters are available in the Microfilm Edition, Harvard University Library, 38 Reels (1966–70). Digital images of the microfilm, in the Robin catalog number sequence, are also available online: https://rs.cms.hu-berlin.de/peircearchive/pages/home.php.

NEM Peirce, C. S. ([1866–1913] 1976), *The New Elements of Mathematics*, 4 vols., C. Eisele (ed.), The Hague: Mouton Press. Cited as NEM, followed by volume number and page number.

PoM Peirce, C. S. ([1888–1908] 2010), *Philosophy of Mathematics: Selected Writings*, M. E. Moore (ed.). Bloomington: Indiana University Press. Cited as PoM.

PPM Peirce, C. S. ([1903] 1997), *Pragmatism as a Principle and Method of Right Thinking: The 1903 Harvard Lectures*, P. Turrisi (ed.), New York: SUNY Press. Cited as PPM, followed by page number.

SS Peirce, C. S. and V. L. Welby ([1903–1911] 1977), *Semiotic and Significs: The Correspondence between Charles S. Peirce and Victoria Lady Welby*, C. Hardwick and J. Cook (eds), Bloomington: Indiana University Press. Cited as SS, followed by page number.

SWS Peirce, Charles S. ([1894–1912] 2020), *Selected Writings on Semiotics, 1894–1912*, F. Bellucci (ed.), Berlin: Mouton De Gruyter. Cited as SWS followed by page number.

W Peirce, C. S. ([1857–92] 1982–2010), *Writings of Charles S. Peirce*, 7 vols. (1–6, 8), Peirce Edition Project (eds), Bloomington: Indiana University Press. Cited as W, followed by volume number and page number.

Introduction

Semiotics in the Arts and Social Sciences

SUSAN PETRILLI AND SOPHIA MELANSON RICCIARDONE

SEMIOTICS, A GLOBAL AND DETOTALIZING ENTERPRISE

This is the third of four volumes constituting *The Bloomsbury Companion to Semiotics*, a state-of-the-art survey of semiotic inquiry, proposing developments and research priorities, as though responding to Sebeok (1991: 97–9) when *à propos* semiosis and semiotics he asks, 'what lies in their future?' The nature of the project is implementation of the 'detotalizing method', thus denominated by Rossi-Landi (1985). Uniting different disciplines, universes of discourse, a multiplicity of voices in an open dialogical totality, the detotalizing method presupposes alterity of signs, language and communication beyond the separatism of specialisms and universalisms, and as such is a dialectical-dialogical method.

A global survey, diachronic and synchronic, historical and transdisciplinary, this project also recalls Morris and his appeal for 'unity of semiotic' ([1938] 1971: 55–64); a *detotalized* unity corresponding to the detotalized and dialogic nature of its object of study in its manifold manifestations – signs and sign systems, semiosis. The aim is not to juxtapose multiple special semiotics syncretically, nor to propose a totalizing transversal language of unified science, nor for semiotics to prevail over different disciplines in the name of philosophical omniscience. Instead, a general and global semiotic vision can perform a detotalizing, critical function towards all claimed totalities, thereby fostering dialogue among specialized disciplines. In this sense semiotics is unique, not merely 'a science among sciences, but an organon or instrument of all the sciences' ([1938] 1971: 67–8).

Based on listening to the other, the detotalizing method favours deconstruction of the larger totality, evidencing interrelationship among its constitutive totalities, *alias* alterities. Otherness and dialogism are intrinsic to the sign, condition of interconnectiveness and interdependency among signs, sign systems and dimensions of semiosis in which human experience is articulated, its sense, meaning and significance. Regarding the arts and social sciences, attention is on verbal and nonverbal semiosis, before and beyond the word. Contrary to reductionist oversimplification, meaning cannot be encapsulated in definitions, pseudo-scientific jargon and improbable typologies. Technical terminology of special languages aside, signifying ambiguity is irrepressible. Alterity, dialogicality and listening are structural to the life of signs and enable semiotic research beyond prescribed boundaries of academic disciplines with their commonplaces and stereotypes, beyond *institutionalized* listening. Such propensity characterizes literary speech genres, and indeed artistic discourse generally.

Semiotic research during the twentieth century evolves across the boundaries of (binary) 'decodification semiotics', focused on intentional meaning, message exchange regulated by codes, through 'signification semiotics' open to unintentional signs, to (triadic) 'interpretation semiotics' (or 'semiotics of significance') conceptualizing interpretive/translative dimensions of meaning, signifying otherness and excess, the ineffable, before and beyond the logic of codes, conventions, intentions and control (Bonfantini 1987, 2004). However, the difference between 'decodification semiotics' and 'interpretation semiotics' is not reducible to opposition between binarism and triadism. As emerges from this volume, Saussurean/Hjelmslvian/Greimasian approaches to semiotics, on one hand, and Peircean approaches, on the other, do not represent two factions siding either with binarism or triadism. Beyond opposition between binarism and triadism, the difference is between a sign model tending towards oversimplification compared to sign models which account for semiosis in its full complexity, like that proposed by Peirce/Morris/Rossi-Landi/Sebeok (Petrilli 2014: 14–46). Sign, sense and significance are in translation. The detotalizing method reveals how 'communication semiotics' presupposes 'signification semiotics' which, in turn, presupposes 'interpretation semiotics', thus how semioses variously objectified by different semiotic disciplines imply one another to varying degrees, as evidenced across the arts and social sciences.

HUMANS TEND BY NATURE TO SEMIOTICS

Considering the range of fields entering his semiotic purview, Sebeok's 'global semiotics' (2001) – semiotics developed as biosemiotics according to a trend evolving since the 1960s, which posits that *signs* and *life* converge – has contributed significantly to shaping general semiotics as a detotalizing interdisciplinary enterprise. As dialogical encounter among different spheres of semiosis in a detotalized totality, global semiotics is the place where we humans reach full consciousness of our constitution as a sign in a universe of signs. Implied here is the double acceptation of 'semiotics', indicating not only the name of the science, but the metasemiosical capacity for reflection upon signs, critical inquiry, taking a stand, intervening upon the course of semiosis, for 'signs about signs about signs' (Morris [1949] 1971: 434–55), specific to the 'semiotic animal' (Deely, Petrilli, and Ponzio 2005). This unique human capacity for metasemiosis puts basic theoretical issues in a new light, as discussed in various chapters in the present editorial project.

At the beginning of *Metaphysics* Aristotle claims that 'all men tend by nature to knowledge'; we now know that *humans tend by nature to semiotics* (*alias* metasemiosis). Semiotics as human semiosis is related to semiotics the discipline, where full awareness is afforded of the human capacity for responsibility. Semiotic inquiry is equipped conceptually to overcome limitations of the psychological subject, measured statistically, reduced to algorithms and pre-established parameters as occurs in the social sciences, thereby favouring interpretation of the subject as a responsible agent interrelated dialogically with other subjects in social practice. The detotalizing method enhances critique of the social reproduction system that social subjects cohabit.

The global semiotic purview expands the boundaries of traditional semiotics, the 'minor tradition', which as semiology was restricted to verbal semiosis and distorted by the *pars pro toto* fallacy, and promotes the 'major tradition' delineated by Peirce, Locke and, in ancient times, Hippocrates and Galen with symptomatology. Semiology, inaugurated by Saussure, focuses on intentional signs in the social. Global semiotics emphasizes their interdependency with unintentional signs, with semiosis generally, human and non-human, verbal and non-verbal. Extended boundaries uniquely cover the vastest possible range of disciplines. Expanding the 'semiosphere' into the 'biosemiosphere' highlights novel aspects of signs and signification, as closed totalities are detotalized. This also means to question the totalities claimed to constitute the semiotic science itself – natural sciences, the human sciences, social sciences, hard sciences, literature, the arts – showing them for what they are: parts in the architecture of an open system, the general science of signs, semiotics.

Semiotics narrates a different story if it begins from Hippocrates, rather than Locke, Peirce or Saussure, or even the biologist Jakob von Uexküll. Objects and models change radically, including our sign models; just as what is considered as central or peripheral (the lower threshold) changes. Nonetheless, sign is inseparable from semiosis – the process, relation, situation whereby something is or becomes a sign, and where for something to be a sign, something else is present to it, an interpreter-interpretant sign, connected to another interpreter-interpretant in a potentially infinite chain of deferrals. Meaning develops in semiosis, as a response, an interpretant that calls for another response, another interpretant. Evolving from such dynamics, semiosis and signification evidence the dialogic nature of sign. Sign and signifying processes are common to all forms of semiosis and to all disciplines that study semiosis in its various configurations. Sign, language and behaviour are engendered in open-ended signifying processes making of meaning and meaning-making processes a determining element in the persistence of semiosis.

The question of meaning is a unifying factor in sign processes and a constant object of reflection throughout this volume, nor could it be otherwise (Petrilli and Ponzio 2005). Different sign models, schools of thought and trends evidence different aspects of meaning. Semiotic research today thematizes the dynamical and dialogical nature of meaning in live communication, resulting from the interrelationship between thinking, speaking and behaving and from the interconnection between the different dimensions of semiosis, including the semantical, syntactical and ethical-pragmatical. Welby ([1896] 1985) proposes the meaning triad 'sense', 'meaning' and 'interpretation', subsequently replaced with 'significance'; Mikhail Bakhtin (in Ponzio, ed., 2014) distinguishes between 'meaning' and 'actual sense'; Morris (1964) differentiates 'significance' from 'signification': does the question 'what is the meaning of life?' interrogate signification of the term 'life', or the significance, value of living?

Peirce claims that the universe globally is a sign, 'a vast representamen, a great symbol [...], an argument', as such 'necessarily a great work of art, a great poem [...], a symphony [...], a painting' (1903: CP 5.119). Association between logic and art underlines how truth value is not reducible to reason understood gnoseologically. 'Truth' is traced in dialogical deferral among signs, in the work of interpretation/translation, in the relation of alterity, in the ethical-pragmatic dimension of semiosis. The quest for truth presupposes Peirce's 'reasonableness' (1901: CP 5.4). And the signifying implications of this vision find developments with Bakhtin's concept of the 'great time', the time of alterity, dialogical participation, unlimited answerability and human responsibility, valorized above all in the arts.

SEMIOTICS AND PHILOSOPHY 'OF LANGUAGE'

As a dialectical-dialogical method, detotalization is intrinsic to (verbal) language, which implies that philosophy is intrinsic. The relation between philosophy and semiotics is a foundational problem subtending all disciplines. Whilst it is not simple to distinguish philosophy that studies signs and language from 'general semiotics', the task is easier when it is a question of 'special semiotics' investigating specific semiosical spheres and their languages. A complication regarding the distinction is that, like philosophy, general semiotics addresses foundations, principles and conditions of possibility, and as such is philosophical. General semiotics does not study a specific sign system, but rather posits general categories in light of which to compare different sign systems. As Eco claims, 'for general semiotics philosophical discourse is neither advisable nor urgent: it is simply *constitutive*' (1984: xii, my trans., S. P.).

The relationship between semiotics and philosophy is pivotal when deciding on problems and perspectives, approaches and methodologies, hi/stories, values and trajectories to pursue as research priorities. Unifying questions concern how the many disciplines involved complement each other, what they share, how they diversify, how philosophy translates into the discourse universe of general semiotics and what semiotics translates from philosophy (Petrilli and Ponzio 2016).

As Deely illustrates in *Four Ages of Understanding*, on realizing that all thought – and before that, sensation – is in signs, the general notion of sign embedded in philosophy's historical development, previously noticed only on the margins if at all, suddenly becomes a central interest, another realization that puts human semiosis and signification in a new light. The action of signs was important from the beginning, but the semiotic animal only realized this with time. Such importance is co-extensive with 'human understanding' and possibly beyond. As illustrated in *Four Ages*, 'the first postmodern survey of philosophy from ancient times to the turn of the twenty-first century', which casts a new perspective on the history of philosophy, semiotics is equipped to revolutionize traditional philosophy representing its most advanced phase of development (Deely 2001, 2002).

The language of philosophy is dialogical with a special inclination for ideologico-verbal detotalization, decentralization, plurivocality, plurilingualism and pluridiscursivity, which equips it for dialectic-dialogic problematization. Even in monological expressions of institutional philosophy, the word's internal dialogism is never completely absent, though it may be deviated or misinterpreted. A unitary philosophical utterance always relates to different languages, even when claiming to unify them in a common language, a language of languages, as physics was elected as the transversal language of 'unified science'. Though the word of philosophy may appear categorical, absolute, monological, it will always look for a surrogate to replace its constitutional dialogicality. Bakhtin (1981) contrasts *formal dialogue* to *substantial dialogue*, where the first is emptied of dialogism (including in rejoinders among multiple interlocutors) and the latter is occasioned by encounter among words based on listening. Substantial dialogism is structural to the utterance in live communication. Monological dialogue favours unilinear, univocal logic, oriented in the direction of ontology recalcitrant to dialogical interrogation. But if we consider the process of its constitution, abstract, monological dialectics is ultimately connected to the dialogical life of the word. In philosophy, an eloquent example of how discourse can be monologized, even inadvertently, with the best of intentions, is offered by no less a figure than Plato and his 'Socratic dialogues'. Rather than foster a dialogical approach to inferential reasoning and argumentation, Plato's dialogues with Socrates are structured through questions, essentially unidirectional, oriented towards a pre-established conclusion, already known to the questioner, as in *Menone* (cf. Bonfantini 2010; Bonfantini, Petrilli and Ponzio 2000).

The philosophical word is structurally dialogic, implying at once question and response. Understanding is constitutively dialogical. Dialogue is discourse, internal or external, where the word of the other (not necessarily another person's) interferes with one's own word. Alterity is the constitutive dimension of the I – that which Welby calls the 'Ident'[1] – of the self's consciousness, which is thought. Alterity is essential to identity, which as such is already dialogue, a relation between 'same' and 'other'. The I is witness to the alterity relationship, whether the alterity of others or self. The philosophical word originates from substantial dialogism. 'Beginning at the beginning', we find at the origins of philosophy neither 'monism' (Deely 2001: 21), nor 'pluralism' (Deely 2001: 25), in accordance with standard philosophical historiography, but *dialogism*. This is dialogism *ante litteram* – a vital relationship with others in the processes of human living and understanding – dialogism antecedent to Plato in his (formal) dialogues.

A general and foundational characteristic of the philosophical word is its vocation for transversa(ti)lity, dialogue across differences, translation, the ability to resist confining discourse within set boundaries, a single discipline, its language, 'regional ontology' (Husserl 1948; Petrilli 2010: 159–92). But philosophy does not transcend regional ontologies alone; it also resists the trap of 'general ontologies'. Truly philosophical discourse rejects constraint to the world as-it-is, the already-given world, the world in contemporaneity. Movement beyond realism of the world, beyond *realpolitik*, transcendence with respect to closed identity and pre-fixed borders, 'material transcendence', the transcendence of 'semiotic materiality', signifying alterity (Petrilli 2010: 137–58), dialogue with the other, search of the otherwise than being (Levinas 1974), in consonance with the alterity dimension of semiosis – such is the philosophical vocation of the word. Thus described, the word rejects limitations of non-dialogic over-specialization, systematization, classification, identity logic unchallenged by critical inquiry and dialogical interrogation. Philosophical analysis cannot be reduced to any one type of specialized analysis, whether linguistic or critical literary analysis. Philosophical discourse is metadiscourse unfolding along the margins of all disciplinary fields, at their points of contact and intersection. As the study of sign and language, philosophy is 'metalinguistic', a 'philosophy of language' where 'of language' resounds as a subject genitive; not language as the object of philosophy, but philosophy as intrinsic to language, philosophy as the structural dimension of language, evoking the dialogical nature of signs, linguistic and non-linguistic. Such is the intrinsic nature of expression and narrativity in the arts and social sciences.

The vocation of the word for dialogue is the vocation of the semiotic science for interdisciplinarity, transdisciplinarity, undisciplinarity. However, the first two phases in twentieth-century developments of the semiotic enterprize, 'decodification semiotics' and 'signification semiotics', are dominated by the structuralist paradigm and its (verbal)-linguistic bias, attributable to Saussure's general linguistics – in truth, to distorted interpretations thereof, but this is another story. As semiotic research progresses and other theoretical paradigms prevail, with Peircean sign theory in the lead, the all-pervasive, foundational and transcendent nature of non-verbal semiosis is at last recognized, moreover as the condition of possibility for verbal semiosis in its multiple expressions. Despite this, glottocentric approaches are not dispelled altogether (cf. Petrilli 2016: 45–68). The chapters of this volume offer insights into the different ways that semiotic theory stemming from both Saussurean and Peircean traditions address (verbal-)linguistic and non(verbal-)linguistic semiosis variously adopting structuralist, post-structuralist and post-human perspectives.

THE CHAPTERS IN THIS VOLUME: SYNOPSIS AND REFLECTIONS

In the first chapter, Vincent Colapietro critiques tendencies among schools of philosophy to question the value of semiotic theory that interrogates philosophical issues, even doubting the possibility of devising a general theory of signs. In alignment with Peirce, he argues against the tyranny of absolute certainty, exactitude or universality. Healthy philosophical discourse requires mutual listening that enhances dialogism and acknowledges diversity as a resource. Colapietro signals the need for critical reasoning, *'reflexive* reason', a 'critique of rationality undertaken in the name of reason itself', criticism of assumptions, methods and conclusions that even interrogate how to understand concepts like 'rationality', 'argumentation' and 'philosophy'. Philosophical discourse engenders 'an ongoing series of contestations in which the most obvious claims, ones seemingly beyond the possibility of doubt [...] generate intense, intricate disputes' (*infra*). The artificial dichotomy between ahistorical canons of rationality and cultural relativism is unproductive. Punctuating the enormity of contributions from phenomenology to contemporary and future philosophers, Colapietro notes that 'it is a sign of an illiberal mind to throw away fertile and ample ideas of a Spinoza, a Kant, or a Hegel or, for that matter, of a Peirce' (*infra*). He describes philosophy as a practice and not simply a body of doctrine, distinguishing between a belief and the argumentative process to reach that belief by the responsible philosopher. 'Critical theory' in modern philosophy is just as ambiguous, covering different trends beginning from the Frankfurt school and now including 'critical race theory', 'queer theory', 'feminism' and 'gender studies'.

Peircean and Saussurean legacies are also outlined in Sally Ann Ness and Steve Coleman's overview of contributions from semiotics to the development of sociocultural anthropology throughout the twentieth century. Semiotic anthropology is an interdisciplinary sub-branch of semiotics and anthropology; the expression 'semiotic anthropology' may appear redundant given the semiotic nature of anthropological research beginning from its founding fathers (including Frazer, Tylor and Morgan), hence their concern with communication systems, writing systems, definition of 'culture' and traditions generally. Nonetheless, Ness and Coleman use 'semiotic anthropology' to refer to the 'application of new theoretical frameworks and methodological tools', in particular the Peircean, 'to subject matter already thoroughly explored from other perspectives'. They dedicate much of their chapter to tracing concurrent shifts in semiotic and anthropological scholarship, as both of these disciplines matured through the transition from early to mid-twentieth-century structuralist paradigms to the poststructuralist 'interpretive turn' in the 1970s. However, despite this paradigm shift, anthropocentrism and dyadic linguicentric models of communication continue influencing sociocultural anthropology. Awareness of the diversity of human culture and communication, the scope of the anthropological project, and perspectives such as Singer's Peircean 'semiotic anthropology', decolonizing orientations and cultural critique, Deacon's biosemiotic turn, Bateson's non-human turn with cybernetics, discovery of the dialogical self, have not yet turned the tide. A challenge for anthropology in dialogue with semiotics is to assume critique of anthropocentrism, ethnocentrism and glottocentrism as the perspective.

Ness and Coleman cite Ogden and Richards's *The Meaning of Meaning* – which includes writings by Malinowski and Peirce from his correspondence with Welby – as a missed opportunity for genuinely semiotic anthropology. Nonetheless, according to the authors, though noteworthy, Malinowski's investigation of language falls short of a unified semiotic framework to describe human culture overall inclusive of both 'civilized' and 'savage' thought, of linguistic and non-linguistic communication systems. Welby, author of *What Is Meaning?* ([1903] 1983), mentored Ogden as a student. But Ogden, author of *The Meaning of Meaning* (1923), by then underestimated Welby's significs. There is irony in this story, considering that she had contextualized her own anthropological reflections in her theory of meaning and evolutionary development of interpretation, translation and significance, moreover in dialogue with Peirce. The beginnings of a possible unified semiotic framework for studies in anthropology and ethnography had been outlined, and, if taken into account, things may very well have turned out quite differently (cf. Reno and Halvorson 2022).

Empirical research in anthropology, ethnography and cognate disciplines calls for philosophical foundations as described above, critique of sense and meaning, and interrogation of the other – such as populations, their histories, socio-economic-political systems and so on. Local European societies have become increasingly multi-ethnic through mass movements more familiar to new world countries in modernity, constitutive of their very configuration. Analyzing post-Second World War developments in Italy, Pasolini discusses the 'anthropological transformation' of the Italian people due to globalization. Migration across the globe demonstrates more than ever the dramatic importance of the relation to the other, the concept of social emergency, and the need to overcome barriers of indifference to the other – who is, after all, our neighbour; certainly in terms of responsibility, if not chronotopically. New sense trajectories in contemporary society associated with the appearance of new actors, languages, cultures and contexts require listening by the anthropologist, focused on interrelations between Western society (a category whose validity in a globalized world requires interrogation) and the other in the dialectics between local and global.

Making sense of the meaning-making customs of people in the past is a central focus in history and archaeology. Marek Tamm and Robert W. Preucel underscore the process of interpreting past events through an historical or archaeological lens as a semiotic act, citing Lotman's assertion that 'the historian begins with the semiotic manipulation of his initial material – the text' (2019: 189–90). Consistent with the previous two chapters in this volume, the authors maintain that Peirce and Saussure inform the two dominant traditions influencing semiotic inquiry in both historical scholarship and archaeology, outlining significant milestones in the recent dialogue among these disciplines: Uspenskji's claim that history is a communication process through which the meaning of a text produces a new text, a perspective characterizing the Tartu-Moscow school of semiotic research of the 1970s; Greimas' typology for historical narrative; Todorov's re-interpretation of the conquest of America; Brooke William-Deely's historical research in a Peircean key; and Pencak's emphasis on the imperative for historians of adopting semiotical instruments. Common features include the focus on meaning-related issues, hence on the importance of understanding, interpretation and communication in investigations concerning the past. As Editor-in-chief of *Semiotica*, Sebeok contributed to the rapprochement between semiotics and history, publishing two special issues on the topic, in 1986 and 1991.

Tamm and Preucel demonstrate the semiotic nature of material culture, thus of our understanding of (verbal and non-verbal) signs from the past, both close and distant, and even remote. The 'objectivity' of knowledge is interpretive, determined in the relation to other signs, whether material or immaterial, whatever the entity, whether things, artefacts or ideas. Thus the 'objectivity' of knowledge is the objectivity of 'semiotic materiality'. The relation to others, including objects become signs on entering our sphere of perception;

relation is always mediated by sign, oriented by previous signifying experience, by the ambiguity of meaning with its 'explicit understandings' and 'implicit assumptions', by value systems. Semiotic mediation is associated with the dialogic nature of signs, meaning and ongoing interpretive work where signs engender new signs and signifying trajectories.

The significance of religion and spirituality for the human condition situates Massimo Leone's examination of the role of semiotics in theology and religious studies along similar theoretical trajectories as those presented in the first two chapters, though semiotic contributions to the interpretation of religious texts extends much further back, to when St. Augustine of Hippo served an instrumental role in shaping the early foundations of the Christian faith (CE 397). Acknowledging that 'it can be safely argued that no discipline today is able to build stronger and more lasting bridges than those that can be built through semiotics', Leone offers a comprehensive historical account of the symbiotic relationship between semiotics, theology and religious studies, culminating in the semiotics of religion as a burgeoning branch of semiotic and religious study. While scripture is a significant component of many religions, the semiotics of religion is not exclusively concerned with linguistic representations. Rather, linguistic representations are rendered increasingly intelligible within the flow of contextual signifying matter from which scripture originates (cf. Heiskala and Selg, *infra*). Leone stresses the importance of accounting for non-linguistic religious texts in order to retain contextual traces of originating contexts of production. To accomplish the task, 'one must adopt a discipline [semiotics] capable of considering simultaneously different expressive means' (Leone, *infra*).

The interconnection between verbal and non-verbal textuality, narrativity and subjectivity is pivotal for an understanding of religious meaning in the history of Western religions. The Protestant Reformation has an important role in the transition from pre-modern 'blind adherence to liturgy and ritual' to 'personal appropriation of the divine word's religious meaning' as a 'prerequisite to believe'. The need for interpreting the sacred scriptures over obedience to dogma is at the origin of Welby's significs.

Leone offers an overview of research at the intersection between studies on language and religion, describing the geography of academic research in semiotics of religion and of different approaches to religious studies. As for other fields of inquiry covered in this volume, signifying trajectories are multiple, and forbid reduction to *all-encompassing* definitions. Greimasian semiotics is amply referenced for interpretation of religious utterances, especially as it resonates in studies by Louis Panier. Philosophies of dialogue with Buber and Levinas are also signalled. Coquet is evoked for his analysis of the Abrahamic style of utterance and the peculiar type of dialogue it performs, seemingly a lack of response. Opening to the other, listening to the other's voice and responding, responsibility in the face of the other who summons me, is intrinsic to religious discourse, including in signs of silence.

A task for semiotics of religion today is to reflect upon the meaning of religious signs and of human action in the name of religious identity and its mystifications. In a world violated by conflict using the alibi of religion and its identities, the real problem is not to refuse violence but to resist the institution of violence. War against terrorism, against fanaticism – not least of all religious fanaticism – confirms, even consecrates, what it is called to defeat: the values of war and violence. The sign's original capacity for unbiased dialogue must be recovered and applied to relationships among people, to interreligious discourse, if the aim is to create multicultural and multi-confessional societies as foreseen by the dialogic nature of the sign beyond ideologico-cultural deviations.

Susan Petrilli's chapter resonates with the themes and trends outlined in the first four chapters, moving beyond the limitations of *theoreticism* and promoting engagement with the *practical* dimensions of the most pressing issues of our era through 'semioethic' inquiry. Referencing Sebeok's global semiotics, she calls for reconciliation between semiotics and life sciences to open both lines of research to a more expansive conception of the ethics of care. The tacit argument undergirding this chapter asserts that there can be no resolution to the dire conditions we find ourselves in without addressing the impact of the semiosphere on the biosphere. Our collective focus must transcend the separatism of specialization in the arts, social sciences and life sciences in order to attend to 'life over the entire planet given that semiosis and life converge, that global semiotics is concerned with the signs of life in all their manifestations, and that human life is objectively part of the global ecosystem interconnected with all others' (Petrilli, *infra*).

Semioethics addresses questions that pertain traditionally to ethics, aesthetics and ideology (cf. Rossi-Landi 1990, 1992). Indications in this sense are traceable in Peirce, who coherently with his pragmatism developed a cognitive approach to semiotics related to human social behaviour and the totality of human interests. From a Peircean perspective, the problem of knowledge necessarily involves valuational and pragmatic considerations. Semioethics extends beyond the logico-cognitive and epistemological boundaries to focus on the axiological dimension of sign activity, which includes the human disposition for critique, creativity, innovation, planning, evaluation, responsibility, and resisting dogmatism and unquestioning acceptance of the world as-it-is.

From a semioethic perspective, semiotics provides a scientific analysis of the foundations of responsibility traceable to two interrelated *global* contexts: biosemiosis and anthroposemiosis, upon which stands social reproduction, a third context, the socio-economic. Contextualization provided by associating global semiotics, semioethics and social reproduction calls for a method of inquiry that is just as global, just as detotalizing. Semiotic inquiry is not limited to partial and sectorial aspects of a given social-cultural formation and its signifying systems, as dictated by internal perspectives functional to persistence of those specific sign systems, whether economic, political, ideological, institutional, national, religious. The totality 'global communication' effectively necessitates a detotalizing and dialogic method of inquiry. Interpretation of contemporaneity and its signs (which do not remain trapped in contemporaneity and its ontologies, whether regional or universal) demonstrates the dialectical interrelationship between alterities, thus between historical-social specificities and life over the planet. The chapter concludes with a brief critique of globalization and its intimate relationship with political economy, stressing the urgency for alternatives to social structures ensnared by the dysfunction of our current globalized world order. Transforming the arrangements of existing political institutions may be a productive point of departure in restoring balance in the relationship between the semiosphere and the biosphere.

Risto Heiskala and Peeter Selg supply a detailed outline of the various ways that political and sociological thinkers have framed questions related to power, governance and democracy across the twentieth century. The social construction of reality involving politics and social institutions is negotiated within patterns of communication (Berger and Luckmann, cited by Heiskala and Selg, *infra*). Media define and standardize shared conceptions of power, solidarity and commitments to values (Parsons, cited by Heiskala and Selg, *infra*). The contours of power structures are increasingly contingent upon the way signs are assembled within communication events. Given that patterns of communication in the twenty-first century are mediated across the global communication network (digital communications more specifically), examination of how semiosis unfolds within information and communication networks (Petrilli and Ponzio 2007: 21–4) is integral to ascertaining how democracy can be preserved within governance in a way that fulfils humanity's responsibility to life.

A dynamical conception of meaning surfaces constantly across the pages of this volume. Here the sign is described as relation rather than entity, intelligible as part of a system of relations with other signs, whose constituent elements are not separable from the flow wherein they are embedded and vice versa. Thus the theoretical framework for their reflections, a working definition of semiotics: 'a research methodology for studying institutions/social facts related to the arbitrariness of the meanings of signs that are contingently articulated in communication' (*infra*). The authors signal two essential tasks for semiotics of social and political action: first, evidence the interconnection between action, signification and sign, 'for meanings do not travel without the material part of the sign or signifier' (*infra*); second, apply semiotic concepts to central problems in sociology and political science.

Another unifying theme in this volume is that of the connection between meaning, language and subjectivity in semiosis. Andrew Stables and Alin Olteanu underline the importance of semiotics as an instrument for the acquisition of such awareness. The social construction of reality is contingent upon the nature of human interactions in social systems (Berger and Luckman, cited by Stables and Olteanu, *infra*). Collectively, humans make sense of one another's interactions through mental representations and concepts that become habituated into normalized social roles over time. The institutionalization of social roles begins at grade school in modern life, where children experience a transition of personal and social becoming. While introducing the term 'edusemiotics' to a growing collection of semiotic subdisciplines, Stables and Olteanu argue that education and learning are inherently semiosic results of communication practices, and advocate for a re-conception of education as a semiosic process rather than a standardized prescription for memorization or mechanical skill development. Edusemiotics focuses on education as process, transformation and growth and not as outcome, where learning trajectories are unique to each person, thus difficult to evaluate. Uniqueness looms in relation to the question of literacy in multimodal communication society, which rather than acquiring a fixed set of skills consists in the ability to quickly acquire new competencies that change even unpredictably in the context of fast mediatic and social transformation.

While the focus in the second half of this volume is on various forms of artistic expression, many of the theoretical themes presented in the first half reappear. The following pages expose readers to a broad and compendious overview of the various theoretical developments in pictorial semiotics, audiovisual semiotics, music semiotics, semiotics of performance and dance, and literary semiotics.

Aiming to delineate a semiotic approach to pictorial-based research, Sara Lenninger and Göran Sonesson draw from previous structuralist studies on children's and apes' understanding of a corpus of images, which incorporated semiotic features to the research design. This ground-breaking work results from two decades of cognitive semiotic research at the University of Lund. Their chapter introduces concepts and terminology, as well as the experimental and theoretical models central to pictorial semiotic analysis. With this objective in mind, the authors explore whether this approach is instrumental to forwarding research in image studies and broadly visual communication, including related phenomena that manifest within the context of digital and social media.

INTRODUCTION 11

Incorporating the audio sensory phenomena of sound to the study of visual texts, Piero Polidoro and Adriano D'Aloia dedicate their chapter to the semiotic examination of audiovisual content, a topic of academic inquiry since the 1960s. During its foundational developments, the semiotic study of audiovisual matter depended on the theoretical principles of linguistic research, later adopting a framework of narratology by the 1980s, and cultural and social semiotics and cognitive semiotics by the turn of the twenty-first century. These advancements in research design resulted in emergent interest in the investigation of audiovisual texts and their effects on social relations and interactions. Polidoro and D'Aloia conclude their chapter by observing that audiovisual texts shape social life through their capacity for narrativity and enunciation along with other semiotic features, forging a new path for inquiry into how digital and social media have generated novel forms of audiovisual texts, presenting new challenges for the semiotician.

Given sound's physical properties, research into the semiotic qualities of music draws on theory of embodiment, cognition, affect and culture. William P. Dougherty and Esti Sheinberg investigate how musical texts signify, while providing an historical overview of this budding semiotic branch of inquiry. Accordingly, they present concepts and theoretical models elaborated by Nattiez, a leading founding figure of music semiotics. Based on structural semantics, Nattiez adapted a taxonomical approach to delineating the nature of music and sound through the lens of semiotics. By the 1990s and 2000s, the incorporation of Peircean principles led to shifts in methodology, indispensable to frame music as a semiotic form of gesture.

Expanding upon this volume's exploration of sensory assemblages as semiosic phenomena, Nikoleta Popa Blanariu presents performative body movement as her primary target of analysis. Dance represents complex semiosic processes involving sound systems, rhythmic patterns, scenography, costume design and composition. As a non-verbal, sense-oriented, embodied mode of expression, an understanding of its communicative value also calls for semiotic analysis of its ineffable qualities. Popa Blanariu presents findings from a broad range of traditions exploring the ways in which performers, choreographers and dancers infuse movement with meaning, exploring themes in performance and dance as semiosis from a cross-disciplinary perspective.

Expanding upon current literature on gesture as a meaningful semiotic act, Irene Mittelberg provides an overview of gesture semiotics, which studies how kinetic action discourse becomes embedded within embodied states. As a branch of gesture studies, an interdisciplinary field of inquiry concerned with how bodily articulations and gestures operate as signs, gesture semiotics borrows from multimodal research into how interactions communicate meaning. Mittelberg consolidates Peircean perspectives with existing approaches to gesture studies to make sense of how visuo-kinetic gestures signify according to similarity (iconicity), contiguity (indexicality) and conventionality or habit (symbolicity), while also proposing Peirce's hypoicons sub-classifications of *image*, *diagram* and *metaphor*, through which visuo-kinetic gesture is expressed in modality-specific ways. Informed by the theoretical paradigms outlined above and borrowing from compatible experimental research on multimodal cognition, Mittelberg looks at how embodied image schema and *gestalt* influence gestural signification.

Stéphanie Walsh Matthews and Paul Perron's chapter offers invaluable insight into the historical evolution of literary semiotics across the twentieth century, from the Russian formalists to post-structural developments. Initially, structural principles of poetry were employed to inform academic notions of literary texts. Within this vein of inquiry, Propp introduced the concepts of form, process and subject to analyse the process of plot construction. Jakobson expanded upon the work of Saussure to examine a text's *literariness* by comparing the nature of literary texts with spoken language. Early to mid-twentieth-century structuralism gradually made way for post-structuralist analyses with 'unprecedented radical rethinking in the social sciences and humanities' (Walsh Matthews and Perron, *infra*), especially in Paris. This shift associated literary semiotics to alternative theoretical modes of analysis, including feminist and gender theory. Greimas's contributions to the Paris School reconceptualized semio-narrative actional and cognitive grammar, integrated with a theory of 'passions' to account for the specificities of literary texts. Walsh Matthews and Perron conclude their chapter by unpacking the ways in which the work of Ricoeur and Greimas depart from dominant structuralist and post-structuralist paradigms, situating narrativity at the heart of human existence as an integral component of social life.

NEW OPENINGS AND FUTURE TRAJECTORIES

To place the humanities and the hard sciences at opposite poles of a spectrum is so widespread as to seem a truism, as Sebeok claims in 'Semiotics as Bridge between Humanities and Sciences' (in Perron et al. 2000: 76–101). Morris believed that an education in semiotics would destroy opposition between the humanities and the sciences ([1946] 1971: 246). While implementing the bridge metaphor, Sebeok warns against recourse to commonplaces and banality in academic discourse and expresses his preference for the web image. Division between 'the two cultures' has led to implementing this metaphor to solve the problem of connecting what is supposedly separate, building bridges between the two sides of a supposed divide essentially non-existent. The 'two cultures' were never separate as semiotics demonstrates. C. P. Snow (1971) thematizes a 'third culture' which Sebeok denominates 'semiotics', a 'universal meta-discourse', Morris's organon. All sciences belong to the same sign 'network' as do all their objects and instruments used to interpret them, according to a vision largely inspired by Peirce's belief that the entire universe is perfused with signs (1905: CP 5.448).

The interplay between artistic genres, human sciences, social sciences and hard sciences has been variously thematized. As emerges in his essay 'The Experimental Novel' (1880), Zola's literary writing was influenced by the physiologist Claude Bernard. Two centuries earlier in his book on *Human(e) Understanding*, Locke proposed a tripartition of the 'Sciences' into Physics, Ethics and Semiotics influenced by Isaac Newton. 'Science' alludes to rationally grounded knowledge and 'human(e) understanding' derives from *Humanitas*, which is not opposed to *Scientia* but subsumes all sciences and is juxtaposed to *Divinitas*. Through Ukhtomsky, physiology influenced Bakhtin who, in addition to the sciences, constructs his philosophical architecture in dialogue with the arts, especially literature. At the interface of multiple disciplines, he invented new terminology or endowed existent terms with new meaning, including the seminal concepts of 'chronotope', 'answerability', 'extralocalization', 'dialogism', 'otherness', 'polyphony', 'depiction' and 'artistic vision' (Petrilli 2019: 157–224; Ponzio 2015).

Whether in the arts or in the social sciences, 'vision' recalls the image which presupposes otherness, dialogue and encounter. As underlined in this volume, the image is not only visual, but sonorous (Saussure's *signifiant*, an 'acoustic image'). The image, in Peirce's terminology *iconicity*, reveals interrelationship between verbal sign, music and painting, and between the verbal and non-verbal generally. The connection among different modalities of the image surfaces not only in the artwork, but in everyday utterances. As general semiotics, semiotics is not limited to investigating different branches of semiosis.

As global semiotics, general semiotics not only extends its gaze beyond (human) social signs, but is committed to evidencing interdependency among different semiosical spheres in which signs are diversified. In the sociocultural sphere the image is a point of encounter among the signs of verbal art, music and painting, visual art, and again between the arts and the 'primary' universes of discourse, characterized by the 'direct word', 'direct discourse', by contrast to the 'indirect word', 'indirect discourse' and its variants. The difference is that between the 'transitive writing' of primary discourse genres and the 'intransitive writing' of artistic genres.

Consciousness of self is interdependent with the vision of others. But vision of the other is not experienced directly, not even in the other's presence. In front of the gaze of the other, the other is always the other-for-me. Beyond psychological, psychoanalytical, even philosophical approaches conducted independently from each other and from other spheres of semiosis, verbal art contributes significantly given its openness to alterity and dialogicality to studies on subjectivity, to semiotics of the self (cf. Sebeok, Petrilli, Ponzio 2001). Bakhtin developed the original categories of his semiotics and philosophy of language with the language of literary writing, with special reference to the language of Dostoevsky's work.

As in the case of the expression 'philosophy of language', the meaning implications of the expression 'of literature' in such propositions as 'the language of literature', 'science of literature' are explicated in terms of the 'subject genitive'. The vision of literature reveals a potential in sign studies for translinguistics, an approach to linguistics that moves beyond limitations not only of traditional Saussurean linguistics, but of language itself. This is possible because the language of literature allows for immanent surpassing internally to language. In this sense, translinguistics is a science 'of literature'. Beyond the system of oppositions that constitute linguistics, beyond alterity determined in relations of opposition, relative alterity, beyond identity determined by deferring to another identity, absolute alterity is endowed with sense in itself. The alterity of verbal art, of literary writing, is not complementary to the assertion of consciousness, to its constitution as a totality. The absolute alterity of verbal art is not alterity functional to finalizing identity, to the sphere of the Same. The alterity of literary writing can be related to Peirce's firstness, orience, originality, as something that is what it is without reference to anything else outside itself, free of external forces or reason.

A characteristic of literary writing is its capacity for 'depiction' in the 'great time' of unlimited answerability, by contrast to 'representation', which implies reproduction of the Same, Identity. The capacity for depiction evolves dialogically from the alterity dimension of semiosis, which it evidences and valorizes. The capacity for depiction, the iconic dimension of semiosis contributes to determining literary value, the artistic quality and uniqueness of the artwork itself, of artistic narrativity, whether verbal or nonverbal.

Institutionalized discourse, whether pertaining to philosophy or the sciences – human sciences, social sciences, exact sciences – reduces the plurilinguistic, pluridiscursive, pluristylistic nature of the word as valorized, instead, by the arts, its propensity for extralocalization, thus our understanding of the world. Dialogical experimentation of truth is replaced by discourse oriented unilaterally, monologically. Instead, detotalized discourse is discourse open to the other, favouring critique based on reasonableness, the reason of alterity and listening, *dialogical reason*, thus understanding and communication. The propensity for dialogical critique is pre-scribed by the human primary modelling device as de-scribed in the dialogue between the sign sciences and life sciences (Sebeok 1991: 49–58).

In the face of present-day planetary emergency, such an attitude, for which as humans we are equipped, and to which as humans we have right, is ever more urgent to assume in response to the problems afflicting our world globally. Though a constant focus in sign studies across the twentieth century, the relation between signs and values has not been a mainstream interest; but today, in a globalized world, this connection is ever more urgent to question and enhance. The historical-theoretical connection of modern semiotics to ancient semeiotics brings new significance to sign studies today, evidencing the semiotician's responsibility as an interpreter/artist/artisan of signs and symptoms, natural and cultural.

NOTE

1   See Welby [1910–11], in Petrilli (2009).

REFERENCES

Bakhtin, M. (1981), *The Dialogic Imagination*, Austin: Austin University of Texas Press.
Bonfantini, M. (1987), *Semiosi e abduzione*, Milan: Bompiani.
Bonfantini, M. (2004), *Semiotica ai media*, Bari: Graphis.
Bonfantini, M. (2010), *Platone*, Naples: Edizioni Scientifiche Italiane.
Bonfantini, M., S. Petrilli A. Ponzio (2000), 'Three Dialogues on Rhetoric, Argumentation and New Media', *Semiotica*, 128 (1/2): 69–112.
Deely, J. (2001), *Four Ages of Understanding*, Toronto: University of Toronto Press.
Deely, J. (2002), *What Distinguishes Human Understanding?*, South Bend: St. Augustine's Press.
Deely, J., S. Petrilli A. Ponzio (2005), *The Semiotic Animal*, Ottawa: Legas.
Eco, U. (1984), *Semiotica e filosofia del linguaggio*, Turin: Einaudi.
Husserl, E. ([1948] 1973), *Experience and Judgement*, Evanston: Northwestern University Press.
Levinas, E. (1974), *Autrement qu'être ou au-dela de l'essence*, The Hague: Nijoff.
Morris, Ch. (1964), *Signification and Significance*, Cambridge: MIT Press.
Morris, Ch. (1971), *Writings on the General Theory of Signs*, The Hague: Mouton.
Ogden, Ch., I. Richards ([1923] 1989), *The Meaning of Meaning*, New York: Harcourt Brace Jovanovich.
Peirce, C. S. ([1866–1913] 1931–58), *The Collected Papers of Charles Sanders Peirce*, vols. 1–6, ed. C. Hartshorne and P. Weiss, vols. 7–8, ed. A. Burks, Cambridge: Harvard University Press. Cited as CP. number.
Perron, P., L. Sbrocchi, P. Colilli M. Danesi (2000), *Semiotics as a Bridge Between The Humanities and the Sciences*, Ottawa: Legas.
Petrilli, S. (2009), *Signifying and Understanding*, Berlin: Mouton De Gruyter.
Petrilli, S. (2010), *Sign Crossroads in Global Perspective*, New Brunswick: Transaction.
Petrilli, S. (2014), *Sign Studies and Semioethics*, Berlin: Mouton De Gruyter.
Petrilli, S. (2016), *The Global World and Its Manifold Faces*, Berne: Peter Lang.
Petrilli, S. (2019), *Signs, Language and Listening*, Ottawa: Legas.
Petrilli, S., A. Ponzio (2005), *Semiotics Unbounded*, Toronto: Toronto University Press.
Petrilli, S., A. Ponzio (2007), *Semiotics Today*, Ottawa: Legas.
Petrilli, S., A. Ponzio (2016), *Lineamenti di semiotica e filosofia del linguaggio*, Perugia: Guerra.
Ponzio, A., ed. (2014), Bachtin e il suo Circolo, *Opere 1919–1930*, bilingual Russian/ Italian, Milan: Bompiani.

Ponzio, A. (2015), *Tra semiotica e letteratura*, Milan: Bompiani.
Reno, J., B. Halvorson (2022), 'The Gendering of Anthropological Theory since 2000: Ontology, Semiotics and Feminism,' *Current Anthropology*, University of Chicago University Press, forthcoming.
Rossi-Landi, F. (1985), *Metodica filosofica e scienza dei segni*, Milan: Bompiani.
Rossi-Landi, F. (1990), *Marxism and Ideology*, Oxford: Clarendon Press.
Sebeok, T. (1991), *A Sign Is Just a Sign*, Bloomington: Indiana University Press.
Sebeok, T. (2001), *Global Semiotics*, Bloomington: Indiana University Press.
Sebeok, T., S. Petrilli A. Ponzio (2001), *Semiotica dell'io*, Rome: Meltemi.
Snow, C. P. (1971), *Public Affairs*, New York: Ssribners.
Welby, V. ([1903] 1983), *What Is Meaning?*, Amsterdam: Benjamins.
Welby, V. ([1985] 1896), *Significs and Language*, ed. H. W. Schmitz, Amsterdam: John Benjamins.

CHAPTER ONE

Semiotics in Philosophy and Critical Theory

VINCENT COLAPIETRO

INTRODUCTION

For the purpose of this chapter, the historical period being considered extends from the closing decades of the nineteenth to the opening ones of the twenty-first century, with emphasis on the time from 1900 or thereabouts to the present. We are dealing with either late modern or arguably postmodern philosophy. But the delimitation is not only chronological: it is also arguably geographical (see, however, Passmore 1985: 11). For the most part, the focus here is on the Anglophone world (above all, North America and the UK), though M. Dummett (1993) certainly has a point in identifying the mainstream of analytic philosophy as 'Anglo-Austrian'.

For roughly the first half of the period considered here, philosophy was more self-contained than during the second half. 'In 1957, when a *Hundred Years of Philosophy* was first published', the author notes, 'the Anglo-American philosophical world was comparatively small, cozy, self-contained, reading very few philosophical periodicals, writing relatively little' (Passmore 1985: 4–5). By the time he turned in 1966 to bring out a second edition of this remarkable history of late modern philosophy, Passmore confessed no one could hope 'to cover the field' as he had endeavoured a decade or so earlier (1985: 5). The 'multiplication of books, the burgeoning of articles', not the mention the proliferation of periodicals had made this impossible. During this period, the history of philosophy encompassed a turn towards history, intensified, if not inaugurated, by T. Kuhn's *The Structure of Scientific Revolution* (1962).[1]

Of course, academic philosophy 'is not a single intellectual community' (Passmore 1985: 11). This goes far beyond specialization. Such philosophy is deeply divided because different philosophers 'have different heroes, different ideas about what constitutes good and bad philosophizing' (1985: 12), indeed, about what simply constitutes philosophy. The heroes of one camp (say, Carnap, Ayer or Quine) might be the villains of another sect. What is possibly worse, they might not even rise to the level of villainy, but simply be deemed utterly negligible. 'At the 1983 World Conference of Philosophy in Montreal it was still true that considerable segments of the participants neither understood nor wished to understand what other segments of participants were doing, or why they were doing it, even when the topics were, to judge from the titles alone, of common interest' (1985: 12). What was true in Montreal in 1983 was true of such gatherings both before and after this. Passmore is not mistaken to insist, 'the division between types of philosophizing no longer corresponds to geographical boundaries even to the degree it once did' (1985: 12). He is also not wrong when he observes, 'the boundaries between "Anglo-American" and "Continental" philosophy are being breached from both directions' (1985: 13). But even he is forced to admit: academic philosophy is 'a striking example of that familiar aphorism: "the more things change, the more they remain the same"' (1985: 13).

Among others, Stanley Cavell (2002) urged that the claim of reason cannot be definitively established at the outset of inquiry, making inquiry simply an exercise in meeting antecedently established criteria. Reason is rather inherently and interminably critical so the only appropriate form of critical rationality is *reflexive* reason. As A. Mahon puts it, 'Cavell urges a critical re-evaluation of rationality *tout court*' (2014: 127). Without implying that Cavell's influence on this or any other point has been especially wide, he is in this respect exemplary of what philosophy is at its best: a reflexively critical exercise of reason without losing sight of substantive issues such as, 'How ought I to act?', 'How ought I to respond to the radical doubts of my own skeptical self?' or even hermeneutic questions such as 'How ought I to read Wittgenstein?' or 'Ought I as a philosopher even to try reading Emerson *as a philosopher*?'

As Hilary Putnam suggests, philosophy has virtually become coextensive with the theory of rationality (1981: 105). He however readily admits, the task of 'giving a sane and human description of the scope of reason' is anything but easy (1981: 126; cf. Smith, especially on the scope of reason). Whatever else philosophical rationality is, it is at least an attempt to avoid dogmatic arbitrariness and, for most professional philosophers, also radical scepticisms (or avowed relativism) (see however Margolis and Stuhr on relativism). In other words, philosophy encompasses a critique of rationality undertaken in the name of reason itself. *Critical rationalism* is an expression used by K. Popper to identify his own position, since for him any rational pursuit is one in which relentless criticism of assumptions, methods and conclusions is a defining feature of that shared practice. *Critical rationality* is an expression used in reference to Cavell's singular undertaking, though it might be used much more widely. Whatever the expression, philosophy is defined in part by its devotion to the ideal of rationality, but even the most basic meaning of this ideal is itself a controversial topic. Of course, one can always find among philosophers dissenting voices even regarding a commitment to reason – the title of one of P. Feyerabend's books, *Farewell to Reason* 1987, alone makes this clear.

Critical theory is, moreover, also ambiguous. The expression has a somewhat narrow meaning, designating an approach inaugurated by the original contributors to the Frankfurt School and continued by such contemporary philosophers as Jürgen Habermas, Axel Honneth, Seyla Benhabib, Nancy Fraser, Amy Allen, Eduardo Mendieta and many others. In a broader sense, it encompasses such approaches as 'critical race theory' and 'queer theory'. Feminism is self-avowedly a critical theory (a theory having at its centre a critique of patriarchy and of allied forms of gender inequality, distortion and violence). The title of an influential anthology, *Feminism as Critique*, edited S. Benhabib and D. Cornell (1987), clearly indicates this as does indeed much else.

An entry such as this cannot avoid being, in part, a series of generalizations. 'Broad generalization is', Peirce stresses, 'glorious when it is the inevitable outpressed juice of painfully matured little details of knowledge; but when it is not that, it is a crude spirit inciting only broils between a hundred little dogmas, each most justly condemning the others' (*c*. 1902: CP 2.14; cf. *c*. 1902: CP 1.224; also, *c*. 1908: CP 5.546). Thus, the author at every turn runs the risk of distortion by indiscriminately lumping together what should be carefully distinguished. And such distortions are certainly going to incite those whose positions have not been accurately or fairly depicted to cry 'foul'. This is especially true given the highly polemical character of contemporary philosophy, beginning with the ongoing 'war' (or *polemos*) regarding what counts as philosophy. Those who have devoted themselves to the study of signs have not only been ridiculed by such philosophers as Simon Blackburn and Roger Scruton. They are not seen by their critics as philosophers at all. Their work is even dismissed as fraudulent, claiming a mastery of concepts when there is an utter absence of minimal competency (see, e.g., Scruton's 1980 criticism of Eco's understanding of philosophical disputes regarding 'possible worlds').

To use W. B. Gallie's concept, philosophy is itself 'an essentially contested concept' (1956). As informed readers know and alert ones are likely to suspect, this concept is itself contested! This much is beyond dispute: professional philosophy is nothing less than an ongoing series of contestations in which the most obvious claims, ones seemingly beyond the possibility of doubt (e.g. an individual holding up his hand and announcing, 'Here is a hand' [Moore]), generate intense, intricate disputes. The very criteria for what would count as success are contested. In his *Pragmatism* (1907), James characterizes the 'manners' of philosophers as 'repugnant'. But the context in which he does so also reveals his appreciation of the value of this discipline:

> Philosophy is at once the most sublime and the most trivial of human pursuits. It works in the minutest crannies and it opens out the widest vistas. It 'bakes no bread' ... but it can inspire our souls with courage; and as repugnant as its manners, its doubting and challenging, its quibbling and dialectics, often are to common people, no one of us can get along without the far-flashing beams of light it sends out over the world's perspectives.
>
> (1907: 10–11)

He could go so far as to claim, this time in a private correspondence (Perry 1935: 2.387): '*Technical* writing on *philosophical* subjects [...] is certainly a crime against the human race!' (1935: 2.697). Such was his commitment to putting his metaphysical views into 'popular form' (1935: 2.387). Even so, James in *Pragmatism* conceded: While 'the philosophy which is so important to each of us is not a technical matter', being 'our more or less dumb sense of what life honestly and deeply means, the philosophy to be presented in these lectures ... to no small extent has to be technically treated' (1907: 10).

Most professional philosophers today eliminate the tension felt by James by addressing themselves solely to other academics. That is, they do what James elsewhere noted: 'the rules of the professorial game' are such that professionalized philosophers 'think and write from each other and for each other and at each other exclusively' (1907, 13). There are of course public intellectuals such as Richard Rorty, Martha Nussbaum, Judith Butler, Cornel West, Eddie Glaude, Jr., who happen to be philosophers.

James, who was in fact an amateur in philosophy, points to what is fundamental. There are, he insists, 'two parts ... in every philosophy – the final outlook, belief or attitude to which it brings us, and the reasonings by which that attitude is reached and mediated' (1907, 11). It is not enough for a philosopher to arrive at the truth ('this being the least of its requirements'). 'What distinguishes a philosopher's truth is that it is *reasoned*' (1907, 11). This even goes for when the truth in question is based ultimately on an appeal to intuition. The legitimacy of an appeal to intuition cannot be simply presumed; it must be argued for – it must be shown by a process of painstaking reasoning why intuition is in a given context acceptable or, more strongly, authoritative (see, e.g., the moral intuitionists). An immediate appeal to immediacy is philosophically suspect. Only an argumentatively mediated case for such an appeal is worthy of serious consideration by responsible philosophers.

This raises an important question regarding philosophy as a commendable activity (or sanctioned practice). Philosophy is, for many professionals, not a body of doctrine but a kind of activity, distinguished by giving and evaluating reasons, drawing and challenging distinctions, more generally, clarifying the meaning of our words, expressions and assertions. Here the contested character of our philosophical endeavours is again on display. This character is *reflexive*, since it not only concerns argument but inevitably takes the form of an argument about the place of argumentation in philosophy. For some, philosophy without argumentation would be analogous to music without sound or a legislature without the means to formulate and pass laws. The essence of the activity would be missing. But the place of argument in philosophy is itself a matter about which philosophers disagree and, thus, argue. Here too an observation by James is worth recalling: 'There is always a blank, opaque something against which we butt; a kind of craving, unassuageable thirst says: "I must get round [or underneath] this thing." … This, however, cannot be done, though some philosophers [e.g., Hegel] say it can' (Perry 1935: 1.484). As a result, we ought to be humble and accept that we 'must fall back on our own divination of truth. … It is chronic humbug of philosophy to prove everything' (1935: 1.484; cf. Holmes quoted in Perry 1935: 2.459, 2.462) or simply to try to prove everything.

This is true of nothing less than what we take Being to be. Being is at bottom either (as James alleges) invincibly opaque or (as Hegel endeavours to demonstrate) infinitely self-luminous to the point of the human mind being able to attain 'absolute knowledge'. On the one side, then, we encounter the pragmatic sensibility, content to accept that approximation must be the fabric out of which our philosophy is woven (*c.* 1890: CP 1.404). This rules out 'absolute certainly, absolute exactitude, absolute universality', and (I would add) absolute closure or finality. On the other side, there is the insistence that nothing short of 'absolute knowledge' ought to be accepted as the ultimate aim of philosophical reflection. Of course, the claim to have attained such knowledge is easy to ridicule but difficult to comprehend fairly. There is nonetheless a deep divide here between (very broadly speaking) 'pragmatists' and 'absolutists' or those who adopt what appears to be a humbler orientation and those who defend what seems to be a more arrogant stance. To James, Oliver Wendell Holmes, Jr., would write: 'philosophy generally seems to me to sin through arrogance' (Perry 1935: 2.459). And he addressed this to James, a philosopher who was tirelessly trying to frame philosophical discourse in a humbler form than the dominant traditions in Western thought.

In more contemporary terms, philosophical projects can be arrayed in reference to the issue of foundationalism, ranging from strong foundationalist projects to anti-foundationalist positions. It can be a matter of debate whether, say, Peirce was or was not a foundationalist. Some argue he was a weak foundationalist, whereas other interpreters cast him as an anti-foundationalist (Nielsen 1992; Liszka 1993; Short 2000).

HISTORICAL CONTEXTS AND RIVAL HISTORIOGRAPHIES

Professional philosophers in the Anglophone world have addressed most of the questions at the centre of semiotics, above all, the question of meaning (Houser 2011, 2020). But they have done so within traditionally defined contexts such as the philosophy of language or the philosophy of mind rather than the theory of signs. These subdisciplines have been and remain today at a distance from semiotics. For the most part, an implicit assumption has governed their treatment of linguistic meaning or mental phenomena. One irony is that, despite the mutual antipathy of 'analytic' and 'Continental' philosophers, the majority on both sides share the assumption that culture – therefore – language – is *sui generis*. A naturalistic account of human language, one wherein the deep affinities between the languages of the human animal and those of other animals, appears to be precluded. When the word *language* is attributed to humans and other animals, it is allegedly being used equivocally. The distinctively human systems of vocal symbolization cannot be assimilated to the systems of communication used by other animals. We cannot naturalistically capture the distinctive features of human language. For decades, then, philosophers have made, at most scant attention to animal communication. That is, we can safely go about exploring the nature of human language in abstraction from consideration of how animals other than humans communicate. The fact of communication is rarely doubted. What is doubted, largely without detailed attention to the biological facts, is that such communication is akin to language as used by humans. Recently, this has changed somewhat. As John Dewey noted in the second decade of the twentieth century, academic philosophy tends to be a conservative discipline (1917: MW 10). It is conservative principally in its adherence to traditional questions, less so in what it is willing to entertain as legitimate answers to allegedly 'timeless' issues.

The linguistic turn taken by Anglophone philosophy has, at most, a tangential relationship to the semiotic turn advocated by Peirce and, in the middle decades of the twentieth century, exemplified by such philosophers as Susanne K. Langer (1930, 1942). The reasons for the marginalization of Langer's contribution to contemporary philosophy are various (the fact that she was a she certainly cannot be discounted), but she was, intellectually if not institutionally, optimally positioned to bring together the concerns of mainstream philosophy and those of sign theory. Alas, even she could do hardly anything to make this happen.

If one opens the influential anthology edited by the young Rorty (1967), one sees that the emphasis, as the subtitle (*Essays on Philosophical Method*) makes explicit, is on method. The genre of philosophizing is, in this tradition, mainly the essay. The method is that of analysis, variously identified as conceptual or linguistic analysis. The paradigms of analysis change over time, from Bertrand Russell's to John Wisdom's to much more recent variants of this activity. To recall, Quine's quip, 'people go into philosophy for one of two reasons: some are interested in the history of philosophy, and some in philosophy' (reported by Rorty 1982: 211). This line of demarcation has proven no less sharp than that between analytic and synthetic judgements or that between theory (Quine himself) and observation (Hanson 1958). With Hegel and other 'historicists', the history of philosophy has increasingly been appreciated as an indispensable resource for philosophical inquiry. Ahistoric and anti-historical postures have given way to self-consciously and unabashedly historical interests (Dummett [1993] and Brandom's [1994] work offer examples of this). These interests are taken to be the work of the philosopher as a philosopher, not merely an historian of ideas.

If one turns back several decades to Langer's *Philosophy in a New Key* (1942), one realizes one is in a quite different world. For she had deeply immersed herself in the literature of the most relevant sciences. *The Linguistic Turn* opens with essays by such positivists such as Moritz Schlick ('The Future of Philosophy') and Rudolf Carnap ('On the Character of Philosophical Problems' 1959). In many cases, the positivists came to philosophy from the sciences. Part of the irony here is that the impact of these philosophers was to drive a wedge between philosophical analysis and experimental inquiry. This was clearly not their intention. This is clear simply from the title of Hans Reichenbach's *The Rise of Scientific Philosophy*. How philosophers use words stands in marked contrast to how scientists use them. It would be desirable if philosophers used words in a more painstaking, careful and responsible manner than all too many have historically done – i.e. if philosophers used words in a manner akin to the rhetorical practices of experimental inquirers. [Significs] The rise of scientific philosophy greatly depends on the reform of philosophical language (cf. Peirce). At least to some extent, philosophers are cast in their Lockean role. Scientists such as Newton and Huygens are the master-builders, a philosopher such as Locke is charged with the humbler but indispensable task of clearing away the rubbish (*Essay on Human Understanding*, 1959 [1690]).

We might now take the work of Ruth Garrett Milliken to be emblematic of a more mature phase in the development of analytic philosophy. In *Language, Thought, and Other Biological Categories* (1984), she in passing notes the work of Peirce (1984, 2004; see Short 2007: esp. 303).

HISTORICIST TWISTS AND LINGUISTIC TURNS

The history of contemporary philosophy, in the sense we are considering it, is full of ironic twists and turns. No twist is more ironic than what is arguably the inaugural act by which analytic philosophy established itself, the thoroughgoing repudiation of the regnant forms of absolute idealism in the British academy (see, e.g., Urmson 1956). At Cambridge, the absolute idealist J. M. E. McTaggart was G. E. Moore's mentor but already in his dissertation one can discern Moore moving away from the idealism of his teacher. This act is not in itself ironic, but, when we consider the resurgence of interest in Hegel during roughly the last quarter of the twentieth century, the irony is impossible to miss (MacIntyre; Bernstein). A philosophical movement predicated on the rejection of Hegelian idealism in the course of three quarters of a century becomes a hospitable ambience in which Hegel's writings, from his *Science of Logic* to his *Philosophy of Right*, from his *Phenomenology of Spirit* to his *Lectures on the History of Philosophy* – and others besides – are taken with the utmost seriousness, this twist of fate can be seen as ironic, if not the cunning of reason!

In 1975, Charles Taylor published *Hegel*. Two years later, Richard J. Bernstein took this as an occasion to address the question, 'Why Hegel Now?' ([1977] 1986). He begins by pointing out the obvious:

> During the past decade, there has been an explosion of interest in Hegel. One can barely keep up with the new editions, translations, commentaries, and articles that have been appearing throughout the world. The reasons for this burst of scholarly activity vary in different cultural milieus, but the question is especially perplexing in the context of Anglo-American philosophy. If there is one philosopher who had been thought to be dead and buried, who embodied all of the vices of the wrong way of philosophizing, who seemed to have been killed off by abuse and ridicule, it was Hegel.
> ([1977] 1986: 141)

The historicist turn in the later phases of late modern philosophy cannot be identified with this Hegelian turn, but the two are not entirely separable. Indeed, the turn towards history was, in many respects, intimately bound up with the turn toward Hegel, a return to an historicist for whom 'the study of the history of Philosophy is an introduction to philosophy itself' ([1977] 1986: 4).

In his response to Kuhn, Karl Popper once again inveighed against 'historicism' and 'sociologism'. 'The idea of turning for enlightenment concerning the aims of science and its possible progress to sociology or psychology or the history of science is', he asserts, 'surprising and disappointing' (*Criticism and the Growth of Knowledge:* Popper 1970: 57). Kuhn is however surprised by Popper's surprise at taking the history of science seriously. In a book significantly entitled *Reason, Truth and History* (1981), H. Putnam announces in the Preface: 'there is no fixed, ahistoric *organon* which defines what it is to be rational' (1981: x). But, he insists, acknowledging this does not lead to relativism. The dichotomy ('either ahistorical unchanging canons of rationality or cultural relativism') is, Putnam claims, 'outdated' (cf. Bernstein 1992, 2010; Margolis 2002, 2003).

Several years later, a collection of sixteen essays by prominent philosophers entitled *Philosophy in History* (1984), edited by Rorty et al., for the most part tries to establish how embracing the historicity of reason is compatible with ideals of objectivity, truth and justice. Within a later phase of those who took the linguistic turn, then, an historical turn is evident. Many of the most prominent contributors to this volume are thinkers who have taken Hegel seriously, at a time when it was still somewhat suspect to do so (see, e.g., MacIntyre's edited volume *Hegel: Critical Essays* [1977] or Taylor's *Hegel* [1975]). As noted, the turn towards history was in some respects linked to that towards Hegel (1982: 224; Rorty et al. 1984).

THE CONTEMPORARY SCENE IN NORTH AMERICAN PHILOSOPHY

In 2007 Kwame Anthony Appiah (2008) gave his Presidential Address to the Eastern Division of the APA. It was entitled 'Experimental Philosophy'. Five years later, Linda Martín Alcoff gave hers in Atlanta, GA. Taking the location of the meeting into account, her address was entitled 'Philosophy's Civil Wars'. The history of professional philosophy can be read through the lens of such address (see Campbell's history of the APA: Campbell 2006). Here I want simply to contrast two tendencies, both illustrative of something critical about philosophy as a discipline.

Contemporary philosophy has been to a great extent defined by a formal division of intellectual labour. Substantive claims were left either to common sense or to scientific inquiry, while questions regarding the meaning of those claims were taken by professional philosophers as their proper concern. First-order discourse about reality thus tended to fall outside of philosophy, making philosophy itself, at least, a second-order discourse. Sharp distinctions were drawn between logical and psychological questions, more generally, between conceptual or linguistic issues and empirical and experimental ones. The cumulative effect of this heavily sanctioned division was that much philosophy became untethered to experience. In James's words, it became excessive thin. It is no surprise then that from time to time professional philosophers feel the urgent demand to 'thicken' the bases of philosophical discourse making directly connecting their activity with what that of experimentalist. Sometimes this might take a modest form: philosophy should become, to some extent, more like the sciences in attending to the disclosures of experience. Sometimes however this would take a more extreme or militant form: philosophy should become, from top to bottom, experimental. What history proved was that dithering about second-order issues of an increasingly abstruse character would not win the respect for the discipline first generation of positivists and analysts had hoped. Recourse to experience, including first-hand acquaintance with the latest discoveries of the experimental sciences (especially such sciences as social psychology), alone afforded a route to respectability. If an individual smelled freshly baked bread on the way to work, that individual was much more likely to do something benevolent in the course of the day. Such discoveries were taken by some even to call into question our conception of character, a more or less enduring set of personal qualities. We were allegedly far more victims of contingent circumstances than our traditional understanding of an abiding character could accommodate. Or so the story goes. The point is that, when discussing moral character, philosophers must take such discoveries into account. Ditto for when they are discussing any other issue: experimental discoveries are always pertinent to philosophical debate. Inspired in part by the Norwegian philosopher Arne Næss, Appiah would seem to have philosophers undertake at least qualitative research of their own. The important point is however the more general one, the one concerning the link between experimental research and philosophical inquiry.

Of course, the response to this proposal was hardly what the more militant advocates of experimental philosophy had hoped. It might even have been the case that, at most, philosophy was moved only slightly in the direction of taking more seriously the salient discoveries of experimental scientists. What needs to be appreciated is that this is nothing less than a perennial tendency in professional philosophy – the call to become experimental and the recoil from this response. There are at least two facets to the call itself. One concerns the animating spirit of experimental inquiry, the other concerns the actual discoveries of experimental scientists. Philosophers should be more like scientists in the way in which they conduct their inquiries and disputes. In an even earlier Presidential Address to the APA, Smith (1982) suggests philosophers might comport themselves more like dispassionate inquiries assessing the strengths and weakness of alternative approaches. His word for such an approach is *dialectical*.

In her presidential address, Alcoff (2012), unlike Smith in 1981 and Bernstein in 1898, does not issue a call for *rapprochement*. She however makes several critical moves clearly aimed at deescalating the 'wars' within her discipline. None is more central than her eloquent endorsement of 'critical rationality'. It is deliberately sounded as a unifying theme.

Though she does not mention him, Popper would of course also exemplify a commitment to 'critical rationality' (human reason as relentless or ongoing criticism). Though she does mention him several times, she does not quote Peirce's characterization of being 'rational': this adjective 'essentially means being self-criticizing, self-controlling, and self-controlled, and therefore open to incessant questions' (n.d.: CP 7.77). For Peirce no less than Alcoff, rationality is defined by such radical and incessant openness.

After noting what appears to be a shared commitment to critical rationality, Alcoff explores how these appeals actually, rather than ideally, operate in philosophy. She is admirably concerned to show how they are used to discredit the philosophical work of committed feminists as merely 'political' rather than truly 'philosophical'. A positive point is tied to her polemical point. Rationality is not sufficiently critical if it fails to examine the historical and institutional conditions in which it is formed, rewarded and operative.

Part of the story is, on Alcof's telling, offering and assessing reasons for accepting a belief. But one of the dichotomies structuring philosophy, that between reasons and causes, tends to deflect attention away from an adequately deep exploration of the actual conditions in which philosophical discourse unfolds. Even on the part of philosophers, who pride themselves on their rationality, causes arguably bear as much as reasons upon the adoption of beliefs, so *critical* attention to the possible causes is an integral part of critical rationality.

To shift our focus for a moment, Jacques Derrida, so often portrayed by analytic philosophers as a fashionable and sophistical nihilist, is happy to join the argument about argument and, by implication, that about rationality itself ('The Principle of Reason: The University in the Eyes of Its Pupils'). He grants the need – indeed, the ideal – to 'exchange arguments as clear, univocal, and communicable as possible' (1996). But he is quick to note that he as a deconstructionist is 'reproached – [more generally] deconstructionists are reproached – with not arguing or not liking argumentation, etc. etc.' His response to this charge is clear, univocal and emphatically communicated: 'This is obviously a defamation.' But, without conceding anything regarding his commitment to argument, he immediately goes on to explain why such a reproach might be made. This defamation

> derives from the fact that there is argumentation and argumentation, and this is often because in contexts of discussion [...] where the propositional form, a certain type of propositional form, governs, and where attention to language is necessarily reduced, argumentation is clearly essential. And what interests me, obviously, are other protocols, other argumentative situations where one does not renounce argumentation simply because one refuses to discuss under certain conditions. As a consequence, I think that the question of argumentation is here central, discussion is here central, and I think the accusations made against deconstruction derive from the fact that its raising the stakes of argumentation is not taken into account. The fact is that it is always a question of reconsidering the protocols and the contexts of argumentation, the questions of competence, the language of discussion, etc.
> (Mouffe [ed.]/Derrida? 1996: 78)

Any philosopher who uncritically accepts the terms of discussion, as they just happen to be configured, would betray thereby one of the defining features of critical rationality. In other words, such a philosopher would be not sufficiently critical. Those terms might be defensible, but, then again, they might be part of the problem (indeed, they might make the problem unresolvable).

Returning to Alcoff, this is precisely the move she makes. Critical rationality must be a self-consciously contextualized capacity exercised in light of the actual historical conditions in which institutionalized games of giving-and-weighing reasons take place. This might mean – for Alcoff it decidedly does mean – taking account, say, of the demographics of the discipline of philosophy. For many, such a consideration of the demography of the discipline would be a diversion from the business at hand (e.g. refuting scepticism or defending some form of coherentism). For Alcoff, however, it *is* decidedly part of the business of the philosopher. This shows that our apparently shared commitment to critical rationality is likely to divide us as sharply as anything else in our discipline. A civil war after all concerns the soul of some human institution. It reaches beyond what counts as good philosophy and extends to nothing less than what simply counts as philosophy. The dismissals, denunciation and disparagements heard among professional philosophers have as their purpose discounting some figure, text or traditional as being philosophical. But, as Alcoff wryly argues, this is of course a philosophical question *par excellence*. As such, it should be argued, not begged in the favour of what anyone happens to have been doing over the course of a career. Moreover, the argument should be constructed with critical attention to information and insights from disciplines such as sociology, anthropology and presumably economics. Though she does not issue a call to make philosophy experimental, Alcoff does display a commitment to taking the social sciences to be *directly* relevant to philosophical self-understanding. As a woman who was born in Colombia, who grew up in the US South, and who is deeply interested in the traditions of Latin American philosophy (2012: 35), she is exemplary in showing how critical rationality drives towards a sophisticated form of reflexive contextualism (my term, not hers). While John Silber might proclaim feminism to be 'an assault on reason' (quoted by Alcoff 2012: 22), her career demonstrates both the irrationality of his form of rationality and the strictly philosophical important of her reflexive contextualism. Given her approach, she is attentive to the way the defenders of the mainstream diligently police the borders of her discipline. But she refuses to be disciplined in ways that shove off her desk important geo-political and indeed personal questions (e.g. her concern, as expressed by the Ghanaian statesman and philosophy Kwame Nkrumah, to improve herself and others). Quoting Nkrumah, she emphatically refuses to 'affect an aristocratic unconcern over the social realities of the day' (quoted by Alcoff 2012: 23).

Of course, semiotics is one of the sites in which such realities are brought into focus, also one in which those social realities manifest themselves everyday life. It has however to an even greater extent fallen victim to the disciplinary policing than, say, feminist philosophy or queer theory. Among those who people 'the army of exiles' in other disciplines, those interested in the study of signs are among them. This 'diaspora', to use Alcoff's word, is part of the reason why the overlap between mainstream philosophy and the best work in sign theory is so slight.

THE LINGERING EFFECTS OF ONE 'CIVIL WAR'

Professional philosophy is a confluence of numerous streams. There are the main tributaries and seemingly minor branchings. Very few of the dominant figures in Anglophone philosophy would unqualifiedly or unabashedly identify themselves as semioticians. But, then, until recently many, perhaps most, would not have identified themselves as metaphysicians or simply philosophers open to granting metaphysics a place in philosophy. Despite this, a semiotic sensitivity is detectable in diverse contexts of academic philosophy (Houser 2020). It is often a deeply sensitive and finely nuanced orientation to whatever phenomena are being explored (e.g. cinema, music, language or mind).

What, if anything, *do* clouds and buttons have in common (Scruton 1980; Eco 1984, also)? Scruton 1980, William Alston (1956, 1967) and others make a strong case against all or even most of the senses of *meaning* being so intimately akin as to offer an opportunity to institute anything like Peirce's comprehensive theory of signs. On the other side of the divide, poststructuralists such as Ricoeur, Derrida, Foucault and Deleuze are not as sceptical about gathering seemingly disparate phenomena within a comprehensive framework. This is however treated in another contribution to this *Companion*. Here let's confine our attention to the dominant tradition of academic philosophy in the Anglophone and, to a great extent, also in the Nordic worlds. The question of whether Scruton, Alston, et al. have actually made a compelling case against a comprehensive theory has been begged, not squarely addressed (Eco 1984, also; Deely 1976).

From a pragmatist perspective, the proof of the pudding is in the eating. The success of a dish cannot be ascertained from the recipe alone; the dish must be concocted and, then, tasted. This holds for a theory of signs.

What, if any, is the pragmatic proof for the viability of such a comprehensive theory as the one to which Peirce devoted so much of his life? The fragmentary uses to which it has been put by such film theorists, deeply rooted in the analytic tradition, suggests such a theory might be even more broadly useful than these limited uses indicate. To a greater extent, the systematic use to which, say, T. L. Short in *Peirce's Theory of Signs* (2007) and Marc Champagne in *Consciousness and the Philosophy of Signs* (2018) or C. F. Delaney's writings on the philosophy of science point to more than the possibility of a truly comprehensive theory. Such use also indicates the form of so intricately elaborated a theory as the one presented by Peirce might prove immensely beneficial to contemporary and indeed future philosophers.

We are not only sign-using but also symbol-making animals whose reliance on language ought not to be gainsaid or minimized. But human semiosis is hardly exhausted by our linguistic resources.

Professional philosophy in the Anglophone world has yet to take a semiotic turn, inclusive of the linguistic turn but also at a critical distance from the duly restrictive assumptions built into the linguistic turn as it was historically taken. We are certainly not at square one. Much good, solid work has been done. But, in most spheres of academic philosophy, it is business as usual. The 'epistemology industry' grinds on, but in what many find to be tedious wrangles of technically sophisticated analysts who belatedly make such discoveries that knowers are embodied and bodies are gendered and gendered bodies are treated differentially – in the very course of these wrangles – critical concerns become intense foci of contemporary dispute. To take but one example, consider Miranda Fricker's *Epistemic Injustice*. To address epistemological issues apart from moral sensitivities condemns us to be unable to give a just account of our epistemic practices.

So, the presence of semiotics in contemporary philosophy is paradoxical, at once marginal and fundamental. The work of John Deely (e.g. 1976, 1982, 2001, 2002) might be taken as emblematic of this state of affairs. No one, with the possible exception of Thomas Sebeok (e.g. 1976, 1991) has done more to advance in the United States and indeed elsewhere the cause of semiotics. His work is however virtually ignored by mainstream philosophers. Such a prolific and influential writer in one arena can be negligible in other spheres. This is far from uncommon.

As a self-consciously adopted framework, semiotics plays a minimal role in the professional discussions of mainstream philosophers. As itself an unmarked signifier, it is, as a sensitivity to the play of signs in the discourse of the human and other sciences, not only pervasive but also profound. There is an irony here. Ordinarily, the unmarked signifier betokens the power in place in a given context. If one refers to the 'female' or 'lack' judge, the signified *judge* is marked. If one simply says *judge*, leaving the signifier unmarked or unqualified, the commonplace assumption is that the occupant of the position is 'white' [Baldwin] and male. In the case regarding semiotics in philosophy, however, the opposite is the case. Being unmarked is not a sign of its power, prestige and privilege, but just the opposite. Even so, the work of Millikan (1984, 2004), and others indicates the possibility that something comparable to Peirce's comprehensive theory of signs will be in upcoming years re-invented. It is impossible, at least for me at present, to ascertain whether Peirce's efforts can be translated into a form recognizable as relevant and useful to contemporary philosophers in the Anglophone world, *or* whether the task must be undertaken anew, with little or no regard to what he tried to accomplish in his semeiotic. In either case, there is the possibility of semiotics becoming more central in the twenty-first century than it has been in the twentieth. Given the politics, fashions and affiliations so much a part of professional philosophy, it should not surprise us that Short's book on Peirce's semeiotic is, in a very qualified sense, a failure. To hope that an independent scholar working to a large extent on the margins of professional philosophy might have had a transformative impact was to hope in vain. A case can be compellingly made but widely ignored.

The point however is not to win a hearing for Peirce. It is rather to win one for semeiotic conceived as a comprehensive framework having direct relevance to various branches of traditional philosophy (most obviously, the philosophy of language, the philosophy of mind and even metaphysics) (again, see Houser 2020). In terms of unquestionable influence, those who, because of their allegiance to Peirce, are aligned with his disposition to examine things *sub specie semioticae*, are not likely to make much of an evident difference. Peirce's life however might be truly exemplary. One labours primarily for the future, without ever knowing whether one's efforts are misguided or futile (CSP). Though we are, even as philosophers, members of a community stretching back centuries, we do much of our work in outward solitude. Of course, in being surrounded by books and articles, we are hardly alone: we are in the company of others, effectively not only standing nearby but also whispering in our ears. The dialogical character of human thought is discernible even when considering the apparently solitary thinker. Given the character of semiosis (CSP), it could hardly be otherwise.

CONCLUSION

In conclusion, then, there is, surprisingly, perhaps no more relevant voice to recall than that of Yehosha Bar-Hillel. He is an Israeli philosopher whose essay 'A Prerequisite for Rational Philosophical Discussion' (1960) was placed by Rorty as the concluding chapter in *The Linguistic Turn* (1967). It is perhaps not widely known that Rorty spent considerable time and effort exploring Peirce's theory of signs. In 'Pragmatist's Progress', his reply to Umberto Eco, he rather bitterly expresses his judgement regarding that undertaking. He eventually abandoned his ambition to be a 'code-cracker' (Rorty 1992: 92). But not before devoting two years of his life to this ambition: It led him to waste his 'twenty-seventh and twenty-eighth years trying to discover the secret of Charles Sanders Peirce's esoteric doctrine of "the reality of Thirdness" and thus of his fantastically elaborate semiotico-metaphysical "System"' (1992: 93). His frustrated ambition prompted his realization that Peirce was 'just one more whacked-out triadomaniac'. Earlier in his Presidential Address to the APA, he took another swipe at 'that infuriating philosopher' (1992: 93), claiming Peirce's 'contribution to pragmatism was merely to have given it a name and to have stimulated James' (1982 [1980]). The basis for Rorty's harsh assessment is based on an interpretive mistake at the most basic level, since he took Peirce to have 'remained the most Kantian of thinkers', convinced that the task of philosophy was to provide 'an all-embracing ahistoric context in which every other species of discourse can be assigned its proper place and rank' (1984 [1980]: 161). In fact, Peirce was as much an historicist as Rorty, a student of the history of science a hundred years before Kuhn's revolutionary work made clear to philosophers of science what Peirce appreciated from the earliest phase of his intellectual development (what science is can only be ascertained from how it has historically evolved and is yet evolving). In addition, it is not likely widely known that Rorty both at the University of Chicago and, then, at Yale University wrote on A. N. Whitehead. Part of him, at least, appears to have been drawn to one of the most speculative philosophers in contemporary times.

It is therefore telling that, in 'A Prerequisite', Bar-Hillel (1960) frames his meta-discussion (his discussion of what is needed for a rational philosophical discussion between logical positivists and linguistic philosophers, on one side, and speculative philosophers, on the other) precisely in these terms (Gallie 1956). The speculative philosopher is pitted here against the analytic philosopher. At the most critical point in this essay, Bar-Hillel announces: 'My insistence [upon speculative philosophers explaining to me and other analytic philosophers their reasons for challenging my standards of intelligibility] is due to the fact that the situation is objectively asymmetrical' (1960: 330). Speculative philosophers are accountable to analysts in a way analysts are not accountable to these philosophers. This is, in Bar-Hillel's judgment, the most basic prerequisite for a rational discussion in professional philosophy. He is aware how 'preposterous' this may sound to those who have not been trained in analytic programs or who do not align themselves with analytic methods. This however does not give him pause, since he is thoroughly convinced that 'the situation is objectively asymmetrical'. He has no doubt that the burden of proof rests on the shoulders of speculative philosophers: they must either prove themselves intelligible to their analytic brethren or accept the neglect their failure entails. For Ben-Hillel, this appears to be a purely logical consideration, not in the least a political situation.

In their respective Presidential Addresses to the APA, John E. Smith in 1981 ('The Need for the Recovery of Philosophy', published in Smith 1982) and Richard J. Bernstein in 1989 ('Pragmatism, Pluralism, and the Healing of Wounds') also called for candid dialogue across 'party' lines. Smith concluded by in effect identifying two prerequisites of his own. We must abandon, first, the claim that 'any single approach is the only legitimate one' (i.e. methodological pluralism should be the default position) and, second, the claim that 'those pursuing philosophical inquiry in any fashion other than one's own are ipso facto not engaged in philosophy at all' (1983 [1981]: 242).

To some extent, professional philosophy will always be what Whitehead described it as: namely, 'a ferocious debate between irritable professors' (quoted by John E. Smith in his Presidential Address 1982: 67; Whitehead 1933: 89). But it might also be more than this. While philosophy frequently aspires to be more than an open-ended Socratic dialogue, it all too often fails to measures up to being even a rigorous exchange in which the various participants commit themselves to mutual understanding, before launching into root-and-branch critique on both sides. As portrayed by Plato, that dramatist of the intellect (Randall), Socratic dialogues most often fail to elicit a sufficiently candid and deep acknowledgement of ignorance, without which the sincere search for the truth cannot even begin. The *doctrinaire*, not the inquirer, is in control.

We can of course turn the question inside out and, rather than asking about semiotics in contemporary philosophy, we can ask about philosophy in contemporary semiotics. This often has the feel of philosophers going on a holiday. But who is to deny the possibility of philosophers when removed from the narrow constraints of their workaday world might reclaim an appropriate (rather than excessive) measure of 'speculative audacity' (Dewey LW 2: 10)? Who can rule out the possibility of semiotics being the site for such a holiday?

With a defence like this, who needs detractors! The criticism that semiotics makes such things as Mikey Mouse, Superman, and advertising jingles 'equally legitimate objects of inquiry' is far from a knock-down punch.

The subject matter of philosophical inquiry at least encompasses everything whatsoever, including nothing (as Wallace Stevens puts it in his poem 'The Snow Man', 'Nothing that is not there and the nothing that is'). It is concerned with everything and anything (Toulmin 1976: 21–2), though of course some matters might be more pressing than others to address.

It is impossible to imagine philosophy abandoning its preoccupation with meaning, in its various senses. Moreover, it is also impossible to suppose the foxes will concede to the hedgehogs or the hedgehogs to the foxes. Finally, the work of many of the most talented and ambitious of professional philosophers, focused on questions pertaining to meaning, mind and shared practices in their diverse forms, can only illuminate, if only by implication, 'problems of the nature, properties, and varieties. of Signs' (Peirce 1913: EP 2.462). Whether semiotics, let alone semiology, can ever become a science of signs – in addition, whether it ought even to aspire to this status – remain at present open questions (Eco 1994). Is the philosophy of science itself a science or is it rather a philosophical reflection upon a wide array of heuristic practices? What however cannot be disputed is that, here as everywhere else, the wheat must be sorted from the chaff. That there is wheat here and that much of it is of very high quality are discernible to everyone but those who are so prejudiced that cannot judge fairly what falls outside the always narrow limits of disciplinary competence, diligently policed. The territorial imperative serving the disciplinary interests of privileged groups is difficult to assess or measure. There is certainly more to it than this. There is a legitimate concern with upholding standards and ideals of an intellectual guild.

In sum, the work of philosophers will be of abiding relevance to that of semioticians. In turn, semiotics, especially outside of the North America, will continue to be a transdisciplinary site in which some very fine philosophical work is encouraged and realized. The enduring effects of earlier waves of intellectual fashion (see, e.g., Blonsky 1985) are, however, likely to work against semiotics winning within philosophy a fair hearing. The institutionalized forms of professional philosophy and the culture of prestige tied to this institutionalization are, in their own way, obstacles. The honest, humble inquirer must ask the question: Is the road of inquiry being thereby blocked or are the talents, energy and indeed lives of especially young scholars being directed to fields of inquiry in which hard work is richly rewarded and solid accomplishments objectively judicable? As Eco notes, nothing precludes the humble inquirer from being obstinate, at least, persistent. Is it an insignificant achievement to illuminate commonplace or everyday experience? Because philosophical discourse in general sounds like so much 'vain babbling' (Scruton 1980, 116; see, however, Eco 1984: 116) in the ears of their hard-headed colleagues in such disciplines as mathematics physics, chemistry, biology and economics, many professional philosophers are motivated to police strenuously their disciplinary boundaries. This might be a sign of insecurity but it also might be indicative of a legitimate concern for the work of professionals to meet exacting standards. The majority of mainstream philosophers have been and continue to be put off by what sounds to them like pretentious and even pompous claims. A minority of professional philosophers however are obstinate in their devotion to the exploration of signs. A much larger number of scholars from a wide range of established disciplines are also devoted to this pursuit. Painstaking, historical work on such figures as the Stoics, Augustine, Scotus, Ockham, Leibniz, Hegel and numerous other important thinkers, concerning signs, by implication, offers evidence how deep and pervasive was the interest of signs, not only linguistic signs. This in itself proves nothing about the possibility that there is a *science* of signs. It might suggest that the study of signs is more than a fashion and those who philosophers who like Eco devote themselves to this study do not deserve to be dismissed as 'Professor Whatever' (Blackburn 2000). In any event, the work by philosophers of language, philosophers of mind and others working in the dominant family of philosophical traditions in the Anglophone world will be raided by 'semioticians' for its aid in illuminating semiosis in its utter generality and myriad forms. Despite the indebtedness of some many inquirers to Peirce, there is little or no investment in the dream of making this study into a science. There are however those willing in effect to stake their intellectual lives on safeguarding this transdisciplinary field as a promising site for fruitful inquiry. We will find philosophers among them. What Peirce said about the lives of early scientists we might, *mutandis mutatis*, say about those of these contemporary future scholars and inquirers: 'their lives were so many experiments in the efficacy of the method of experimentation' (1893: CP 4.31). Without any pretence of semiotics being or ever becoming a science, their lives are so many experiments in making the study of signs into a responsible and fruitful arena of inquiry. Many appear not to have any concern for respectability. Each such devotee of semiotics is in the judgement of the overwhelming majority of their philosophical colleagues what Peirce was in the eyes of his friend James (at least in some respects) 'a hopeless crank' (Perry 1935: 2.375). To repeat, the work of philosophers will continue to prove an invaluable resource for the ongoing inquiry into a wide array of seemingly disparate phenomena, whatever philosophers might in turn take to be the value of this inquiry. Unlike the writings of Foucault, Derrida, Deleuze, Guattari and Baudrillard as well as Husserl, Heidegger, Merleau-Ponty, Ricoeur, Kristeva, the most important thinkers in the Anglophone world will keep a studied distance from the 'vain babblings' of what they often judge to be intellectual frauds. Two broad streams will continue for the most part running parallel, rarely, if ever, intersecting. The relationship between mainstream philosophy in the Anglophone world and semiotic inquiry will be 'asymmetrical'.

The deep scepticism towards the very project of semiotics, however modestly conceived, coexists alongside of an intense interest in exploring signs in their manifest heterogeneity, but without jettisoning too quickly all hope of discerning hidden affinities and possibly a unifying conception among these phenomena.

Among highly educated people, alas, there is no less deep scepticism regarding the project of philosophy itself. The interminable disputes among professional philosophers are, in the judgement of these sceptics, apparently different from the typical agreements in other disciplines. The charges go back centuries: philosophy makes no progress. Its devotees appear to be content tearing the arguments of one another apart rather than contributing anything constructive to the intellectual community or the broader culture.

The dream of instituting a method whereby philosophers might rationally resolve their disagreements is one that stands at the origin of virtually all of the important movements in contemporary philosophy. Even though this dream has proven to be unattainable, much of value has been accomplished in its pursuit. What William James said about philosophy, already noted, might be recalled once more: 'no one of us can get along without the far-flashing beams of light it sends out over the world's perspectives.' Or what John Dewey stressed near the outset of 'The Need for a Recovery of Philosophy' might even better serve as a conclusion to this entry: 'In the course of the development of unreal premises and the discussion of artificial problems, points of view have emerged which are indispensable possessions of culture. The horizon has been widened; ideas of great fecundity struck out; a sense of the meaning of things created' (1917: MW 10.5). It is surely a sign of an *undisciplined* mind 'to treat their contributions to culture as confirmations of premises with which they have no necessary connection', especially premises rendered fanciful in light of social, intellectual, technological and other developments. But, then, 'it is a sign of an illiberal mind to throw away the fertile and ample ideas of a Spinoza, a Kant, or a Hegel' (Dewey 1917: MW 10.5) or, for that matter, of a Peirce. One of these fertile and ample ideas just might yet turn out to be, in the judgement of more philosophers than at present, his conception of semiosis or some analogous understanding of sign-action in an extremely general sense. The family resemblances among widely disparate practices are suggestive and numerous enough to gather these practices together under the rubric of 'language-games'. So, too, might the resemblances among sign-exchanges come more widely to be viewed in such a way.

However else philosophy, in any distinct epoch in its contested history, might be defined, it will always be (in Langer's memorable phrase) 'the pursuit of meaning'. Ongoing, intense, debates about the very meaning of this pursuit – also ones about the meaning of meaning – point to possibilities for intersections between those committed to the dominant paradigms in Anglophone philosophy and those exploring signs in partially overlapping, partially divergent ways. A fuller, deeper engagement, however unlikely, promises to enrich both sides.

NOTE

1   More regarding this turn below.

REFERENCES

Alcoff, L. M. (2012), 'Philosophy's Civil Wars', [Presidential Address to Eastern Division of the APA]. *Proceedings and Addresses of the APA*.

Alston, W. (1967), 'Meaning', in P. Edwards (ed.), *Encyclopedia of Philosophy*, vol. 5, 233–41, New York: Macmillan & Free Press.

Alston, W. (1956), 'Pragmatism and the Theory of Signs in Peirce', *Philosophy and Phenomenological Research*, 17: 79–88.

Appiah, K. A. (2008), 'Experimental Philosophy' [Presidential Address to the Eastern Division of the APA], *Proceedings and Address of the APA*, 82: 7–22.

Bar-Hillel, Y. (1960), 'A Prerequisite for Rational Philosophical Discussion', Reprinted in Richard Rorty (ed.), *The Linguistic Turn*, 356–9, Chicago: University of Chicago Press, 1992.

Benhabib, S. and Drucilla Cornell, eds (1987), *Feminism as Critique: On the Politics of Gender*, Minneapolis: University of Minnesota Press.

Bernstein, R. J. (1986), *Philosophical Profiles*, Philadelphia: University of Pennsylvania Press.

Bernstein, R. J. (1989), 'Pragmatism, Pluralism, and the Healing of Wounds', *Proceedings and Address of the APA*, 63 (3): 5–18.

Bernstein, R. (1992), 'The Resurgence of Pragmatism', *Social Research*, 59 (4): 813–40.

Bernstein, R. (2010), *The Pragmatic Turn*, Cambridge: Polity Press.

Blackburn, S. (2000a), 'Professor Whatever' (review of Umberto Eco's *Kant and the Platypus*), *The New Republic* (February), 34–40.

Blonsky, M., ed. (1985), *On Signs*, Baltimore: JHU Press.

Brandom, R. (1994), *Making It Explicit*, Cambridge, MA: Harvard University Press.

Campbell, J. (2006), *A Thoughtful Profession: The Early Years of The American Philosophical Association*, Chicago: Open Court.

Carnap, R. (1959), 'On the Character of Philosophical Problems', *Philosophy of Science*, 1 (1): 5–19.
Cavell, S. (2002), *Must We Mean What We Say?*, updated edn, Cambridge: Cambridge University Press.
Deely, J. (1976), 'The Doctrine of Signs: Taking Form at Last', *Semiotica*, 18 (2): 171–93.
Deely, J. (1982), *Introducing Semiotics: Its History and Doctrine*, Bloomington: Indiana University Press.
Deely, J. (2001), *Four Ages of Understanding*, Toronto: University of Toronto Press.
Deely, J. (2002), *What Distinguishes Human Understanding*, South, Bend, IN: Saint Augustine's Press.
de Lauretis, T. (1984), *Alice Doesn't: Feminism, Semiotics, Cinema*, Bloomington: Indiana University Press.
Derrida, J. (1996), 'Remarks on Deconstruction and Pragmatism', trans. Simon Critchley, in Chantal Mouffe (ed.), *Deconstruction and Pragmatism*, 77–87, New York: Routledge.
Dewey, J. (1917), 'The Need for a Recovery of Philosophy', in B. H. Bode et al. (eds), *Creative Intelligence: Essays in the Pragmatic Attitude*, 3–69, New York: Henry Holt & Co. All references in this entry are to The Middle Works of John Dewey, vol. 10, 4–48. Cited as MW 10.
Dummett, M. (1993), *Origins of Analytic Philosophy*, London: Bloomsbury.
Eco, U. (1986), *Semiotics and the Philosophy of Language*, Bloomington: Indiana University Press.
Eco, U. (1994), *The Limits of Interpretation*, Bloomington: Indiana University Press.
Feyerabend, P. (1987), *Farewell to Reason*, London: Verso.
Frege, G. (1892a), 'On Sinn and Bedeuting', in M. Beaney (ed.), *The Frege Reader*, 151–71, Malden, MA: Blackwell Publishing.
Frege, G. (1892b), 'On Concept and Object', in M. Beaney (ed.), *The Frege Reader*, 181–93, Malden, MA: Blackwell Publishing).
Gallie, W. B. (1956), 'Essentially Contested Concepts', *Proceedings of the Aristotelian Society*, 56: 167–98.
Hanson, R. N. (1958), *Patterns of Discovery: An Inquiry into the Conceptual Foundations of Science*, Cambridge: Cambridge University Press.
Hegel, G. W. F. (1975), *Hegel's Logic: Part One of the Encyclopædia of the Philosophical Sciences (1830)*, [Lesser Logic], trans. W. Wallace, Oxford: Clarendon Press.
Houser, N. (2011), 'Action and Representation in Peirce's Pragmatism', in R. Calcaterra (ed.), *New Perspectives on Pragmatism and Analytic Philosophy*, 61–9, Amsterdam: Rodopi.
Houser, N. (2020), Semiotics and Philosophy, *The American Journal of Semiotics*, 36 (1/2): 135–64.
James, W. (1907), *Pragmatism: A New Name for Some Old Ways of Thinking*, New York: Longman Green and Co.
James, W. (1976), *Essays in Radical Empiricism*, Cambridge: Harvard University Press.
Kuhn, T. (1962), *The Structure of Scientific Revolution*, Chicago: University of Chicago Press.
Langer, S. K. (1930), *The Practice of Philosophy*, New York: Henry Holt.
Langer, S. K. (1942), *Philosophy in a New Key*, Cambridge: Harvard University Press.
Liszka, J. (1993), 'Good and Bad Foundationalism: A Response to Nielsen', *Transactions of the Charles S. Peirce Society*, 29 (4): 573–9.
Locke, J. (1959 [1690]), *An Essay on Human Understanding*, New York: Dover Publications.
MacIntyre, J. (1977), 'Epistemological Crises, Dramatic Narrative, and the Philosophy of Science', *The Monist*, 60 (1) (October): 453–72.

Mahon, Á. (2014), *The Romantic and the Ironist: Reading Richard Rorty and Stanley Cavell*, London: Bloomsbury.
Margolis, J. (2002), *Reinventing Pragmatism: American Philosophy at the End of the Twentieth Century*, Ithaca: Cornell University Press.
Margolis, J. (2003), *The Unraveling of Scientism: American Philosophy at the End of the Twentieth Century*, Ithaca: Cornell University Press.
Milliken, R. (1984), *Language, Thought, and Other Biological Categories*, Cambridge, MA: MIT Press.
Nielsen, Kai (1993), 'Peirce, Pragmatism, and the Challenge of Postmodernism', *Transactions of the Charles S. Peirce Society*, 29 (4): 513–60.
Passmore, J. (1985), *Recent Philosophers*, London: George Duckworth & Co., Ltd.
Peirce, C. S. ([1866–1913] 1931–58), *The Collected Papers of Charles Sanders Peirce*, vols. 1–6, ed. C. Hartshorne and P. Weiss, vols. 7–8, ed. A. Burks, Cambridge: Harvard University Press. Cited as CP.
Peirce, C. S. ([1893–1913] 1998), *The Essential Peirce: Selected Philosophical Writings*, vol. 2, ed. Peirce Edition Project, Bloomington: Indiana University Press. Cited as EP 2.
Perry, R. B. (1935), *The Thought and Character of William James*, 2 vols, Boston: Little, Brown & Co.
Popper, K. (1970), 'Normal Science and Its Dangers', in I. Lakatos and A. Musgrave (eds), *Criticism and the Growth of Knowledge*, 51–8, Cambridge: Cambridge University Press.
Putnam, H. (1981), *Reason, Truth and History*, Cambridge: Cambridge University Press.
Rorty, R., ed. (1967), *The Linguistic Turn: Essays in Philosophical Method*, Chicago: University of Chicago Press.
Rorty, R. (1982), *Consequences of Pragmatism*, Minneapolis: University of Minnesota Press.
Rorty, R. (1992), 'The Pragmatist's Progress', in S. Collini (ed.), *Interpretation and Overinterpretation*, 89–108, Cambridge: Cambridge University Press.
Rorty, R., J. B. Schneewind and Q. Skinner, eds (1984), *Philosophy in History*, Cambridge: Cambridge University Press.
Scruton, R. (1980), 'Possible Worlds and Premature Sciences', *London Review of Books*, 2 (2) (February): 44–16.
Sebeok, T. (1976), *Contributions to the Doctrine of Signs*, Bloomington: Indiana University Press.
Sebeok, T. A. (1991), *Semiotics in the United States*, Bloomington: Indiana University Press.
Short, T. L. (2000), 'Was Peirce a Weak Foundationalist?', *Transactions of the Charles S. Peirce Society*, 36 (4) (Fall): 503–28.
Short, T. L. (2007), *Peirce's Theory of Signs*, Cambridge: Cambridge University Press.
Smith, J. E. (1982), 'The New Need for a Recovery of Philosophy', *Proceedings and Addresses of the American Philosophical Association*, 56 (1): 5–18.
Strawson, P. F. (1959), *Individuals: An Essay in Descriptive Metaphysics*, London: Routledge.
Taylor, C. (1975), *Hegel*, Cambridge: Cambridge University Press.
Taylor, C. (1984), 'Philosophy and Its History', in Rorty et al. (ed.), *Philosophy in History*, 17–30, Cambridge: Cambridge University Press.
Toulmin, S. (1976), *Knowing and Acting: An Invitation to Philosophy*, New York: Macmillan.
Urmson, J. O. (1956), *Analytic Philosophy: Its Development between the Two Wars*, Oxford: Oxford University Press.
Whitehead, A. N. (1933), *Adventures of Ideas*, New York: Macmillan.

CHAPTER TWO

Semiotics in Anthropology and Ethnography

SALLY ANN NESS AND STEVE COLEMAN

INTRODUCTION

The story of how semiotics, broadly defined, has emerged and evolved along multiple trajectories within the subdisciplines of anthropology can be and has been told in many different ways (Sebeok, Hayes, and Bateson 1964; Sebeok 1969, 1986; Singer 1984; Sonesson 2004, 2012, 2016; Mertz 2007; Portis-Winner 2009, 2103; Sicoli and Wolfgram 2018).[1] The present narrative will proceed along a somewhat unusual path in its attempt to tell one portion, the cultural anthropological portion, of this complicated story. It will track the history of what has been explicitly recognized as 'semiotic anthropology' (as opposed to 'symbolic' or 'semiological' or 'structural' or 'semiotics in/of' anthropology/ culture), and it will do so specifically with regard to research in the subdiscipline of sociocultural anthropology.[2] In so doing, it will briefly take into account the emergence of biosemiotics within anthropology as it has influenced ongoing research in sociocultural anthropology.

This focus may well be judged overly narrow by some, given all that the term 'semiotics', broadly defined, has come to mean and to interrelate within the discipline. The broader, all-inclusive meaning of the concept, the one that anthropologist, Margaret Mead, advocated for in 1962 when she became the first to recommend the interdisciplinary use of the term 'semiotics' (Sebeok, Hayes and Bateson 1964; Sebeok 1986; Mertz 2007), has more often served as the central focus of essays such as this one. It has been a focus that typically has led into intricate discussions of competing definitions, along with their respective intellectual legacies and their various applications and findings (Portis-Winner and Umiker-Sebeok 1979, Portis-Winner 2014; Sonesson 2016). The present strategy is adopted to serve an alternative purpose. It is intended to throw into high relief the pivotal role that semiotic anthropology, *narrowly* defined, has played and continues to play in relation to the discipline's broader history of theory and practice in semiotic anthropology *broadly* defined. The strategy is also meant to illuminate how semiotic theory, both narrowly and broadly defined, has manifested as a salient and influential approach to the study of human cultural diversity precisely in moments when disciplinary paradigm shifts of major import have been in the early stages of unfolding, moments when what might count as the 'leading edge' of anthropological theory and inquiry has not been easy to identify. By narrowing the focus in this way, a clearer understanding of the relationship of semiotics both broadly and narrowly defined to the larger subdiscipline of sociocultural anthropology may be forthcoming.

After providing a somewhat extended introduction to the disciplinary context that set the stage for semiotic anthropology's arrival, the chapter will survey what will here be termed the 'main wave' of sociocultural anthropological research that was produced under this rubric, a wave that waxed and waned during the 1980s and early 1990s. In the third section of the essay, work that has characterized a more recent, second wave of semiotic anthropology, a wave that is still largely potential in its formation, will serve as an additional focus of discussion. Together these movements track into the present moment the co-evolution of sociocultural anthropological practice and semiotic theory as they have adapted to the ongoing transformation of the social sciences from its mid-twentieth-century 'Interpretive Turn' through the late-century 'Culture Wars' and into the current era of twenty-first-century post-humanism.

THE EMERGENCE OF 'SEMIOTIC ANTHROPOLOGY': THE DISCIPLINARY CONTEXT

The study of humankind's semiotic endeavours, that is, of all that humanity has found or made meaningful, and of the myriad ways in which it has managed to convey and elaborate such findings and makings, has been of central interest to the discipline of anthropology from its earliest days. In the comparative investigations of such foundational figures as James Frazer ([1890] 1981) and Lewis Henry Morgan ([1878] 1985) concern with phenomena that at present would be classified unambiguously as semiotic – communicative systems of myth and kinship reckoning, ritual practices and paraphernalia, traditions of architecture, exchange, and written and oral literature to mention only a few – are not only apparent, but motivate and guide inquiry. One sees in the pioneering British anthropologist Edward B. Tylor's initial anthropological definition of the concept of 'culture' a focus directly on the workings and contents of such sign phenomena as art, moral codes and legal systems, and on their social acquisition as well ([1871] 1973: 63).[3] Indeed, the further back one goes in the history of the discipline, the more the idea of a specifically 'semiotic' anthropology seems redundant. In all its constituent subdisciplines, the distinctly human story of sign creation, assemblage, manipulation, evolution, conflict, transmission and diversification has been at the heart of what has mattered most to anthropological theory and practice.

In this disciplinary regard, the explicit use of the qualifier 'semiotic' to define a subfield of research within the discipline of anthropology has occurred in order to reference, not the recognition of new subject matter, but the application of new theoretical frameworks and methodological tools to subject matter already thoroughly explored from other perspectives. It is crucial, then, to note what preceded 'semiotic anthropology' proper within the discipline when it actually did arrive, so as to appreciate how the intellectual stage was set for the theoretical framework that it was to introduce. This setting shaped and continues to shape – some might say mis-shape in certain respects – anthropology's distinctive sociocultural applications and theoretical explications with regard to the semiotic of Charles Sanders Peirce insofar as that semiotic can be seen to define this particular disciplinary field.

THE 'EMPIRE OF GRAMMAR' IN ANTHROPOLOGY

The year 1923 saw a missed opportunity for establishing a genuinely semiotic anthropology. Ogden and Richards' *The Meaning of Meaning* included a 'supplement' – Bronislaw Malinowski's (1923) essay, 'The Problem of Meaning in Primitive Languages', and an appendix featuring a description of Peirce's semiotic and selections from his late correspondence with Victoria Lady Welby. In *The Meaning of Meaning*, Malinowski, Ogden and Richards, although hampered by functionalist and evolutionary assumptions, struggled towards a truly triadic semiotics. Malinowski's contribution, written from the perspective of an anthropological fieldworker, included both a critique of the scholarly conceit of 'the empire of Grammar', as a putatively autonomous realm of purely linguistic form, and a strong argument for the investigation of language use in context, prefiguring both the critical investigation of language ideologies (Schieffein, Woolard and Kroskrity 1998) and the ethnography of speaking (Bauman and Sherzer 1974). As a fieldworker, Malinowski had a finely developed sense of language-in-use as a means towards social ends – as one utilitarian object among others in the 'savage' toolkit. But his evolutionary and psychologistic bent precluded recognizing the possibility and desirability of a unified semiotic framework with which to describe human culture in general, encompassing 'civilized' and 'savage' thought as well as linguistic and non-linguistic cultural forms. The relativist linguistic anthropological tradition stemming from Boas and Sapir had meanwhile overcome evolutionary biases, developing an ethnographically rich account of the interanimation of linguistic forms and social life, but, for its own reasons, avoided developing any cross-culturally generalizable descriptive/analytic system for human culture as a whole. It was left to Malinowski's 'Grammarians' – in a tradition extending from Saussure through Bloomfield and Chomsky, to develop a powerful, formal, descriptive system, based on a dyadic semiotics featuring the unity of abstract sound-patterns and mental concepts, which became the dominant model for the analysis of human language, thought and culture in the twentieth century. This 'empire of Grammar' featured a clearly demarcated disciplinary object, not consciously accessible to the speaking subject but objectively observable by a detached, impartial analyst. It was immensely attractive as a scientific model, but in spite of Saussure's hopes that it could form the basis of a general semiotics, it proved problematic as a tool for understanding human social life. Nonetheless, the model of autonomous grammar, and its methodological after-image, in which unitary, bounded, 'languages' seem to be reflexes of similarly demarcatable 'cultures' or 'societies', was influential in structural-functionalist-derived anthropology from the 1950s until the 1980s. This model also provided the possibility of an anthropological linguistics based on the Saussure-Bloomfield legacy. Descriptive linguistics afforded anthropologists working in any location in the world the methodological and technological means to document and record, dissect, analyse and classify what were now referred to as 'field languages' (Burling 1984) – even and especially those languages for which no written traditions existed. Field languages could, from this point onward be understood as isolatable objects of cultural inquiry, suitable for comparative analysis. The new capacity forthcoming from this development – the capacity to *specialize* exclusively in the anthropological study of linguistic objects that this theoretical/methodological/technological apparatus made knowable, produced a class of experts of a particular language-centred kind within the modern discipline of twentieth-century anthropology.[4] In its most influential guise – that which generated the 'etic/emic' distinction (Pike 1967) so widely disseminated both within and beyond the discipline of anthropology during its cognitively oriented period[5] – this model defined linguistic signs as minimal 'units' of significance constituted by contrasting relations, asserting that a sign's identity was entirely a function of binary oppositional markings evident only within the linguistic system in which it was employed. This theoretical perspective, instituted with regard to the study of human language – language here assumed to be the quintessential form of all sign phenomena and uniquely human in character – was firmly entrenched by the time of semiotic anthropology's arrival.

LÉVI-STRAUSS

Claude Lévi-Strauss's structuralist revolution in sociocultural anthropology effectively extended the theoretical perspective previously applied specifically to linguistic signs to the whole of what comprised the subject matter of sociocultural anthropology (and much of archaeology as well). 'Culture', anthropologically speaking, was defined by Lévi-Strauss as a closed system of internally definitive, binarily oppositional relations of significance whose relationship to biological ('natural') aspects of life was arbitrary as far as any governing influence on the signs' formal or conceptual character was concerned (1963). Initially, Lévi-Strauss made this case specifically with regard to kinship reckoning, where he demonstrated that the 'natural' kin grouping, which he took to be the nuclear family kin group (mother, father and their children), was not in actuality the fundamental *cultural* kin group, which he argued, through comparative analysis, to be a group that necessarily included male kin on the mother's side as well. What he found to be true of kinship, Lévi-Strauss quickly extended to all of human social relations. All were argued to be governed by the cultural equivalent of *langue* in the case of language: that shared, finite, rule-governed system of comprehension-creating relations that in the case of culture formed a system, not of grammar, but of myth. Lévi-Strauss's structuralist revolution served to reinforce and re-establish the structuralist model of the linguistic sign as the standard theoretical perspective on human sign phenomena generally, deeply embedding it in the anthropological definition of culture.

THE COMPLEX ROLE OF JAKOBSON AND THE RISE OF LINGUISTIC ANTHROPOLOGY

Lévi-Strauss' structuralism stemmed from a misapprehension of Roman Jakobson's linguistics, being based on the phoneme – the only level of language structure which involves binary oppositions between forms which aren't meaningful in and of themselves. Jakobson was a key figure in both the rise of structuralist sign theory and in the project of its disassembly. Already in 1950 Jakobson identified the role of the context of utterance, as manifested in indexical signs, within the system of grammar itself (Jakobson 1971). Jakobson noted the pertinence of several Peircean concepts – especially the icon/index/symbol trichotomy and the classifications of Interpretants – for researching human cultural forms, including language, and he appeared to recognize the importance of the triadic nature of Peirce's semiotic (Portis-Winner 2002). Nonetheless, he regarded Peirce as a 'structuralist,' (Jakobson 1977) but in Jakobson's own particular sense of structuralism, which included various triadic aspects which he claimed were fundamental to the nature of Saussurean grammar itself, e.g. the role of the Interpretant in phenomena such as markedness (Shapiro 1983; Andrews 1990). A few of Jakobson's students led efforts to apply Peircean semiotic concepts to linguistic phenomena, consolidating the new field of linguistic anthropology out of the Boasian legacy and in contrast to a grammatically centred 'anthropological linguistics' (Silverstein 1976). Peircean categories were partially abstracted from their original theoretical context, becoming powerful analytic principles (iconicity, indexicality, etc.) with which to investigate the relationships between language in use and its wider contexts. There followed several decades of important research in which the 'broader contexts of verbal utterance' (as Malinowski had put it) were found to be limitless, and language use itself, increasingly understood as an integral part of consequential human action, was found to be constitutive of those very contexts. As the field has matured, researchers have become more adept at situating language use within a broader cultural semiotics (see for example, Stasch 2003), and there is some movement towards the articulation of general semiotic theory in a Peircean vein, e.g. Gal and Irvine (2019) who use an altered terminology motivated by a strict disciplinary focus (e.g. 'conjecture' for Peirce's 'Interpretant').

In tracing the Jakobsonian legacy within linguistic anthropology, we have gotten a bit ahead of ourselves. Linguistic anthropology developed in parallel to and influenced what we term below 'the main wave' of semiotic anthropology, but has only recently become explicitly semiotic within a relatively Peircean framework, and its influence on the rest of the discipline is only now becoming significant. At the time the term 'semiotic anthropology', with its reference to Peircean semiotic theory, began to appear in the anthropological literature of the 1970s, structuralist linguistic theory, as developed in the work of Saussure ([1916] 2009) and Bloomfield (1935), was firmly in place to broker its admission, not only with regard to the subject matter of linguistics, but with regard to the subject matter of sociocultural anthropology as well. This situation would have critical consequences with regard to what aspects of semiotic theory would be emphasized when it was imported into the discipline, and what aspects would largely be ignored or even misrepresented. Semiotic anthropology's sign theory, in other words, was destined to be read by sociocultural anthropologists, in relation to, and generally through the theoretical lens of structuralist semiology. Even after the discipline embraced interpretive social science theory in the 1980s (Rabinow and Sullivan 1979) and structuralist anthropology was deemed thoroughly defunct, only influential in its 'post' guises, nonetheless this structuralist approach remained the received wisdom of the day insofar as semiotic anthropology was to be concerned.

More will be said below about exactly how this legacy of structuralist sign theory shaped the anthropological understanding of Peirce's pragmaticist sign theory when it was eventually introduced into the discipline under the label of semiotic anthropology. However, before moving on to this topic, it is worth pausing momentarily to consider, as one looks back on this particular disciplinary history, that the arrival of this semiotic into the discipline of anthropology was relatively late. The arrival of semiotic anthropology might well have occurred much earlier – actually a full century earlier, given that its theoretical framework was in existence, at least in its early phases, from the 1860s onward and was well known to philosophers, including the philosopher, John Dewey, who was a close colleague of Boas. This theoretical framework was fully elaborated to its final stages by the 1910s, nearly sixty years before any of its concepts were first adopted into anthropological studies. Had this theory of signs arrived in anthropology when it was newly minted – that is *before* the emergence of the twentieth-century developments of descriptive linguistics and the subsequent structuralist revolution – the history of the discipline of anthropology in its entirety, and certainly the identity of linguistic anthropology as it related to sociocultural anthropology, might well have been substantially different. However, anthropology did not so discover this semiotic when it was itself 'breaking news'. Its discovery, rather, was motivated instead by a decline that gave opening to the interpretive movement in the discipline, along with its reinvention and valorization of ethnography. It is to this moment and this movement that we now turn in earnest.

SEMIOTIC ANTHROPOLOGY: THE MAIN WAVE

The use of the explicit label, 'semiotic anthropology', dates to the late 1970s, and most directly to the path-breaking work of sociocultural anthropologist, Milton Singer (Singer 1978, 1980, 1984). In 1978, in a publication that appeared first in Thomas Sebeok's edited collection, *Sight Sound and Sense,* and reappeared in Singer's 1984 landmark volume, *Man's Glassy Essence,* Singer called for a 'semiotic anthropology', connecting this phrase specifically and explicitly to the pragmaticist sign theory of C.S. Peirce. Given the philosophical density and logical complexity of Peirce's thought, as well as Peirce's lack of overt work in or reference to the social sciences generally (in high contrast, it might be noted, to the other leading pragmatists of Peirce's time, William James and Josiah Royce), this call was an extraordinary feat for an anthropologist to undertake. Singer was, perhaps, uniquely qualified to attempt it. His doctoral training in philosophy, in particular his understanding of formal logic, and his intensive work with G.H. Mead during a period when Mead himself was focused on pragmatic dimensions of human communication, prepared Singer as no other cultural anthropologist of his time to read Peirce's semiotic comprehensively and with deep philosophical understanding.

Singer saw Peirce's semiotic as the approach that could complete what he recognized as an ongoing paradigm shift of historic proportions occurring in the social sciences. These disciplines, in his view, in recent decades had been collectively moving away from methodological and theoretical approaches grounded in the empirical sciences in which the objects of scientific inquiry were conceived of and studied from fundamentally atomistic orientations. As the social sciences entered into their full autonomy and modernity in the twentieth century, Singer saw them adopting relational models of social and cultural phenomena, developing approaches that, in their very reliance on relationality rather than objective discreteness as the theoretical and methodological basis of inquiry, were understood to be more appropriate to primordially social phenomena. The growth of research focusing on symbolic and otherwise communicative phenomena in anthropology that began in the 1940s, and which 'exploded', as he characterized it (Singer 1980: 486), in the 1960s, was part of this transformation. It gave rise to the broader field of 'symbolic anthropology' (1980: 486; 1984: 32, 72), and fuelled Lévi-Strauss's structuralist revolution as well.

While this paradigm shift was well underway by 1978, Singer noticed that it was hindered by limitations inherent in the relational models it had employed, specifically those grounded in the dualisms of Saussurian semiology. While these approaches served well enough to enable a shift to relationality with regard to the study of the macro-phenomena of 'society' and 'culture' – two of the three main foci of the social sciences in Singer's view (1980: 486) – it had proved inadequate, with regard to the third foci, that is, to the study of 'the self'. The self, socially constructed, presented certain insurmountable problems for structuralist social scientific approaches. This stemmed from the fact that the self included micro-phenomenological dimensions of subjective and bodily experience, learning and meaning-making. Dualistic models could not, in Singer's view, effectively articulate and integrate into macro-social and cultural relational processes such micro-phenomenological components. To complete the transformation of the social sciences so that they might effectively base all of their forms of inquiry in relational method and theory, Singer called for the introduction of the triadic relational theory of Peirce's pragmaticist semiotic. Peirce's sign theory, with its close alignment to phenomenological philosophical approaches, possessed the capability in Singer's view to deal comprehensively and realistically with the elusive third member of the social science triad, the social and significantly phenomenological self.

The case that Singer made for this triadic Peircean advantage, both within the discipline of anthropology and beyond, was grounded in a recognition of both Peirce's early and later writings. It began with a close examination of some portions of the 1866 Lowell lectures and moved all of the way through to Peirce's post-1903 letters to Victoria Lady Welby. Singer drew not only from Peirce's semiotic triads, in particular, the icon/index/symbol triad, but also, and with masterful philosophical understanding, from Peirce's broader theory of the universal categories. Singer's explication of Peirce's semiotic and his comparative analysis of its triadic relationality, which he contrasted with what he termed the 'dyadic' structuralist theories of Lévi-Strauss and Edmond Leach among others (1984: 42), set a standard for Peircean semiotic explication that arguably remains unsurpassed within the discipline of anthropology even until today. His primary concern was to show that the triadic relationality Peirce recognized in the semiotic 'self' – that is in the semiotic sign considered as a self – led to a definition of the self as inherently processual, dialogical, social and public, a definition that did not equate the self with an individual organism or empirical body, even while it recognized the significance of the self's involvement with corporeality and organismic life experience. In this way, Singer championed Peircean semiotic theory as the means by which the social sciences in general and anthropology in particular could at last fully engage and integrate the social scientific study of the self into the larger whole of social scientific inquiry, remaining true to the fundamental micro-phenomenological aspects of the social self while at the same time illuminating their relations to collective social structures and processes.

Singer was not alone, of course, in this effort. Among the anthropologists he acknowledged in developing his call were prominent figures in symbolic and linguistic anthropology such as Clifford Geertz, James Boon, Thomas A. Sebeok, Michael Silverstein, Melford Spiro and M.N. Srinivas (1984: xiii). As Singer's work was developing, leading anthropologists of art and ritual studies, such as Roy Rapapport (1979), Stanley Tambiah (1979), and Nancy Munn (1973, [1986] 1992), among others, also had turned to various aspects of Peirce's pragmaticist sign theory as well. Rappaport's (1979) study of what he termed 'the obvious aspects' of ritual bears special mention here, as he employed Peirce's semiotic to develop an evolutionary theory of ritual that was comparable to Singer's work in its efforts to intervene in and move beyond the limitations of prevailing dyadic approaches employed in structural anthropology. Rappaport focused on the habit-taking character of ritual practices, which communicated merely by the voluntary participation of those involved the acceptance of the social commitments therein entailed. Peirce's processual orientation enabled Rappaport to diagram in given cases of ritual practice how social relations were understood and enacted performatively rather than through the media of doctrine or canonical (linguistic) communication (1979). While Rappaport's and various other applications of Peirce's semiotic served to further extend and refine the scope of symbolic anthropology, however, none set forth as clearly as Singer's call the programmatic advantages of the Peircean approach for the overall advancement of the discipline's progressive shift to fully anti-Cartesian relational method and theory. In this regard, it was largely Singer's vision that provided the theoretical and topical foundation for the work that for the next two decades was to follow from this initial main wave of semiotic anthropology.

The body of research that issued forth after Singer's call focused predominantly on various forms of what Singer had identified as 'cultural performance', a label he adopted from the ethnographic work of anthropologist, Lloyd Warner, on public festivals (1963). The main topics of inquiry focused on public displays of symbols, whether in ritual or secular contexts, that were considered to be emblematic of given ways of life, endeavouring to show precisely how these performance processes achieved their meaningful ends in relation to their diverse sociocultural and historical contexts.

As it happened, Singer's call for a semiotic anthropology came at a critical moment for the larger field of symbolic anthropology, which by the late 1970s had come under increasing fire within the discipline, both for its failure to yield the universal laws of cultural symbolism that its prevailing structuralist semiological approaches had promised to deliver and also for what were increasingly viewed as the neocolonial politics of representation that structuralist anthropology's very mission appeared to espouse in its intent to articulate determinative symbolic patterns of which cultural subjects were unaware and evidently unable to articulate for themselves. Semiotic anthropology's emergence and development, in this regard, provided a pragmatic alternative to carry symbolic anthropology forward out of this structuralist predicament. It aligned effectively both with an 'interpretive' turn the discipline was taking away from structuralism, as well as with the rise of the movement within sociocultural anthropology championing decolonizing orientations to inquiry and which supported the subdiscipline's growing interest in becoming a form of anti-imperialistic 'cultural critique' (Fischer 1984). With regard to the former, the interpretive turn, particularly as it was articulated in the influential work of symbolic anthropologist, Clifford Geertz (1973), created, among other things, a new and central role for ethnography in the subdiscipline of sociocultural anthropology. Ethnography, being the form of anthropological practice and representation in which indepth, participant-observation methodology was employed for the purpose of providing detailed, comprehensive accounts of given traditional ways of life, was inherently set up to enable the inclusion of a plurality of subjective voices and perspectives as opposed to providing a reductive universalist argument. In this interpretive ethnographic regard, the emergence and evolution of semiotic anthropology in sociocultural anthropology, with its capacity to recognize and represent the experiences and interpretations of various selves involved in its research, became a viable analytical support for interpretive ethnographic approaches. Likewise, in its definition of the self as fundamentally dialogic, public and social, a definition that applied equally to the subjects of anthropology as well as to its ethnographers, semiotic anthropology, employed strategically, avoided the charges of neo-imperialism to which structuralism had fallen prey.

The work of E. V. Daniel well exemplifies these features of semiotic anthropology's main wave.[6] Daniel produced two major works in semiotic anthropology during this period (1984, 1996). Each work adapted Peirce's semiotic to the prevailing trends of its respective decade. The first, *Fluid Signs: Being a Person the Tamil Way*, appeared in 1984 at the height of the interpretive turn. The second, *Charred Lullabies: Chapters in an Anthropography of Violence*, appeared in 1996, when anthropology as cultural critique was well established and a shift to large-scale, globally focused research was underway as well. *Fluid Signs* carried forward the interest in the social, dialogic self, analysing a variety of cultural performances traditional of the Sri Lankan Tamil ethnic group. Peirce's semiotic was employed to analyse and describe these performances as they were experienced by Tamil subjects and by Daniel himself in dialogue with them. *Charred Lullabies*, in contrast, examined manifestations and subjective experiences of violence occurring in relation to the Tamil–Sinhala conflict in Sri Lanka during the 1980s and 1990s, following the movements of the subjects of violence beyond the boundaries of Sri Lanka into English and American contexts. Peirce's semiotic in this context was again used to describe subjective experiences of violence and its aftermath, as well as to characterize the inter-ethnic (mis)understandings that each group tended to hold about the other.

Daniel's work illustrates the relative adaptability of semiotic anthropology to the changing theoretical and ideological orientations that were occurring during the end of the twentieth century in the discipline. However, despite attempts such as Daniel's to address issues and debates revolving around neo-imperialism and decolonization, semiotic anthropology was nonetheless due to wane as the new millennium approached. It remained identified with Singer's work and the pre-critical era of interpretive ethnography in which it had emerged. As new theoretical paradigms appeared designed to address globally focused issues of political-economy, a shift to analytical lenses that were closely associated with Foucauldian critical theory gained prestige. Judith Butler's Derridian theory of gender performativity is, perhaps, one of the most influential examples of such an approach gaining popularity in sociocultural anthropology at this time (Butler 1990). As a consequence, research under the rubric of semiotic anthropology declined as the twenty-first century dawned. It would require yet another fundamental disciplinary shift for it to once again resurface.

MILLENNIAL SIGNS OF RESURGENCE: (BIO)SEMIOTIC ANTHROPOLOGY IN THE ERA OF POST-HUMANISM

In recent years, there has been a renewed interest on the part of some sociocultural anthropologists in semiotic anthropology. Although it is occurring in a markedly different guise, this resurgence, if it, in fact, eventually achieves that status, can be seen to echo in certain respects, the initial pattern of semiotic anthropology's emergence. It has come about in part as a consequence of the increasing concern and attention paid across academic disciplines to climate change. Sociocultural anthropology is currently participating in a movement sweeping the humanities that seeks to develop new ecologically minded orientations towards cultural inquiry. It is adopting a more critical stance towards human-centred or 'anthropocentric' interpretive approaches in favour of approaches that challenge what is now sometimes termed human exceptionalism – the idea that human intelligence is superior to that of all other lifeforms. The vast majority of anthropological research on human communication, learning and symbolism since its inception would fall into this human exceptionalist category, given its tacit acceptance of the superiority of human language to all other communicative systems.

In this broader context of the 'non-human turn' (Grusin 2015), the cybernetic theory of Gregory Bateson (1972) has enjoyed a resurgence of interest in sociocultural anthropology, being one of the very few theoretical approaches developed by a twentieth-century sociocultural anthropologist that kept the theoretical door open, as it were, for the study of non-human-centred forms of learning. The cyborg post-humanist theory of Donna Haraway and the rhizomatic orientation of sociologist Bruno Latour's Actor Network Theory have been influential within the subdiscipline as well. Additionally, however, the emergence and rapid growth of the field of biosemiotics (Hoffmeyer 2008) also has provided ethnographic research with yet another means of preserving its capacity to study human meaning-making in cultural performances and practices, while at the same time responding to the criticisms of post-humanism. In this regard, semiotic anthropology, with a biosemiotic emphasis, has again offered sociocultural anthropology a means of carrying forward its research agenda on human symbolism in the face of a fundamental shift away from theoretical paradigms that might otherwise have come to impede it.

A noteworthy example of recent interpretive ethnographic research on human cultural symbolism undertaken from an explicitly biosemiotic perspective is Eduardo Kohn's 2013 study, *How Forests Think: Toward an Anthropology beyond the Human*. Kohn's analysis of the ecological life and thought of the Runa cultural group of Ecuador's Upper Amazon has been given outstanding recognition for its theoretical innovation. *How Forests Think* was awarded the Bateson Prize in 2014 by the Society for Cultural Anthropology and heralded by reviewers as 'marking a decisive moment' in the history of anthropology in which the discipline began to move beyond anthropocentric views of humanity (Pandian 2014: 245). Kohn's interest in this study is to show that the human capacity to achieve this shift in perspective may rest upon the ability to imagine the perspectives of non-human beings, beings to which Kohn assigns the status of 'selves'. Kohn's ethnography documents traditional Runa understandings of this very kind, understandings evident not only in oral tradition but also in dreams and in actual incidents of human-non-human interaction with animals of the Amazonian forest such as monkeys, dogs, wild boar and, most significantly, jaguars.

Kohn's theoretical perspective features most prominently Peirce's semiotic, aligning closely with Peirce's pansemiotic view that, as Kohn expresses it, 'all life is semiotic' (2013: 78). Kohn employs Peirce's icon/index/symbol triad in particular to reveal various ways in which the forest and its life forms can be seen to exhibit the properties of such 'living thought' (2013: 99). Images are iconic signs of particular importance in this regard. Positioning this semiotic analysis as a means of demonstrating the crucial importance of nonhuman perspectives for human life, Kohn's study can be read as a leading example in the new field of multispecies ethnography that seeks to bring the perspectives of nonhuman living subjects into ethnographic research in more active capacities.

While Kohn identifies Peirce as his philosophical champion, his biosemiotic reading of Peirce follows most closely the work of biological anthropologist, Terrence Deacon. In this respect, Kohn's study also illustrates a divergence from Peirce's thought that is itself a hallmark feature, not only of Deacon's reading of Peirce, but also of the vast majority of anthropologists who have worked under the rubric of semiotic anthropology, including Singer, Daniel, Rappaport and Geertz, among others, as well as the linguistic anthropological tradition as discussed above (e.g. Gal and Irvine). Its presence in Kohn's work, however, given its post-humanist alignment, is particularly telling. This divergence occurs, as reviewers of Kohn's work have noted (Herrera and Palsson 2014: 238), in regard to Peirce's definition of the symbol. Kohn, following Deacon (1997) and the standard anthropological reading, narrows the definition of the symbol to a 'sign of convention', omitting Peirce's broader conceptualization of the symbol as a sign of habit, conventional or otherwise. Kohn then approximates the Peircean symbol to the Saussurian linguistic sign, a move that Singer did not make, but which the majority who have followed in his footsteps did, including Deacon. Rather than remaining consistent with Peirce in this symbolic theoretical regard – or with biosemioticians other than Deacon, for that matter, who have recognized Peirce's symbol classification as broader than Saussure's linguistic sign – Kohn followed the standard ethnographic position, arguing that the thinking of nonhuman lifeforms is entirely iconic and indexical in character. Kohn considers humans to be exceptional with regard to their capacity for symbol usage.

Kohn's position, which, again, echoes closely one that Deacon has repeatedly taken and defended (Deacon 1997, 2012), is indicative of how deeply rooted the semiological linguicentric perspective is and remains in sociocultural anthropological thought. While it has been challenged by biosemioticians outside of anthropology (Stjernfelt 2012, 2014; Patee 2007), the perspective remains the predominant view within the discipline.[7]

CONCLUSION

In closing, it remains to acknowledge the resilience of semiotic theory, broadly defined, within the subdiscipline of sociocultural anthropology. It would be difficult to identify another set of theoretical perspectives on any topic of anthropological inquiry that have managed to survive the discipline's various reversals of theoretical fortunes with equal tenacity. However, it must also be recognized that semiotic anthropology, narrowly defined, has remained, and most likely will remain on the margins of cultural anthropological research, in the role of David facing the Goliath of semiology and its (post)structuralist allies. These latter continue to remain at its core, even if somewhat submerged at various moments. This may in large part be due to the strength of anthropocentrism on which the anthropological subdisciplines have been founded, and which ultimately may prove impossible to transcend. Or, it may be due to a sympathy with and for dyadic models of communication, which are models of relative clarity in many respects, compared to the slippery (or 'glassy' in Singer's perspective) processual intricacies of triadic, pragmaticist semiotics. Whatever the reason, it seems unlikely that any single theoretical approach will ever prevail once and for all over the others. The diversity of human cultural and communicative practice and the breadth of the anthropological project itself make this outcome very hard to imagine, let alone bring about.

NOTES

1 This review is focused primarily on semiotic anthropology which takes a Peircean orientation; See Sedda and Padoan (2018) for an overview of Continental semiotic traditions in anthropology.
2 Particularly in the American context (to which this chapter in the main stays confined), the discipline of anthropology comprises the subdisciplines of biological/physical anthropology, linguistic anthropology, archaeology and a fourth subdisciplinary area dedicated to the study of human diversity in living human populations transmitted via means that are social and learned. This fourth subdiscipline has acquired different labels in different geographical regions and intellectual schools of thought, the most common being 'social' and 'cultural' anthropology. This chapter will employ the phrase 'sociocultural anthropology' with the intent of referring relatively inclusively to the entirety of anthropological work in this fourth subdisciplinary area.
3 Tylor's definition of culture reads, 'Culture or Civilization, taken in its wide ethnographic sense, is that complex whole which includes knowledge, belief, art, morals, law, custom, and any other capabilities and habits acquired by man as a member of society' ([1871] 1973: 63).
4 Ironically, much of the opposition to this model came from within the field of linguistic anthropology itself (e.g. Hymes 1983).
5 'Etic', derived from the term 'phonetic', refers to a universal view point such as that of the International Phonetic Alphabet as it categorizes the whole array of sounds that are used in

languages worldwide, while 'emic', derived from the term 'phonemic', refers to a culture bearer's learned perspective of functionally significant sounds used in a given language.
6 Other texts that also exemplify this 'first wave' of semiotic anthropology include Parmentier (1987); Lewis (1992); Ness (1992); Keane (1997); Portis-Winner (2002); and Mines (2005).
7 Perspectives adopting Peirce's broader definition of the symbol have been taken within the discipline by Ness (2016, 2020) and Pandian (2014), among others.

REFERENCES

Andrews, E. (1990), *Markedness Theory: The Union of Asymmetry and Semiosis in Language*, Durham: Duke University Press.
Bateson, G. (1972), *Steps to an Ecology of Mind*, New York: Ballantine Books.
Bateson, G. (1976), *Mind and Nature: A Necessary Unity*, New York: Dutton.
Bauman, R. and J. Sherzer, eds (1974), *Explorations in the Ethnography of Speaking*, Cambridge: Cambridge University Press.
Bloomfield, L. (1935), *Language*, London: G. Allen & Unwin, Ltd.
Burling, R. (1984), *Learning a Field Language*, Ann Arbor: University of Michigan Press.
Butler, J. (1990), *Gender Trouble: Feminism and the Subversion of Identity*, New York: Routledge.
Daniel, E. V. (1984), *Fluid Signs: Being a Person the Tamil Way*, Berkeley: University of California Press.
Daniel, E. V. (1996), *Charred Lullabies; Chapters in an Anthropography of Violence*, Princeton: Princeton University Press.
Deacon, T. (1997), *The Symbolic Species*, New York: W.W. Norton.
Deacon, T. (2012), 'Beyond the Symbolic Species', in T. Schilhab, F. Stjernfelt and T. W. Deacon (eds), *The Symbolic Species Evolved*, 9–38, The Netherlands: Springer.
Fischer, M. M. J. (1984), 'Film as Ethnography and Cultural Critique in the Late Twentieth Century', in D. Carson and L. D. Friedman (eds), *Shared Differences: Multicultural Media and Practical Pedagogy*, 29–56, University of Illinois Press.
Frazer, J. G. ([1890] 1981), *The Golden Bough; The Roots of Religion and Folklore*, New York: Avenel Books.
Gal, S. and J. T. Irvine (2019), *Signs of Difference: Language and Ideology in Social Life*, Cambridge: Cambridge University Press.
Geertz, C. (1973), *The Interpretation of Cultures*, New York: Basic Books.
Grusin, R., ed. (2015), *The Nonhuman Turn*, Minneapolis: University of Minnesota Press.
Herrera, C. E. G. and G. Palsson (2014), 'The Forest and the Trees', *HAU: Journal of Ethnographic Theory*, 4 (2): 237–43.
Hoffmeyer, J. (2008), *Biosemiotics: An Examination into the Signs of Life and the Life of Signs*, Scranton: University of Scranton Press.
Hymes, D. (1983), *Essays in the History of Linguistic Anthropology*, Philadelphia: J. Benjamins.
Jakobson, R. ([1950] 1971), 'Shifters, Verbal Categories, and the Russian Verb', in S. Rudy (ed.), *Selected Writings*, vol. 2, 130–47, The Hague: Mouton.
Jakobson, R. (1977), 'A Few Remarks on Peirce, Pathfinder in the Science of Language', *Modern Language Notes*, 92 (5): 1026–32.
Lewis, J. L. (1992), *Ring of Liberation; Deceptive Discourse in Brazilian Capoeira*, Chicago: University of Chicago Press.
Keane, W. (1997), *Signs of Recognition; Powers and Hazards of Representation in an Indonesian Society*, Berkeley: University of California Press.

Kohn, E. (2013), *How Forests Think: Toward an Anthropology Beyond the Human*, Berkeley: University of California Press.
Lévi-Strauss, C. (1963), *Structural Anthropology*, New York: Basic Books.
Malinowski, B. (1923), 'The Problem of Meaning in Primitive Languages', in C. K. Ogden and I. A. Richards (eds), *The Meaning of Meaning: A Study of the Influence of Language Upon Thought and of the Science of Symbolism*, 296–336, New York: Harcourt, Brace & World, Inc.
Mertz, E. (2007), 'Semiotic Anthropology', *Annual Review of Anthropology*, 36: 337–53.
Mines, D. (2005), *Fierce Gods; Inequality, Ritual, and the Politics of Dignity in a South Indian Village*, Bloomington: Indiana University Press.
Morgan, L. H. ([1878] 1985), *Ancient Society*, Tucson: University of Arizona Press.
Munn, N. (1973), *Walbiri Iconography: Graphic Representation and Cultural Symbolism in a Central Australian Society*, Ithaca: Cornell University Press.
Munn, N. ([1986] 1992), *The Fame of Gawa: A Symbolic Study of Value Transformation in a Massim (Papua New Guinea) Society*, Durham: Duke University Press.
Ness, S. A. (1992), *Body, Movement, and Culture: Kinesthetic and Visual Symbolism in a Philippine Community*, Philadelphia: University of Pennsylvania Press.
Ness, S. A. (2016), *Choreographies of Landscape; Signs of Performance in Yosemite National Park*, New York: Berghahn.
Ness, S. A. (2020), 'Diagnosing with Light; the Semiotics of Acupoint Biophoton Emissions Testing', *The American Journal of Semiotics*, 35 (3–4): 365–400.
Ogden, C. K. and I. A. Richards, eds (1923), *The Meaning of Meaning: A Study of the Influence of Language Upon Thought and of the Science of Symbolism*, New York: Harcourt, Brace & World, Inc.
Parmentier, R. J. (1987), *The Sacred Remains; Myth, History, and Polity in Belau*, Chicago: University of Chicago Press.
Patee, H. H. (2007), 'The Necessity of Biosemiotics: Matter-symbol Complementarity', in M. Barbieri (ed.), *Introduction to Biosemiotics*, 115–32, New York: Springer.
Pandian, A. (2014), 'Thinking Like a Mountain', *HAU: Journal of Ethnographic Theory*, 4 (2): 245–52.
Pike, K. L. (1967), *Language in Relation to a Unified Theory of the Structure of Human Behavior*, The Hague: Mouton.
Portis-Winner, I. (2002), *Semiotics of Peasants in Transition; Slovene Villagers and Their Ethnic Relatives in America*, Durham, NC: Duke.
Portis-Winner, I. (2009), 'Facing Emergences: Past Traces and New Directions in American Anthropology (Why American Anthropology Needs a Semiotics of Culture)', *Sign Systems Studies*, 37 (1/2): 114–68.
Portis-Winner, I. (2014), *Semiotics of Culture and Beyond*, Bern: Peter Lang.
Portis-Winner, I. and J. Umiker-Sebeok, eds (1979), *Semiotics of Culture*, Paris: Mouton, The Hague.
Rabinow, P. and W. Sullivan (1979), *Interpretive Social Science: A Reader*, Berkeley: University of California Press.
Rappaport, R. A. (1979), *Ecology, Meaning, & Ritual*, Berkeley: North Atlantic Books.
Saussure, F. de ([1916] 2009), *Course in General Linguistics*, trans. R. Harris, ed. C. Bally, A. Sechehaye and W. A. Riedlinger, Chicago: Open Court.
Schieffelin, B. B, K. A. Woolard and P. V. Kroskrity, eds (1998), *Language Ideologies: Practice and Theory*, Oxford: Oxford University Press.
Sebeok, T. A., ed. (1969), *Approaches to Semiotics 1*, The Hague: Mouton.

Sebeok, T. A., ed. (1978), *Sight, Sound, and Sense*, Bloomington: Indiana University Press.
Sebeok, T. A., ed. (1986), '"Semiotics" and Its Congeners', in J. Deely, B. Williams and F. E. Kruse (eds), *Frontiers in Semiotics*, 255–63, Bloomington: Indiana University Press.
Sebeok, T. A., A. S. Hayes and M. C. Bateson, eds (1964), *Approaches to Semiotics: Cultural Anthropology, Education, Linguistics, Psychology*, The Hague: Mouton.
Sedda, F. and T. Padoan (2018), 'Sémiotique et Anthropologie', in A. Biglari and N. Roelens (eds), *La Sémiotique en Interface*, 37–68, Paris: Éditions Kimé.
Sicoli, M. A. and M. Wolfgram (2018), 'Charles Sanders Peirce and Anthropological Theory', *Oxford Bibliographies*, online. doi: 10.1093/OBO/9780199766557-1087.
Shapiro, M. (1983), *The Sense of Grammar: Language as Semeiotic*, Bloomington: Indiana University Press.
Silverstein, M. (1976), 'Shifters, Linguistic Categories, and Cultural Description', in K. H. Basso and H. A. Selby (eds), *Meaning in Anthropology*, 11–55, Albuquerque: University of New Mexico Press.
Singer, M. (1978), 'For a Semiotic Anthropology', in T. Sebeok (ed.), *Sight, Sound, and Sense*, 202–31, Bloomington: Indiana University Press.
Singer, M. (1980), 'Signs of the Self: An Exploration in Semiotic Anthropology', *American Anthropologist*, 82 (3): 485–507.
Singer, M. (1984), *Man's Glassy Essence: Explorations in Semiotic Anthropology*, Bloomington: Indiana University Press.
Sonesson, G. (2004), 'The Globalization of Ego and Alter; an Essay in Cultural Semiotics', *Semiotica*, 148: 153–73.
Sonesson, G. (2012), 'Between Homeworld and Alienworld: A Primer of Cultural Semiotics', in E. W. B. Hess-Lüttich (ed.), *Sign Culture=Zeichen Kultur*, 315–28, Würzburg: Verlag Königshausen & Neumann.
Sonesson, G. (2016), 'Epistemological Prolegomena to the Cognitive Semiotics of Evolution and Development', *Language and Semiotic Studies*, 2 (4): 46–99.
Stasch, R. (2003), 'The Semiotics of World-making in Korowai Feast Longhouses', *Language & Communication*, 23: 359–83.
Stjernfelt, F. (2012), 'The Evolution of Semiotic Self Control', in T. Schilhab, F. Stjernfelt and T. W. Deacon (eds), *The Symbolic Species Evolved*, 9–38, The Netherlands: Springer.
Stjernfelt, F. (2014), *Natural Propositions; the Actuality of Peirce's Doctrine of Discisigns*, Boston: Docent Press.
Tambiah, S. J. (1979), 'A Performative Approach to Ritual', *Proceedings of the British Academy*, 65: 113–69.
Tylor, E. B. ([1871] 1973), 'Primitive Culture', excerpts printed in P. Bohannan and M. Glazer (eds), *High Points in Anthropology*, 63–78, New York: Alfred A. Knopf.
Umiker-Sebeok, J. (1977), 'Semiotics of Culture: Great Britain and North America', *Annual Review of Anthropology*, 6: 121–35.

CHAPTER THREE

Semiotics in History and Archaeology

MAREK TAMM AND ROBERT W. PREUCEL

INTRODUCTION

Semiotics has enjoyed a limited, but enduring interest in history and archaeology. Projects like 'semiotics of history', 'historical semiotics', '*historia sub specie semioticae*', 'semiotics of archaeology', 'archaeology of semiotics' and 'archaeological semiotics' have been proclaimed periodically since the heyday of semiotics in the 1970s. Although never a dominant focus, semiotic approaches have opened many important new theoretical vistas and produced some important empirical studies in history and archaeology and their potential is definitely not yet exhausted.

This chapter provides a short history of joining semiotics to historical and archaeological research featuring separately Saussurean and Peircean perspectives. We shall present some major achievements and discussions in historical and archaeological semiotics, primarily in theoretical, but also in empirical terms, and describe some key questions and research perspectives for the future of semiotics in these two fields. But first, we will offer a general framework for the semiotic analysis of past societies.

The study of the past, both in history and in archaeology, is a semiotic enterprise in at least two senses. First, most archaeologists and historians agree that understanding meaning is a main goal of their research. Estonian-Russian semiotician Juri Lotman has explained this particularly well:

> In order to understand the *meaning* of the behaviour of past people and literary characters we have to know their culture, their everyday life, their habits and customs, their systems of representations, etc. [...] Namely to understand, because to know facts and to understand these are two different things in history. Events are driven by people. People behave according to the motives and habits of their epoch. If we don't know these motives, then the acts of the people start to look inexplicable and senseless.
> (Lotman 1994: 9, 13)[1]

Put differently, the past reality can be considered as semiotic by its very nature, the past does not consist of events (and things, etc.), but of their meanings, and the goal of the historians and archaeologists alike is to investigate the systems of symbolization people have developed in the past to give meaning to their existence.

But the study of the past is semiotic also in the sense that archaeological or historical interpretation is itself a semiotic act. 'All historians are semioticians: from an infinite number of occurrences, they select those, which they consider meaningful, hoping to convey the importance of that interpretation to their readers,' American historian William Pencak (2011: 77) has written to the point. As we cannot study the past directly, because, by definition, it does not exist anymore, we can study only the traces the past has left. This means that semiotic interpretation is at the core of each exploration of the past. Lotman explains this again very well:

> Standing between an event 'as it was' and the historian is a *text* [in the widest semiotic sense of the term, i.e. every kind of sign system – M.T., R.P.], which fundamentally alters the scholarly situation. A text is always created by someone and represents a past event translated into another language. One and the same reality differently encoded will yield different – often contradictory – texts. Extracting a fact from a text or an event from a story about an event requires an act of decoding. And so, whether this is acknowledged or not, the historian begins with the semiotic manipulation of his initial material – the text.
>
> (Lotman 2019: 189–90)

As widely known, there are two main traditions of semiotics, one derives from the work of Charles Sanders Peirce and the second from Ferdinand de Saussure. Accordingly, we can detect also two different tracks of historical and archaeological semiotics: one of Peircean and the other of Saussurean tradition. Following Mihhail Lotman (2002), we could call these two traditions also as atomistic (or semiotics of sign) and holistic (semiotics of language). From the standpoint of the Peircean semiotics, sign is elementary and, semiotically, the smallest element. Although Peirce's definition of sign is relativistic (the sign is formed by the system of relations), it is nevertheless semiotically an elementary object, it does not consist of any smaller components. For Saussure, on the contrary, the starting point or a primary reality is language and its structure; the individual elements of language do not play an important role in his theory. Saussure conceptualizes language as a system of relationships between elements defined only by their differences. Within the tradition of atomistic semiotics, the researchers' attention is focused on the sign in isolation, that is, on the relationship of sign to meaning, to addressee and so on, whereas in the case of the holistic tradition, the researchers concentrate their attention on a language, that is, a mechanism which uses a certain set of elementary signs for the communication of content (Lotman and Uspenskij 1984: ix).

SEMIOTICS IN HISTORY

The early attempts to introduce a semiotic perspective in history date back to 1970s.[2] The first programmatic effort was made by Russian semiotician and linguist Boris Uspenskij at the First All-Soviet-Union Symposium on Secondary Modelling Systems held at the University of Tartu in early February 1974. In his paper titled '*Historia sub specie semioticae*' Uspenskij proposed to consider history as a communication process in which new information (text) is interpreted by the addressee (society), and the meaning ascribed to this text generates a new text, communicated in the addressee's reflexive reaction. The paper was published in the same year in the proceedings of the symposium, a rotaprint booklet with a small print run (Uspenskij 1974). Two years later, a slightly modified version appeared in the collective volume *Kul'turnoe nasledie Drevnej Rusi* [Cultural Heritage of Old Rus'], published in Moscow (Uspenskij 1976a). Since Uspenskij's paper, the project of a semiotics of history became an important avenue of research in the Tartu-Moscow School of Semiotics (see below).

But next to the work of the Tartu-Moscow semioticians, there were some other examples of joining history and semiotics in late 1970s and early 1980s. For instance, Algirdas Julien Greimas, leader of the so-called Paris School of Semiotics, called in his book *Sémiotique et sciences sociales* (1976) for a foundation of a 'historical semiotics' (*une sémiotique historique*), which 'would have the task of establishing a typology of historiographic narrative structures' (Greimas 1976: 169). Unfortunately, his call did not find many followers; but Greimas's ideas inspired many semiotically minded scholars around the world, not least Peter Haidu, who was among the first to plea for linking history and semiotics in the English-speaking world in the early 1980s (see below). But one of the best examples of French historical semiotics in practice, although not in the spirit of Greimas, is Tzvetan Todorov's *The Conquest of America*, published in 1982. This study offers an original interpretation of the discovery of America by Columbus and of the subsequent conquest and colonization of Mexico by the Spaniards. According to Todorov, what took place in America after 1492 was not merely a subjugation of the local population by the Spanish conquistadors, but it was also an encounter between two semiotic systems. The Spaniards defeated indigenous peoples by means of signs, not of arms, the author argues, this means that in order to understand the conquest of America, it is imperative to study the semiotic behaviour of both parties, i.e. their ways of comprehension, interpretation and communication (Todorov 1982).

Semiotics of history in the United States: A Peircean tradition

In the early 1980s we can witness an increasing rapprochement of semiotics and history in the United States (see Williams 1990), reflected primarily on the pages of the journal *Semiotica*, edited by Thomas A. Sebeok, including two special issues, in 1986 (Boklund-Lagopolous and Lagapoulos 1986) and in 1991 (Pencak and Williams 1991). As mentioned above, Peter Haidu, a scholar of medieval literature, was among the first to advocate 'coordination of semiotics and history' in the English-speaking world (Haidu 1982: 188; but see also Finlay-Pelinski 1982). In his article 'History and Semiotics', published in *Semiotica* in 1982, he aims 'to demonstrate the availability, within the present stock of semiotic techniques, of procedures that can found a historical semiotics' (Haidu 1982: 191). According to Haidu, 'semiotics must consider history, not as phenomenal event, but as an entity producing meaning, as a signifier capable of being assigned a signified. The events of history, that is, must be considered as "event-messages"; it is their meaningfulness that allows the imposition of semiotic analysis' (Haidu 1982: 198). Haidu is clearly inspired by the semiotic theories of Greimas (see also Haidu 1980, 1981, 1985), but his proposition to consider 'history as text' (Haidu 1982: 199) also comes very close to the ideas of the Tartu-Moscow School.

Another American historian who contributed prominently to the converging of history and semiotics in the 1980s was Brooke Williams (Deely). She started a Peircean tradition in American semiotics of history, with a focus on theoretical and epistemological issues. Educated in history, she discovered her semiotic calling in October 1978 while attending the third annual meeting of the Semiotic Society of America, becoming the first historian who joined the society (Williams Deely 2011: 372). Five years later, already deeply engaged in semiotic discussions, Williams declared at the 8th annual meeting of the Semiotic Society of America, held in Snowbird, Utah, on 6–9 October 1983: 'The time has come for history to be classified within semiotics according to its proper characteristics both as a discipline in its own right and in terms of its transdisciplinary place in the development of signs' (Williams 1987b: 409, see also Williams 1987a). In a more detailed way, Williams presented her ideas on the relationship between history and semiotics in the article 'What Has History to Do with Semiotics', published in *Semiotica* in 1985. For Williams, semiotics permits us to rethink the very concept of history: 'History in its proper being is not first of all a discipline, but precisely is the anthroposemiotic transmission and generation of culture wherein nature and mind mutually influence each other in the shaping and constitution of "reality"' (Williams 1985: 281; cf. Williams 1986: 219). Historical past is an outcome of semiosis, of semiotic mediation and transmission, and the study of history is therefore crucial in order to understand the question how and why sign systems change. She draws an important conclusion: 'History is always being rewritten because that is its semiosic role in culture' (Williams 1985: 321).

On the initiative of Williams, a session on history and semiotics was presented in December 1987, as part of the 102nd Annual Meeting of the American Historical Association in Washington, DC. The purpose of the session, Williams reported next year, was to initiate dialogue between the discipline of history and the transdisciplinary movement of semiotics concerning how a semiotic understanding of history can enhance communication across fields within the discipline, as well as open up avenues of understanding between history and semiotics (Williams 1988: 821).

In 1991, Williams, together with William Pencak edited what has so far remained the last special issue on history and semiotics of *Semiotica* (Williams and Pencak 1991). Unlike the previous special issue *Signs of the Past: Semiotics and History*, edited by Karin Boklund-Lagopolous and Alexandros-Phaidon Lagopoulos in 1986, it was written exclusively by practising historians, in order to show, as Pencak (1993: 1) would explain it a few years later, 'how historians can use semiotics to ask and answer better the sorts of questions and interpret the sorts of data they usually do, rather than using history as a springboard for semiotic theorizing'. Pencak was indeed the second key figure in the United States to promote the dialogue between history and semiotics in the late 1980s and early 1990s. In 1993 he gathered his relevant publications in a volume titled *History, Signing in: Essays in History and Semiotics*. From the outset, he declared that his main aim with this volume was to show 'how a historian aware of semiotics but unwilling to become a semiotic theorist – or drown his writing with semiotic jargon incomprehensible to his normal audience – can employ semiotics in historical work' (Pencak 1993: 1). Unlike Williams, who was interested in 'what has history to do with semiotics', Pencak would like to inquire into 'what has semiotic to do with history', while suggesting 'to historians wary wading too deeply into the waters of semiotic theory the reverse propositions' (Pencak 1993: 86). To his mind, too 'much of the work on "history and semiotics" [...] consists of the musings of non-historians about the meaning of history' (Pencak 1993: 1) and therefore there is a need for a serious engagement of professional historians in semiotic theories and methods (see also Pencak 1998).

Some other American examples from the same period can be mentioned, especially the work of the Yale literary scholar Thomas M. Green, who in 1986 formulated a need for 'historical semiotics' (Green 1986). However, ten years later he had to admit that very little progress had been made in developing this new (sub)discipline:

> One purpose of the essay, in fact, is to dramatize the effective absence of a missing sub-discipline which the humanities grievously need – namely, historical semiotics. We possess many sketchy contributions like the forgoing paper which this future sub-discipline might incorporate, but to my knowledge we have no organized effort, no single scholarly journal, no academic program, which might focus the cross-disciplinary collaboration that is required.
> (Green 1996: 33)

When historical semiotics is nowadays evoked in the English-speaking world, the dominant mood is still longing for a semiotic approach in history, considered very promising, but somehow always in the state of emerging. In 1999, the historian Luisa Passerini published an article 'History and Semiotics', trying to integrate the historical semiotics of Uspenskij with contemporary approaches in cultural history and historical theory. But in her conclusion she points once again to the old desiderata:

> We would argue [...] that much is left to be done in order to draw out the full consequences of a semiotic conception of history as a communicative process. [...] The development of a semiotics of history might be the essential step that historians have to take in order to assume their role on the cultural scene of the present.
> (Passerini 1999: 19)

So, in a recent article Youzheng Li (2017: 49) still talks about historical semiotics in terms of 'a recently emerging new discipline'.

Semiotics of history in the Tartu-Moscow School: A Saussurean tradition

The Saussurean tradition of the semiotics of history is best represented by the work of the Tartu-Moscow School of Semiotics. The two main representatives of the field, Juri Lotman and Boris Uspenskij, make very explicit their adherence to the holistic semiotics of language, in opposition to the atomistic semiotics of sign:

> There is a crucial difference between the understanding of non-semiotic reality in the Peircean and the Saussurean approaches. If in the former it exists as the object of logical models, then in the latter it acquires features of empirical reality. For this reason, the first approach opens the way only to logical models, while the second affords the hope of reconstructing extratextual empirical reality by means of the text. At this point the aims of semiotics converge with traditional aims of historical research.
> (Lotman and Uspenskij 1984: x)

The Tartu-Moscow semioticians proceed from the basic premise that the domain of semiotic phenomena is coextensive with that of culture. Culture is seen as a system of semiotic relationships between humans and the world and this relationship can be regarded as a communicatory dialogue. 'This approach', Lotman and Uspenskij (1984: x–xi) argue, 'makes it possible to look at history from the semiotic perspective: from this angle the historical process appears as a system of communications between the social group and the reality surrounding it – in particular between various social groups – and, at the same time, as a dialogue between the historical personage and the social group.'

When in the early phase of the Tartu-Moscow School, in 1960s, the main paradigm was structuralism and the emphasis was on synchronic and static aspects of culture, since the early 1970s, the dynamic and diachronic aspects became increasingly important. Retrospectively, Lotman (1993: 41) admitted that 'the semiotic movement began from a denial of historical studies', but immediately added that 'abandoning the historical study was necessary in order *to return* to it later'. In his last, posthumously published book, *The Unpredictable Workings of Culture*, he explains the argument in more detail:

> At the inception of semiotic studies, the isolation of the field of culture from the sphere of history was in part necessary and in part polemical in nature. The dissemination of the object of semiotics within the broad field of the science of history has made the very border between semiotics and the world outside it an object of study. At this stage it is possible to define semiotics as the study of the theory and history of culture.
> (Lotman 2013: 53)

In 1971, Lotman and Uspenskij postulated in a joint article the fundamental principle of culture as a dynamic system, connecting it with the dynamism of the social life of human society: 'The necessity for continual self-renewal, to become different and yet remain the same, constitutes one of the chief working mechanisms of culture' (Lotman and Uspensky 1978: 226). It is in this context of dynamic study of cultural semiotics that Uspenskij and Lotman formulated their programme of semiotics of history. Both together and separately they wrote in the 1970s and 1980s an extended series of studies in the semiotics of Russian cultural history.

Although in many ways similar and developed in close collaboration, Lotman's and Uspenskij's approaches to the semiotics of history present some important differences (see Kalinin 2003, 2009; Pern 2012; Hałas 2017; Trunin 2017). In the centre of Uspenskij's theory of semiotics of history stands the concept of communication. Uspenskij departs from the principle that in various fields of culture, including history, we can see the same mechanisms that operate in language. Therefore, he builds his model of semiotics of history on the basis of an analogy with the linguistic act or communication in a natural language. Uspenskij depicts history as a cultural process, consisting in communication, in which new text (information) is interpreted by the addressee (society), and the meaning attributed to this text produces a new text. This process takes place in a specific historical-cultural context, where acts of communication are founded in a certain code (Uspenskij 1976b: 64, 1996: 10). In other words, a semiotic model of history constructed in this way consists in linking two planes – of action or performance and of thought or interpretation (Hałas 2013: 70). Uspenskij is primarily interested in the study of the second plane, 'the cultural semiotic approach to history presupposes the emphasizing of the inner viewpoint of the participants in the historical process: only what is important from *their* perspective matters' (Uspenskij 1996: 9). Historical events are therefore communicative events, the meaning of which changes along with the emerging new present and new addressees.

From this point of view, it is thus not the objective meaning of events (if anything of the kind be presumed to exist) that matters, but the way they are perceived, the way the events are read. Under these circumstances, the fact that some events are perceived as momentous – regardless of whether they are products of symbolic activity or not – gains key importance: the way a sequence of events is interpreted determines the further course of events (Uspenskij 1996: 10, 2017: 233). In an introduction to a new book series, *Fakty i znaki: issledovaniya po semiotike istorii* (Facts and Signs: Studies in Semiotics of History), that Uspenskij established in 2008 together with his son Fedor Uspenskij, he succinctly summarizes his take on the semiotics of history:

> The semiotic approach [...] involves the reconstruction of the system of representations that determine both the perception of certain events in a given society, as well as the reaction to these events, which is the direct impulse of the historical process. In this case, the historian is interested in the cause-effect relationships at the level that is directly related to the event plan, directly and not indirectly. Thus, the historian tries to see the historical process through the eyes of its participants, deliberately distracting from the objectivist historiographical tradition retrospectively describing events from an external point of view.
>
> (Uspenskij and Uspenskij 2008: 8)

Juri Lotman's more specific interest in the semiotics of history arose from his critical discussion of historical sources in the mid-1970s (Boyko 2014: 63, 2015: 272, 2022). In a short article 'On the Problem of Dealing with Unreliable Sources', Lotman (1975) shows that the widely used notion of 'reliability' in textual studies is inherently relative, and that even a deliberate forgery can offer valuable information. Some years later, in his discussion with the mathematicians Mikhail Postnikov and Anatoly Fomenko, Lotman (1982: 44–5) argued in the same vein that historical documents had a potentially varied semiotic nature, and therefore any quantitative account should be preceded by a semiotic analysis of each particular document.

According to Lotman, 'facts' and 'events' are not given to historian but are outcomes of textual encoding and decoding:

> The idea of what constitutes a historical event is the product of a given type culture and is itself an important typological indicator. And so, when historians pick up a text, they must distinguish between what constitutes an event from their point of view and what was an event worthy of remembering from the point of view of the author of the text and his or her contemporaries.
>
> (Lotman 2019: 190)

Lotman argues that every historical text is encoded on at least three levels. First, each text is an utterance in a natural language and, as a result, is organized according to the laws structuring a given language. Second, on a super-phrasal level, each text is subjected to the laws of rhetoric and to the logic of narrative. And third, on the highest level, each text must be ideologically encoded: 'The laws of the political, religious, and philosophical order, genre codes, and representations of etiquette, which the historian must reconstruct on the basis of those very texts, occasionally falling into a logical vicious circle, all leads to supplemental encoding' (Lotman 2019: 191). In brief, as stated earlier, in Lotman's mind every historian is by definition also a semiotician, even if unwittingly.

Alongside the historian's dependence on textual mediation, Lotman underlined another important aspect of the historian's work – its retrospective character:

> The historian regards an event from a point of view which is oriented from present to past. This view, by its very nature, transforms the object of description. The picture of

events, which appears chaotic to the casual observer, leaves the hands of the historian in the form of a secondary organisation. It is natural for the historian to proceed from the inevitability of what has occurred. However, his creative activity is manifested in other ways: from the abundance of facts stored in memory, he constructs a sequential line, leading with the utmost reliability towards this conclusive point.

(Lotman 2009: 17)

The retrospective gaze of the historian creates the illusion of a linear and causal stream of time and excludes all unpredictable and random elements from the past. 'By removing the moment of unpredictability from the historical process, we make it totally redundant,' Lotman contended (Lotman 2009: 14). From the standpoint of the semiotics of history, the event that has occurred is only one of the possible versions; thus, historical research cannot be reduced to merely investigating the circumstances and the inevitability of the historical event.

According to Lotman, random events or elements in the historical process can cause unpredictable situations, cultural explosions, that completely change the whole semiotic situation, but these accidental elements can also act as a reserve for future reorganizations of the culture. In this approach, Lotman was greatly inspired by the work of Ilya Prigogine and Isabelle Stengers, especially by their ideas regarding complex systems, dissipative structures and irreversible processes in chemistry and physics. Lotman decided to apply some of these ideas to the realm of historical processes as well as to the study of history in general. Particularly important for Lotman is the concept of bifurcation, which is a point of development of a system when it reaches the point of 'choice' between two possible scenarios. Proceeding from this idea, Lotman proposed a basic assumption that a historical event should be seen as the result of one of multiple alternatives, meaning that, at a certain point (the point of bifurcation), the same circumstances in history might not have identical consequences: 'History is not a unilineal process but a multi-factored stream. When a point of bifurcation is reached, movement appears to stop so as to permit contemplation over which path to take' (Lotman 2019: 184).

The historian is a prophet who predicts the past, Lotman reminds us, quoting Friedrich Schlegel's aphorism; that is, the gaze of the historian inevitably transforms the past. In retrospect, that which has occurred is declared uniquely possible, and all other (untaken) paths are declared to be impossible (Semenenko 2012: 72). This allows Lotman to conclude:

Therefore, we can conclude that the necessity of relying on texts leaves the historian unavoidably facing a double distortion. On the one hand, the syntagmatic directionality of the text transforms the event by placing it into a narrative structure while, on the other hand, the contradictory directionality of the historian's gaze deforms the written object.

(Lotman 2019: 198)

In 1992, shortly before Lotman's death, the thematic issue of *Trudy po znakovym sistemam* (*Sign Systems Studies*) – the oldest journal of semiotics in the world, established by Lotman in 1964 – was published, dedicated to 'Semiotics and History'. The editorial preface of the volume, written by Lotman, declared in a programmatic way the need for a new connection of history and semiotics: 'Semiotics has changed during the past decades. One of its accomplishments along its difficult path was its joining with history.

The perception of history has become semiotic, and semiotic thinking has acquired historical features' (Lotman 1992: 3). Since Lotman's death, the new generation of Tartu (and Moscow) semioticians has not dedicated much attention to developing dialogue between history and semiotics. However, one can mention a recent special issue of *Sign Systems Studies* (vol. 45, no. 3/4), titled 'Semiotics and History' and exploring some new perspectives of the semiotics of history (Tamm 2017a).

SEMIOTICS IN ARCHAEOLOGY

Archaeology's relationship with semiotics began in the 1960s with the structuralist encounter.[3] As is well known, Claude Lévi-Strauss elaborated upon Saussure's linguistic approach and applied it to the study of social and cultural phenomena in his pursuit of cognitive universals. Several leading French archaeologists were influenced by his ideas and adopted his methods to understand the origins of art during the Upper Palaeolithic period. Structuralism was a foundational approach in the early development of historical archaeology in the United States. In the late 1970s, processual archaeology developed in the United States as an explicitly scientific approach grounded in positivism. Archaeologists interested in the study of adaptive systems were drawn to developments in cognitive science, computation and language models. In early 1980s, a counter movement, known as post-processual archaeology, emerged as a critique of processual archaeology. It was strongly influenced by contemporary developments in the humanities and social sciences represented by poststructuralism, feminism and neo-Marxism. Of special interest were hermeneutics and the text model. In the early 2000s, some archaeologists turned the semiotics of Peirce as a measured response to the excesses of post-processual archaeology, particularly the idea of radical ambiguity. These scholars regarded Peirce's model of the sign to be especially suitable to the study of material culture and as a way of being more explicit about the logic of archaeological interpretation.

Archaeology and structuralism: A structural linguistics approach

The French paleoarchaeologist André Leroi-Gourhan advocated a holistic science of humanity, integrating the fields of biology, psychology, sociology and ethnology. Although he was reluctant to ally himself to structuralism because of his interest in the diachronic, he adopted aspects of Lévi-Strauss' structuralist methodology in his study of Palaeolithic cave art. He proposed that the distribution of the animal representations was not random and could be analysed into groups according to their location within the cave (Leroi-Gourhan 1965, 1968). He interpreted some of the groupings from the perspective of gendered differences such as male/horse/spear versus female/bison/wound. He concluded that 'without overly forcing the evidence, we can view the whole of Palaeolithic figurative art as the expression of ideas concerning the natural and supernatural organization of the living world' (Leroi-Gourhan 1968: 173). Leroi-Gourhan's student, Annette Laming-Empèraire (1962), wrote her doctoral thesis on Lascaux cave art. She implemented a structuralist methodology that involved the detailed documentation of the distribution of animal species with respect to such variables as gender, associations and orientation.

In the United States, James Deetz, a historical archaeologist, applied structural linguistics to the study of material culture and justified it on the grounds of a universal cognitive structure underlying human behaviour. He proposed the existence of structural units in artefacts which correspond to phonemes and morphemes in language, a correspondence which goes beyond simple analogy, reflecting an essential identity between language and objects in a structural sense (Deetz 1967: 87). He then identified factemes (the minimum class of attributes which affects the functional significance of an artefact) and formemes (the minimum class of objects that has functional significance) as the basic units of material culture appropriate for structural analysis. He also proposed a method for analysing artefact assemblages using a linguistic method. He noted that when linguists compare two languages they often determine whether they are related by the degree to which they share the same vocabulary. However, if they share the same grammatical rules, their relationship is virtually certain. He then postulated that this method might be applied to archaeology. Two artefact assemblages can be compared and shown to be related, if they share a high degree of similarity in individual attributes. However, our confidence in this relationship is increased, if it can be shown that they also share the same rules of combining the attributes.

In the late 1970s, processual archaeology developed in the United States as an explicitly scientific approach. Research areas included systems theory, network analysis, linguistic approaches, design studies, information exchange and complexity theory (Conkey 1978; Fritz 1978; Nordbladh 1978; Washburn 1977). These theories all shared a commitment to the idea that there exist overarching structures that govern and regulate social interaction and communication. Conkey (1978), for example, argued that Palaeolithic art could be understood as symbolic behaviour that involves culturally standardized systems of visual representation that function as mechanisms to order experience and segment it into manageable categories. Because the production of art is labour intensive and competes with other activities, she suggests that it must have had some adaptive value for the individual artist as well as the group. For her, those societies that maximized the intergenerational transmission of information may have enjoyed an adaptive advantage in terms of increased life spans, delayed maturation processes and/or encoding strategies. She regarded style in Palaeolithic art to be an informational process that favours behavioural redundancy and predictability and assists in the common organization of different behavioural domains. This, in turn, permits groups to establish identities and maintain social boundaries in relations to other groups.

Inspired by Deetz's work, symbolic and structural approaches became important components in the development of historical archaeology. Peter Schmidt (1978) adopted structuralism in his integration of archaeology and African oral history. He reasoned that since the African people valued genealogical ordering in their historical accounts of clans and kingdoms, structural analysis focusing on the rapid expansion of binary oppositions would facilitate an understanding of cultural change. He found this to be the case with Kiziba royal history where the creation of a new royal cult emerged to counter the influence of Bacwezi spirit mediums. The paradigmatic relations he identified included expensive/cheap, white/black, dangerous/benign, Bacwezi/Bito royal. Mark Leone (1984) drew from the structural Marxism of Louis Althusser to argue that our dominant ideas about nature, causality, time and personhood serve to mask and naturalize inequalities in the social order. In this sense, ideology hides the arbitrariness of social relations, making them appear natural and inevitable. In his study of William Paca's garden, Leone argued that Paca, a wealthy Maryland planter and signatory of the Declaration of Independence, negotiated contradictory values consisting of his inherited wealth based on slavery and his passionate defence of liberty. Paca's parterre garden with geometric pathways and a 'wilderness' area acted to link these values to nature, making them seem part of an ordered and natural world.

Several of Deetz's students have continued his structuralist legacy. Mary Beaudry (1988), for example, has conducted an innovative linguistic analysis of foodways vessels in seventeenth- and eighteenth-century probate inventories from the Chesapeake Bay region. Drawing from structural linguistics, she employs marked versus unmarked distinctions. Her results indicate the use of a greater frequency of functional markers towards the middle of the eighteenth century. She interprets this to mean that there was a greater need to differentiate special function vessels from one another. She also finds that items associated with individual users increase while those associated with communal use decrease. She concludes that her results are consistent with Deetz's findings in architecture and ceramics, namely that there is a shift from natural and emotion in the seventeenth century to a focus on the artificial and intellectual. In a study of eighteenth-century English and American ceramics, Ann Yentsch (1991) argued that a culture/nature opposition underlying ceramic manufacture and use was part of the negotiation of social inequality.

From language to text: Post-processual archaeologies

In early 1980s, Ian Hodder (1982b) and his students at Cambridge University initiated a series of trial explorations of practice theory, structuration theory, semiotics, gender and ideology. Hodder (1982a), himself, had prior experience with structuralism using it to interpret ethnic boundary formation and exchange of material culture in the Baringo district of Kenya. However, he became dissatisfied with its inability to explain social practice. This caused him to argue that

> culture is to be studied as meaningfully constituted – as the framework through which adaptation occurs – but the meaning of an object resides not merely in its contrast to others within a set. Meaning also derives from the associations and use of an object, which itself becomes, through the associations, the node of a network of references and implications. There is an interplay between structure and content.
> (Hodder 1982c: 9)

Semiotics was initially deployed in the critiques of structuralism and functionalism. Daniel Miller, for example, questioned whether 'the division within linguistics of syntax, semantics and pragmatics, which is in any case hard to maintain, would be at all plausible in the study of material forms, and the actual use of any such "grammar" would probably be limited in archaeology and social anthropology to the study of formal systems such as designs' (Miller 1982: 21). He then called for an approach to categorization that links langue and parole in order to provide a realist explanation of the past. Alison Wylie provided a deeper evaluation of the linguistic model. She suggested that material culture does not produce 'meaning effects' in the sense of conveying specific messages of states of mind similar to sentences or speech acts (Wylie 1982: 40). She concluded on a cautious note observing that additional work is needed to develop methodological procedures that address cognitive, semiological and symbolic aspects of material culture.

Hodder (1986) introduced the idea of considering the archaeological record as a 'text to be read'. He noted that the idea of material culture as a text has long been tacitly assumed in archaeology. This is evidenced by the fact that archaeologists often refer to their data as a record or as a language. For him, 'the importance of such an analogy increases when the concern is to discover the meaning content of past behaviour' (Hodder 1986: 122).

He explained that the text analogy means 'in association' or 'in context' and that artefacts are silent only when they are 'out of their texts'. For Hodder (1987a, 1987b) semiotic approaches are incapable of dealing with contextual meanings. This follows because they depend upon an arbitrary relationship between the signifier and signified and neglect the associated meanings of the signified. Thus semiotic analyses ultimately fail in engaging with the relationships between signs and the world of material action.

Hodder then proposed, following Paul Ricoeur, that human action can be conceived as having the properties of discourse and text. He wrote, 'any material action, such as the forming of a pot or the discarding of an artefact, has a "propositional" content which can be identified and reidentified as the same' (Hodder 1988: 257). He continued with the poststructuralist insight that meaning is not determined by the author or actor and becomes linked to the intentions and practical contexts of the reader, user or viewer. Christopher Tilley (1989) also advocated the move from language to text. He held that

> each act of material culture production and use has to be regarded as a contextualized social act involving the relocation of signs along axes defining the relationship between signs and other signs which reach out beyond themselves and towards others becoming amplified or subdued in specific contexts.
>
> (Tilley 1989: 188–9)

One especially generative research area has been the semiotic study of the landscape. An early and highly influential study was Tilley's (1991, 1997) phenomenological approach to the British Neolithic landscape. Inspired by Michel de Certeau's idea of walking as a 'reading' of a narrative structure, he argued that our own embodied experiences of landscapes and monuments today allow us access to some of the experiences of the people who once inhabited those same places in the past. His interaction with the Dorset cursus, two parallel embankments extending over six miles in east Dorset, led him to offer a provisional interpretation of it as mysterious, exciting and frightening passageway in which young initiates processed as part of an initiation ceremony. Children and Nash (1997: 1) also emphasized the phenomenological, arguing that landscapes are socially constructed entities and that are 'reliant on the cognitive processes of perception, recognition, and the acknowledgement of certain phenomena'. Nash and Children (2008: 1) have extended this position holding that it is possible to identify an underlying grammar of landscape and that semiotics, in its different varieties, offers considerable potential in its interpretation.

Towards a pragmatic archaeology: A Peircean approach

A number of archaeologists have drawn inspiration from the semiotics of Charles Sanders Peirce. Perhaps, the first systematic engagement was in 2001 when the second author proposed a semiotic or pragmatic archaeology building upon pragmatic anthropology (Preucel and Bauer 2001; Preucel 2006). Pragmatic anthropology adopts a pragmatic perspective on language and culture and is well established in the subfields of linguistic anthropology and sociocultural anthropology (Mertz 2007). To a large extent, this movement can be seen as a response to the limitations of symbolic, structural and cognitive anthropology. In addition, it is also a critique of certain excesses of poststructuralism, particularly the notion of radical ambiguity. Pragmatic anthropology offers several advantages for archaeology. First, it draws attention to the fact that all fields and indeed all knowledge seeking activities share a common logical structure. Second, it has the potential to contribute to the current semiotic discourse on cultural pragmatics through a consideration of materiality in the processes of semiotic mediation.

Semiotic mediation can be considered at a number of levels and scales (Preucel 2016). Artefacts were and are produced in the context of explicit understandings and implicit assumptions about how material culture communication works. These understandings and assumptions were and are themselves products of social institutions that regulate usages, impose canons and codify belief systems (Parmentier 1994: 142). In this respect, material culture signs are no different from linguistic signs. And because of the inherent ambiguity in interpreting some of these meanings (not all interpreters share the same understandings and assumptions), they also have the potential to generate new meanings. When actors offer their 'non-standard' views of meanings, these can be used to challenge existing conventions and even interpretive frames. Archaeologists need to attend closely to the canons governing the articulation of words and things in ethnographically documented cultural performances. These then can be used as provisional analogies with which to interpret past social practices.

Carl Knappett has reviewed Peircean semiotics as contributing to a sociosemiotic theory of material culture. He notes that the production of signs need not correspond to a motivated, language-like attempt to communicate a message (Knappett 2005: 88). Rather, it may very often constitute a practical action occurring in the material world. The value of Peircean semiotics is thus in its role as a middle way between the extremes of materialist and idealist approaches. Moreover, he observes that the Peircean perspective is congruent with the pragmatic, action-centred, approach to material meanings embodied in the Gibsonian notion of 'affordances'. He thus celebrates Peirce's approach as allowing us to merge the pragmatic and the significative domains of meaning.

The second author has applied Peircean semiotics to reveal new insights into how Pueblo Indian people reconstituted their world after the Pueblo Revolt of 1680 (Preucel 2006). Borderlands historians have documented that Pueblo Indian leaders espoused a revitalization discourse that circulated widely among Indigenous people. This discourse advocated the renouncement of Spanish beliefs and customs, ritual purification and the reinstatement of traditional ceremonies. The ideological frame for this discourse was given by the belief that these practices would allow people to live 'in accordance with the laws of their ancestors' and enjoy future health and prosperity. Archaeological research revealed that this popular discourse was materialized in a range of media including village architecture and pottery design. These material and linguistic practices mutually supported one another and collectively mediated a new temporal sensibility. This, in turn, allowed the creation a new form of Pan-Pueblo Indian identity, one that transcended genealogical ties.

Joanne Baron (2016) has also urged archaeologists to consider the complex interrelationships of language and material culture. In her study of the ancient Maya, she holds that the materiality of artefacts, both linguistic and non-linguistic in nature, can play a part in the efficacy of those objects in social life. For example, the iconicity of material objects links them to other similar objects, giving them meaning in certain social situations. The indexicality of objects associates them with co-occurring objects, also affecting their interpretation and efficacy. In the case of the ancestral Maya town of La Corona, patron deity temples iconically referenced other patron deity temples throughout the Maya world and indexically pointed to older funerary shrines that they replaced. The physical care and handling of patron deity effigies indexically pointed to the status of rulers who carried out these rituals and iconically signified the similarities between rulers and gods. For her, Peircean semiotics provides a method for understanding how social norms and models become widespread and allows for the meaning of signs to be empirically assessed through a consideration of their interpretants.

Rosemary Joyce (2007) has drawn upon Peirce's notion of the index to examine the hierarchy of the interpretive process and the degree to which it corresponds with past interpretations. She is particularly interested in the recursive, experiential aspects of figurine use in northern Honduras between 1100 and 200 BC. She notes that her study is, properly speaking, a study of meaning-making rather than meaning *per se*, a response to the 'how' question rather than the 'why' question. She starts with the idea of indexicality, holding that the figurines themselves point towards the existence of active social agents making marks that we recognize as meaningful. She argues that the bidirectionality of the index implies that just as a ceramic figure indexed a maker's labour, the personhood of the maker also indexed the figurines he or she made. She then identifies hair treatment as a special locus of iconic significance, and finds that hair-styles appear to vary with the age of the represented person. She then notes that the symbolic meaning of these figurines remains elusive because of the difficulties associated with understanding conventions associated with their community of production and use. Her analysis thus reveals the limits of interpretation, and multiple levels in which signs can understand by both contemporary scholars and past actors.

Julia Hendon, Rosemary Joyce and Jeanne Lopiparo (2014) have used Peircean semiotics to interpret social practices related to pre-Hispanic Honduran marriage figurines and Ulúa Polychrome ceramics. They begin from the perspective that meaning is constructed in the sense that 'it is made historically, at specific points in time, by specific human agents, in relation to preceding agents, moments of time, things, and meanings' (Hendon, Joyce and Lopiparo 2014: 35). They further note that meanings of these mould-made figurines developed in complex ways, often functioning as semiotic indices that afforded people different ways of representing social connections and allowed their distribution across time and space. They also observe that contemporary Ulúa Polychrome ceramics, made in the same area, exhibit considerable standardization in terms of motif, design layout and vessel shape. The motifs are iconic in the sense that they are recognizable as images of humans and animals. They interpret the depiction of essentially identical designs as a way for the different pottery manufacturing communities to reiterate a common identity. For them, the advantages of a Peircean view are that it draws attention to how signs are productive in multiple ways at once.

Alexander Bauer (2013) has adopted a Peircean perspective to critique and expand theories of material agency in his study of standardization of in Early Bronze Age pottery in the Black Sea region. Archaeologists often treat theories of material agency in a utilitarian fashion, the ways in which specific objects act in social life to bring about specific ends. More recent studies of agency look it not as an individual property but as a distributed one, extended across social networks. Bauer proposes that Peirce's concept of habit provides a new way of viewing agency. It 'turns agency around and implies that we are not what we do (or eat or wear), but rather what others see' (Bauer 2013: 17). It even calls into question whether agency is the right concept to investigate since it is grounded in the problematic subject-object dichotomy. He provocatively holds that agency might be better understood as a 'theory of self' in the sense that 'the self is the sum of how it is semiotically encountered, perceived, and responded to' (Bauer 2013: 18).

CONCLUSIONS

The study of the past is doubly semiotic by its nature, as we argue in this chapter. It involves the attempt to understand the meanings held by past social actors, as well as the recognition that the interpretation of the past is itself a semiotic process. As Boris Uspenskij has written, historical research 'involves a certain semiotization of reality – transformation of non-sign into sign and non-history into history' (1996: 11). This fundamental recognition has not been widely appreciated among archaeologists and historians, but has however produced some innovative and important research since 1970s. Our brief review of semiotics in history and archaeology has highlighted some of the different ways that Saussurean and Peircean perspectives have been incorporated into the study of past meanings. In both cases the initial engagement has been on the holistic or linguistic perspective developed by Saussure. This has led to explorations of reading the past as text. Alongside this holistic approach, has emerged a Peircean or atomistic tradition that seeks to consider the role of material culture in actively constituting past meanings. Despite these parallel trajectories and common interests, history and archaeology have seen few collaborations on semiotic issues. This is a generative area for future growth.

NOTES

1. All translations are our own, unless otherwise noted.
2. The following overview of semiotics in history draws importantly on the first author's previous articles on the topic (Tamm 1995, 2015, 2017b, 2019).
3. This overview of semiotics and archaeology is based on the second author's publications (Preucel and Bauer 2001; Preucel 2006, 2016).

REFERENCES

Baron, J. P. (2016), *Patron Gods and Patron Lords: The Semiotics of Classic Maya Community Cults*, Boulder: University Press of Colorado.

Bauer, A. A. (2013), 'Objects and Their Glassy Essence: Semiotics of Self in the Early Bronze Age Black Sea', *Signs and Society*, 1 (1): 1–31.

Beaudry, M., ed. (1988), *Documentary Archaeology in the New World*, Cambridge: Cambridge University Press.

Boklund-Lagopoulos, K. and A.-Ph. Lagopoulos, eds (1986), '*Signs of the Past: Semiotics and History*', *Semiotica*, 59 (3/4)s: 209–386.

Boyko, T. (2014), 'Tartu-Moscow School of Semiotics and History', *Historein*, 14 (2): 51–70.

Boyko, T. (2015), 'Describing the Past: Tartu-Moscow School Ideas on History, Historiography, and the Historian's Craft', *Sign Systems Studies*, 43 (2/3): 269–80.

Boyko, T. (2022), 'History', in M. Tamm and P. Torop (eds), *The Companion to Juri Lotman: A Semiotic Theory of Culture*, 245–56, London: Bloomsbury Academic.

Children, G. and G. Nash (1997), 'Establishing a Discourse: The Language of Landscape', in G. Nash (ed.), *Semiotics of Landscape: Archaeology of Mind*, 1–4, Oxford: Archaeopress.

Conkey, M. W. (1978), 'Style and Information in Cultural Evolution: Toward a Predictive Model for the Paleolithic', in C. L. Redman et al. (eds), *Social Archaeology: Beyond Subsistence and Dating*, 61–85, New York: Academic Press.

Deetz, J. (1967), *Invitation to Archaeology*, Garden City: The Natural History Press.

Finlay-Pelinski, M. (1982), 'Semiotics or History: From Content Analysis to Contextualized Discursive Praxis', *Semiotica*, 40 (3/4): 229–66.

Fritz, J. M. (1978), 'Paleopsychology Today: Ideational Systems and Human Adaptation in Prehistory', in C. L. Redman et al. (eds), *Social Archaeology: Beyond Subsistence and Dating*, 37–60, New York: Academic Press.

Green, T. M. (1986), 'Post-Feudal Rhetoric and Historical Semiotics', in R. Hagenbüchle and L. Skandera (eds), *Poetry and Epistemology: Turning Points in the History of Poetic Knowledge*, 46–56, Regensburg: Friedrich Pustet.

Green, T. M. (1996), 'Ritual and Text in the Renaissance', in J. Hart (ed.), *Reading the Renaissance: Culture, Poetics, and Drama*, 17–34, New York and London: Garland.

Greimas, A. J. (1976), *Sémiotique et sciences sociales*, Paris: Seuil.

Haidu, P. (1980), 'Towards a Socio-Historical Semiotics: Power and Legitimacy in the "Couronnement de Louis"', *Kodikas/Code*, 2 (2): 155–71.

Haidu, P. (1981), 'Text and History: The Semiosis of Twelfth-Century Lyric as Sociohistorical Phenomenon (Chrétien de Troyes: "D'Amors qui m'a tolu")', *Semiotica*, 33 (1/2): 1–62.

Haidu, P. (1982), 'Semiotics and History', *Semiotica*, 40 (3/4): 187–228.

Haidu, P. (1985), 'Considérations théoriques sur la sémiotique socio-historique', in H. Parret and H.-G. Ruprecht (eds), *Exigences et perspectives de la sémiotique: Recueil d'hommages pour A. J. Greimas*, 215–28, Amsterdam: John Benjamins.

Hałas, E. (2013), 'The Past in the Present: Lessons on Semiotics of History from George H. Mead and Boris A. Uspensky', *Symbolic Interaction*, 36 (1): 60–77.

Hałas, E. (2017), 'The Future Orientation of Culture and the Memory of the Past in the Making of History', *Sign Systems Studies*, 45 (3/4): 361–79.

Hendon, J. A., R. A. Joyce and J. Lopiparo (2014), *Material Relations: The Marriage Figurines of Prehispanic Honduras*, Boulder: University Press of Colorado.

Hodder, I. (1982a), *Symbols in Action: Ethnoarcheological Studies of Material Culture*, Cambridge: Cambridge University Press.

Hodder, I., ed. (1982b), *Symbolic and Structural Archaeology*, Cambridge: Cambridge University Press.

Hodder, I. (1982c), 'Theoretical Archaeology: A Reactionary View', in I. Hodder (ed.), *Symbolic and Structural Archaeology*, 1–16, Cambridge: Cambridge University Press.

Hodder, I. (1986), *Reading the Past*, Cambridge: Cambridge University Press.

Hodder, I., ed. (1987a), *The Archaeology of Contextual Meanings*, Cambridge: Cambridge University Press.

Hodder, I. (1987b), 'The Contextual Analysis of Symbolic Meanings', in I. Hodder (ed.), *The Archaeology of Contextual Meanings*, 1–10, Cambridge: Cambridge University Press.

Hodder, I. (1988), 'Material Culture Texts and Social Change: A Theoretical Discussion and Some Archaeological Examples', *Proceedings of the Prehistoric Society*, 54: 67–75.

Joyce, R. A. (2007), 'Figures, Meaning, and Meaning-Making in Early Mesoamerica', in C. Renfrew and I. Morley (eds), *Image and Imagination: A Global Prehistory of Figurative Representation*, 107–16, Cambridge: McDonald Institute.

Kalinin, I. (2003), 'The Semiotic Model of a Historical Process: History – Between Grammar and Rhetoric', *Sign Systems Studies*, 31 (2): 499–509.

Kalinin, I. (2009), 'Tartusko-moskovskaya shkola: semioticheskaya model' kul'tury/kul'turnaya model' semiotiki', *Novoe literaturnoe obozrenie*, 98: 27–56.

Knappett, C. (2005), *Thinking through Material Culture*, Philadelphia: University of Pennsylvania Press.

Laming-Empèraire, A. (1962), *La signification de l'art rupestre paléolithique*, Paris: Picard.

Leone, M. P. (1984), 'Interpreting Ideology in Historical Archaeology: Using Rules of Perspective in the William Paca Garden in Annapolis, Maryland', in D. Miller and C. Tilley (eds), *Ideology, Power and Prehistory*, 25–36, Cambridge: Cambridge University Press.

Leroi-Gourhan, A. (1965), *Treasures of Paleolithic Art*, New York: Abrams.
Leroi-Gourhan, A. (1968), *The Art of Prehistoric Man in Western Europe*, London: Thames and Hudson.
Li, Y. (2017), 'General Semiotics as the All-round Interdisciplinary Organizer – General Semiotics (GS) vs. Philosophical Fundamentalism', in K. Bankov and P. Cobley (eds), *Semiotics and its Masters*, 45–57, Boston and Berlin: Walter de Gruyter.
Lotman, J. (1975), 'K probleme raboty s nedostovernymi istochnikami', *Vremennik Pushkinskoj komissii*, 13: 93–8.
Lotman, J. (1982), 'Redaktsionnoe primechanie k stat'e "Novyye metodiki statisticheskogo analiza narrativno-tsifrovogo materiala drevnej istorii"', *Trudy po znakovym sistemam*, 15: 44–8.
Lotman, J. (1992), 'Ot redkollegii', *Trudy po znakovym sistemam*, 25: 3–4.
Lotman, J. (1993), 'Zimnie zametki o letnih shkolah', *Novoe literaturnoe obozrenie*, 3: 40–2.
Lotman, J. (1994), *Besedy o russkoi kul'ture: Byt i traditsii russkogo dvorianstva (XVIII–nachalo XIX veka)*, Saint Petersburg: Iskusstvo–SPB.
Lotman, J. (2009), *Culture and Explosion*, trans. W. Clark, Berlin: Mouton de Gruyter.
Lotman, J. (2013), *The Unpredictable Workings of Culture*, trans. B. J. Baer, Tallinn: Tallinn University Press.
Lotman, J. (2019), *Culture, Memory and History: Essays in Cultural Semiotics*, ed. M. Tamm, trans. B. J. Baer, London: Palgrave Macmillan.
Lotman, M. (2002), 'Atomistic versus Holistic Semiotics', *Sign Systems Studies*, 30 (2): 513–27.
Lotman, Yu. M. and B. A. Uspensky (1978), 'On the Semiotic Mechanism of Culture', trans. George Mihaychuk. *New Literary History*, 9 (2): 211–32.
Lotman, Yu. M. and B. A. Uspenskij (1984), 'Authors' Introduction', in Yu. M. Lotman and B. A. Uspensky (eds), *The Semiotics of Russian Culture*, trans. A. Shukman, ix–xiv, Ann Arbor: Department of Slavic Languages and Literatures, University of Michigan.
Mertz, E. (2007), 'Semiotic Anthropology', *Annual Review of Anthropology*, 36: 337–53.
Miller, D. (1982), 'Artifacts as Products of Human Categorisation', in I. Hodder (ed.), *Symbolic and Structural Archaeology*, 17–25, Cambridge: Cambridge University Press.
Nash, G. and G. Children (2008), 'Archaeology of Semiotics and the Social Order of Things', in G. Nash and G. Children (eds), *Archaeology of Semiotics and the Social Order of Things*, 1–8, Oxford: Archaeopress.
Nordbladh, J. (1978), 'Images as Messages in Society: Prolegomena to the Study of Scandinavian Petroglyphs and Semiotics', in K. Kristiansen and C. Paludan-Muller (eds), *New Directions in Scandinavian Archaeology. Studies in Scandinavian Prehistory and Early History*, vol. 1, 1–16, Copenhagen: The National Museum of Denmark.
Parmentier, R. J. (1994), *Signs in Society: Studies in Semiotic Anthropology*, Bloomington: Indiana University Press.
Passerini, L. (1999), 'History and Semiotics', *Historein*, 1: 13–20.
Pencak, W. (1993), *History, Signing In: Essays in History and Semiotics*, New York: Peter Lang.
Pencak, W. (1998), 'History and Semiotics', in R. Kevelson (ed.), *Hi-fives: A Trip to Semiotics*, 103–23, New York: Peter Lang.
Pencak, W. (2011), 'History and Semiotics: Preliminary Thoughts', in J. M. Broekman and F. J. Mootz III (eds), *The Semiotics of Law in Legal Education*, 77–80, Dordrecht al.: Springer.
Pencak, W. and B. Williams, eds (1991), *History and Semiotics, Semiotica*, 83 (3/4)s.
Pern, T. (2012), 'History as Communication in the Works of Tartu-Moscow School', in *Proceedings of the 10th World Congress of the International Association for Semiotic Studies (IASS/AIS)*, 453–8, A Coruña: Universidade da Coruña.

Preucel, R. W. (2006), *Archaeological Semiotics*, Oxford and Malden, MA: Blackwell.
Preucel, R. W. (2016), 'Pragmatic Archaeology and Semiotic Mediation', *Semiotic Review*, 4: 1–8.
Preucel, R. W. and A. A. Bauer (2001), 'Archaeological Pragmatics', *Norwegian Archaeological Review*, 34: 85–96.
Schmidt, P. R. (1978), *Historical Archaeology: A Structural Approach in an African Culture*, Westport: Greenwood Press.
Semenenko, A. (2012), *The Texture of Culture: An Introduction to Yuri Lotman's Semiotic Theory*, New York: Palgrave Macmillan.
Tamm, M. (1995), 'The Dynamics of Medieval Culture: Some Problems of Historical Semiotics', in M. Lotman and T. Viik (eds), *Uurimusi keelest, kirjandusest ja kultuurist*, 195–219, Tallinn: Eesti Humanitaarinstituut.
Tamm, M. (2015), 'Semiotic Theory of Cultural Memory: In the Company of Juri Lotman', in S. Kattago (ed.), *Ashgate Research Companion to Memory Studies*, 127–41, Farnham: Ashgate.
Tamm, M., ed. (2017a), Semiotics and History, *Sign System Studies*, 45 (3/4)s.
Tamm, M. (2017b), 'Introduction: Semiotics and History Revisited', *Sign Systems Studies*, 45 (3/4): 211–29.
Tamm, M. (2019), 'Introduction: Juri Lotman's Semiotic Theory of History and Cultural Memory', in J. Lotman (ed.), *Culture, Memory and History: Essays in Cultural Semiotics*, trans. B. J. Baer, 1–26, London: Palgrave Macmillan.
Tilley, C. (1989), 'Interpreting Material Culture', in I. Hodder (ed.), *The Meaning of Things*, 185–94, London: Unwin Hyman.
Tilley, C. (1991), *Material Culture and Text: The Art of Ambiguity*, London: Routledge.
Tilley, C. (1997), *A Phenomenology of Landscape: Places, Paths and Monuments*, Oxford: Berg.
Todorov, T. (1982), *La Conquête de l'Amérique*, Paris: Seuil.
Trunin, M. (2017), 'Semiosphere and History: Toward the Origins of the Semiotic Approach to History', *Sign Systems Studies*, 45 (3/4): 335–60.
Uspenskij, B. (1974), 'Historia sub specie semioticae', in J. Lotman (ed.), *Materialy vsesoyuznogo simpoziuma po vtorichnym modeliruyushchim sistemam*, 119–30, Tartu: TGU.
Uspenskij, B. (1976a), 'Historia sub specie semioticae', in V. G. Bazanov (ed.), *Kul'turnoe nasledie Drevnej Rusi (istoki, stanovlenie, traditsii)*, 286–92, Moscow: Nauka.
Uspenskij, B. (1976b), 'Historia sub specie semioticae', in H. Baran (ed.), *Semiotics and Structuralism: Readings from the Soviet Union*, 64–75, White Plains: International Arts and Sciences Press.
Uspenskij, B. (1996), 'Istoriya i semiotika', in B. Uspenskij, *Izbrannye trudy*, vol. 1, 9–70, Moscow: Gnozis.
Uspenskij, B. (2017), 'Semiotics and Culture: The Perception of Time as a Semiotic Problem', *Sign Systems Studies*, 45 (3/4): 230–48.
Uspenskij, B. and F. Uspenskij, eds (2008), *Fakty i znaki: Issledovaniya po semiotike istorii*, vol. 1, Moscow: Yazyki slavyanskih kul'tur.
Washburn, D. K. (1977), *A Symmetry Analysis of Upper Gila Area Ceramic Design*, Cambridge, MA: Peabody Museum of Archaeology and Ethnology, Harvard University.
Williams, B. (1985), 'What Has History to Do with Semiotic?', *Semiotica*, 54 (112): 267–333.
Williams, B. (1986), 'History in Relation to Semiotic', in J. Deely, B. Williams and F. E. Kruse (eds), *Frontiers in Semiotics*, 217–23, Bloomington: Indiana University Press.

Williams, B. (1987a), 'The Historian as Observer', in J. Deely and J. Evans (eds), *Semiotics 1982*, 13–25, Lanham: University Press of America.

Williams, B. (1987b), 'History as a Semiotic Anomaly', in J. Evans and J. Deely (eds), *Semiotics 1983*, 409–19, Lanham: University Press of America.

Williams, B. (1988), 'Opening Dialogue between the Discipline of History and Semiotics', in T. A. Sebeok and D. J. Umiker-Sebeok (eds), *The Semiotic Web 1987*, 821–34, Berlin: Mouton de Gruyter.

Williams, B. (1990), 'Uma década de debates: história e semiótica nos annos 80', *Face. Revista de Semiótica e Comunicação*, 3 (1): 11–28.

Williams Deely, B. (2011), 'Thomas A. Sebeok: On Semiotics of History and History of Semiotics', in P. Cobley, J. Deely, K. Kull and S. Petrilli (eds), *Semiotics Continues to Astonish: Thomas A. Sebeok and the Doctrine of Signs*, 371–418, Berlin, Boston: Walter de Gruyter.

Wylie, A. (1982), 'Epistemological Issues Raised by a Structuralist Archaeology', in I. Hodder (ed.), *Symbolic and Structural Archaeology*, 39–46, Cambridge: Cambridge University Press.

CHAPTER FOUR

Semiotics in Theology and Religious Studies

MASSIMO LEONE

INTRODUCTION: RELIGION(S) AND MEANING

In the French novel *Le Royaume* [*The Kingdom*] (2014), acclaimed author Emmanuel Carrère questions religious belief from two intertwined perspectives: on the one hand, he autobiographically recalls first his own conversion, then the subsequent disaffection; on the other hand, he narratively reconstructs, with brio and humour, the exceptional diffusion of Christianity in the first centuries of the Common Era. At several stages, perhaps involuntarily, he adopts a semiotic point of view towards early Christian texts. As he analyses the relation between Luke the Evangelist and Paul the Apostle, for instance, Carrère detects, albeit without using the metalanguage of generative semiotics, a significant shift from '*débrayage*' to '*embrayage*', as Franco-Lithuanian semiotician and father of structuralist and generative semiotics Algirdas J. Greimas would define the opposite strategies of distancing or approaching the text from the abstract source of its utterance (enunciation). An evangelist who never knew Jesus in person, Luke strategically hides in his own account of Jesus's life through the adoption of a systematic '*débrayage*': in Luke's narrative, Jesus is always pronominally represented by 'He', never by 'You'. As soon as Luke tells the story of his encounter with Paul, however, and especially that of his own adhesion to the new Christian faith, he adopts an '*embrayage*' that immediately situates the person of the narrator (or rather, his linguistic proxy in the enunciate) solidly within the 'us' of the Christian community.

In another passage, Carrère offers a further insight on the Christian enunciation: one of the first texts in Western history thoroughly describing the formation of a religious subjectivity, Augustine's *Confession* constantly resorts to the vocative. The semiotics of Émile Benveniste, as well as the philosophies of dialogue of Martin Buber and Emmanuel Levinas, have long underlined that the construction of an 'I' depends on that of a 'You' to which the former is addressed. Semiotics – for instance, the semiotics of enunciation by Jean-Claude Coquet (1984) – formalizes this intuition and draws from it a whole series of theoretical consequences: the peculiarity of the dialogic regime of the Abrahamic style of utterance consists in the fact that interlocutors only exceptionally exchange their roles in the enunciation. The Christian utterer, thus, is an 'I' eternally in search of a 'You' that rarely answers back.

Although Emmanuel Carrère is not a semiotician, his narrative shows that, for the modern and contemporary sensibility, the religious experience involves an understanding of its meaning. Yet that has not always been the case. The ancient and, in any case, pre-modern feeling of religion was often limited to a blind adherence to liturgy and ritual, without the need to probe its mysteries individually. In Christianity, it is just as a consequence of the Protestant Reformation that the personal appropriation of the divine word's religious meaning becomes a prerequisite to believe. Future understandings of religions, including Christianity, might not necessarily confirm such attitude: contemporary fundamentalisms, for example, advocate an improbable collective hermeneutic ignorance of the religious text; that is, perhaps, the main reason for their success.

The modern approach to religions, on the contrary, cannot get rid of a typically semiotic concern, expressing itself in the quintessential semiotic enigma: 'what does it mean?' That is the unavoidable question that the contemporary believer asks; in order to answer it, semiotics begins to tackle a preliminary issue: 'how does it mean?'; from the 1960s, all the theoretical and analytical resources of the discipline have been devoted to this explanatory task.

THE SEMIOTICS OF RELIGION(S)

This chapter does not aim at opening up new paths for the interdisciplinary field at the intersection of research on language and studies on religion; rather, it attempts to provide an overview, as complete as possible, on the history, the present, and the likely prospects of this field of investigation. First, it is important to focus, albeit briefly, on the meaning of the word 'semiotics' itself. The variety of methods, references, theoretical instruments and analytical practices that it entails is such that it is impossible to produce a single all-encompassing definition of it. It is wiser, perhaps, to refer to its history, at least in relation to the development of the denomination (the history of semiotics begins, in fact, long before the appearance of its name, but the attempt at retracing the prehistory of the discipline would lead to a rather difficult ground, which it would be preferable to approach in another context).

Modern semiotics has two fathers: the US philosopher Charles Sanders Peirce and the Swiss linguist Ferdinand de Saussure. It suffices to recall that the first borrowed the term 'semiotics' from John Locke and made it the label of his own philosophy of the sign, while the second created the neologism 'semiology' in order to designate a generalization of linguistics. Both terms derive from the same Greek word '*semeion*', which means 'sign'. Peirce's semiotics and Saussure's semiology inquire about the same object, namely the sign, but from two different perspectives, which reflect the backgrounds of the two scholars. Peirce's thought has given rise to a philosophical study of the sign and its mechanisms, whilst Saussure's thought resulted in a study of the sign carried on according to the paradigms of linguistic research. One must be careful not to confuse semiotics and semiology with semeiotics: the latter also derives from the Greek word *semeion*, but it only designates a part of general semiotics, namely, the study of medical signs or symptoms.

Before moving on to the semiotics of religion, it should be added that, although the founders of the two main currents of semiotics lived between the nineteenth and the twentieth centuries, it was in the sixties and the seventies of the last century that the discipline experienced its greatest development. On the one hand, the US semiotician of Hungarian origins, Thomas A. Sebeok, interpreted and developed the thought of Peirce, thus inaugurating a semiotic school that has been represented almost everywhere in the world, but that had its main centre at the University of Indiana in Bloomington,

United States. On the other hand, Saussure's thought exerted a decisive influence on French semiology, and especially on the work of Roland Barthes and on that of the Franco-Lithuanian semiologist Algirdas Julien Greimas. The latter, in particular, a researcher in linguistics, lexicology, semantics and mythology, succeeded in blending together the theoretical contributions of the linguistics of both Saussure and the Russian researcher Roman Jakobson, but also certain intuitions of the linguistics of Noam Chomsky, the anthropology of Claude Lévi-Strauss, folklore studies by Vladimir Propp and comparative mythology by Georges Dumézil, into a very articulated and complex semiotic system, with the ambition to describe all the phenomena of meaning, independently of the accidents of their manifestation. This project, which maintained a constant dialogue especially with the hermeneutics of Paul Ricoeur and with the phenomenology of Maurice Merleau-Ponty, continues to be pursued today by several researchers mainly in France, Italy, continental Europe and Latin America.

In summarizing the history of semiotics one cannot forget to mention Umberto Eco, who was able to weave the US and the French-speaking semiotic traditions and is also the creator of one of the most concise and effective definitions of semiotics. This discipline, Eco wrote in his 1976 *A Theory of Semiotics*, first published in Italian in 1975 as *Trattato di semiotica generale*, studies 'everything that can be used to lie'. This shrewd formula reveals a truth: when lying is impossible, there is no possibility of meaning either. For there to be meaning, for there to be signification, and for there to also be a semiotics that studies them, there must be a space for lying and, therefore, for interpretation.

The theoretical principles, epistemology, analytical instruments and technical lexicon of semiotics being very abstract and general, they have been applied to some extent to all fields of research, in the human sciences as well as in the social and natural sciences. A disciplinary crossing has also manifested itself between semiotics and religious sciences: on the one hand, certain semioticians sought to put their knowledge and the power of their interpretive instruments to the test of a new context of study; on the other hand, some researchers in religious sciences longed for using a new method of analysis. It must be admitted that the results of semiotic research, in the field of religious sciences as well as in the other areas of investigation, have not always lived up to the expectations. On the one hand, semioticians have applied their method without first acquiring a deep knowledge of their object and without grasping its specificity, thus producing generic or even misleading results, albeit dressed in a pseudo-scientific jargon, often incomprehensible to non-specialists. On the other hand, researchers in religious sciences have sometimes yielded to the fascination exercised by this hermetic lexicon, without however fully understanding the real issues of an application of semiotics to the study of religions.

Perhaps today that is almost inconceivable, but there was a time in which bookstore shelves were filled with works such as *Letture strutturaliste dell'Antico Testamento* ['Structuralist Readings of the Old Testament'], by Rémi Lack (1978) or *Introduzione alla lettura strutturalistica della Bibbia* ['Introduction to the Structural Reading of the Bible'] by Etienne Charpentier *et at.* (1978). In the preface to the first volume, the author writes, quoting the French intellectual Jean Starobinski:

> What is structuralism, in its most general definition, if not an attempt at taking into account the interdependence and the interaction of the parts within the whole? A faithful and passionate attention to show not what gave birth to the text, in the past and from the outside, but the way in which the text is produced and unfolds from within and today. It is a contemplative method. (1978: 6; author's translation)

In the second, thinner book – an introduction to the structural analysis of the Bible for high-schools – the author writes: 'Traditionally, men are in search of meaning. Well, meaning – that is, roughly speaking, ideas, what we want to express – does not exist in its purest form: it must be expressed' (1978: 7; our translation). It was the innocence of structuralism and nascent semiotics. Later, semioticians, but mostly non-semioticians, started to be wary of readings ignoring 'what gave rise to the text', and to reincorporate in their interpretations both the philology of writing and the phenomenology of reading; similarly, semiotic anthropology started to question the universality of the relation between a hidden meaning and the need for its expression, for example through highlighting the anthropological and often the religious roots of this preconception (see, for instance, the work of Webb Keane on the Christian-Protestant presuppositions of the Saussurean ideology of the sign, Keane 2007).

A VARIETY OF APPROACHES

Nevertheless, besides these mediocre results – which are rather the legacy of the 'disciplinary imperialism' of a certain arrogant semiotics of the past – there has also been more in-depth research, which has produced an interesting literature. These studies can be classified according to the semiotic school to which they refer, namely the one resulting from the philosophy of Peirce or that which is connected with the linguistics of Saussure. Referring to either of these two thought systems influenced not only the answers researchers gave, but also the questions they asked. Two texts have tried to survey the variety of semiotic approaches to religion: the first is the article 'Religious Studies', written by two eminent semioticians of religion, namely, Daniel Patte and Gay Volney, and included in the three-volume encyclopaedic dictionary of semiotics edited by Thomas A. Sebeok (Patte and Volney 1986). The second is an article by Jean Delorme and Pierre Geoltrain, included in the collective work edited by a collaborator of Greimas, the semiotician Jean-Claude Coquet: *Sémiotique: L'École de Paris* ['*Semiotics: The School of Paris*'] (Delorme and Geoltrain 1982).

In the first text, the authors identify three groups of semiotic studies on religion: theories of religion that implicitly use a semiotic theory; those that use one explicitly; analyses of religious texts that employ semiotic methodologies. As regards the first category, i.e. that of studies on religion that implicitly contain semiotic elements, certain researchers have attempted to find, within the classics of the history, sociology and anthropology of religion(s), intuitions about religious signs, forms and languages that could be described as 'semiotic'. Éliade, Durkheim, Weber, Schmidt, Tylor, Marett, Freud and so on would therefore have been semioticians without knowing it, semioticians of religion *ante litteram*. This type of research is not without interest, if it is not reduced to the attempt at reconstructing a long and prestigious pedigree for a relatively new discipline. On the contrary, it is undoubtedly useful to reread the classics of thought on religion(s), trying to find in them elements that can be reappraised into the framework of semiotic theory. Yet, this operation runs the risk of producing extremely general results: what researcher in the study of religion has never reflected on the signs, forms and languages of the spiritual dimension of human life? For this kind of study to be effective, such negative question should be asked, so as to reduce its scope to thinkers who have given priority, in their studies, to the semiotic (or proto-semiotic) component of their object of investigation.

The second group of studies, that is, the one in which a semiotic theory is used explicitly, lends itself, on the contrary, to a more specific discourse. Some of these studies are inspired by the semiotic theory of Peirce and, in particular, by his theological writings or, more generally, by his writings on religion. It should be noted that the theology of Charles Sanders Peirce is still fairly unexplored, although some scholars, especially in the United States, are now turning it into the primary object of their research (Raposa 1989). Indeed, is it not doubtful enough that an author so preoccupied with cosmological, religious and downright theological questions has been read as the creator of a quite secular discipline, detached from all confessional influence and capable, therefore, to deploy a neutral metalanguage, able to describe with certainty and without parochial barriers any religious phenomenon? Here is a subject for a thesis to be written: the secularization of Peirce in the construction of modern semiotics. Umberto Eco would figure there prominently. But perhaps this would be a file to review: can Peirce's model of semiosis be really understood without taking into account his theological ambitions?

In this second group of studies, one or more semiotic theories are used in order to propose a new interpretation of the ethnology, anthropology and sociology of religion (Leone 2014a), but also of that part of the theological thought that is centred on the concept of sign. In this regard, another dichotomy can be identified: on the one hand, semiotic theories that deal with the role of language in such or such religious culture. This approach, which is traditional in this type of survey, leads to questions such as the following ones: is there, in the teachings of a religious culture, a traditional explicit description of what language is and how communication takes place? If the answer is positive, are, then, words distinguished from other types of signs? Is there a specific conception of the origins of language and of the other forms of communication? Do religious authorities believe they speak the true, original, or genuine language? Or, on the contrary, is their language seen in some way as arbitrary? Are there secret languages or secret codifications of the natural language? How are changes in language explained? If the god or gods communicate with human beings, do they do so in an ambiguous or in a transparent way? Is the divine word interpretable only by a few adepts? Is it a variant of other hyerophanies? (Patte and Volney 1986: 798–9). One could multiply and articulate questions of this kind, which mainly concern the role of (verbal) language within a religion. The scope of these questions may be more or less extensive depending on the type of language conception that one adopts. In current semiotics, for example – in the Peircean school as well as in the Saussurian tradition – there is a tendency not to restrict the meaning of the word 'language' to the verbal expression only, but to broaden it, instead, to any semiotic phenomenon that presents the formal features of a language. Consequently, the scope of questions concerning the relation between a religion and its languages widens too.

Alongside this kind of study, there are other trends of research that do not focus so much on the role of language in a religion but, rather, on the possibility of interpreting a religion, and even the religious dimension as a whole (or 'the sacred') as a semiotic phenomenon and, more specifically, as a phenomenon of communication. To this category belong less numerous studies that try, for example, to construct a linguistic or semiotic model of the Christian theology. One could mention, in order to describe this perspective, a work that adopts it, for instance, John Milbank's collection of essays *The Word Made Strange: Theology, Language, Culture*, wherein the author asserts that his intention is to analyse language not only as an unavoidable means or, better, event of truth, but also as a matter of reflection (Milbank 1997). Hence the work aims, first, at developing a specifically theological description of language and, second, at showing how a theology that considers language – within such theological interpretation – as one of its central concerns, can approach the traditional themes of God and the Creation, the Incarnation, the Holy Spirit, Christian life and society. Milbank's book exemplifies a theological study that is cross-fertilized by linguistics and philosophy of language. A parallel perspective is expressed by the works of those semioticians who, through reflection on language and communication, aim at establishing a new conception of religion (Yelle 2013).

The difficulties presented by this approach have been highlighted by one of the most active semioticians in the field of the application of the Greimasian semiotic theory to the study of religion, namely, Louis Panier (1973, 1983, 1984, 1991, 1993, 1996, 1999). In his work *La naissance du fils de Dieu : Sémiotique et théologie discursive – Lecture de Luc 1–2* ['The Birth of the Son of God: Semiotics and Discursive Theology: A Reading of Luke 1–2'], Panier asserts that 'faire de la théologie avec la sémiotique, c'est sans doute s'exposer à ne satisfaire ni les sémioticiens ni les théologiens' ['doing theology with semiotics without a doubt runs the risk of satisfying neither semioticians nor theologians'] (Panier 1991: 361). But he also adds, at the end of his analysis, that the role of semiotics (in this case, that of the semiotics of the discourse of the Bible) is not to actualize its message by expressing its values today (and in today's terms) but, on the contrary, to work on (and in) the forms of meaning, thus opening and leaving open a place for the Word. Paradoxically – Panier concludes in his work – it is through the detour of forms that it is possible to make the word in the message heard. Panier's analysis contains an explicit reference to Michel de Certeau, an author who turned semiotics, and the sciences of language in general, into a theoretical framework through which the approach of religious sciences could be reformulated (see, for instance, his study on the mystical fable and his numerous works on the religious discourse (Certeau 1982, 1989a, 1989b, 2003)). The works of Mino Bergamo (1984, 1991), Louis Marin (1972, 1992, 1994, 1995a, 1995b), and Giovanni Pozzi (1987, 1993, 1997) also follow the same line.

Regarding the classification of the different types of semiotics of religion, two elements should be retained from the works of scholars such as Michel de Certeau, Louis Marin and Giovanni Pozzi: first, the epistemological flexibility of the semiotic method enables them to compare verbal texts with texts composed through other languages, and above all, with images. Second, these researchers are able to combine, thanks to the semiotic method – as well as by means of their personal interpretive intelligence and the contributions of other disciplines – the general level of the interpretation of religion in semiotic terms with the particular level of the semiotic analysis of religious texts.

As regards the third of the three groups of semiotic studies on religion, it is arguably the most fruitful category, and also the one in relation to which the adoption of the semiotic perspective is the most promising. It comprises those works that seek to analyse, through semiotics, one or more texts belonging to the corpus of a religious tradition. Works in this category do not interpret religion according to the semiotic perspective, but use it in order to analyse the texts and discourses of a religion. Yet, these ad hoc analyses produce repercussions also from the point of view of the general interpretation of religion(s). This third group should be described according to its typical questions and especially in relation to its analytical qualities. Some indications about the geography of the academic research will be useful to survey this literature. This third branch of the semiotics of religion was developed especially in France, Germany and the United States. With regard to France, in 1967 the research centre 'ASTRUC' was established (an acronym of 'A-nalyse Struc-turale', hinting at the name of Jean Astruc, a doctor of Louis XV and one of the first modern biblical exegetes);

CADIR ('Centre pour l'analyse du discours religieux', ['Centre for the analysis of the religious discourse']) has been the most important centre of research in this field for several decades; it was directed by Louis Panier at the University of Lyon, France. In the United States, this type of study was carried out mainly at Vanderbilt University, by a team of researchers led by Daniel Patte (1976, 1981, 1983, 1990a, 1990b). In Germany, another research group was created around the linguist and semiotician Erhardt Güttgemans, who formulated an eclectic and original theory of the religious sign. These three research groups have produced several studies, which were published in the form of monographs, articles or collections of essays as issues of the magazines related to the three research centres: respectively, *Sémiotique et Bible* ['*Semiotics and Bible*']; *Structuralist Research Information*; and *Linguistica biblica*.

THE BENEFITS OF SEMIOTICS

As for the problems tackled by the abovementioned research groups, it should be noted that they have mainly focused on biblical texts, and especially on the New Testament. They applied themselves, therefore, to the classification of literary forms and typologies of discourse in the Gospels (as well as on their developments and metamorphoses); on the narrative organization of the biblical text; on the cognitive dimension of the story; on veridiction (i.e. on how the biblical text organizes the values of truth in its narrative structures); on enunciation; on the transformation of semantic values. Although the biblical text has predominantly attracted the attention of scholars, they have at least considered the theoretical interest of other types of discourse and other investigative *corpora*: the prophetic discourse, the apocalyptic discourse, the epistolary literature, psalms, the liturgical discourse (Sadowski and Marsciani 2020), the theological, mystical (Solís Zepeda 2016) and even the diabolical discourse.

The fact that semiotics inquires about these types of texts does not deny the importance of other more traditional kinds of research, such as biblical philology or hermeneutics. On the contrary, an effective interpretation of a religious culture and of the texts that it produced can only arise from a cooperation between historical knowledge and semiotic interpretation or, to put it in the words of the Italian historian of culture Carlo Ginzburg, a collaboration between history and morphology (Ginzburg 1983). It is impossible to determine in advance to what extent these two types of knowledge, the first, concerning time and its chronologies, the second, forms and their semiotics, should contribute to the analysis of a religious text; on the contrary, a heuristic equilibrium must be established according to the coordinates of the research within a semiotics of religious cultures.

The use of the semiotic method has, however, undeniable advantages. On this occasion only a few of them can be mentioned: the ability to establish and analyse intertextual links; that of drawing comparisons between texts that use different expressive means (a fundamental operation both in iconology and in cultural history when it uses images to construct its arguments); the possibility of developing complex interpretative frameworks, which avoid the triviality of common sense. But, as Delorme and Geoltrain argued in their overview of the semiotics of religion, it is above all in the field of the history of religious ideas that the science of signs can make a fundamental contribution, mainly because 'what the historian of ancient ideologies feels as an obstacle – a literary documentation often disconnected from his precise production contexts – the semiotician considers as one of the usual conditions of his analysis'[1] (Delorme and Geoltrain 1982: 116).

The analytical tools of semiotics make it possible, first of all, to develop an interdisciplinary discourse on the history of religious ideas, according to a model of theoretical cross-fertilization; second, the semiotic method can help building both an original interpretation of religious phenomena and a meticulous analysis of the religious texts that represent them. In addition, when conducting research that attempts at reconstructing the role of a certain idea in the religious culture of an epoch, it is essential not to confine the study to the analysis of verbal texts; therefore, one must adopt a discipline capable of considering simultaneously different expressive means. It can be safely argued that no discipline today is able to build stronger and more lasting bridges than those that can be built through semiotics (Leone and Parmentier 2014).

WHAT FUTURE FOR THE SEMIOTICS OF RELIGION(S)?

The semiotics of religion of the future will be, first of all, humble: the subject that it investigates is one of the most studied in the history of mankind. The idea of sweeping everything away (history, anthropology, psychology, theology, etc.) in order to start everything anew is presumptuous and foolish. From the excesses of semiotics in the 1970s and 1980s, it should be learned that an object of study must be known in-depth, in constant contact with the other disciplines that deal with it, while preserving the specificity and richness of the semiotic approach. In addition, it will be necessary to take advantage of the gradual evolution of semiotics towards more and more complex units of analysis. If signs are still of central importance in religions, it is inconceivable today not to analyse religious symbols within their cultures and practices. The semiotics of cultures by Youri M. Lotman, that of practices and life forms by Jacques Fontanille, the socio-semiotics of Eric Landowski, the semiotic anthropology of Richard Parmentier, Webb Keane, Michael Silverstein and Robert A. Yelle, are all assets that the semiotics of religion can use to both complexify and clarify its analyses.

The comparative approach will play an essential role in this. Thanks to the studies of Bernard Jackson (2000), Peter Ochs (1998) and Ugo Volli (2012; 2019) on the semiotics of Jewish culture, Fabio Rambelli (2013) and Tatsuma Padoan (2021) on the religions of Japan, the current semiotics of religion develops more and more in the direction of comparative research, although that it is still limited to the major world religions, with some exceptions (Baron 2016; Huang 2018; Laack 2019).

The most recent trends of scholarship in the field concern the semiotics of religious cultures (Leone 2004, 2010; Ponzo 2019); the comparative semiotic study of different forms of religious mediation (Ponzo, Yelle and Leone 2021); semiotic-oriented research on the philosophy of signs in religious authors (Marmo 1997; Cary 2008; Angelici 2019; Gramigna 2020); textual studies of the Bible adopting a semiotic framework (Leone 2001; Odell-Scott 2018).

The semiotics of religion of the future, moreover, will also have to seek to satisfy the social demand of knowledge. The world is increasingly worried about religions. The religious sciences and even theology, which were considered as purely academic disciplines in the epoch of triumphant structuralism, today become, again, the object of a more and more pressing curiosity. In a world where hundreds of innocent people are murdered every year using religion as pretext, investigating the individual and collective dynamics of religious meaning and denominational identity becomes essential (Leone 2014b). The semiotics of religion, from this point of view, can constitute one of the strongest ramparts against any fundamentalist drift. Showing that there may be inspired meaning in religious discourse, while admitting that it must nevertheless always manifest itself through social language, and that, in this sense, it is always subject to the variability of interpretations, means advancing in the direction of a less antagonistic and more plural understanding of religious life forms (Leone 2012). Contrary to relativistic deconstructions, and yet also opposed to everything that freezes interpretation without rational appeal to the text, semiotics today offers a third way to build a more harmonious equilibrium for the multi-confessional societies of the future.

In order to achieve this objective, the semiotics of religion is called to a paradoxical exercise of introspection too (Leone 2021). It will be necessary to recognize the religious presuppositions of semiotics (Leone 2013), without however reaching a paralysis of the semiotic process; questioning, thus, the relation between conceptions of religious meaning internal to communities and the ideologies of external observers and analysts. Is it always true that understanding a religion comes down to grasping its meaning? Surrendering to the ignorance of meaning is not perhaps a fundamental dimension in all religious experience? Moving, hence, from the quest for what means to the fusion with what is? Semiotics cannot answer these questions without recovering its deep links with one of the disciplines that, ultimately, were at its origins: philosophy.

NOTE

1 'Ce que l'historien des idéologies antiques ressent comme un obstacle, – une documentation littéraire souvent déconnectée de ses situations précises de production – le sémioticien le considère comme une des conditions habituelles de son analyse.'

REFERENCES

Angelici, R. (2019), *Semiotic Theory and Sacramentality in Hugh of Saint Victor: Contemporary Theological Explorations in Mysticism*, London and New York: Taylor and Francis.

Baron, J. (2016), *Patron Gods and Patron Lords: The Semiotics of Classic Maya Community Cults*, Boulder: University Press of Colorado.

Bergamo, M. (1984), *La scienza dei santi: Studi sul misticismo secentesco*, Florence: Sansoni.

Bergamo, M. (1991), *L'anatomia dell'anima: Da François de Sales a Fénelon*, Bologna: Il Mulino.

Cary, P. (2008), *Outward Signs: The Powerlessness of External Things in Augustine's Thought*, Oxford and New York, UK: Oxford University Press.

Carrère, E. (2014), *Le Royaume*, Paris: POL; trans. J. Lambert (2017), *The Kingdom*, New York: Farrar, Straus and Giroux.

Certeau, M. de (1982), *La fable mystique, 1–XVI–XVII century*, Paris: Gallimard.

Certeau, M. de (1989a), *La Possession de Loudun*, Paris: Gallimard.

Certeau, M. de (1989b), *Il Parlare angelico*, Florence: Olschki.

Certeau, M. de (2003), *La Faiblesse de croire*, Paris: Seuil.

Charpentier, E. et al. (1978), *Introduzione alla lettura strutturalistica* [sic] *della Bibbia* (1976) [Introduction to the Structural Analysis of the Bible], Turin: Piero Gribaudi Editore.

Coquet, J.-C. (1984), *Le Discours et son sujet*, Paris: Klincksieck.

Delorme, J. and P. Geoltrain (1982), 'Le discours religieux', in J.-C. Coquet (ed.), *Sémiotique: l'École de Paris*, 103–26, Paris: Hachette.

Eco, U. (1975), *Trattato di semiotica generale*, Milan: Bompiani; English version (1976) *A Theory of Semiotics*, Bloomington, IN: Indiana University Press.
Ginzburg, C. (1983), *Indagini su Piero: Il Battesimo, il Ciclo di Arezzo, la Flagellazione di Urbino; con l'aggiunta di quattro appendici*, Turin: Einaudi.
Gramigna, R. (2020), *Augustine's Theory of Signs, Signification, and Lying* [series 'Semiotics of Religion', 3], Berlin and New York: Walter De Gruyter.
Huang, L. [黄丽云著] (2018), 龙, 船, 水与端午竞渡: 龙神信仰的文化符号 ['Dragon, Boat, Water, and Racing: Cultural Semiotics of Dragon-God Belief'], Beijing: She Hui Ke Xue Wen Xian Chu Ban She.
Jackson, Bernard S. (2000), *Studies in the Semiotics of Biblical Law*, [Series 'Journal for the study of the Old Testament'; Supplement series, 314], Sheffield, UK: Sheffield Academic Press.
Keane, W. (2007), *Christian Moderns: Freedom and Fetish in the Mission Encounter*, Berkeley: University of California Press.
Laack, I. (2019), *Aztec Religion and Art of Writing: Investigating Embodied Meaning, Indigenous Semiotics, and the Nahua Sense of Reality*, Boston: Brill.
Lack, R. (1978), *Letture strutturaliste dell'Antico Testamento*, Rome: Edizioni Borla.
Leone, M. (2001), 'Divine Dictation: Voice and Writing in the Giving of the Law', *International Journal for the Semiotics of Law*, 14 (2): 161–77.
Leone, M. (2004), *Religious Conversion and Identity: The Semiotic Analysis of Texts*, New York and London: Routledge.
Leone, M. (2010), *Saints and Signs: A Semiotic Reading of Conversion in Early Modern Catholicism*, Boston and New York: Walter de Gruyter.
Leone, M. (2012), 'The Semiotics of Fundamentalist Authoriality', in M. Leone (ed.), *The Authoriality of Religious Law*, monographic issue of *International Journal for the Semiotics of Law*, 26 (1): 227–39.
Leone, M. (2013), 'The Semiotic Ideology of Semiotics: A Vertiginous Reading', in M. Stausberg and S. Engler (eds), *Research Symposium on Robert Yelle's Semiotics of Religion*, monographic issue of *Religion*, 43: 1–7.
Leone, M. (2014a), *Annunciazioni: Percorsi di semiotica della religione* ('I saggi di *Lexia*', 13), Rome: Aracne.
Leone, M. (2014b), *Sémiotique du fondamentalisme religieux: Messages, rhétorique, force persuasive*, Paris: L'Harmattan.
Leone, M. (2021), 'Beyond Meaning: Prospections of Suprematist Semiotics', in R. A. Yelle and J. Ponzo (eds), *Representing Transcendence* (Religion and Reason 61), 215–42, Berlin and Boston: Walter de Gruyter.
Leone, M. and R. J. Parmentier (2014), 'Representing Transcendence: The Semiosis of Real Presence', in M. Leone and R. J. Parmentier (eds), *Representing Transcendence*, special issue of *Signs and Society*, 2, S1,.1–22, Chicago, IL: The University of Chicago Press.
Marin, L. (1972), *Études sémiologiques, écritures, peintures*, Paris: Klincksieck.
Marin, L. (1992), *Lectures traversières*, Paris: Albin Michel.
Marin, L. (1994), *De la représentation*, Paris: Gallimard-Seuil.
Marin, L. (1995a), *Philippe de Champaigne ou la présence cachée*, Paris: Hazan.
Marin, L. (1995b), *Sublime Poussin*, Paris: Seuil.
Marmo, C. and J. Jolivet, eds (1997), *Vestigia, Imagines, Verba: Semiotics and Logic in Medieval Theological Texts (XII–XIV Century)* (Semiotic and Cognitive Studies 4), Turnhout, Belgium: Brepols.
Milbank, J. (1997), *The Word Made Strange: Theology, Language, Culture*, Oxford: Blackwell Basil.

Ochs, P. (1998), *Peirce, Pragmatism, and the Logic of Scripture*, Cambridge, CA: Cambridge University Press.

Odell-Scott, D. W. (2018), *The Sense of Quoting: A Semiotic Case Study of Biblical Quotations* (series 'Brill Research Perspectives'), Leiden: Brill.

Padoan, T. (2021), *Towards a Semiotics of Pilgrimage: Ritual Space, Memory and Narration in Japan and Elsewhere*, [Series: 'Semiotics of Religion', 1 and 'Religion and Reason', 56], Berlin and New York: Walter De Gruyter.

Panier, L. (1973), *Écriture, foi, révélation : Le Statut de l'Écriture dans la révélation*, Lyon: Profac.

Panier, L. (1983), *La Vie Éternelle : Une Figure dans la 1ère Épître de Saint Jean*, Paris: Groupe de recherches sémiolinguistiques.

Panier, L. (1984), *Récit et commentaires de la tentation de Jésus au désert : Approche sémiotique du discours interprétatif : Étude*, Paris: Cerf.

Panier, L. (1991), *La naissance du fils de Dieu : Sémiotique et théologie discursive ; Lecture de Luc 1–2*, Paris: Cerf.

Panier, L., ed. (1993), *Le Temps de la lecture : Exégèse biblique et sémiotique. Recueil d'hommages pour Jean Delorme*, Paris: Cerf.

Panier, L., ed. (1996), *Les Lettres dans la Bible et dans la littérature : Actes du Colloque de Lyon, 3–5 juillet 1996*, Paris: Cerf.

Panier, L., ed. (1999), *Récits et figures dans la Bible : Colloque d'Urbino*, Lyon: Profac–Cadir.

Patte, D. (1976), *What Is Structural Exegesis?*, Philadelphia: Fortress Press.

Patte, D. (1981), *Carré sémiotique et syntaxe narrative : Exégèse structurale de Marc, ch. 5*, Besancon: Groupe de recherches semio-linguistiques.

Patte, D. (1983), *Paul's Faith and the Power of the Gospel: A Structural Introduction to the Pauline Letters*, Philadelphia, PA: Fortress Press.

Patte, D. (1990a), *The Religious Dimensions of Biblical Texts: Greimas's Structural Semiotics and Biblical Exegesis*, Atlanta, GA: Scholars Press.

Patte, D. (1990b), *Structural Exegesis for New Testament Critics*, Minneapolis: Fortress Press.

Patte, D. and G. Volney (1986), 'Religious Studies', in T. Sebeok (ed.), *Encyclopedic Dictionary of Semiotics*, 3 vols, 3, 797–807, Berlin: Mouton de Gruyter.

Ponzo, J. (2019), *Religious Narratives in Italian Literature after the Second Vatican Council: A Semiotic Analysis*, Berlin and Boston: Walter De Gruyter.

Ponzo, J., R. A. Yelle and M. Leone, eds (2021), *Mediation and Immediacy: The Semiotic Turn in the Study of Religion* (Semiotics of Religion 4). Berlin and Boston: Walter de Gruyter.

Pozzi, G. (1987), *Rose e gigli per Maria: Un'antifona dipinta*, Bellinzona: Casagrande.

Pozzi, G. (1993), *Sull'orlo del visibile parlare*, Milan: Adelphi.

Pozzi, G. (1997), *Grammatica e retorica dei santi*, Milan: Vita e pensiero.

Rambelli, F. (2013), *A Buddhist Theory of Semiotics: Signs, Ontology, and Salvation in Japanese Esoteric Buddhism*, series 'Bloomsbury Advances in Semiotics', London and New York: Bloomsbury Academic, An imprint of Bloomsbury Pub. Plc.

Raposa, M. L. (1989), *Peirce's Philosophy of Religion* (book series 'Peirce Studies', 5), Bloomington: Indiana University Press.

Sadowski, W. and F. Marsciani, eds (2020), *The Litany in Arts and Cultures*, Turnhout, Belgium: Brepols.

Solís Zepeda, M. L. (2016), *Decir lo indecible: Una aproximación semiótica al discurso místico español*, Rome: Aracne.

Volli, U. (2012), *Domande alla Torah: Semiotica e filosofia della Bibbia ebraica*, [serie 'Bereshit', 2], Palermo: L'epos.

Volli, U. (2019), *Il resto è interpretazione: Per una semiotica delle scritture ebraiche*, Livorno: Salomone Belforte & C.

Yelle, R. A. (2013), *Semiotics of Religion: Signs of the Sacred in History*, London and New York: Bloomsbury.

CHAPTER FIVE

Semiotics in Ethics and Caring

SUSAN PETRILLI

SEMIOTICS, SEMEIOTICS, SEMIOETHICS

The ethical dimension is implicit in human semiosis but has surfaced only recently as a consistent object of study in semiotic research. *Global semiotics* (Sebeok 2001) facilitates the development by reconnecting semiotics with the life sciences, on one hand, and extending it beyond the boundaries of knowledge theory reduced to gnoseology, thus opening to ethics, on the other. Our topic has a major reference in 'semioethics', a neologism forming the title of a monograph co-authored with Augusto Ponzio (2003, also 2010). This expression originated in the early 1980s by contrast with 'cognitive semiotics', and was privileged over others including 'tel(e)osemiotics', 'ethosemiotics', 'ethical semiotics' (Petrilli 2012a: 185–6). Semioethics researches the ethical dimension of semiosis in the framework of semiotics of life.

Semiotics is 'global semiotics' following Thomas Sebeok, who contributed to shaping semiotic history from the second half of the twentieth century, in contrast to Ferdinand de Saussure's '*sémiologie*' (1916) and its focus on conventional-intentional signs in human communication. John Locke (1690) used 'semiotic' for the general sign science, as did the pioneers of modern 'semiotics', Charles Peirce (alternatively to 'semeiotic') and Charles Morris. To the constitution of semiotics as a science a major contribution came from the Moscow-Tartu School with Jurij Lotman; also Roman Jakobson who led scholars in the United States to rediscover Peirce. Important landmarks in the history of modern semiotics include the International Association for Semiotic Studies, founded in 1969 (Paris), followed by the first international semiotic congress in 1974 (Milan).

A possible beginning in the genesis of semiotics as a discipline is *symptomatology* in a tradition originating with Hippocrates (*c.* 460–377 BCE) and developed by Galenus (*c.* 129–200 CE). Ethics is explicit in the Hippocratic oath, but not simply as a professional issue concerning the physician as physician. The ethical demand concerns the single individual in everyday life, beyond social roles and functions (Hippocrates 1990: *Decorum*, VII, *Precepta*, VI). Hippocrates prescribed that the physician help citizens and foreigners alike – if necessary without payment, for where there is love for art, there is love for humanity and where there is love for humanity, there is love for art. Galenus also claimed that science and ethics should not be separated.

To identify *cryptosemioticians*, sign masters who practice semiotics without knowing it, is not only to recover historical memory and boast ancient origins. Reconnecting *semiotics* and *semeiotics*, or *symptomatology* is not just a historiographical issue. Semiotic research is shaped differently depending on whether its history begins with Hippocrates or Locke, even Saussure, or includes Jakob von Uexküll. To search for the origins of semiotics in *symptomatology*, reconnecting with medicine and biology, conditions what objects and models for semiotics, including sign models; what to consider central, what peripheral, the 'lower threshold'. Moreover, historico-theoretical reconnection between the new semiotic science and ancient medical semeiotics results in interdisciplinary extension of semiotic research from the human sciences to the clinics to the biological sciences.

Semioethics underlines the need to overcome separatism among the sciences, for specialism stands upon interconnectivity. Different sciences and disciplinary fields are interrelated, from the natural, logico-mathematical sciences to the historico-social, human sciences, hence the different spheres of semiosis elected as their object of investigation.

Amplification of the interdisciplinary scope of semiotics is a prerequisite for recovering its early vocation as symptomatology and *care for life*, a major issue for semioethics. As global semiotics that distinguishes between 'semiosis' (sign activity) and 'semiotic' (reflection on signs, not just a synonym for 'semiotics'), 'semiotics' reconnecting with 'semeiotics' refines its capacity to interpret symptoms of social disease, e.g. 'alienation' – social, linguistic economical, political, ecological (Petrilli 2014a: 322–42). Committed to understanding social practice in the global communication world, interrogating its signs, implications, perspectives, risks and responsibilities, and considering that, as biosemiotics (global semiotics, semiotics of life) avers, semiosis and life coincide, a semioethical approach is urgent in a globalized world where communication between the semiosphere (Lotman 1984) and the biosphere (Vernadsky 1926) is compromised at a planetary level. To counteract alienation disalienating discourse involves analyzing and transforming social structures oriented by 'false ideas', 'false consciousness', expressed through 'mental illness', mystified by a 'clean conscience'. This requires alternative social planning, theory of social practice to transform social structures that capitalize on linguistic alienation. Disalienation calls for a critique of political economy.

The term 'symptom' is extended from *symptomatization* semiosis to *information* and *communication* semiosis (Petrilli and Ponzio 2007: 21–4). The verbal sign emerges as a symptom thanks especially to Freud. For semioethics, symptomatization is omnipresent, first, because of the centrality of life and health; second, relatively to historico-social context. Like all worldviews that read signs, global semiotics is associated with a specific model producing a specific world (*Umwelt*) – today's, the historico-social specification of primary modelling, where secondary modelling (languages) and tertiary modelling (economico-cultural formations) assume specific configurations: the current phase of development in communication-production tagged *globalization*. Semioethics is particularly concerned with symptoms of planetary life in globalization, where interrelation of each single portion of life with every other, between the totality and its parts has reached the highest degrees ever of mutual implication.

To recognize *semeiotics* at the origin of *semiotics*, seemingly distant disciplines, is not only to recount the history and range of a discipline, but to search for its original sense, a question of *ends*: the health of semiosis, thus of life. General semiotics becomes 'semioethics', neither a branch of semiotics, nor a discipline in its own right. Rather, semioethics emphasizes the original vocation of semiotics as semeiotics for life, and focuses on symptoms. Semioethics fosters the *quest for sense* – relatedly to both special semiotics and general semiotics – the *ultimate vocation of semiotics*.

The implications for semiotics and the semiotician are enormous in terms of *human responsibility*. Though deriving from theoretical reason, the commitment is to surpass the limits of theoreticism and engage in *practical reason*: such engagement is of an ethical-pragmatic order, ultimately to concern the *health of life*. Recovery of the vocation of semiotics for health and the study of symptoms, which (for *global semiotics*) include the physical-chemical, biological, environmental, somatic, psychic, linguistic, economico-social, political, is justified not only in genealogical terms, but the theoretical. Reference is to life over the planet given that semiosis and life converge, that global semiotics addresses the signs of life in all their manifestations, and that human life is objectively part of the global ecosystem, interconnectedly with all other lifeforms (Petrilli and Ponzio 2001a, 2002a, 2002b).

That semiotics should focus on signs in terms of ethics beyond the boundaries of knowledge theory and overcome gnoseology, implies the capacity to critique positivistic accommodation to the world as-it-is, the being of things, worse still servile reproduction of relations of power and control over the communication-production system.

If the concern is for the health and quality of life, merely to describe signs investigating their function, utility, efficiency, productivity without engaging in *critique*, as though human semiosis were neutral, unaccentuated by *values*, *ideologies* and *worldviews*, is inadequate. Social practice is oriented by *social planning*; sociosemiosis is never neutral. To neglect the need for *critique* and *care* involves *indifference* to the other which can only lead to global disaster, as testified by current ecological and humanitarian crises (e.g. most recently the Covid-19 pandemic, Black Lives Matter movement; but, for decades, mass migrations, war, famine, unemployment) (Petrilli 2021c). If semiotics is concerned with life throughout the biosphere and health is at the origin of studying signs, a non-negligible task for semiotics today, particularly arduous in the era of globalization, is to call attention to the need of caring for life in its global diversity and multifaceted globality. And to this ethical demand in semiotics is added another, again traceable in its original vocation as symptomatology, for *life* and *care of the other*, evoking *agape*, a demand for *love* and *responsibility*.

PREFIGURATIONS OF SEMIOETHICS IN THE HISTORY OF SEMIOTICS

Semioethics as formulated in *Semioetica* (Petrilli and Ponzio 2003) is the arrival point of our semiotic research stemming back decades, and launching pad for ongoing studies. Signposts in our travels include Victoria Welby, Charles Peirce, Giovanni Vailati, Edmund Husserl, Charles Morris, Ferruccio Rossi-Landi, Thomas Sebeok, Emmanuel Levinas and Mikhail Bakhtin – whose works we have contributed to circulating internationally through translations, edited volumes, monographic studies. 'Semioethics' is a term that evolves from the margins of their discourses, at the crossroads of texts and ideas, aiming to convey a sense of the interrelation between signs and values, semeiotics and semiotics, meaning and significance. It somehow translates Welby's 'significs', the expression she coined for her special approach to sign and meaning.

As a global sign science, concerned with *signification* and *significance*, the term 'semiotics' should suffice. If the ethical-valuative dimension of signifying processes is related to the operative-pragmatic, further specifications for semiotics are superfluous. But given the tendency to gnoseologism, an expression emphasizing the pragmatic-valuative component of sign models and signifying processes is in place. Like significs, semioethics signals extension of semiotic research beyond logico-gnoseological boundaries of semiotic processes, and focus on problems of the axiological order, thus developing the orientation of significal research on signs and language, sense, meaning, significance at the end of the nineteenth century.

As the study of significance, significs contributes to broadening the semiotic vision: it designates the propensity for signifying practical action, i.e. human involvement in the life of signs at a theoretical level as much as the pragmatic-operative (Welby [1903] 1983: 8). In significs, as in semioethics, meaning as infinite potential for signification and interpretation, for conscious and critical representation constitutes the condition and measure of semantic-pragmatic validity of all experience, knowledge and behaviour. In a letter to Peirce dated 18 November 1903, Welby describes 'Significs' as a 'practical extension' of 'Logic proper' (SS p. 6). Significs facilitates critique of practical reason united to critique of pure reason, for responsible human behaviour. Translation of thought into practice converges with sign interpretation associated with sense and value, urged by the question 'what does it signify?' As the study of significance, significs promotes what we could designate as a *methodics of everyday life* consisting in the development of a responsible, reasonable, questioning attitude, 'scientific' and 'ethical', free of blinding and anaesthetizing dogmatism.

Significs is semioethics not because it studies ethics as a separate discipline, or human behaviour in moral terms, but because like semioethics *it elects alterity, the other as its viewpoint*. The link between meaning and value subtends the human capacity to relate to things and objects, to self and others, to translate interpretation into new spheres of knowledge and action, where the overriding movement is other-oriented, unequivocally testifying to the sign's vocation for the other. All this leads to associating significs to the proposal of a new form of humanism, effectively inscribed in signifying processes and production of other-responsive values.

Coherently with pragmatism, Peirce also connected cognitive semiotics to social behaviour and the totality of human interests, dedicating what turned out to be the final phase in his studies to the normative sciences, ethics and aesthetics. The *summum bonum*, ultimate end of semiosis is 'reasonableness' (Peirce 1905: CP 5.520, 1901: CP 5.4), reason and its development as open process, characterized by synechism (1896: CP 1.72). Reasonableness regulates evolutionary development. With Mikhail Bakhtin this is reason free of prejudice, dialectical-dialogical, other-oriented sign interpretation process, never complete, unfinalizable (Petrilli 2012b; Bachtin e il suo Circolo 2014).

The ethical orientation of Peirce's semiotics is already traceable in his sign model. With his conception of interpretation resulting from dialogue among 'interpretants', Peirce assumes alterity as the condition of the sign's signifying potential, of its identity. His notion of thought-sign evidences the dialogical structure of the self, involving dialogue between a thought acting as a sign and another sign acting as interpretant. All this occurs in semiosical processes where the growth of knowledge necessarily involves valuation.

The relation of signs to values, considered as two faces of the same signifying process, is the specific topic of Morris's *Signification and Significance* (1964). He was concerned with values almost as much as with signs and opposed the idea that it was enough to describe signs to make value judgements about them. Morris focused his research on a fact of communication: that between the order of signs and the order of values and among operators in disciplines relative to these dimensions of human behaviour. Consequently, he investigated correspondences among notions established in the context of sign theory, value theory and theory of human action (Mead) (Rossi-Landi [1953] 1975, 1992; Petrilli

2014a), dedicating many of his writings to the topic with special attention on ethical and aesthetical value considered from a semiotic perspective: in addition to *Signification and Significance* and after *Foundations* (1938) and *Signs, Language and Behavior* (1946), other book titles include *The Open Self* (1948) and *Varieties of Human Value* (1956).

The sign value relationship was also at the centre of Saussure's attention (1916). He explored the relation between linguistic value and economic value, with reference to Marginalistic economic theory (Walras, Pareto), which influences his sign model. Saussure associated language with the market in an ideal state of equilibrium. He applied to language the same procedures that 'pure economy' employed to study the laws of the market, which meant to neglect the social relations of production, social linguistic work, its social structures. Rossi-Landi had already critiqued the notion of value subtending Saussure's sign model, the 'official Saussure', in *Language as Work and Trade* (1968). Based on his interpretation of language as work, 'linguistic work', Rossi-Landi related linguistic value to economic value as analyzed in the Ricardian-Marxian tradition.

Rossi-Landi's research can be associated to Bakhtin and his Circle (2014), particularly Valentin Vološinov's *Marxism and Philosophy of Language* (1929, only translated into English in 1973, after the long 'silence' imposed during the Stalinist era). Vološinov critiqued Saussure's *Cours* through the concept of 'utterance', maintaining that his writings did not account for the live processes of communication, nor adequately describe the specificity of human language, its characterizing aspects – plurilingualism, plurivocality, ambiguity, polysemy, dialogism and otherness. In real signifying processes the sign neither subsists in an ideal state of equilibrium, nor functions in terms of equal exchange between signified and signifier. The complex life of language is not contained between two poles, the unitary system of language and individual speech, no one-to-one relation between signifier and signified, nor is meaning pre-established outside signifying processes. Bakhtin described the utterance as a *response* to preceding utterances, a standpoint in the context of communication, structurally dialogical, socially interactive, expressive of the voice of others, filled with polyphonic overtones, with echoes of utterances of the other (Bakhtin [1952–1953] 1986: 84–100).

Interpretive work is not limited to decodification, mechanical substitution of the interpreted sign with the interpretant sign, to mere recognition of the interpreted sign, but develops through complex processes of infinite semiosis (Peirce), of deferral in the dialogical relationship among signs. Bakhtin (1981) places the sign in the context of dialogism, which implies intercorporeity, responsive understanding, otherness: interpretive work develops in terms of dialogical response, mutual alterity among parts in communication, and presupposes the propensity for responsibility/answerability towards the other (Petrilli and Ponzio 2000b; Petrilli 2019c). Interpretation occurs through deferral among signs in open-ended semiosical chains, sustained by signifying excess over communicative intentionality, production of signifying surplus-value in the dialogical dynamics between interpreted and interpretant signs.

FROM SEMIOSIS TO METASEMIOSIS: THE SEMIOTIC ANIMAL, A SEMIOETHICAL ANIMAL

Endowed with a species-specific capacity for *metasemiosis*, the human being is a *semiotic animal*, expression introduced as the title of a book co-authored by Deely, Petrilli and Ponzio (2005; Deely 2010). The human being is a *semiotic animal*, capable not only of 'semiosis', but also of 'metasemiosis' or 'semiotics', of using signs to reflect on signs, of conscious awareness. Aristotle begins *Metaphysics* positing that *man tends by nature to knowledge*. We now claim that *man tends by nature to semiotics* (or *metasemiosis*).

'Semiotics' means both the *specificity of human semiosis* and the *general science of signs*. In the first case semiotics is *metasemiosis* characteristic of human semiosis. Signs are not only object of interpretation undistinguished from our responses to them. The human use of signs is endowed biosemiosically and phylogenetically with a unique capacity for suspending action and deliberating, thus for critical thinking, taking a standpoint, making choices, intervening creatively in semiosis throughout the biosphere and taking responsibility. It follows that humans can care for semiosis, for life in its joyous and dialogical multiplicity. In this sense, the 'semiotic animal' is also a 'semioethical animal' with an original propensity for *listening* to the other.

'Semiotics' as 'metasemiosis' is connected to 'semiotics' the discipline, the study of signs at the highest levels of conscious awareness and human responsibility for life over the planet. As *semioethics* semiotics provides a scientific analysis of the foundations of responsibility, traceable in two closely interconnected global contexts: the biosemiosic and anthroposemiosic contexts of global communication. 'Global' in 'global semiotics' emphasizes the wide-ranging, totalizing nature of sign studies, crossing over multiple disciplines and, at once, its detotalizing nature as *open semiotics*. In fact, the global semiotic method is characteristically a 'detotalizing' method, responsive to otherness, heterogeneity, difference, distinctions in the great sign network. Semiotics takes account of progress in the sciences – human, social, natural, logico-formal – always ready to renew itself, interrogating its own methods and categories. The ethical demand for care evolves out of semiosis in its extension and vitality, in its interconnectedness and dialogicality.

The relation between semiotics and ethics is based on the possibility of founding ontology in ethics and helps us understand the question of responsibility. Beyond the limits of special responsibility, restricted to social function, role, gender, etc., human responsibility implies responsiveness to the other transcending the boundaries of being and identity, to concern human existence as such. According to this description (Levinas [1935] 1982), responsibility is *ethics* antecedent to all justifications of the cognitive, apophantic order where the existent is situated in a horizon of being, relative to a given regional ontology, limited by the logic of *relative otherness* in contrast to *absolute otherness*.

The problem of being, the fundamental problem of philosophy and a moral problem, is that of the relation to others, *autrui*. When being justifies its existence, it justifies itself to others. With Levinas (1982) and Bakhtin (1993), both of whom proceed from the critique of gnoseologism, first philosophy is ethics. Semioethical discourse begins from this ethical founding of ontology, where ontology is conceived semiotically and semiotics is revisited as global semiotics. Following such theoretical trajectories, semioethics restores semiotics with its original sense as a science concerned with the health of life, perhaps the only sense possible for semiotics today in the situation of global communication.

Life is a specifically human problem. And it is an ethical problem. Responsibility is human responsibility, only humans can take responsibility for life. As the capacity to reflect on signs, *metasemiosis* is inevitably concerned with responsibility: the human being is the only *semiotic animal*, the only animal capable of accounting for sign behaviour, for self. The human is subject *to* responsibility and subject *of* responsibility. The question is 'what is our responsibility towards life?' As a capacity exclusive to humans, semiotics as *metasemiosis* provides the key to a full understanding of why, in what sense each human being is responsible for semiosis *alias* life over the entire planet. In fact, as a unique semiotic animal, the human being can adopt a global and at once detotalized vision of life and its signs, assuming global responsibility/responsiveness beyond short-sighted identity and self-interest, beyond the boundaries of identity-difference, and indifference to other differences. The semiotic animal not only experiences signs in their immediacy, but reflects on signs, answers to and for them, even with one's own life. The human has a singular responsibility for life and its signs, hence for the quality of life. Beyond *limited, relative responsibility with alibis, responsibility indifferent to the other*, the type of responsibility summoned is *unlimited, absolute responsibility, unindifferent responsibility without alibis*.

The ethical dimension of semiosis concerns the human as a *semiotic animal*. After Sebeok and his global semiotics, reflection on semiosis must clearly involve the ethical component. 'Ethical' and not simply 'moral'. The ethical dimension of semiosis transcends morality circumscribed to an individual standpoint, doctrine, faith, religious confession, credo, ideology. Before all else, ethics assumes otherness as its viewpoint and concerns the human capacity to use signs with *conscious awareness* and *responsibility*.

But the semiotician's responsibility is even greater. If semiotics as metasemiosis characterizes humanity, semiotics as a science is *metasemiotics* specific to semioticians. So if the human, a semiotic animal, is a *metasemiosical animal*, the semiotician is a *metametasemiosical* or *metasemiotical animal*. The semiotician (even more so the global semiotician), a metasemiotician, is doubly responsible and is called to care not only for self and the known, familiar other, but for all life, the alien other included. This is a far cry from *global indifference* as it characterizes global communication today.

THE DETOTALIZING METHOD

Cognitive semiotics provides theoretical systems to study signs, but the task of understanding requires a global vision. This implies detotalization, i.e. critique of claims to totality, including the totality 'worldwide global communication'. Like all surface phenomena, a condition for understanding communication is understanding range and complexity: first, communication is not reduced to intentional message exchanges; and consequently, to avoid is the *pars pro toto* fallacy, exchanging the part (human verbal, intentional communication) for the whole (total communication, human/nonhuman, verbal/nonverbal, intentional/unintentional). Among the risks of communication today is the end of communication, not in the sense of message exchange, or of incommunicability and social alienation – a social symptom of our times (Petrilli and Ponzio 2000a). Well beyond communicative needs and message exchanges, communication is far broader such that from a global semiotic perspective the end of communication is tantamount to the end of life.

All environments are part of larger contexts both in the biosphere and historico-cultural anthroposphere, and are not separable as long-term ecological crisis and today Covid-19 pandemic evidence all too clearly. Despite efforts to build barriers, there is no respite from the other, no shelter, we are necessarily exposed, subject to the other: impossible to live and act separately from the other (Petrilli 2021a). Any totality fits into a larger totality, is exposed to the other; impossible to discern internal characteristics, logics, needs, dynamics of the totality, or plan new totalities remaining inside its boundaries. The totality relates to larger totalities, such that what appears as a self-sufficient unit is only a piece or result of a larger totality. Understanding requires a detotalizing method, awareness of the relation of interdependency with the other, with another detotalized totality.

Globalization is a historical-social-economic phenomenon characterized by interpermeability between two totalities, represented by technology and the world market, effects of a larger totality, formed by the social relations of production and social reproduction. Community habitats, natural environments, the body's bio-psychic health belong to the same level of technological production and to the same global market. The intricacies of micro-architecture are revealed in light of a system's overarching architectonics.

The detotalizing method traces profound homological, i.e. genetico-structural similarities among objects seemingly unrelated, independent of each other, passing from the metaphors and analogies of surface similarities to homologies of the logico-structural and historico-genetic level. The transition is from the limited programs of pseudo-totalities to ever larger programs in which the former are inserted. Such a description affords an understanding of control by communication-production programs over each other in concentric circles and trajectories that are not only unidirectional, but retroactive. This is the general communication system, the global communication semiosphere, a sign network hosting all cultures, languages, productions on the planet Earth.

Architectonics as the art of a system (Kant, 'Architectonics of pure reason', in *Critique of pure reason*, [1787] 1963) facilitates critique of the social system of global communication. Thus understood architectonics is detotalizing architectonics: it involves the cognitive and practical-operative spheres, and the aesthetic and ethic, all interrelated. From an other-oriented detotalizing perspective, logic, aesthetics and ethics implicate each other; nor is ethics separable from the Kantian categorical principle of the other as end and not means. From this perspective, *critique of dialogical reason*, *critique of pure reason* and *critique of practical reason* unite (Ponzio 1993).

Semioethics of globalization is founded on critique of dialogical reason and foresees precategorial perception as listening to the other. Critique of globalization is based on the restlessness of responsibility for the other. The detotalizing method involves accounting for the other beyond the barriers of identity and difference, identity-difference (by contrast with alterity-difference) safeguarded by alibis.

Associating different conceptions that underline how the interpersonal relation is not reducible to a cognitive relation, and characterizing it instead as a relation of responsibility, the philosophy of alterity connects responsibility to singularity, to the uniqueness of one's place in the world in a relation of implication with the other. Responsibility is responsibility for the other, *autrui*. Singularity implies that responsibility cannot be delegated. That the relation to the other is not reducible to cognitive relations implies that it is not reduced exclusively to relations among roles, professions, competences and their special responsibilities delimited by alibis. The relation to the other as absolute alterity, singularity, is a relation of proximity, of mutual and at once asymmetrical implication, which the cognitive subject neither chooses, nor premises to behaviour. The relation among singularities in their absolute otherness concerns what cannot be equalled, 'incomparables' (Levinas 1974: 239–52).

SEMIOSIS AND OTHERNESS: DIALOGISM, LISTENING, CARING

Semiosis is modelling, communication and dialogism. A major reference for the notion of modelling in semiotics is Sebeok (1986a, 1991, 1994) and for dialogism Bakhtin (1963, 1965, 1981). Moreover, dialogism and intercorporeity (grotesque body) are two faces of the same coin. Bakhtin studied biology and authored 'Contemporary Vitalism' (signed by biologist Kanaev, in *Bachtin e il suo Circolo* 2014: 215–69). Peirce too evidenced the dialogical nature of the sign. The relation between interpreted sign and interpretant is *dialogic* (Ponzio 2006a). Dialogism not only concerns reasoning, nor is it circumscribed to anthroposemiosis: dialogism invests communication semiosis, but also symtomatization and information (or signification) semiosis. The general logic of semiosis where the interpretant is a response is dialogical.

Dialogism, the functional cycle (Uexküll 1982, 1992), autopoiesis (Maturana and Varela 1980) are part of a global vision that keeps account of organisms (macro, micro) as components of the biosphere (Vernadsky 1926), and of the relation established by Sebeok between communication and modelling. Sebeok as well as Bakhtin cite Vernadsky and Uexküll, both of whom are present in the archaeology of biosemiotics.

Singularity, uniqueness is characterized by unrepeatability, but occurs in space-time, in diachronic and synchronic relations. These are inscribed in singularity constitutively, through the functional cycle and autopoiesis, hence singularity is always relational. Uniqueness is the uniqueness of an organism. Unrepeatability is the unrepeatability of relations involving organisms in specific space-time relations.

This means that identity and alterity are inseparable. It also means that dialogism is not reducible to speaker initiative. Dialogism is part of the organism's structure: 'Life by its very nature is dialogic. To live means to participate in dialogue' (Bakhtin 1963, [1961] 1984: 293). In this sense dialogism and intercorporeity converge: the organism is part of synchronic and diachronic relations that enter its autonomous, singular, unique constitution.

Dialogism is not a question of a subject's good intentions, tolerance, respect towards the other. More than openness to the other as decided by the subject, dialogue is impossible exclusion of the other, impossible indifference even when a question of hostility, hatred. Impossibility is not only of the psychological-cultural order, but also biosemiotic. One's own word is always involved in the word of the other, even passively, despite itself (consider Dostoevsky's tales from the underground). Dialogue is composition of viewpoints and identities, recalcitrant to synthesis, including one's identity, which too is dialogically deconstructed, implicated with the other to varying degrees.

Insofar as it interprets the semiotic universe, interrogates its signs, critiques signs of illness, including separatism, technicalism, overspecialization, semiotics takes a listening attitude towards the other, intending to answer responsively, in the sign of critical awareness and ethical responsibility. As Umberto Eco (1984: xii) says in his Preface to *Semiotics and Philosophy of Language*, semiotics is philosophical in nature because it does not focus on a single system, but on the general categories in light of which to compare different systems. And as philosophical discourse, semiotics practised as semioethics shares a fundamental attitude with philosophy of language – listening to the other, the other's word, a recurrent theme in Bakhtin's writings (Petrilli and Ponzio 2016).

The propensity for critique in philosophy of language, free of prejudice, recognizes the word of the other in my own. The fundamental problem of general semiotics and philosophy of language is the problem of the other, and the problem of the other is that of the word, the word as voice, a demand for listening. Augusto Ponzio describes *philosophy of language as the art of listening* (Petrilli 2007). Listening is constitutive of the word, which general linguistics tends not to evidence unless practiced as metalinguistics. As a part in unending dialogue, the word demands listening, responsive understanding, a response and in turn responds to the response, *ad infinitum* (Bakhtin [1960–61] 1986: 127).

Symptoms are social and at once specific to the single individual, relatively to one's unique relation to the other, the world, self. All ideas, desires, affects, values, interests, emotions, needs examined as symptoms find expression in the singular, embodied word, the unique voice. Semioethics listens to voices.

Listening and *dialogical interrelatedness* imply each other: dialogue is not a condition granted through generosity towards another, but the structure of life itself, the condition for its flourishing. Singularity implies alterity-difference, and alterity implies dialogism.

What distinguishes 'semiotics' from 'semeiotics' phonetically is an 'e' which shifted forward (with the additon of an 'h') obtains 'semioethics' (in Italian 'semeiotica' and 'semioetica'), evoking the *semeiotic vocation of semiotics*. *Semioethics* recovers the sense, scientific and humane, of *semeiotics*, proposing to revisit semiotics – traditionally understood as cognitive semiotics and now global semiotics – in an ethical key. In other words, we have imagined a new approach to semiotics associated with the propensity to recover the ancient vocation of semeiotics for life and well-being, strong in qualitative theor-et(h)ical-pragmatic implications as much as the quantitative, extensive: to safeguard the quality of life is only possible remembering that encounter with the other is inevitable, that the condition of intercorporeity and interdependency among all lifeforms on earth cannot be escaped. Health is totally dependant upon this vital sign network, such that the destiny of each single individual is determined relatedly to every other, human and nonhuman (bacteria and viruses included), and involves the propensity for care: caring for the other. Given its anthropocentric overtones (Bouissac 1991: 168), the human-nonhuman binomial fails to reveal the other in the fullness of its complexity and variation, in phenomenological terms as excess with respect to the totality, to identity, where the intended projection is the detotalized totality, and the context our environing universe in its cosmic infinity. Reading Levinas (1961), interpreter of Descartes, the infinite in the relation to totality alludes to the idea of more in less, alterity in identity, where the 'in' of 'infinite' means at once 'non' and 'within'.

Considering Sebeok's axiom that semiosis and life converge, a major issue for semioethics is care for life across the global ecological system. What to understand by 'care', in what sense? An important specification distinguishes between *care* and *cure*. The propensity for *caring* in the double sense of 'caring' and 'curing' is conveyed in English with these two terms; in Italian contained in the single expression *cura* (care/cure; verb form *curare*: to care/to cure). Semioethically, to care is to care without 'patients', without reducing the human being to the status of 'object' of care/cure.

'We must be brought up to take for granted that we are diagnosts, that we are to cultivate to the utmost the power to see real distinctions and to read the signs, however faint, which reveal sense and meaning. Diagnostic may be called the typical process of Significs' (Welby [1903] 1983: 51). Analogically, we associate diagnostic to the ethical attitude of semiotics for listening and caring for the other, for unindifference and solidarity, inspired by Welby's significs and focus on sense, meaning, significance, Peirce's ethics and aesthetics, Morris's studies on the relation between semiotics and axiology, Levinas's alterity, Bakhtin's dialogism.

The semiotician focused on symptoms, preoccupied with semiosis, therefore life, does not engage as a physician, general practitioner or specialist of some sort. S/he does not prescribe treatments or drugs; nor apply the healthy/ill, normal/abnormal paradigm. The semiotician critiques widespread medicalization in present-day society.

Concern with symptoms recalls Freudian analysis given the centrality of interpretation and listening in his work. This is not medical auscultation, but listening to the other – which is not simply to auscultate. If semiotic analysis of symptoms can be associated to Freudian analysis, it shares nothing with psychiatry, psychiatrized psychoanalysis, psychiatric patients, psychiatric treatment, use of drugs and sundry concoctions; it shares nothing with psychiatrization of human life (Petrilli 2012: 237–65). Under this aspect the psychiatrist and cryptosemiotician Thomas Szasz critiqued psychiatry and psychoanalysis unequivocally, notoriously since his book *The Myth of Mental Illness* (1961) (Petrilli and Ponzio, 'In dialogue with Thomas Szasz', in Schaler et al. 2017: 25–8).

Care is *caring for the other,* unindifference towards the other, where otherness is the perspective, outside binary oppositions – 'healthy/sick', 'normal/abnormal', 'sane/insane', etc. – before and beyond them. *To care* is not only to auscultate the other in the medical sense, to establish diagnoses, preventive therapies, posologies. Semioethically *to care* is *to listen* to the other, with whom self is inexorably interconnected, in relations of mutual exposition, without refuge, shelter (Petrilli 2021a).

Semioethics is raising interest internationally and across disciplines including philosophy, literature, translation studies, theology, anthropology, legal studies, medicine, psychiatry, cultural studies, recognizing care for the diversified other as a unifying concern (Arnett 2017). In medicine, for example, Gary Goldberg (2017) approaches ethical dilemmas in brain injury care in a semioethical framework, 'biosemiotically informed ethics', aiming to overcome the limits of mind-matter dualism, still influential in modern science, to proceed with the ethical-pragmatic instruments of 'dialogical practice' and 'reasonableness' in the search of humanizing solutions in the healing relationship with injured persons, a far cry from medicine functional to 'bio-power', to subordination of the body to biopolitical technology and knowledge-power (Foucault 1977).

In 'semiotics of music', the perspective is music *alias* listening, 'semiotics of music' is '(general) semiotics of listening' and vice versa (music since antiquity is considered therapeutic) (Ponzio 2018). Likewise, medicine today plagued by the separatism of technologies and specialisms should recover concern for the individual's health in a holistic framework, sensitive to detotalized unity, thus push beyond auscultation in the technical sense to investigate symptoms in terms of listening and caring. This means to recover a global vision of humanity and its materiality, which is first *semiotic materiality*, where each human, as both individual body and member of the larger community, evolves in the dialectics between totality and singularity. Bodies are not self-sufficient entities, independent of each other; instead, the body and its parts, like the larger community and its members are part of ever larger interrelated and interdependent totalities and as such are detotalized totalities. The propensity for listening and dialogism means to open to otherness and interrogate pre-existing categories, stereotypes, prejudices, to overcome the indifference of specialisms, to question bodies and signs, including symptoms, to the end of recovering and safeguarding the health and vitality of each one as a part in the living open totality (Petrilli 2010). A pathway in this sense is reconnection with the other in dialogical terms, whether a question of self as other or the external other in ever larger detotalized totalities, in relations characterized at once by singularity and co-dependency among agents and actors. By contrast with the unquestioning believer, disciple, patient, this attitude involves dialogical listening to the other and care in the sign of interrogation, investigation and responsive understanding (Barthes and Havas 1977: 990), as prescribed by ancient medical semeiotics.

Caring for the other, though not mainstream ideology, is necessary for human survival. The notion of 'ecological civilization', introduced in the early 1980s, is at the centre of numerous projects across the globe from East to West, aware that care for life over the planet and human survival are interrelated (Gare 2009). The notion of 'ecological civilization' develops from dialogue between scientists, philosophers and politicians.

Social practice should be founded in ethics, otherness engendering vital semiosic activity, such that ethics is semioethics comprehensive of bioethics (Petrilli and Ponzio 2001b). All lifeforms are co-implicated in a holistic ecological system; ultimately, health is one health, global health, and at once detotalized and multifaceted. Healthy human semiosis evolves as a detotalized totality of alterity-differences.

Care is a central theme in Genevieve Vaughan's gift economy (1997, 2015). But in a world dominated by exchange economy, the regulating value is exchange value, *do ut des*. However, exchange could not subsist without the gift economy, beginning from the gift of life and caring for life itself – necessarily care by others, maternal, parental, social care.

Gift economy is the condition for our social reproduction system to function, as all others. First, it concerns the mother-infant relationship. Mother nurtures child, cares for its growth and education. Gifting is central in language learning. Not incidentally the 'first language' is named 'mother tongue'. Maternal care includes what Vaughan tags 'verbal nurturing'. 'Maternal' by definition recalls mother as possessing all the peculiar characteristics thereof, *paradigmatic* for *un-self-interested* behaviour, in a movement without return, without repayment, what Levinas calls *œuvre* ('Le sens et l'œuvre', in *Humanisme de l'autre homme*, 1972). Peirce conceptualizes 'mother wit', Victoria Welby 'maternal sense' without *gender* distinctions. To avoid misunderstanding Welby further proposes the expressions 'primal sense', 'racial sense', 'original sense', 'native sense'; Vaughan speaks of 'nurturers', 'carers' and 'motherers'.

In *The Gift in the Heart of Language*, Vaughan observes how to maternal gift-giving corresponds *gifting from the child*. This relation transcends exchange logic: an 'amorous' relation where, in mutual gifting, love for the child generates expansion of the motherer/nurturer/carer's experiential space – visual, acoustic, imaginative – giving new sense to life. Not only *her* life: maternal gifting enters the behavioural modalities of receivers, who understand its essential, vital nature, beneficial to self and others, contributing significantly to that condition of *unindifference*, involvement, co-implication, responsibility towards the other that characterizes the human being.

Maternal caring contributes to preparing the child and future adult to understanding the importance, indeed 'vitality' of 'love for one's neighbour', of giving for nothing, receiving for nothing, of perceiving this as a right, a *natural* right, the most important of 'human rights': the right of each single individual to 'nonfunctionality' (Ponzio [1997] 2004), to being loved for nothing, un-self-interested love, hospitality, listening; the right to help and support *in return for nothing*. This right to 'nothing', to 'nonfunctionality' is surely what we each acknowledge as the condition *sine qua non* of true friendship, true love.

'Education to gifting' occurs in the first instance through family, 'recognized' by the Italian Constitution as a 'natural society', through the *maternal*, which is not limited to the female, the mother – though inevitably beginning from her, from the gestation phase, before the birth of each single individual, which only the 'other' can recount, communicate. Education to gifting includes linguistic education; not only as education to speaking, but also *to listening*, to *responsive understanding*, education to *responsibility for the other*. Without this type of basic 'education', all the *Organon* of Aristotelian logic, as Levinas claims, serves nothing, is useless ('La Bible et les Grecques', in Levinas, *À l'heure des Nations*, 1988). Rhetoric is entirely useless if not based on listening to the other, not only to the other's word, but also to what the other says simply by existing, through presence, through uniqueness of the face, in the face-to-face relationship (*de visu*), as much as at a distance.

Life is based on gift-giving, material and verbal maternal nurturing. And gifting is not symmetrical exchange, equal exchange, but is rather a broad process of response and anticipation of what is perceived as need, also desire of the other, well beyond *do ut des* boundaries, according to a natural propensity for unilateral gifting, where the offer precedes the request, and is always bidding higher in open interactive processes. All the social is originally constructed on gifting and care economy, the maternal gift economy, and must necessarily continue in such terms.

HUMAN RIGHTS AND THE RIGHTS OF THE OTHER

Semioethics proposes a new form of humanism, inseparable from the question of alterity, which evidences the extension and consistency of the sign network connecting every human to every other, synchronically and diachronically, pragmatically and ethically: not 'humanism of identity', but 'humanism of alterity'. This 'new humanism' has a major reference in Levinas's *Humanisme de l'autre homme* (1972).

Human rights are traditionally oriented by identity logic, conceived in terms of 'identity humanism', neglecting the other's rights in favour of one's own rights, identity rights. But human rights must include the rights of the other, not just the other *beyond self*, but the other *of self*. Paradoxically, the concept of 'human rights' tends to neglect the rights of the other, including my own rights as other (Petrilli 2019b). The I characteristically removes and segregates alterity, sacrificing it to the cause of identity. But built on sacrifice and repression of otherness, identity is fictitious such that efforts to maintain or recover it are ultimately destined to fail (Ponzio 2006b, 2019).

In globalization where encounter among cultures is inevitable, signs of the relation between identity and alterity call for interpretation in a semioethical key (Petrilli and Ponzio 2019a, 2019b). Identity is a pivotal issue in global society today, and ever more difficult to assert. Consequently, the search for identity has reached paroxysmal degrees, such that obsession with identity leads to forms of self-exaltation, on one hand, together with vilification of the other, on the other hand. In this context, the rights of the other are mostly denied, excluded, to the advantage of identity rights, passed off as human rights *tout court*. Under the title 'Les droits de l'homme et les droits d'autrui' (*Hors sujet*, 1987), Levinas emphasizes the paradox of human rights when understood as identity rights, neglectful of responsibility for the other, the other's rights, the rights of alterity. But the health of semiosis and communication generally, cultural and biosemiosical, demands that we counteract this tendency with the 'humanism of alterity', where the rights of the other are the first to be recognized.

Human rights derive from an original relation with the other, antecedent to all legislation and justification. In this sense they defer to a relation of unindifference to the other, involvement with the other, responsibility for the other. This original relation is an *a priori* of the 'declaration of human rights', antecedent and independent of roles, functions, merits and acknowledgements. Human rights inclusive of the other's rights precede all permissions, concessions, authorities, all claims to identity rights; thus conceived they precede all traditions, jurisprudences, privileges, affiliations, all reason (Petrilli 2021b, 2022). If we recognize that like *humilitas*, *humanitas* derives from *humus*, humid mother earth, cultivated together, and not from *homo*, then truly *human* rights are inevitably the rights of alterity.

The relation between human rights and ethics, law and ethics passes through Georg W. F. Hegel and his philosophy of the Spirit. The Spirit represents the idea that returns to itself. It is divided into the subjective, objective and absolute spirit. In the dialectics of the spirit, the final phase, the absolute spirit, is philosophy. The intermediate phase, the objective spirit, is analyzed dialectically as law, morality and ethics. Ethics is manifest in the form of family, civil society and the State. In Hegel's view, the State is the maximum manifestation of ethics. This is the ethical State theorized by Thomas Hobbes even before Hegel. Institution of the State is described as the concrete manifestation of the universal good. Thus interpreted, the State is the ultimate end towards which single individuals must direct their actions.

The immediate question is whether ethics (especially when considered as an end) can be related to law (the means) without contending with Hegel. Substantially, does the unique individual have no other choice but to submit to the State as the maximum expression of ethics?

From a semioethical perspective, keeping account of figures who have valorized ethics, this particular view of the world can be avoided. Consider Peirce's 'interpretation semiotics' in contrast to 'code' or 'decodification semiotics'; Welby who viewed ethics as the ultimate end and foundation of 'significs' thus named to highlight the fundamental question concerning signs and language – 'what does it signify?', 'what signifying value?'; Bakhtin author of an early essay *Toward a Philosophy of the Act*, published (posthumously), which discusses ethics as first philosophy; Levinas, a philosopher of language who like Bakhtin valued Dostoevsky and posited that responsibility for the other is the original modality of the I-other relationship. This orientation as delineated by such figures contrasts with Hobbes's conception of the human as '*homo homini lupus*'. For Levinas the I-other relationship implies a relation of unindifference to the other, where the I is placed in the accusative, instead of the nominative. The I is called to answer for self, but in answering for self the appeal is first to answer for the other.

Contrary to the 'ethical State' and Hobbes's conception of the I/other relation, for Levinas the State does not establish responsibility for the other, but limits it: the law establishes from where to where I am responsible. My responsibility is delimited and at once guaranteed by alibis provided by the law. For Levinas, as demonstrated in *Autrement qu'être* (1974), the legal system is an inevitable institution because in the social the relation is not between self and another: there is always a third, a fourth, etc. This other not only relates to me, but to the other as well, to another and yet another. All this calls for a legal system committed to equalling what cannot be equalled: our singularities. The implication is that law, and with law the State, is perfectible, never definitive or absolute.

FOR A CRITIQUE OF IDENTITY: ECOLOGICAL CRISIS AND HUMAN SURVIVAL

As regards social roles, human rights, individual identities, their internal and external indifference, regulated by equal exchange logic, sanctioned by the order of discourse, semioethics is specifically concerned with the other.

This other is not the other understood as a means but as an end, not the other of *relative otherness*, but rather *absolute otherness*; the other as a value in itself, non-functional, unproductive, excess with respect to the dominant order, difference unindifferent to the otherness of others; the other involved in the 'play of musement' (an expression adapted by Sebeok from Peirce, as the title of his book of 1981).

The concept of 'hors lieu', 'out of place', 'exo-topos', 'u-topos' (Levinas 1972; Ponzio 2007), with its spatio-ethical resonations, indicates singularity, alterity irreducible to identity, to the individual (Petrilli, Ponzio and Sebeok 2001). Singularity is involved in the relation with others, without alibis or substitutes. Self is unique, incomparable, irreducibly other: 'U-topos' with respect to role, position, function, community, belonging, identity. 'Out of place' means to find oneself in a position of exposition, vulnerability, without shelter, protection, justification, without excuses, a way out, without alibis (Lat. *alibi* = somewhere, another place), exposed to the other; out of genre, not to belong; it implies existence, interrelation, involvement in the life of others outside the role of subject and its identity; before and beyond affiliation as an individual to a class, group, agglomerate, community.

'Out of place' implies outside the places of discourse, outside judgement, definition, stereotypes, predication of being. To listen to the voice of the other 'out of place' – as in the case of Levinas's 'hors sujet', 'otherwise than being' – implies outside the order of discourse, a return to the word that listens and gifts time to the other, for the other.

'Out of place' is the place of encounter with the other, of unlimited responsibility for the other, unlimited answerability to the other.

Caring for life in human semiosis, semioethics investigates the 'properly human' outside the space, time and values of the already-constituted-world.

The 'properly human' refers to that dimension of human semiosis where interhuman relationships are not reduced to closed identity, to relations among predefined subjects and objects, or to relations of exchange, equality, functionality, productiveness, self-interest.

Semioethics explores the possibility of responding in a dimension beyond the horizon of being, that of 'otherwise than being' (Levinas 1974). By contrast with 'being otherwise', 'otherwise than being' indicates the outside with respect to the already-given-world, the world as-it-is. This is the capacity for earthly transcendence beyond the already-given-world, a dimension of sense other than sense of this world. In sum, by contrast to identity humanism, a new humanism based on alterity is possible.

As evidenced by Sebeok's 'global semiotics', interpreting Jakob von Uexküll, 'communication' and 'environment' are inseparable. All species communicate in a given environment, a species-specific *Umwelt*. All species – and certainly the animal – have a specific 'modelling device' through which to model their world, with the difference that the human species-specific modelling device, what Sebeok also tags 'language', language-as-modelling, is syntactical. Semiotic animals are thus endowed to model their *Umwelt* variously, to create multiple possible worlds, a capacity traceable back to the early hominid, and which explains human development through to what we are today.

To global semiotic research is associated another internationally renowned semiotician, Paul Bouissac (1998). Contrasting with the destructive nature of anthropocentric and ethnocentric positions, Bouissac avers that through science, including semiotics, humankind nonetheless is capable of modelling a different culture, shaped by different knowledge and value systems. Bouissac is directly concerned with the ethical dimension of semiosis, oriented in an ecological sense. Global semiotics developed as semioethics signals the need for a radical shift in worldview, particularly obvious in recent decades.

Bakhtin is a careful observer of semiosis in the 'great time', by contrast with the 'small time' of individual life, lived and experienced as a function of one's *conatus essendi*. My body is interconnected with every other body, synchronically and diachronically, with the body of all other living beings, human and nonhuman. Hence Bakhtin's theory of 'dialogism' is not reducible to formal dialogue, nor to dialogue in verbal communication. Bakhtinian dialogism is synonymous to 'intercorporeality' and tells of the capacity for 'unindifferent response' to the other. Human responsibility, which implies *responsiveness*, is projected towards the whole biosphere and is the *condicio sine qua non* for the global health of semiosis, thus life, human and nonhuman – which, as Bouissac observes, share the same cosmic niche.

For an adequate understanding of today's communication-production world from a global semiotic perspective, a third context to consider beyond the phenomenological and ontological is the socio-economic (Petrilli and Ponzio 2000a). Phenomenological, ontological and socio-economic contexts are closely interrelated from the viewpoint of ethics, important to consider when investigating the relation between communication and environment. Global semiotics practiced as semioethics in the global communication-production system has an enormous responsibility, that of revealing and critiquing the threats it presents to life over the planet.

Australian philosopher Brian Medlin (1927–2004) had already denounced the connection between 'ecological disaster' and 'social order', nature and culture from mid-XXth century onward (Medlin 2021), clearly foreseeing planetary ecological disaster, exacerbated by ideological contest about climate action and human survival in present-day neo-imperialism and neo-colonialism. His writings are pervaded by an appeal to safeguarding the 'environing universe' in its multiform diversity, urging the need to acknowledge and act upon the inevitability of interrelatedness among all lifeforms for the sake of human survival: impossible life in an egocentric world revolving around the myopic self, neglectful of interdependency with the overarching ecosystem.

Developing from the conjunction between the search for 'cosmic significance', the practical conduct of 'human affairs', and the 'life of reason', Medlin's worldview can be associated with Sebeok's global semiotics and biosemiotic research today. Moreover, like Welby before him, Medlin was critical of the poor use of language, which in the best of philosophical tradition he associated with muddled thinking and confusion, if not straight-out mystification.

Social practice calls for *cooperation* and *responsibility*, in the dialogue between global and local, based, in Medlin's terminology, on 'reason' and 'rationality'. Peirce the pragmatist thematized 'reasonableness', creative inferential procedure unbiased by prejudice, dialectical and dialogical, open to action regulated by otherness. In Medlin reason practised as passionate argument is necessary for logical rigour associated with a strong ethical and political commitment. Medlin promoted eco-action and the potential to do well collectively:

> [T]he fact is that without passions and desires reason is simply undirected, goal-less. Thought needs motivation and this applies to scientific thought as well as to any other. In fact, given the daily tides of ideological sludge against which we must make way, it is so hard to be reasonable that only a passionate person can hope to bring it off.
> ('Objective Despair', in Medlin 2021 [1988]: 103)

Problems afflicting Medlin's day such as to fear for 'human survival' have since assumed planetary dimensions. With reference to risks generated by the socio-economic system for life, not only human life but the global Earth system, the semiotic animal is called to quickly transform from a 'rational animal' into a 'reasonable animal', reason inspired by otherness, and commit to cooperative enterprise. Not the arrogance of smug certainty, but 'dissatisfaction' and 'disagreement' animate discussion and scientific inquiry, again with Peirce the 'play of musement', imagination (1896: CP 1.47, 1877: CP 6.461), innovative reason oriented by otherness, dialogism, listening (Petrilli 2013, 2019a). Rather than satisfaction with things as they are, dissatisfaction and disagreement favour the development of discernment, the restlessness of critical thinking, the interpretive-signifying capacity, the capacity to imagine the unimaginable, necessary for progress in the sciences, the arts, for the humanities overall, for rational development of experience and conscious awareness inspired by the humanism of alterity.

Among the conditions for human survival, Medlin indicates 'non-expanding economies'. Considering that globalization is planned in terms of 'expanding economies' and that the global social reproduction system challenged by Medlin is still firmly in place, in spite of current ecological emergency, the implications of this determination are no less than apocalyptic for dominant political economical systems. All the same, with the world threatened by the Covid-19 crisis and wars in course awareness of intercorporeal interrelatedness, of interdependency among all lifeforms is slowly rising (albeit too slowly), and human mishandling of affairs human and nonhuman, is now more cogently interrogated (albeit not cogently enough) – to echo Terrence, *humani nihil a me alieno puto* (nothing human is alien to me).

Contrary to Hobbes and the principle he promulgated of *homo homini lupus*, 'man a wolf for the other man', the original relationship between one human and another is not based on fear, as predicated by Levinas. Science has not indicated genetic limitations on human nature, as Medlin observed, whereas changed social circumstances can prove to be therapeutic. The primordial propensity is not for violence and conflict, not for 'selfishness', but for 'cooperation', without which human societies simply could not exist. Medlin promoted the need to build a 'new polity', oriented by values characteristic of *humane humanity*, responsible difference and caring, unselfishness, social justice and global prosperity, the condition for human survival, and not merely a moral imperative: 'probably the hardest task that the human species has ever set itself', but a challenge and a hope in the face of catastrophe threatening life in present-day emergency.

'Hope' as auspicated by Medlin is level-headed and down to earth, an appeal to goals towards which humanity must strive, to common knowledge, common sense, as afforded by global experience of the world – such as we can extrapolate from history through reasoning honestly and resolutely, being values within the human reach – and to act as a consequence:

> I don't hope that I'm going to tell you much that you don't know already. I do hope, though, that I can get you to *believe* what we all know. For most of us who are preoccupied with the developing global crisis, what's hard is seriously to believe what we know very well. The reason for this is obvious: honestly and resolutely to act out our belief would seem to demand that we unravel and re-weave the whole fabric of our lives. Not only our own personal lives, but the whole of human life as it is currently lived on the planet. And nobody knows how to do that – even how to start doing that.
>
> ('Ecological Crisis and Social Disorder', in Medlin 2021 [1991]: 116)

Referring to the historical condition of his day, Medlin observes how humanity works towards its own destruction. Impending ecological disaster is co-opted to the cause of human extinction as 'career politicians', 'corporate hucksters' and other 'ideological chameleons' turn fashionably green. Nor can we deny that world events since Medlin confirm and amplify global emergency on all fronts. It is necessary to listen to the voice of scientific research over that of a short-sighted, greedy market. At the same time, however, though striving towards objectivity scientific research is not neutral, but too is oriented by values and worldviews, if not by motivations of the ideological order. Even dialogue with biology is not always a guarantee of scientific validity given that it too like other sciences can be oriented, and often is, by ideology in a narrow sense (Petrilli and Ponzio, 'Biologia, ideologia e semioetica', in Petrilli 2015: 353–72). A significant example of the mystifications pervading scientific discourse is the 'Lysenko case', identified in the title of a renown book by Dominique Lecourt (1977), prefaced by Louis Althusser. All this underlines the central importance of dialogical critique, otherness, cooperative responsibility in the architecture of worldview and social practice.

On valorizing the life-world in its multifaceted totality, Medlin observes that the non-human should not be reduced to the mere status of resource and annex, a function of humankind, or extension thereof. The other, whether friend, comrade, opponent, human or non-human is a value *in itself*. Against reductive anthropomorphism, he warns that 'until we win our way back to a proper reverence for non-human nature, we shall remain lost in a world growing ever more hostile to us' ('Ecological Crisis and Social Disorder', in Medlin 2021 [1991]: 142).

This observation rings just as true applied to the human other considered as alien – to relationships among human beings based on fear *of the other*, rather than fear *for the other* (Levinas 1987), for the other's well-being, for 'happy humanity' (van Eeden 1912). Life, a value in itself, embedded in death is made meaningful by the human propensity for cooperation and love, friendship and comradeship, caring and peace. For all its 'ugliness' and 'horror', the world remains 'various' and 'beautiful'.

Hope presupposes the malleability of human nature, with Sebeok thanks to 'primary modelling' – the human specifies-specific device whose main characteristic is syntactics –, thus the capacity for creativity, innovation, construction, deconstruction and reconstruction of new possible worlds, cultivation of the imagination, accompanied by development of our metasemiosical capacity for conscious awareness and responsibility/responsiveness. In fact, the potential for transformation, innovation, improvement, even for perfectibility of the world, is associated with the semiotic animal's capacity not only to use signs, but to reflect upon signs: the human is the only life-form capable of using signs on the basis of deliberation and decision-making. It follows that the human animal *is endowed with a capacity for responsibility*: responsible not only for the (species-specific) construction and transformation of the social environment, but also for effects and consequences on the natural environment, on our 'environing universe' *tout court*. Conscious awareness, responsibility and hope are not only philosophically legitimate, artistically inspirational, semioethically urgent, but they are also scientifically and biosemiosically founded.

Medlin's writings may be read as practical philosophy in a semioethical key, in dialogue with scientific research, concerned with the question of human responsibility for life over the planet. Though this focus is a feature of twentieth-century studies in the philosophy of language and general science of signs, it has not been a mainstream interest. But today, in a globalized world, a focus on the relation between signs, language and behaviour from the perspective of ethics and values is urgent. We have described semioethics as the propensity in 'semiotics' to recover its ancient vocation as 'semeiotics' for 'care'. This goes together with the capacity for 'listening' to the other, surveying symptoms of sickness and unease throughout the great ecosystem, now ever more urgent for communication and survival in the face of growing interference between the 'biosphere' and the 'semiosphere'.

The Western worldview is traditionally anthropocentric, based on the dualism human and other organisms, described by Bouissac (1991: 169) as one of the fundamental – albeit tacit – tenets of Western metaphysics, epistemology and ethics, one that has provoked an ontological gap used to legitimize discrimination not only between human and nonhuman, but within the domain of the human itself. Such is the case towards difference, the 'alien' other whether a question of gender, disability, dysfunctionality, ethnicity, skin colour, religion, class, etc. Semiotics is a significant indicator of a worldview emerging from science, emancipated from dogmatic metaphysical and religious frameworks, and capable of modelling a new culture, different knowledge and value systems. Ultimately, the hope is for development of an ethical system based on environmental philosophy (Bouissac 1991: 177, cf. 1988). Global semiotics and semioethics may be considered as contributions in this direction (Posner et al. 1997–2004; Sebeok 1986b).

SEMIOTICS OF LIFE AND HUMAN RESPONSIBILITY

The sign network includes the semiosphere constructed by humankind, a sphere in turn inclusive of culture, its signs, symbols, artefacts. But global semiotics teaches us that the semiosphere is far broader than human culture. It converges with the great biosphere, if we accept Sebeok's axiom that semiosis and life coincide. The semio(bio)sphere constitutes humanity's habitat, the matrix whence we sprang, the stage upon which we are destined to perform. Semiotics has the merit of demonstrating that whatever is human involves signs. Even more: from a global semiotic perspective we know that whatever is living involves signs (Merrell 1996, 1999). This is as far as cognitive semiotics and global semiotics reach.

But semioethics develops awareness beyond extension and complexity of the semiosic network in the direction of ethics. It relates semiosis to values with a focus on human responsibility for life over the planet, radical, inescapable responsibility inscribed in our very own bodies insofar as we are 'semiotic animals', with the task of defining values and commitments for practical action.

Semioethics interprets human sign behaviour on the principle that if all the human involves signs, all signs in turn are human. This humanistic commitment does not mean to reassert (monologic) identity, nor propose yet another form of anthropocentrism. What is implied is a radical operation of decentralization and detotalization, a Copernican revolution. As Welby would say, 'geocentrism' must be superseded, then 'heliocentrism', to approximate a truly 'cosmic' perspective (Petrilli 2009: 7–40), at the intersection between global semiotics and semioethics. In human responsibility, at stake more than anything else is otherness, not only my neighbour's otherness, whether spatially close or distant, but otherness of the alien other, of living beings distant genetically even. Semioethics emphasizes how indifference to difference is impossible, delusory.

Semioethics does not propose programs, goals and practices, no decalogue or formula to apply, whether sincerely or not, contrasting with stereotypes, norms and ideologies. Its special vocation is to evidence sign networks where it seemed there were none, bringing to light inescapable connections and implications, where it seemed there were only separations, boundaries, distances and relative responsibilities safeguarded by alibis, hypocritical responsibilities of a 'clean conscience': the semioethical approach implies the exquisitely human capacity for critique.

Contrary to strictly cognitive, descriptive, ideologically neutral approaches, semioethics evidences the axiological dimension of human semiosis. With Levinas and Bakhtin the human individual is valorized as concrete singularity interrelated with other singularities. Semioethics starts from the assumption that the individual as concrete singularity, whatever the specific object of study, however specialized the analysis, is implicated in the destiny of every other inextricably, without alibis.

Given its broad scope, semiotics accounts for the 'reason of things'. The propensity for detotalization is the condition of critical and dialogical totalization, such that for healthy social practice *reason* is not separated from *reasonableness*.

The critical capacity, social awareness, responsible behaviour are central themes in semiotic studies intending to interrogate not only the sense of science, but of life for mankind.

Beyond Sebeok, semioethics evidences the ethical implications of global semiotics and relevance to education, particularly for comprehensive and critical interpretation of communication under present-day conditions, i.e. communication in globalization, global communication.

In global communication converging with life, dialogism is not reduced to the exchange of rejoinders among interlocutors, but indicates the permanent condition of intercorporeal involvement and reciprocal implication among bodies and signs throughout the semiosical universe. Vital biosemiosic dialogism is a necessary condition for the emergence of more specialized forms of dialogue in human semiosis.

Today's socio-economic world is a 'global communication' world and calls for instruments of analysis just as global, which 'global semiotics' associated with 'semioethics' can provide. Today's world is characterized by a computer-driven industrial revolution, global free markets, and pervasiveness of communication through the production-exchange-consumption cycle, exploited for capitalist profit.

Another characteristic of globalization is its destructive potential. The risk of destruction over the planet is increasing and requires to be recognized if semiosis and life are to flourish. The appeal is to *global responsibility*, just as global as the dominant socio-economic order at least.

Sebeok's 'global semiotics' evidences interconnection between communication and life. His planetary perspective lays the condition for an approach to contemporaneity capable of transcending the limits of contemporaneity itself, from a semioethical perspective the condition for assuming responsibility without alibis.

Capitalism today imposes ecological conditions that render communication between self and body, self and environment ever more difficult and distorted (Ponzio and Petrilli 2000a). In a world governed by the logic of production and market exchange, where everything is liable to commodification, humanity risks becoming desensitized, anaesthetized towards the signs of non-functionality and ambivalency: from signs of the body to seemingly futile signs of phatic communication with others. But for the quality of life, such signs must be recovered. In terms of narrativity, a task for semioethics is to reconnect rational worldviews to myth, legend, fable, popular tradition, to the places of discourse that valorize humanity and its relations to the surrounding world.

The main function of semiotics of life, the ethical, is rich with implications for human behaviour: the signs of life that we cannot read, don't want to read, no longer know how to read require to be recovered in their importance and relevance to the health of humanity and life globally (Petrilli and Ponzio, 'Bioetica, semiotica della vita, e comunicazione globale', in Petrilli 2019b: 87–103).

Well before the advent of global communication in capitalist and globalized society and the worldwide spread of the communication network through progress in artificial intelligence and technology supported by the global market, global communication was already a fact of life. From a biosemiosical perspective, global communication characterizes the evolution of life from its origins, something we cannot ignore if life, including the human, is to flourish globally, as inscribed in the nature of sign activity. Human communication is part of a global biosemiosical network where all life-forms are interrelated and interdependent with respect to each other.

Instead, global communication understood in socio-economic terms, investing social reproduction in all its phases (production-circulation-consumption), the expression of corporate-led capitalist globalization, is neither inevitable nor desirable, threatening even to destroy life on earth as we know it, as denounced by its oft-devastating effects over the planet.

SIGN MASTERS AND PEACEMAKERS, THE PHILOSOPHICAL VOCATION OF SEMIOTICS

Considering recent developments in sign and language studies and historical-social context, all figures so far denominated contribute together to scientific research and social practice, whether explicitly as sign masters or implicitly as cryptosemioticians, and as peacemakers (Petrilli 2017b). Sign and language scholars know that to make a sign takes another sign which interpreting the former develops its meaning, such that one sign only flourishes and functions in relation to another. The sign's 'vocation' is the other, the other's interpretation, encounter with other signs, words, dialogue, listening. In this sense, orientation towards 'preventive peace' is in the 'nature' of signs and words (Levinas 1961; Ponzio 2009, 2019).

The basic method for using signs is translation already within the same sign system, the same language, even before encounter with other sign systems and languages. Speaking, communicating, signifying and translating occur in the relation between identity and alterity. This explains the interest and orientation of scholars in semiotics, philosophy of language, the sign sciences generally for dialogue and encounter with the other, for living together, for relation to the other, whatever the identity or community affiliation.

Levinas interrogates the relation to the other in terms of 'face', clarifying that the *face of the other* is not only that of the 'face-to-face' relationship. The 'face' is metaphor and metonymy of the other. The 'I' whether directly or indirectly is always in front of the 'other'. The I must *answer for the other*, and at once *to the other*. In this sense the I is always in front of the face of the other: always, in all circumstances, in all decisions, outside relations of both the spatial and temporal order. The other is not only the contemporary other, the other whose gaze weighs directly upon the I in all deliberations, decisions, actions. The other whose face is always and inevitably in front of the I, the face from which the I cannot distract its gaze, is also the other to come, the other from subsequent generations with a right to life and to the quality of life. To stand in front of the face of the other, to have to answer for the other and to the other, indicates the inevitable relationship of unindifference, involvement, complicity, compromise with the other.

This attitude contradicts the idea of 'preventive war', promoted in dominant communication ideology circuits, considered 'just and necessary', even 'humanitarian', as justification of military intervention. Levinas proposes 'preventive peace.' This is not the peace of the end of war, peace of cemeteries, silence imposed by conquerors over the vanquished. Peace is my peace, a relation that extends from self to other, desire and goodness, where self finds itself and at once lives without selfishness (Levinas 1961: 342).

The *said*, with its names, concepts, universals, assemblages, types, genres and species, with its 'communication' as the transition of messages from 'sender' to 'receiver', arises, as amply demonstrated by Levinas (1974: 200–3; 1987: 145–51) in *saying*, in the relation of proximity and responsibility without alibis for the other, one's neighbour. As emerges from his *Cours*, Saussure too maintained that verbal language cannot be reduced to nomenclature, which also results from the system of language (*langue*). But this is not enough. Language cannot be reduced to nomenclature in another sense as well.

The *said* is nomination, knowledge, abstraction, attribution, allocation, appropriation, identification; *saying* is movement towards the other provoked by the other, involvement, participation, unindifference, finding oneself implicated in another's situation even. As proximity, responsibility for the other, one-for-the-other, saying requires putting oneself at the other's disposal, on the side of the other, given that the first case in which self presents itself, as Levinas claims, is not the nominative, but the *accusative*, the I questioned, summoned by the other. This gives rise to a one-way movement towards the other, to the necessity of responding to the other, before the face of the other, antecedently to the conventional sign, the letter, the verbal. Saying is the immediacy of proximity, restlessness of responsibility for the other who summons me, calls me to question, even before taking the initiative to do so. 'La responsabilité pour l'autre est une immediateté anterieure à la question' (Levinas 1974: 245). Even before being summoned, challenged, interrogated, the other's face, that regards me, is already interrogation, demand for consideration, appeal.

With respect to the condition of one-for-the-other, the relationship between I and other, my neighbour, yet another intervenes, a third: the third interferes, disturbs the relationship. The I, the other and the third are all neighbours, and the third is also the neighbour of my neighbour. The third puts the dual asymmetrical relation into crisis, a one-way irreversible relation of self for the other, with the simple question, with no need to be uttered: 'What about me?', thereby placing a limitation, the *other* other, on the self's absolute responsibility for the other. This is how consciousness and the problem of justice arise in original saying; and, consequently, the need for abstraction of the concept, equalization, comparison among incomparables, thematization; the problem arises of equality, of social convenience; the need for law presents itself, of the State and its institutions – an origin altogether different from that presented by Hobbes. Justice, society, the State rise to safeguard the third, to guarantee social justice; they presuppose the condition of otherness as proximity, unlimited responsibility for the other.

Knowledge, know-how, science all rise from the need to equate, compare, abstract. With respect to saying, such phenomena as the said, language as organization and classification, relative to a given reality, representation of the objective world, all rise from the need for justice. But even before this, they rise, including justice itself, from unindifference towards the other, towards one's neighbour, not just the first comer, but another, and yet another, not only the next in a spatial sense, my neighbour, but also my neighbour in a temporal sense, the immigrant, the newly arrived, those to whom we are not related at the moment, but could be subsequently, those who are not present yet, but who could arrive, those who come after us, to whom we are connected affectively or not, future generations. At the basis of justice, there is ethics; at the basis of laws that establish rights and duties, that regulate giving and receiving, that permit equal exchange, there is concern for the other, fear for the other, hospitality of the other, care for the other. The *said* arises from *saying*, and originally *saying* is *giving*.

As noted by Levinas, dialogue as exchange of rejoinders, however important in the I-other relationship, is not a fundamental modality in the verbal relation. Dialogue comes subsequently, with the *said*. But before being dialogue and materializing in the said, language is gifting. In front of the other's face, the other who engages and concerns me, language rises as a gift, so that saying is essentially gifting-giving, availability, not thanks to a subject's initiative, but as provocation that the subject endures, as responsibility urged by the other, as involvement, unindifference, in a word, *proximity*, which is not decided by me. Language is witness, even *substitution* of the I for the other, in that range of modalities associated by Levinas under the expression 'hostage' ('Langage et Proximité', in Levinas 1967: 217–36).

Knowledge, know-how, science rise from the need for abstraction caused by equating the incomparable, demanded by justice, required in turn by the irreversible relationship of responsibility for the other, by an original ethical relation. And what about philosophy?

To ask this question means to ask it for semiotics as well, given that, as the general sign science, semiotics too is philosophy. According to Eco (1984), philosophy is constitutive of semiotics.

Philosophy is search for sense introduced to sociality with the origin of justice and order, search for sense in being for the other, in proximity, in living together as sociality, as infinite responsibility of one for the other, to the point of substitution of one with the other.

Semiotics studies the sign in general, the sign characterized by the 'relation of this as that', by exchange between *signifiant* and *signifié*, between *sign* and *interpretant*. But because of its 'philosophical vocation', semiotics cannot limit itself to the *said*, whatever the sign system, verbal or nonverbal. Because of its 'philosophical vocation', general semiotics shifts reflection from the level of the *said*, to *saying*, and *giving*. The 'semiotician-philosopher' Peirce – unlike Saussure, who, influenced by the Marginalist conception of value (School of Lausanne) conceived the *signifiant-signifié* relation as an equal exchange relation – evidenced the uneven, asymmetrical relation between interpreted sign and interpretant sign, revealing how the interpretant adds something more to the interpreted sign which it somehow translates, transfigures and develops. The 'philosophical vocation' of semiotics, the general sign science, entails that reflection and planning (inevitable in knowledge and science) shift from exchange to gifting without return, without a counterpart, from indifference in the relation between one and another, to difference of one and the other, and unindifference for the other, care for the other.

It is in this sense that semioethics aims to develop the philosophical orientation of semiotics, with Levinas (1974: 207) *philosophia* as 'wisdom of love in the service of love', *agape* the evolutionary principle of life (Peirce 1893: CP 6.287–317), thus of all semiosis at a planetary level given that, as results from Sebeok's global semiotics and from biosemiotics, *semiosis and life converge*.

Ethics and care are topics that should characterize semiotics today and those who practise it. At stake is its coherence, its professionality even. And, in fact, the term 'semioethics' indicates neither a trend, nor a special branch of semiotics, but simply an orientation now necessary for semiotics to become a truly human science. Human is understood here in the sense of humanism, the humanism of alterity, where the other is not reduced to the status of object, but is our perspective, pointing to the need for listening and caring for the other.

LIVING TOGETHER IN THE TIME OF COVID-19 CORONA CRISIS

The search for sense presupposes a commitment to survival, thus to goodness, beauty, love and truth. Perception, sensibility, experience, belief, knowledge, orientation, perspective and value vary extraordinarily, depending on the actors involved and context. But the overriding goal that is life and its health can only be reached together, united in diversity, as we interpret, translate, imagine, create, critique and communicate.

This is the time of Covid-19 corona crisis: humanity is hostage to a menacing ecosystem which it has contributed to creating. In the effort to resist the deadly virus, as it freely circulates across borders – national, economical, political, racial, social, gender, religious, no passport required, no citizenship – the world in the effort to interrupt communication channels has quickly shut down. With few 'trumpeting' exceptions, the appeal from those who command and represent us, the politicians (sometimes elected democratically, sometimes our jailor tyrants), is to cooperation and responsibility. Despite the global order to lock doors for fear *of* the other, the human other, the non-human other, our environing universe, the appeal is necessarily to the *open community*, to global collaboration, oriented as never before by *otherness* and *listening*: for the sake of the other, in the name of the other – including myself as other, the condition of human survival.

Against myopic economical-ideological reason, each single individual is summoned, not the self-interested market individualist, but single individuals in their otherness and singularity, each called to cooperation if not for love and generosity towards the other, if not for the sake of community health and survival, local and global, simply for one's own sake, one's own other. The condition of intercorporeal co-implication, of dialogical interrelatedness cannot be escaped, underlining the demand for cross-community solidarity, worldwide, beyond walls and barriers: isolated humanity is delusory as Peirce had already explained in semiotic terms even before the advent of global semiotics. Global emergency – ecological, humanitarian, political, economic – reveals the extent to which my body, your body is entangled with the other's body, the extent to which your body is compromised by mine, the other's, beyond walls and barriers – whether we like it or not, together forever.

The beauty of Covid-19 corona crisis is how it tells us that we all count, each one of us valuable, an end, in care and responsibility for the other, ever more so in our globalized world: not fear *of* the other, but fear *for* the other is the condition for the other's health and security, my own. The global threat to life and appeal to co-participative responsibility emphasizes how each single individual in this world makes a difference, for self and for the other, each single individual interrelated in the life and destiny of every other. Intercorporeality and interdependency across the biosemiosphere is the condition for human historico-socio-cultural communities to flourish.

This is the fundamental understanding called upon to govern politics, economics, finance and law intending to lead rational and reasonable social practice in a global world. Anything less is at the best misconception, but most often political propaganda at the service of dominant ideology: the fascist ideology of a greedy consumerist global market and its communication circuits. But the human propensity for caring, gifting and responsibility is not contained by equal exchange market logic. Encounter and dialogue with the other is the original human capacity before and beyond the limits of any socio-economic order.

Life is communication and communication is learning, life-long learning, before and beyond new-learning, e-learning, this is learning as it evolves from the processes of semiosis, evolutionary learning, also re-learning what we already know, but have forgotten, always investigating and discovering, whether new discovery or re-discovery. Let us listen to the earth, water, air, to the other, human and nonhuman, together in the beauty of one diversified, multi-voiced world. Paraphrasing Shakespeare (in *The Merchant of Venice*), 'Mark the music'.

REFERENCES

Arnett, R. (2017), 'Communicative Ethics: The Phenomenological Sense of Semioethics', *Language and Dialogue*, 7: 80–99.
Bakhtin, M. ([1963] 1984), *Problems of Dostoevsky's Poetics*, trans. and ed. C. Emerson, Minneapolis: University of Minnesota Press.
Bakhtin, M. (1965), *Rabelais and His World*, trans. H. Iswolsky, ed. K. Pomorska, Cambridge: The Massachusetts Institute of Technology.
Bakhtin, M. (1981), *The Dialogic Imagination*, trans. C. Emerson and M. Holquist, Austin: University of Texas Press.
Bakhtin, M. (1986), *Speech Genres & Other Late Essays*, trans. V. W. McGee, C. Emerson and M. Holquist (eds), Austin: Austin University Press.
Bakhtin, M. (1993), *Toward a Philosophy of the Act*, trans. V. Liapunov, ed. M. Holquist, Austin: Austin University Press.
Bachtin, M. and his circle (2014), *Opere 1919–1930*, trans. and ed. A. Ponzio, Milan: Bompiani.
Barthes, R. and R. Havas (1977), 'Ascolto', *Enciclopedia*, vol. 1, 340–52, Turin: Einaudi.
Bonfantini, M., S. Petrilli and A. Ponzio (2009), 'Semiotics and Dialogue between Logic and Ethics', in Eero Tarasti (ed.), *Communication: Understanding/Misunderstanding* (Acta Semiotica Fennica 34), 1372–84, Tartu: Greif.
Bouissac, P. (1989), 'What Is a Human? Ecological Semiotics and the New Animism', *Semiotica*, 77 (4): 497–516.
Bouissac, P. (1991), 'Semiotics and the Gaia Hypothesis: Toward the Restructuring of Western Thought', in *Philosophy and The Future of Humanity*, 1 (2): 168–84.
Bouissac, P. (1998), *Encyclopedia of Semiotics*, New York: Oxford University Press.
Cobley, P., J. Deely, K. Kull and S. Petrilli, eds (2011), *Semiotics Continues to Astonish: Thomas A. Sebeok and the Doctrine of Signs*, Berlin: De Gruyter Mouton.
Deely, J. (2010), *Semiotic Animal*, South Bend: St. Augustine's Press.
Deely, J., S. Petrilli and A. Ponzio (2005), *Semiotic Animal*, Ottawa: Legas.
Eco, U. (1984), *Semiotica e filosofia del linguaggio*, Turin: Einaudi.
Eeden, F. van (1912), *Happy Humanity*, Garden City: Doubleday.
Foucault, M. (1970), *L'ordre du discourse*, Paris: Seuil.
Foucault, M. (1977), *Power/Knowledge*, Hemel Hemstead: Harvester.
Foucault, M. (1996), *Biopolitica e territorio*, Millepiani 9, Milan: Mimesis.
Gare, A. (2009), 'Barbarity, Civilization and Decadence', in M. Weber and R. Desmet (eds), *Chromatikon V. Yearbook of Philosophy in Progress*, 167–90, Louvain: Presses universitaires de Louvain.
Goldberg, G. (2017), 'Toward a Postmodern Pragmatic Discourse Semioethics for Brain Injury Care', *Physical Medicine Rehabilitation Clinic of North America*, 28 (2): 393–411.
Hegel, G. W. F. ([1807] 1976), *Phenomenology of Spirit*, trans. A. V. Miller, Oxford: Oxford University Press.
Hippocrates ([460–377 BCE] 1952), *Hippocratic Writings*, trans. and ed. F. Adams and A. J. Brock, Chicago: Encyclopædia Britannica.

Hobbes, T. ([1651] 1909), *Leviathan*, London: Oxford University Press.
Kanaev, I. I. (1926), 'Sovremennyj vitalizm', *Chelovek i prioda*, 1: 33–42; 2: 9–23.
Kant, I. ([1787] 1963), *Kritik der reinen Vernunft* (Zweite hin und wieder verbesserte Auflage; Riga: Johann Friedrich Hartknoch), trans. Norman Kemp Smith, *Kant's Critique of Pure Reason*, New York: St. Martin's Press.
Lecourt, D. (1977), *Il caso Lysenko*, Rome: Editori Riuniti.
Levinas, E. (1961), *Totalité et Infini*, Dordrecht: Martinus Nijhoff, Kluwer Academic.
Levinas, E. (1967), *En découvrant l'existence avec Husserl et Heidegger*, Paris: Vrin.
Levinas, E. (1972), *Humanisme de l'autre homme*, Montpellier: Fata Morgana.
Levinas, E. (1974), *Autrement qu'être ou au-ela de l'essence*, Dordrecht: Martinus Nijoff, Kluwer Academic.
Levinas, E. ([1935] 1982), *De l'évasion*, ed. Jacques Rolland, Montpellier: Fata Morgana.
Levinas, E. (1982), *Éthique et Infini*, Paris: Fayard.
Levinas, E. (1987), *Hors Sujet*, Montepellier: Fata Morgana.
Locke, J. ([1690] 1975), *An Essay Concerning Human Understanding*, ed. P. H. Nidditch, Oxford: Clarendon Press.
Lotman, J. (1984), '0 Semiosfere', *Trudy po Znakovym Sistemam*, 17: 5–23.
Lotman, J. (1991), *Universe of Mind*, trans. A. Shukman, Bloomington: Indiana University Press.
Maturana, H., F. Varela (1980), *Autopoiesis and Cognition*, Dordrecht: D.Reidel.
Medlin, B. (2021), *The Level-Headed Revolutionary*, S. Petrilli, G. Dooley and W. McKitrick (eds), Adelaide: Wakefield Press.
Merrell, F. (1996), *Signs Grow: Semiosis and Life Process*, Toronto: University of Toronto Press.
Merrell, F. (1999), 'Living signs', *Semiotica*, 127 (1–4): 453–79.
Morris, C. (1938), 'Foundations of the Theory of Signs', in O. Neurath, R. Carnap and C. Morris (eds), *International Encyclopedia of Unified Science*, vol. 1, no. 2, 1–59, Chicago: The University of Chicago Press.
Morris, C. (1948), *The Open Self*, New York: Prentice-Hall.
Morris, C. (1956), *Varieties of Human Value*, Chicago: University of Chicago Press.
Morris, C. (1964), *Signification and Significance*, Cambridge: MIT Press.
Peirce, C. S. ([1866–1913] 1931–58) *The Collected Papers of Charles Sanders Peirce*, vols. 1–6, ed. C. Hartshorne and P. Weiss, vols. 7–8, ed. A. Burks, Cambridge: Harvard University Press. Cited as CP.
Peirce, C. S., V. Welby ([1903–1911] 1977), *Semiotic and Significs: The Correspondence between Charles S. Peirce and Victoria Lady Welby*, ed. C. Hardwick and J. Cook, Bloomington: Indiana University Press. Cited as SS.
Petrilli, S., ed. (2007), *Philosophy of Language as the Art of Listening: On Augusto Ponzio's Scientific Research*, Bari: Edizioni dal Sud.
Petrilli, S. (2009), *Signifying and Understanding: Reading the Works of Victoria Welby and the Signific Movement*, Boston: De Gruyter Mouton.
Petrilli, S. (2012a), *Expression and Interpretation in Language*, New Brunswick: Transaction.
Petrilli, S. (2012b), *Altrove e altrimenti*, Milan: Mimesis.
Petrilli, S. (2013), *The Self as a Sign, the World, and the Other*, New Brunswick: Transaction Publishers.
Petrilli, S. (2014a), *Sign Studies and Semioethics*, Berlin: De Gruyter Mouton.
Petrilli, S., ed. (2014b), *Semioetica e comunicazione globale*, Milan: Mimesis.
Petrilli, S., ed. (2015), *Scienze dei linguaggi e linguaggi delle scienze*, Milan: Mimesis.

Petrilli, S. (2016), *The Global World and Its Manifold Faces*, Bern: Peter Lang.
Petrilli, S., ed. (2017a), *Challenges to Living Together*, Milan: Mimesis International.
Petrilli, S., ed. (2017b), *Pace, pacificazione, pacifismo e i loro linguaggi*, Milan: Mimesis.
Petrilli, S. (2019a), *Significare, interpretare e intendere*, Lecce: Pensa Multimedia.
Petrilli, S., ed. (2019b), *Diritti umani e diritti altrui*, Milan: Mimesis.
Petrilli, S., ed. (2019c), *Signs, Language and Listening. Semioethic Perspectives*, New York: Legas.
Petrilli, S. (2021a), *Senza ripari. Segni, differenze, estraneità*, Milan: Mimesis.
Petrilli, S. (2021b), 'Beyond Signs of Identity as Justification for Conflict. A Semioethic Approach', *Listening: Journal of Communication Ethics, Religion, and Culture*, 54 (3): 92–143.
Petrilli, S. (2021c). 'Migration, an Inescapable demand. The Responsibility of Hosting and the Right to Hospitality', *Calumet. Intercultural Law and Humanities Review*, 1–43, 4 February 2021.
Petrilli, S. (2022), 'The Law Challenged and the Critique of Identity with Emmanuel Levinas', *International Journal for the Semiotics of Law*, 35: 31–69.
Petrilli, S., A. Ponzio (2000a), *Il sentire della comunicazione globale*, Rome: Meltemi; now in S. Petrilli 2014b.
Petrilli, S., A. Ponzio (2000b), *Philosophy of Language, Art and Answerability in Mikhail Bakhtin*, New York: Legas.
Petrilli, S., A. Ponzio (2001a), *Thomas Sebeok and the Signs of Life*, Duxford: Icon Books.
Petrilli, S., A. Ponzio (2001b), 'Bioethics, Semiotics of Life, and Global Communication', *Sign Systems Studies*, 29 (1): 263–75.
Petrilli, S., A. Ponzio (2002a), *I segni e la vita. La semiotica globale di Thomas Sebeok*, Milan: Spirali.
Petrilli, S., A. Ponzio (2002b), 'Sign Vehicles for Semiotic Travels: Two New Handbooks', *Semiotica*, 141 (1–4): 203–350.
Petrilli, S., A. Ponzio (2003), *Semioetica*, Rome: Meltemi; now in S. Petrilli 2014b.
Petrilli, S., A. Ponzio (2005), *Semiotics Unbounded*, Toronto: Toronto University Press.
Petrilli, S., A. Ponzio (2007), *Semiotics Today*, Toronto: Legas.
Petrilli, S., A. Ponzio (2010), 'Semioethics', in P. Cobley (ed.), *The Routledge Companion to Semiotics*, 150–162, London: Routledge.
Petrilli, S., A. Ponzio (2016), *Lineamenti di semiotica e di filosofia del linguaggio*, Perugia: Guerra.
Petrilli, S., A. Ponzio (2019), *Identità e alterità*, Milan: Mimesis.
Petrilli, S., A. Ponzio (2019), *Dizionario, Enciclopedia, Traduzione fra César Durmarsais e Umberto Eco*, Bari: Parigi, L'Harmattan.
Petrilli, S., J. Deely, ed. (2010), *Sign Crossroads in Global Perspective: Semioethics and Responsibility*, New York: Routledge.
Ponzio, A. (1993), *Signs, Dialogue and Ideology*, Amsterdam: John Benjamins.
Ponzio, A. (1996), *Sujet et altérité. Sur Emmanuel Lévinas*, trans. N. Bonnet, Paris: L'Harmattan.
Ponzio, A. (1998), *La revolución bajtiniana*, trans. M. A. Florez, Madrid: Catedra.
Ponzio, A. ([1997] 2004), *Elogio dell'infunzionale*, Milan: Mimesis.
Ponzio, A. (2006a), *The Dialogic Nature of Sign*, trans. S. Petrilli, Ottawa: Legas.
Ponzio, A. (2006b), 'The I Questioned: Levinas and Critique of Occidental Reason', *Subject Matters*, 3 (1): 1–45.
Ponzio, A. (2009), *Emmanuel Levinas, Globalisation, and Preventive Peace*, Ottawa: Legas.

Ponzio, A. (2010), *Rencontre de paroles*, Paris: Alain Baudry et Cie.
Ponzio, A. ([2007] 2013), *Fuori luogo*, Rome: Mimesis.
Ponzio, A. ([1992] 2015), *Tra semiotica e letteratura. Introduzione a Michail Bachtin*, Milan: Bompiani.
Ponzio, A. (2018). 'Musica, immagine, scrittura', in S. Petrilli (ed.), *L'immagine nella parola, nella muscia e nella scrittura*, 11–88, Milan: Mimesis.
Ponzio, A. (2019), *Con Emmanuel Levinas*, Milan: Mimesis.
Posner, R., K. Robering, T. Sebeok, eds (1997–2004), *Semiotik/Semiotics*, 3 vols., Berlin: Walter de Gruyter.
Rossi-Landi, F. ([1953] 1975), *Charles Morris e la semiotica novecentesca*, Milan: Feltrinelli Bocca.
Rossi-Landi, F. (1968), *Il linguaggio come lavoro e come mercato*, Milan: Bompiani.
Rossi-Landi, F. (1992), *Between Signs and Non-Signs*, S. Petrilli (ed.), Amsterdam: John Benjamins.
Saussure, F. de (1916), *Cours de linguistique générale*, C. Bally and A. Séchehaye (eds), Paris: Payot.
Schaler, J., H. Lothane, R. Vatz, eds (2017), *The Man and His Ideas*, London: Routledge.
Sebeok, T. (1981), *The Play of Musement*, Bloomington: Indiana University Press.
Sebeok, T., ed. (1986a), *I Think I Am a Verb*, New York: Plenum.
Sebeok, T., ed. (1986b), *Encyclopedic Dictionary of Semiotics*, 3 vols, Berlin: Mouton deGruyter.
Sebeok, T. (1991), *A Sign Is Just a Sign*, Bloomington: Indiana University Press.
Sebeok, T. (1994), *Signs*, Toronto: University of Toronto Press.
Sebeok, T. (2001), *Global Semiotics*, Bloomington: Indiana University Press.
Sebeok, T., S. Petrilli, A. Ponzio (2001), *Semiotica dell'io*, Rome: Meltemi.
Szasz, T. (1961), *The Myth of Mental Illness*, New York: HarperCollins.
Uexküll, J. von ([1940] 1982), 'The Theory of Meaning', *Semiotica*, 42: 1–87.
Uexküll, J. von ([1934] 1992), 'A Stroll through the Worlds of Animals and Man', *Semiotica*, 89 (4): 319–91.
Vaughan, G. (2015), *The Gift in the Heart of Language*, Milan: Mimesis.
Vernadsky, V. (1926), *Biosfera*, Leningrad: Nauka.
Vološinov, V. (1929), *Marxism and the Philosophy of Language*, trans. L. Matejka and I. R. Titunik, New York: Seminar Press.
Welby, V. ([1903] 1983), *What Is Meaning?*, Philadelphia: John Benjamins.

CHAPTER SIX

Semiotics in Sociology and Political Science

RISTO HEISKALA AND PEETER SELG

INTRODUCTION

In the most general sense, sociology is the discipline of studying the social dimension of human relations. More technically, it aims to describe and explain social interaction as it is embedded in social facts or institutions, such as the family, associations, markets and the state. Similarly, political science is the study of the political dimension of human relations, aiming at explaining and describing political action as it is embedded in structures of power, governance and democracy. Semiotics originates from the works of Ferdinand de Saussure (1857–1913) in the European continent and from those of Charles Sanders Peirce (1839–1914) in America. It revolves around the notion of 'sign'. Both Saussurean and Peircean concepts of sign presume it to be a relation rather than an entity: signs are presumed to be intelligible always as a part of a system of relations with other signs. In addition, unlike in the stereotyped depictions of semiotics as a form of structuralism, this system of relations is a phenomenon that is a dynamic process unfolding in communication whose constituent elements cannot be grasped separately from the flows within which they are embedded and vice versa. Thus, we provide a working definition of semiotics for the following reflection as follows: semiotics is a research methodology for studying institutions/social facts related to the arbitrariness of the meanings of signs that are contingently articulated in communication.

The task of the semiotic study of social and political action is twofold. First, it shows that these activities would not be possible at all without human signification, which takes place through signs. The object of the disciplines of sociology and political science is thus semiotic in itself. That is an important point to make in these disciplines because the mainstream has omitted it and even after 'the cultural turn' it has been rarely understood that meanings do not travel without the material part of the sign or signifier. The second task is thus to apply technically developed semiotic conceptions to the core problems of the disciplines and show how it is possible to dig deeper with them than without such concepts. In this chapter we record the ways in which sociology and political science have dealt with meanings and suggest some ways in which semiotics could be brought closer to the core of these disciplines. Since these two social scientific disciplines have different historical and contemporary encounters with semiotics, our conclusions and suggestions regarding them are likewise different, but overlapping nevertheless.

HISTORY

In this section we deal first with the ways in which sociologists and social theorists have tried to tackle the phenomenon of meaning. It will turn out that despite its many potential benefits, a genuine semiotic approach has not yet made its way to the field. We then turn to political science where the core categories of power, governance and democracy are analysed as forms of meaning-generating practices.

Interpretation of meaning in sociology

Even if the study of signification is older than sociology, and in the most part studied elsewhere, all important sociological traditions have developed specific ways to deal with meanings. In the French tradition this happened in the work of one of the founding fathers of sociology, Émile Durkheim, who in his later work, and especially in *The Elementary Forms of Religious Life*, presented totemic symbols of the Australian aboriginals as collective representations of their community and its subgroups (Durkheim 1912). That was also the path followed by his son-in-law Marcel Mauss in his social anthropological studies on the *kula* exchange in the Trobriand Islands in his *The Gift* (Mauss 1925). The cornerstone of this tradition is the interpretation that all symbols are sacred and in the sacred the community idolizes itself and affirms its conceptual system ritually.

Durkheim's career was timewise parallel to that of Ferdinand de Saussure (both extending from the 1850s to the 1910s), but no references to Saussure can be found in his work. Such references only found their way to social theory later when anthropologist Claude Lévi-Strauss, Marxist cultural analyst Roland Barthes, and A.J. Greimas, a Lithuanian literary scientist working in Paris, developed what has been called the structuralist code theory (Heiskala 2014). The approach was a limited interpretation of Saussure's *oeuvre* because it interpreted structures (*la langue*) as closed codes, which consisted of strictly binary paradigmatic relations with no relation to syntagmatic relations interpreted to prevail in the sphere of speech (*parole*). That interpretation was parallel to the development of mathematical tools such as Boolean algebra and other models making it possible to program computers, which all needed to be binary because the technical application requires unequivocal binarity (electricity either goes through the gate or its flow is blocked). Lévi-Strauss (1958) learned that model from linguist Roman Jakobson whom he met during a stay in New York and whose axiomatization of phonology followed the maxim of binarity. Without paying any attention to the possibility that such binarity does not necessarily characterize more complex levels of signification such as syntax, semantics or pragmatics, Lévi-Strauss transferred the phonological model to the study of anthropological myths baptizing the smallest signifying unit of myth a *mytheme* following the example of Jakobson's *phoneme*. Lévi-Strauss also interpreted the mythological structure to be universal so that individual cultures and their myths were its actualizations. As he was a poet who often disguised his art in seemingly scientific formulas and parlance, he was able to make his example world famous even if his actual interpretations of myths were quite far from anything resembling controlled scientific practices.

Another code theorist was Roland Barthes, whose *Elements of Semiology* and *Mythologies* provided a way to analyse ideological signification as a second order language built on the first order of signification in ordinary language (Barthes 1957, 1964). A famous example is Barthes's analysis of the cover image of *Paris Match* magazine in which an Algerian soldier is pictured saluting the tricolour (see Figure 6.1).

FIGURE 6.1 Front cover of the *Paris Match* magazine that Barthes analyses (Getty Images).

According to Barthes's quite convincing analysis the second-order ideological signified to these first-order signifiers taken together is that the French reign in Algeria is doing well and accepted by the local population. Finally, the literary models of A. J. Greimas developed more and more extensively to the point that in his *Structural Semantics*, and work following it, he tried to create such an extensive world model, based on binary relations on several levels, that it would have covered the whole of reality (Greimas 1966, 1976).

The French audience that had gotten tired of the post-war subjectivist existentialism of Sartre and others welcomed the structuralist code theory in the 1950s. Yet fame in Paris rarely lasts, and already in the 1960s and 1970s not to mention the 1980s it was time for the 'poststructuralists' to flourish. This included Jacques Lacan's mystifying version of psychoanalysis according to which the subconscious is structured like language but is still beyond our interpretive reach. Especially, it was epitomized in the work of two theorists. One was Michel Foucault who wanted in his social and intellectual histories to replace the concept of structure with that of *dispositive* which served the same purposes but gave more leeway to the process of articulation than the idea of structure as a code (Foucault 1975, 1976). The other was Jacques Derrida whose discourse moved somewhere in the border of philosophy and literary theory and used the term *differance* instead of Saussure's *difference* to emphasize the continuity and primacy of the process of articulation over any solid codification (Derrida 1967). These and similar attacks against the structuralist code theory in the work of feminist theoretician Julia Kristeva (1969) or the Pope of Postmodernism Jean-Francoise Lyotard (1979) were theoretically justified; but, strictly speaking, even if they were against structuralist code theory they often meant returning to problems which had already been present in Saussure's original semiology that had been buried under the success of the structuralist code theory. So, semiologically speaking, French social semiotics is largely now back in the phase from which it started in the early twentieth century. Yet one exception can be mentioned, i.e. Pierre Bourdieu's cultural 'theory of practice', the task of which has been to unify sociology and anthropology into one field and then analyse how hierarchies are constituted and reproduced through symbolic practices (Bourdieu 1980). In the analysis of modern societies, his *Distinction* has been a path breaking account of the symbolic practices through which hierarchies are maintained (Bourdieu 1979). Semiotically speaking, though, it too leaves something undone because the understanding of symbolization is more Durkheimian than Saussurean. Judgements of taste and signifying distinctions are thus understood as representations of their holders' status and position in society. This is already a big step towards a culturally sensitive sociology and thus for a reason famous within the international sociological community but still only halfway to a genuinely semiotic sociology.

The German tradition starts already from Marx's theory of ideology as false consciousness, on the one hand, and Neo-Kantian emphasis on the vital role of categories in the interpretation of reality, on the other. Here, however, we start from the German founding father of sociology, Max Weber, whose interpretive sociology was a 'science concerning itself with the interpretative understanding of social action and thereby with a causal explanation of its course and consequences' (Weber 1922: 4). Understanding of the meaning of social action was to utilize theoretically constructed concepts that Weber called 'ideal types', which were based on 'one-sided accentuation of one or more points of view' (Weber [1904] 1949: 90). The most famous of Weber's classification of ideal types is that concerning action, which he divides into two completely rational types, i.e. end-rational and value-rational action, and two bordering types, i.e. traditional and affectual action (Weber 1922: 24–5). Actual explanation of people's action, then, is to be done in the light of all these types constructed by the scholar by asking how rational, and in what sense, is the behaviour of a small entrepreneur, for example.

That is where Weber left the interpretation of meaning, and that is from where Alfred Schütz found it and started to develop it further in his *Die sinnhafte Aufbau der sozialen Welt* (Schütz 1932, later translated by the title *Phenomenology of the Social World*). Schütz was a young scholar who was inspired first by Bergson and later by Husserl and he set as his task in the book to develop 'mundane phenomenology', which would study interpretation of meaning on the level of everyday, which Heidegger called the reign of 'das Man' and which Husserl marginalized by taking it just as a starting point of his numerous phenomenological reductions bracketing everything not immediately related to the validity of scientific categorization. Schütz, instead, was interested in exactly the mundane dimension, which he saw sociologically important. His strategy was to develop Weber's ideal types into real types or prototypes of interpretation grounded on everyday interpretation and this way provide for Weber's sociology the foundation in the theory of meaning that it lacked. To realize that objective, much of the book goes through the mundane processes of interpretation and concentrates especially to the problem of intersubjectivity of interpretations. To that effect Schütz develops several concepts such as 'growing older together' (sharing a segment in the flow of time) and 'we-relation' (situation of mutual and shared interpretation of meaning). As the starting point of theorizing following the phenomenological tradition is the solipsistic Ego intersubjectivity never quite arises even if the author is capable to illuminate mundane interpretation of meaning in versatile ways. Yet at the time of publication the author had great expectations concerning Husserl's *Cartesian Meditations*' ability to solve the problem of intersubjectivity and he planned to base his future work to that solution (Husserl 1931). We now know that the solution was never delivered because all that Husserl managed to deal with was the meaning but not the being of another Ego (see Hammond, Howarth and Keat 1991: 222–35). The cunning of history in the form of the rise of the Nazis, threw Schütz to New York where he earned his living as a bank lawyer and could be only a part-time teacher in the New School for Social Research and had to limit his publications into articles. Yet we will soon report some important encounters he had in the United States.

Explication of the North American tradition should naturally start from the pragmatists, and especially from the early institutionalists and the social psychology of G. H. Mead. However, as we lack space, and since both traditions were marginalized, we start straight from the marginalizer (see Camic 1986): i.e. the sociology of Talcott Parsons. He was a great synthesizer of sociology who worked in Harvard and was in addition to that educated in London School of Economics and Heidelberg University. It was Parsons's first *magnum opus* titled *The Structure of Social Action* that established Durkheim and Weber so firmly as the classics of sociology that this status is scarcely doubted even today (Parsons 1937). But Parsons was not a historian of ideas. Instead, he was prone to develop a synthesis of his own. In the book mentioned, it circulated around what he called 'the unit act' which was the smallest unit into which action could be reduced without it losing its nature as action. The unit act was meant to serve as a kind of nuclear model of sociology and combined elements from the work of Durkheim, Weber, Alfred Marshall (an economist) and Vilfredo Pareto (mainly treated as an economist too). To make a long story short, it combined the actor's effort and ends in an action situation in which the actor's doings were constrained by environmental factors (scarcity), on the one hand, and normative factors (values and social norms), on the other hand. Later on, Parsons developed his approach further to structural functionalism in *The Social System* and numerous other publications (Parsons 1951). After the publication of *Economy and Society* (Parsons and Smelser 1956) the AGIL field was formed into the privileged means of analysing the ways systems could respond to the four tasks of adaptation to environment: (A), goal attainment (G), integration (I) and latent pattern maintenance (L). On the field of the social system these tasks were maintained by economy (A), polity (G), social norms and communities (I) and socialization institutions such as schools and churches keeping up values (L).

The closest to semiotics is Parsons's claim that the subsystems develop their specific media of communication and are involved in systemic exchanges with each other through these media, which on the level of the social system are money (A), power (G), influence or solidarity (I) and commitment to values (L). Yet his take on theories of meaning was remote. That gave Alfred Schutz (whose name lost the umlaut dots over the *u* during his trip over the Atlantic) a reason to contact him with the same idea in his mind as he had had with Weber's sociology. Schutz now thought that he could provide Parsonian sociology that basis in mundane phenology which it lacked. An exchange of letters followed between Parsons and Schutz who once even visited Harvard to give a lecture, but the end result was that neither of the gentlemen understood each other that well (for the compiled letters see Grathoff 1978). Yet Schutz managed to catch the attention of some other sociologists such as Harold Garfinkel, who was a critical PhD student of Parsons's and become later famous with his *Studies in Ethnomethodology*, the central concept of which is 'accounting' of meaning, which can be understood as a lay version of the 'intentional act' of Schutz and other phenomenologists (Garfinkel 1967; on his relationship to Schutz see Wagner 1983).

While Garfinkel and his less theoretically oriented and more anarchistic colleague Erving Goffman (1959, 1967, 1974) have sometimes been said to set up a 'micro revolution' against Parsons's macro sociology (Alexander 1987), which they thought to have forgotten actors' creativity, Schutz was also able to give a creative impulse for another current in sociology. We have in mind *The Social Construction of Reality* by Berger and Luckmann (1966), which was a comprehensive culturally oriented macro theoretical account of sociology. The authors had been following Schutz' lectures in the New School and it can be said that they picked up their understanding of knowledge and culture from Schutz, socialization theory from Mead and macrosociology from several sources the most important of which they said to be Weber. The emerging conception was more robust than Schutz's, but it covered the whole area of sociology and because Schutz, despite his plans, never managed to write a similar book it has represented the approach in sociology since the sixties.

After that time North American cultural sociology has spent most of its time in importing European theorists such as Foucault, Derrida, Kristeva and other poststructuralist feminists and Bourdieu from France and Habermas (1981a, 1981b), Luhmann (1984) and Honneth (1992) from Germany and Giddens from the UK. When it comes to the UK as a sociological field of its own it first rather passively imported French structuralist code theory in the form of Althusser's Marxism (Althusser 1965a, 1965b) and Barthes's semiology but then, in addition to importing poststructuralists, developed some more actor-centred forms of meaning analysis such as the youth studies of the Birmingham School and Giddens's and Archer's versions of structuration theory (Willis 1977; Giddens 1984; Archer 1988). None of these, however, developed any real invention in the field of meaning analysis.

To gather the above together it can be said that even if meanings and culture have been central in sociology during the whole time of its existence, the topic of sign has almost completely been avoided. Sociology has, therefore, largely been in a state of 'metaphysics of presence' (Derrida 1967) also after the 'cultural turn' because only a genuinely semiotic understanding of signification would make it clear that, even if the sender and receiver of a sign relate to the same material bearer of meaning, their interpretations may differ from each other in ways relative to the more extensive meaning structures in both ends of the transmission. That again would make semiotically informed empirical study necessary, but in its stead sociologists have usually *naively* taken the hermeneutical circle to be unproblematic and meanings transparent. This is an issue to be recalled in the section on the state-of-the-art.

Political science and the conceptualization of power, governance and democracy as meaning practices

Political science is the study of the political dimension of human relations. This dimension can be divided into three major subdimensions: power, governance and democracy (see Selg and Ventsel 2020). Since from the semiotic point of view meaning is essentially relational – meaning *emerges* from communication, and is not only something transmitted through communication – all perspectives on power, governance and democracy that see the latter as dependent on *mutual* action, have at least tacitly a semiotic component in them. True, it is almost never articulated in the terms proposed by the tradition of semiotics. This is, however, not a conceptual issue, but one of lack of communication, gate keeping or just plain illiteracy. Semiotics is part and parcel of most conceptualizations of power, governance and democracy in political science, but people who have training in semiotics almost never have corresponding background in political science; and, of course, political scientists almost never have any background in semiotics. Before engaging with relational understandings of power, governance and democracy we should ask what is the alternative to such conceptualizations. Basically, it is seeing those phenomena, as being certain objects (recourses) or properties and dispositions of entities (individuals, groups, institutions). This is in many ways our common sense view. Let's start with power. If we were to analyse power as being analogous to an object or property, then we would be interested in questions such as: What features or recourses of A make A powerful? This strategy of analysing power has been around since Thomas Hobbes, who, in Chap. 10 of his *Leviathan* (1651) famously uttered: 'THE "POWER of a man," to take it universally, is his present means, to obtain some future apparent good.' Various rational choice perspectives in political science and realism in international relations have this kind of implicit theory of power informing their analyses.

When it comes to governance then all the modern state-centric perspectives are pertinent here (usually referred to as 'government' in the 'from government to governance' literature – see Fukuyama 2016: 94–7; Jessop 2016; Rhodes 2017). It is the reified view of state system and/or government as an actor with certain resources and properties acting on its subjects (Jessop 2016, ch. 2) through commands in the widest sense, including bureaucratic directives, enforced laws, performance assessments and immediate coercion by force structures which is one of the functions of the police.

In democratic theory the recourse/property-based understanding reveals itself in approaches that compare a large number of countries along a small set of variables (e.g. Przeworski et al. 2000) who have analysed the influence of regime type to its economic performance). Insightful here is that democracy is defined as a property of certain structure – the existence of contested elections. These kinds of models leave aside the everyday (meaningful) action that forms the practice of democracy. Generally, we could distinguish at least three such strategies of defining democracy in which the existence of certain structures is presumed to determine whether a setting (usually a regime) is to be counted as democracy. One of the oldest approaches, leading back to at least Aristotle, is to see the constitution as the structure of democracy. As is well known the proclaimed constitutions can often hide starkly different political reality. This is why sometimes a more substantive approach is adopted by focusing on whether the structure of society promotes certain outcomes often associated with democracy (human welfare, individual freedom, equity, social equality, public deliberation, etc.). This approach begs the question: 'What if all those outcomes are achieved through undemocratic means?' That is why another property/resource-based approach in democratic theory proposes a procedural definition of democracy focusing on the existence/non-existence of some governmental practices for determining whether a regime is democratic. Often this procedure is related to elections (Tilly 2007: 8). Besides the already mentioned example of Przeworski et al. (2000) various democracy indexes (e.g. Freedom House) work with procedural definitions. On the whole, whether one sees democracy in terms of constitutions, substantive aims or procedures, s/he is working with a resource/property model just the same.

There is little room for conceptualizing meaning practices in these models of power, governance and democracy. The properties of certain bounded entity – regime that has democratic structure, an actor who has power as means for certain ends, or state that has capacities to govern – are the objects of scrutiny. Meaning starts to enter the scene of political analysis when power, governance and democracy are seen as emerging from social action – an action that is oriented towards responses of (potential or actual) actions of *others*. Meaning, power, governance and democracy can be seen in static or dynamic terms.

Thus, if we treated power as being basically a static *relation* rather than a *thing* – then we would be interested in questions like: Which A's are having power and to which extent and by which actions of B's over whom they have power? Since Max Weber defined power as 'the probability that one actor within a social relationship will be in a position to carry out his own will despite resistance' (1978: 53), this has been a social scientific mainstream understanding of power in the Anglo-Saxon world.

In governance terms this static-relational understanding would be a movement from seeing government as a 'one-way traffic' (top-down approach) to a 'two-way traffic' (Kooiman 1993: 4) mode of governance which is often associated with networks as a third way between hierarchy of state and anarchy of the market (Jessop 2016: 167–9).

When it comes to democracy, Dahl (1998: 37–8) distinguishes five criteria for a process to qualify as democratic: 'effective participation', 'voting equality', 'enlightened understanding', 'control of the agenda' and 'inclusion of all adults'. Here democracy is seen as a dimension of social action rather than that of structures or actors – their *inter*-action rather than their individual properties deserves the qualifier democratic. Even though Dahl's criteria for process evaluation go well beyond the constitutional, substantive and procedural definitions of democracy as a property of certain entities, it is still dichotomous and static: certain social (inter-)action either is or is not democratic and there is no question of the processual movement and change – the practice of democracy-making through meaning-making in this model. Several eminent theorists (e.g. Tilly 2007) have tried to move in this direction through their process-oriented definition of democracy. What is often missed there is the presumption of organic relationship between democratic process and meaning-making process.

Over-all the question is, what if we viewed power, governance and democracy as certain logics of communication and meaning-making in society or culture. What would power, governance and democracy as continuous processes look like if they did not have their own specific region (government, citizens, parties), but were, rather, a set of processual relations organizing certain settings? For responding to this question, we have to move first from the idea that those notions can be conceptualized as sets of structures or institutions to an idea of power, governance and democracy as dynamic meaning-making practices.

This research strategy for studying power would focus on the network of dynamic relations through which certain actions by the A's emerge as subjugation through meeting certain reactions of the B's, and through which A's and B's are constituted as dominators, subordinates, resisters and so on and are in a constant process of mutual (re)constitution, elements of which can be considered separately, but not as being separate. Perspectives on power that take Michel Foucault's insistence on 'the strictly relational character of power relationships' (1978: 95) as their starting point, are relevant here. Power in these treatments is conceptualized as an unfolding, dynamic and constitutive process of meaning-making.

Several recent developments in theories of policy making have taken the turn to seeing discursive, cultural or argumentative process as constitutive of governance. In their discussion of the 'argumentative turn' in policy analysis (see Fischer and Forester 1993; Fischer and Gottweis 2012a) Fischer and Gottweis point to importance of focusing on communication and argumentation in our contemporary world. The reason for that in their view is that 'policy analysis can no longer afford to limit itself to the simplified academic models of explanation. Such methods fail to address the nonlinear nature of today's messy policy problems' (Fischer and Gottweis 2012b: 6). Similarly, in a more generalist perspective for what they call 'epistemic governance', Alasuutari and Qadir propose that whichever governance relies on 'epistemic work' such as defining the 'ontology of the environment'; 'actors and their identifications' and 'norms and values' (2019, chapter 2; see also Alasuutari and Qadir 2014). The key to governance is, in other words, meaning production in terms of investigating the widespread public views of reality. Finally, we point to a development in public administration that sees Mary Douglas's and Aaron Wildavsky's cultural theory (1982) as an important framework for making sense of policy process and governance in terms of different forms of policy and political cultures organized in terms of different mixtures of hierarchical, egalitarian, individualist and fatalist tendencies in decision-making and communication (see Swedlow 2002, 2011).

Thus, in the conceptualization of governance, we have tendencies to see this phenomenon in terms of meaning-making, argumentation and culture. The same holds for democracy. One of the promising pathways towards conceptualizing democracy as a dynamic process of meaning making is to be found in cultural approach to politics that sees culture not in terms of some 'sedimented essences' of groups or certain 'group traits', but rather as 'practices of meaning-making' or as 'semiotic practices' (Wedeen 2002). The notion of culture as 'semiotic practices' is a key to this approach to democracy.

The principal promoter of this kind of approach, Lisa Wedeen, points out that there are several important consequences in seeing culture as consisting in semiotic practices (Wedeen 2004: 714):

1. 'culture as semiotic practices refers to what language and symbols do – how they are inscribed in practices that operate to produce observable political effects.'
2. '"semiotic practices" is also a lens. It offers a view of political phenomena by focusing attention on how and why actors invest them with meaning.' In other words: '[w]hether one does or does not explore processes of meaning-making will depend on the particular research problem one confronts.'

This entails not seeing democracy in terms of a regime composed of certain formal institutions, and a movement to meaning-making as the research object for analysing democratic process or practice. These steps are of paramount importance for a semiotic approach to democracy. Wedeen is not, of course, alone in taking them, although she has probably moved the furthest in developing an empirical methodology consistent with these steps. There is, however, a noteworthy tradition in taking what could be called 'the discursive turn' in democratic theory, which conceptualizes democracy as a 'discourse' – that is, a system of meaning – rather than as a checklist of formal criteria.

The discourse-theoretical approach to democracy, informing the normative ideal of deliberative democracy is probably the most widely known among the intellectual movements taking these steps. Habermas (1996: 26), the leading figure of this movement, explicitly criticizes both the liberal and the republican model of democratic politics for presupposing 'a view of society as centered in the state – be it as guardian of market-society [liberalism] or the state as the self-conscious institutionalization of an ethical community [republicanism]'. What he calls 'discourse theory of democracy' or 'deliberative model of politics' has a 'decentered' view of society (Habermas 1996: 29). Formal political institutions (the parliament, the cabinet, etc.) are not the fundamental political elements of society through which the crucial features of democracy (such as popular sovereignty) work. This non-state-centric or 'discourse-theoretical' understanding of democracy started out originally with Habermas's early discussion of the 'public sphere' or '*Öffentlichkeit*' as it emerged in the eighteenth-century Europe. It is crucial here that we are talking about certain practices of meaning making that are important for conceptualizing democratic 'moments', 'situations' or 'processes' within an historical setting in which there was no formal democracy in place at all (eighteenth-century Europe) with its usual features revolving around competitive elections. This is crucial for semiotic approach to democracy. The feature 'democratic' as attributed to certain action makes sense in potentially infinite number of settings – whether they happen to be in a formally democratic or undemocratic regime. Thus, there can be even extensive or regular democratic processes in a formally non-democratic country. This makes sense from the 'discursive' or 'meaning-making' perspective on democracy, seeing democracy in terms of 'semiotic practices'. This is a de-centred notion of democracy. From the viewpoint of democratic theory, it sees democracy as a 'mode of being' (Wolin 1996; cf. Lefort 1988; Mouffe 2000) rather than set of (formal) rules or procedures.

This conceptualization of democracy as a 'mode of being' lies at the foundation of the political theory that critically engages with post-structuralist social ontology, most notably the so-called Essex School (Laclau, Mouffe and others). Important to note is that the idea of democracy as a mode of being rather than a certain form of rule or even a certain form of deliberation, comes, for the Essex school, from the understanding that the very idea of democracy is based on the acknowledgement of the *contingency* of whichever social relations. Democracy is a certain mode of contingent articulation of social relations. In fact, a great representative of the Essex School, Ernesto Laclau, has even established the general tendencies that the democratic mode of articulation has taken throughout its modern history (drawing, of course, on their earlier joint work, e.g. Lalcau and Mouffe 1985, 1987):

> I see the history of democracy as divided by one fundamental cleavage. On the one hand, we have democracy as the attempt to construct the people as 'one', a homogeneous social actor opposed either to 'power' or to an external enemy – or to a combination of both. This is the *Jacobin* conception of democracy, with its concomitant ideal of a transparent community unified – if necessary – by terror. This is the tradition that runs, with very analogous structural features, from Robespierre to Pol

Pot. The discourses around which this democratic ideal is constructed are, obviously, predominantly *metaphoric* – although [...] they cannot conceal their metonymic foundations. On the other hand, we have democracy as respect of difference, as shown, for instance, in *multiculturalism* or in the new *pluralism* associated with contemporary social movements. Here we have discourses that are predominantly *metonymic*, for although – given the impossibility of a pure differential, nontropological closure – some effect of metaphoric aggregation is inevitable, it will be an aggregation that always keeps the traces of its own contingency and incompleteness visible. Within this basic polarity there are, obviously, all kinds of possible intermediate combinations that we can start exploring through the variety of *tropoi* to be found in classical rhetoric.

(Laclau 2001b: 250, italics added)

The appeal to general tropes of democratic discourse – metaphor and metonymy – is crucial for making sense of Laclau and Mouffe's idea of democracy and the political. Basically they argue that there is an inherent tension in every democratic discourse: a pull towards presenting society (or 'the people') as a unified whole with a singular voice – a tendency characteristic of various populist political discourses – or a tendency to present society as full of diversities and different voices – as in various forms of pluralism. The former pull is overwhelmingly metaphoric in its strategy and tactics, the latter metonymic. But what grounds Laclau and Mouffe to put forth this kind of understanding of democracy as a discourse between tendencies towards metaphoric and metonymic articulation? A quick answer is that they see every contingent articulation of discourse as essentially a hegemonic articulation, and metaphoric and metonymic just refer to different forms of hegemony. In addition, in their usage the notions of 'discursive' and 'social' are co-terminus: articulation of discourse is articulation of social relations. Therefore, they do not see 'discourse' as some sort of regional category reduced to merely text and talk, but as synonymous with systems of meaning that constitute (social) action. Thus, the 'linguistic' or 'semiotic' categories of metaphor and metonymy are also to be understood as general logics of the social, not just figures of speech or writing. Somewhat exaggeratedly, we can speak of metaphorical or metonymical societies, social formations, social action and acts, not just metaphorical expressions or works of art, poetry or speech. Analysing different forms of hegemony could thus be one of the central tasks of semiotic approaches to the political, since hegemony is a notion that lies in the intersection of the three key political concepts discussed in this section: power, governance and democracy. In fact, this is one of the starting points for Selg and Ventsel who in their works over the previous decade (e.g. 2008, 2010, 2019, 2020) have been developing the argument that power, governance and democracy can all be analysed along the same metaphor/metonymy axis as proposed by Laclau and Mouffe for making sense of democracy. They call their approach 'political semiotics' and argue that it is a deep relational approach to political analysis. We will return to their contribution in the 'State-of-the-art' section in more detail.

METHODOLOGIES

Most often semiotics is used in social analysis as an essayistic viewpoint as happens in books such as McCannell (1976) and Eco (1983, 1986). More rigorous approaches include Greimas' (1966, 1976) approach, which has been developed further by Sulkunen and Törrönen (1997) and Törrönen (2002) who show that sometimes ontologically wanting conceptions such as Greimas's rigorous binarism can provide more useful methodological tools for reducing complexity than ontologically more sophisticated approaches such as Peirce's semiotics or poststructuralist semiology. Methodologically advanced conceptions have also been developed for discourse analysis (cf. Fairclough 2003; Van Dijk 2008). More general introductions to semiotic methodologies include Hodge and Kress (1988), Sebeok and Danesi (2000), Kress (2010), Hodge (2016) and Danesi (2018).

STATE-OF-THE-ART

As was said in the section on history above, concepts such as 'meaning' and 'culture' have been central to sociology and social theory; but genuinely semiotic accounts to these concepts have been almost completely missing. One attempt to bring in semiotic concepts was made in Risto Heiskala's *Society as Semiosis* (Heiskala 2003, 2014). It is an attempt to build up a synthesis in the field of sociological analysis of meaning so that the starting point is action theory in the form present in Weber and rational choice theories. That approach is in the book seen to have an area of competence covering many explicit choices often made in well-organized contexts in business and administrative organizations. However, its validity erodes when we reach the typical problem setting of phenomenological sociology (in the work of Schutz, Berger & Luckmann, Garfinkel, and in many senses Goffman). A paradigmatic way of reacting to that situation has been strife between action theorists and phenomenological sociologist, and it has been thought that a choice should be made between the approaches. What Heiskala suggests, however, is an alternative approach in which a synthesis is sought so that phenomenological sociology is interpreted as a more extensive approach than action theory but, at the same time, action theory is recognized to be a valid approach in that enclave where explicitly defined choices are made in well-defined contexts. The benefit of that solution is that it saves researchers' energy in cases where the relatively laborious phenomenological methods of determining meaning are not necessary and, at the same time, makes it possible for the researcher to move to phenomenological sociology whenever there is a benefit from that in sight. But in addition to this first synthetic step there is another to be taken.

The second step is the introduction of semiotic concepts into the basis of the model so that semiotics would be in the same relation to phenomenological meaning analysis as phenomenological sociology is to action theory. This is required because the starting point in phenomenology is the solipsist Ego and its intentional acts and phenomenology; therefore both turn all meaningful material into the Ego's knowledge (cf. 'everyday knowledge' in Berger & Luckman and 'accounting' in Garfinkel) and have difficulties in conceptualizing intersubjectivity (cf. Schutz). The move itself can be made in several ways. Heiskala's solution is a synthesis of Pearce's semiotics and Saussure's semiology based on the idea that phenomenological sociology can be connected to semiology by understanding Saussure's *articulation* as a *prereflective intentional act* in the phenomenological sense, and that again can be understood as an *interpretant* in Peirce's semiotics. This makes it possible to interpret the semiotic base layer of the synthetic construction in such an extensive way that it completely covers the areas of action theory and phenomenological sociology and, in addition, makes possible such analyses of unconscious or preconscious habitualization of meanings which the two other approaches are not capable of committing because they understand meanings through the concepts of conscious action or everyday knowledge. Here a similar relationship emerges between the semiotic layer and the two other approaches as previously between action theory and phenomenological sociology: in principle it would be possible to replace all action theoretical and phenomenological analyses by semiotic analyses but because thorough semiotic analyses tend to be even more laborious than analyses in phenomenological sociology it is for practical reasons not wise to follow that path but instead commit action theoretical or phenomenological sociological analyses in those contexts in which semiotics would not bring significant benefits in the form of different research results.

By taking one term from the Saussurean and another from the Peircian tradition Heiskala calls the synthetic conception 'neostructuralist semiotics' and also represents it as a figure (see Figure 6.2). The synthetic conception would be one way to make semiotic concepts relevant and omnipresent in sociology and social theory (for the most recent codification of this program see Heiskala 2021). As we are not aware of others moving on the level of basic concepts (even if there is a Renaissance of pragmatism going on in the social sciences – one that may well mean a Renaissance of Peirce's semiotics; see Hodgson 1988; Joas 1997; Kilpinen 2000), we now take a slightly different view to semiology and semiotics: i.e. because there is no doubt that relations are the subject matter of both schools we discuss them in the light of the recent rise of 'relationalism' in the social sciences.

Currently (Spring 2020) the only full-fledged monograph on both relational political analysis and political semiotics is the book *Introducing Relational Political Analysis: Political Semiotics as a Theory and Method* by Selg and Ventsel (2020). The book has an ambition to put forth a theory, methodology and method for political analysis that is relational, empirically oriented, and can be utilized for both critical and analytical research of power, governance and democracy and the topics related to these core categories of

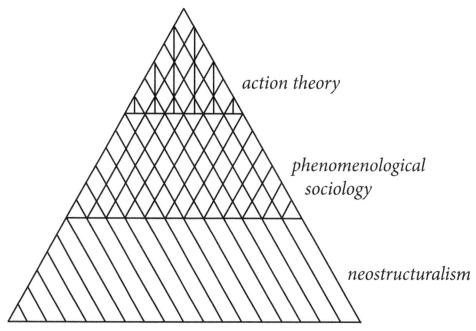

FIGURE 6.2 The field and subfields of neostructuralist semiotic sociology (Heiskala 2003: 321, reprinted by permission of Peter Lang).

the political (wicked problems, problematization and de-problematization, populism and democratization and de-democratization, etc.).

The metatheory that is proposed in the book is pretty simple: the major difference between relational and non-relational approaches is not in their emphasis on the importance of social relations in their analyses, but the fundamentally different understanding of those relations. Relational approaches view relations as *constitutive* and therefore the entities and their relations cannot be considered as being separate from one another. A non-relational approach presumes the primacy and givenness of entities that might or might not enter relations with other such entities. In most cases the relations in that sense are presumed to be *causal*, which entails considering relations and entities as being separate from one another. This simple thesis informed the authors' discussion on the differences between self-actional, inter-actional and trans-actional approaches in conceptualizing different perspectives in political science and governance, semiotics, and later in different views of (social) scientific explanation.

The authors highlight that all the three major phenomena of interest for political analysis can be conceptualized in terms of meaning-making and cultural and communicative processes by distinguishing self-actional, inter-actional and trans-actional approaches to power, governance and democracy. This needs to be complemented with the pertinent discussions of simple, complex, wicked and de-problematized political/governance problems and the processes of problematization and de-problematization as forms of politics/governance. In addition, the book argues that the notion of 'hegemony' as elaborated by the Essex School of political theory (Laclau, Mouffe and others) lies at the intersection of the three core notions of relational political analysis and that it is at the same time defined in terms of the constitution of meaning systems that are defined in thoroughly relational manner. The authors also point out that the political needs to be conceptualized mostly in terms of process rather than certain 'arena' (parliaments, governments, etc.) where it takes place. At the same time, we should not ignore the historically relevant connotation of 'publicness' when it comes to conceptualizing the political.

Selg and Ventsel put forth a relational theory of meaning and its constitutive connection with hegemony – the latter being a crucial category lying at the intersection of power, governance and democracy. The authors demonstrate that the core categories of the Essex school of political analysis (Laclau, Mouffe and others) are congenial to the core categories of the Tartu-Moscow school of cultural semiotics (Lotman and others). Through this synthesis it was possible to provide a general relational theory of the political. Essentially the authors put forth a theory that every meaning-system is constituted through establishing a core or centre ('empty signifier' in Laclau's sense) through which discrete elements are translated into a unified whole or system that has boundaries which entails excluding (or pushing to the periphery) of certain other meanings of that whole or system. Such a constitution is inherently political in the sense that it involves privileging and exclusion of different meanings through establishing a certain centre for the system which dominates as a hegemonic core of the system, giving it its major identity. But how does this constitution work? Here the authors pointed out the crucial connection between meaning and communication and highlighted it, besides recourse to cultural semiotics, through neostructuralism (Heiskala) that sees the original Saussurean project of semiotics to be mainly a research of the contingent articulation of meaning in communication. Yet, could something more concrete be said on this articulation? For this Selg and Ventsel put forth a concrete conceptual framework for political semiotic analysis of the political based on the Essex/Tartu school synthesis and Roman Jakobson's model of communication. They relate theories of power, governance and democracy to the Jakobsonian model of communication that distinguishes six aspects of each communicative act: emotive aspect (orientation towards the addresser), phatic aspect (orientation towards contact), poetic aspect (orientation towards message), conative aspect (orientation towards the addressee), referential aspect (orientation towards context) and metalingual aspect (orientation towards code). In addition, these aspects can be positioned along the two fundamental tensions in each meaning-system or communication: the tendency towards metonymic articulation of meaning and the tendency towards metaphoric articulation. The authors relate the latter tendencies to the topics of problematization and de-problematization of policy issues. Consequently, political semiotic categories are outlined that could be used for empirical analyses of political phenomena. These categories are not meant for merely describing different forms of communication, but for *explaining* them. But what kind of explanation is implied here?

This question leads Selg and Ventsel to the core distinction between causal and constitutive *explanation*, research *methodology* and *design*. The authors explicate in more detail the notion of constitutive explanation and demonstrate that this is what is at stake in relational understanding of social sciences. They provide a comparison with causal explanation that is characteristic of variable-centred approaches in the social sciences. Also, the authors explicate why constitutive explanation always entails abductive research logic and untangle the specificity of abduction in view of the two prevalent logics in scientific and theoretical thinking – induction and deduction. It is important that the authors highlight the essentially processual and relational character of abduction which they call the 'context-sensitive code-selection' and demonstrate why semiotic explanation is essentially constitutive and abductive. How should one conduct research in view of the methodological proposals that, in turn, grow out from our theoretical and metatheoretical background? This is reflected in the last parts of the book where the authors attempt to illustrate, through empirical examples and more theoretical positions, the political semiotic method they call 'political form analysis'.

CONCLUSION

Astonishingly semiotics is still a small-scale business in sociology and political science even though both disciplines have gone through a sea of change called 'the cultural turn' from the 1980s onwards. Together with the increasing density of the semiosphere on the surface of the globe, which is the prime cause of developments such as 'the cultural turn', the turn has given birth to an abundance of cultural studies of this and that, first in sociology and a bit later in political science. Yet very few of the cultural approaches are semiotically enlightened and are thus incapable of digging as deep into the core of the cultural dimension as is semiotics. Modest signs of development in this sense emerge here and there. Examples include the popularity of Bourdieu's sociology, some methodological approaches in cultural sociology (such as Sulkunen and Törrönen 1997; Törrönen 2002) and some critical approaches in political theory (such as Laclau and Mouffe 1985a, 1985b; Jessop 2004). Still, the prevailing situation is that semiotics would have much to give to the study of society but thus far its resources have not been utilized in a sufficient degree.

Various approaches in both political science and sociology that have implicit semiotic approaches built into them have been discussed in this chapter. In addition, a couple of attempts to outline an explicitly semiotic approach in political science (e.g. Selg and Ventsel) and sociology (e.g. Heiskala) have been reviewed. One of the conclusions from our analysis is that although generally speaking meaning-making is recognized as an important topic in both sociology and political science most of the current approaches in these disciplines either ignore or mention in passing the major achievements of semiotics as the discipline of analysing meaning-making in general. The situation seems more promising for semiotics in political science which is enjoying an upsurge of 'interpretive' or 'argumentative' turns in recent years (see Fischer and Gottweis 2012; Bevir and Rhodes 2015; Wagenaar 2015) that set a methodological primacy of studying communication in explaining politics and policy. When it comes to sociology, the cultural turn set the table for rigorous semiotic approaches to come; but few signs of such development have been seen thus far. Yet an optimist would think that the explosive increase and intensivization of the semiosphere on the surface of the globe will in due time make the rise of semiotic sociology a necessity.

ACKNOWLEDGEMENTS

Writing of this chapter was supported by the Academy of Finland (Heiskala, grant 308740) and the Estonian Research Council (Selg, grant PUT1485). A draft of the chapter was discussed in the weekly seminar of the Institute for Advanced Social Research, Tampere University, and we are grateful for all the brilliant comments.

REFERENCES

Alasuutari, P. and A. Qadir (2014), 'Epistemic Governance: An Approach to the Politics of Policy-making', *European Journal of Cultural and Political Sociology*, 1 (1): 67–84.
Alasuutari, P. and A. Qadir (2019), *Epistemic Governance: Social Change in the Modern World*, Cham: Palgrave Macmillan.
Alexander, J. C. (1987), *Twenty Lectures. Sociological Theory since World War II*, New York: Columbia University Press.
Althusser, L. (1965a), *For Marx*, London: Allen Lan.
Althusser, L. (1965b), *Reading Capital*, London: NLB, 1970.
Archer, M. (1988), *Culture and Agency. The Place of Culture in Social Theory*, Cambridge: Cambridge University Press.
Barthes, R. (1957), *Mythologies*, English edn, London: Paladin.
Barthes, R. (1964), *Elements of Semiology*, New York: Hill & Wang.
Berger, P. L. and T. Luckmann (1966), *The Social Construction of Reality. A Treatise in the Sociology of Knowledge*, New York: Anchor, Books/Doubleday.
Bevir, M. and R. Rhodes, eds (2015), *Routledge Handbook of Interpretive Political Science*, London: Routledge.
Bourdieu, P. (1979), *Distinction: A Social Critique of the Judgement of Taste*, Cambridge: Harvard University Press.
Bourdieu, P. (1980), *The Logic of Practice*, Stanford: Stanford University Press.
Camic, C. (1986), 'The Matter of Habit', *American Journal of Sociology*, 91 (5): 1039–87.
Dahl, R. (1998), *On Democracy*, New Haven: Yale University Press.
Danesi, M. (2018), *Understanding Media Semiotics*, London: Bloomsbury.
Derrida, J. (1967), *Of Grammatology*, Baltimore: Johns Hopkins University Press.

Douglas, M. and A. Wildavsky (1982), *Risk and Culture: An Essay on the Selection of Technological and Environmental Dangers*, Berkeley: University of California Press.
Durkheim, É. (1912), *The Elementary Forms of Religious Life*, New York: Collier.
Eco, U. (1983), *The Name of the Rose*, San Diego: Harcourt.
Eco, U. (1986), *Faith in Fakes: Travels in Hyperreality*, London: Minerva.
Fairclough, N. (2003), *Analysing Discourse: Textual Analysis for Social Research*, London: Routledge.
Fischer, F. and H. Gottweis, eds. (2012a), *The Argumentative Turn Revisited: Public Policy as Communicative Practice*, Durham: Duke University Press.
Fischer, F. and H. Gottweis (2012b), 'Introduction: The Argumentative Turn Revisited', in F. Fischer and H. Gottweis (eds), *The Argumentative Turn Revisited: Public Policy as Communicative Practice*, 1–27, Durham: Duke University Press.
Fischer, F. and J. Forester (1993), *The Argumentative Turn in Policy Analysis and Planning*, Durham: Duke University Press.
Foucault, M. (1978), *The History of Sexuality, Volume I: An Introduction*, New York: Pantheon Books.
Foucault, M. (1975), *Discipline and Punish: The Birth of the Prison*, New York: Pantheon.
Foucault, M. (1976), *The History of Sexuality I: An Introduction*, New York: Pantheon.
Fukuyama, F. (2016), 'Governance: What Do We Know, and How Do We Know It?', *Annual Review of Political Science*, 19: 89–105.
Garfinkel, H. (1967), *Studies in Ethnomethodology*, Cambridge: Polity Press.
Giddens, A. (1984), *The Constitution of Society: Outline of the Theory of Structuration*, Berkeley: University of California Press.
Goffman, E. (1959), *The Presentation of Self in Everyday Life*, Harmondsworth: Penguin.
Goffman, E. (1967), *Interaction Ritual: Essays on Face-to-Face Behavior*, New York: Pantheon.
Goffman, E. (1974), *Frame Analysis: An Essay on the Organization of Experience*, Boston: Northeastern University Press.
Grathoff, R., ed. (1978), *The Theory of Social Action: The Correspondence of Alfred Schutz and Talcott Parsons*, Bloomington: Indiana University Press.
Greimas, A. J. (1966), *Structural Semantics: An Attempt at a Method*, Lincoln: University of Nebraska Press.
Greimas, A. J. (1976), *The Social Sciences: A Semiotic View*, Minneapolis: University of Minnesota Press.
Habermas, J. (1996), 'Three Normative Models of Democracy', in S. Benhabib (ed.), *Democracy and Difference: Contesting the Boundaries of the Political*, 21–30, Princeton: Princeton University Press.
Habermas, J. (1981a), *Theory of Communicative Action, Volume One: Reason and the Rationalization of Society*, Boston: Beacon Press.
Habermas, J. (1981b), *Theory of Communicative Action, Volume Two: Lifeworld and System: A Critique of Functionalist Reason*, Boston: Beacon Press.
Hammond, M., J. Howarth and R. Keat (1991), *Understanding Phenomenology*, Oxford: Blackwell.
Heiskala, R. (2003), *Society as Semiosis: Neostructuralist Theory of Culture and Society*, Frankfurt am Main and New York: Peter Lang.
Heiskala, R. (2014), 'Toward Semiotic Sociology. A Synthesis of Semiology, Semiotics and Phenomenological Sociology', *Social Science Information*, 53 (1): 35–53.
Heiskala, R. (2021) Semiotic Sociology. Cham: Palgrave Macmillan.
Hobbes, T. (1651), *Leviathan*, London: A&C Black.

Hodge, R. (2016), *Social Semiotics for a Complex World: Analysing Language and Social Meaning*, Cambridge: Polity Press.
Hodge, R. and G. Kress (1988), *Social Semiotics*, Cambridge: Polity Press.
Hodgson, G. (1988), *Economics and Institutions: A Manifesto for a Modern Institutional Economics*, Cambridge: Polity Press.
Honneth, A. (1992), *The Struggle for Recognition. The Moral Grammar of Social Conflicts*, Cambridge: Polity.
Husserl, E. (1931), *Cartesian Meditations: An Introduction to Phenomenology*, The Hague: Martinus Nijhoff.
Jessop, B. (2004), 'Critical Semiotic Analysis and Cultural Political Economy', *Critical Discourse Studies*, 1 (2): 159–74.
Jessop, B. (2016), *The State: Past, Present, Future*, Cambridge: Polity.
Joas, H. (1997), *G.H. Mead: A Contemporary Re-Examination of His Thought*, Cambridge: MIT Press.
Kilpinen, E. (2000), *The Enormous Fly-Wheel of Society: Pragmatism's Habitual Conception of Action and Social Theory*, Helsinki: University of Helsinki, Department of Sociology, Research Reports 235.
Kooiman, J. (1993), 'Social-political Governance: Introduction', in J. Kooiman (ed.), *Modern Governance: Government-Society Interactions*, 1–8, London: Sage.
Kress, G. (2010), *Multimodality. A Social Semiotic Approach to Contemporary Communication*, London: Routledge.
Kristeva, J. (1969), *Desire in Language: A Semiotic Approach to Literature and Art*, Oxford: Blackwell.
Laclau, E. (2001), 'The Politics of Rhetoric', in T. Cohen, B. Cohen, M. J. Hillis and A. Warminskij (eds), *Material Events: Paul de Man and the Afterlife of Theory*, Minneapolis: University of Minnesota Press.
Laclau, E. and C. Mouffe (1985a), *Hegemony and Socialist Strategy: Towards a Radical Democratic Politics*, London: Verso.
Laclau, E. and C. Mouffe (1985b), *Hegemony and Socialist Strategy*, London: Verso.
Laclau, E. and C. Mouffe (1987), 'Post-Marxism without Apologies', *New Left Review*, 166 (1): 79–106.
Lefort, C. (1988), *Democracy and Political Theory*. Translated by David Macey, Cambridge: Polity Press.
Lévi-Strauss, C. (1958), *Structural Anthropology*, New York: Doubleday Anchor Books.
Luhmann, N. (1984), *Social Systems*, Stanford: Stanford University Press.
Lyotard, J. F. (1979), *The Postmodern Condition: A Report on Knowledge*, Manchester: Manchester University Press.
Mauss, M. (1925), *The Gift: The Form and Reason for Exchange in Archaic Societies*, London: Routledge.
McCannell, D. (1976), *The Tourist*, Berkeley: University of California Press.
Mouffe, C. (2000), *The Democratic Paradox*, London: Verso.
Parsons, T. (1937), *The Structure of Social Action*, New York: The Free Press.
Parsons, T. (1951), *The Social System*, New York: The Free Press.
Parsons, T. and N. Smelser (1956), *Economy and Society*, New York: The Free Press.
Przeworski, A., M. A. Alvarez, J. A. Cheibub and F. Limongi (2000), *Democracy and Development: Political Institutions and Well-Being in the World, 1950–1990*, Cambridge: Cambridge University Press.

Rhodes, R. (2017), *Network Governance and the Differentiated Polity: Selected Essays, Volume 1*, Oxford: Oxford University Press.

Schutz, A. (1932), *Phenomenology of the Social World*, London: Heinemann.

Sebeok, T. A. and M. Danesi (2000), *The Forms of Meaning. Modelling Systems Theory and Semiotic Analysis*, Berlin: Mouton de Gruyter.

Selg, P. (2011), 'An Outline for a Theory of Political Semiotics', PhD diss., Tallinn: Tallinn University.

Selg, P. and A. Ventsel (2008), 'Towards a Semiotic Theory of Hegemony: Naming as Hegemonic Operation in Lotman and Laclau', *Sign Systems Studies*, 36 (1): 167–83.

Selg, P. and A. Ventsel (2010), 'An Outline for a Semiotic Theory of Hegemony', *Semiotica*, 182: 443–74.

Selg, P. and A. Ventsel (2019), 'What Is Political Semiotics and Why Does It Matter? A Reply to Janar Mihkelsaar', *Semiotica*, 231: 27–37.

Selg, P. and A. Ventsel (2020), *Introducing Relational Political Analysis: Political Semiotics as a Theory and Method*, Cham: Springer.

Swedlow, B. (2002), 'Toward Cultural Analysis in Policy Analysis: Picking up where Aaron Wildavsky Left Off', *Journal of Comparative Policy Analysis: Research and Practice*, 4 (3): 267–85.

Swedlow, B. (2011), 'A Cultural Theory of Politics, Editor's Introduction: Cultural Theory's Contributions to Political Science', *PS: Political Science & Politics*, 44 (4): 703–10.

Tilly, C. (2007), *Democracy*, Cambridge: Cambridge University Press.

Törrönen, J. (2002), 'Semiotic Theory on Qualitative Interviewing Using Stimulus Texts', *Qualitative Research*, 2 (3): 343–62.

Van Dijk, T. A. (2008), *Discourse and Power*, Houndsmills: Palgrave.

Wagenaar, H. (2015), *Meaning in Action: Interpretation and Dialogue in Policy Analysis*, London: Routledge.

Wagner, H. R. (1983), *Alfred Schutz: An Intellectual Biography*, Chicago: Chicago University Press.

Weber, M. ([1904] 1949), 'Objectivity in Social Science and Social Policy', in E. A. Shils and H. A. Finch (eds and trans.), *The Methodology of the Social Sciences*, 289–93, New York: Free Press.

Weber, M. (1978), *Economy and Society: An Outline of Interpretive Sociology, Vol 1*, Berkeley: University of California Press.

Weber, M. (1922), *Economy and Society: An Outline of Interpretive Sociology*, Berkeley: University of California Press.

Wedeen, L. (2002), 'Conceptualizing Culture: Possibilities for Political Science', *American Political Science Review*, 96 (4): 713–28.

Wedeen, L. (2004), 'Concepts and Commitments in the Study of Democracy', in I. Shapiro, R. M. Smith and T. E. Masoud (eds), *Problems and Methods in the Study of Politics*, 274–306, Cambridge: Cambridge University Press.

Willis, P. (1977), *Learning to Labour: How Working Class Kids Get Working Class Jobs*, Aldershot: Gover.

Wolin, S. (1996), 'Fugitive Democracy', in S. Benhabib (ed.), *Democracy and Difference: Contesting the Boundaries of the Political*, 31–45, Princeton: Princeton University Press.

CHAPTER SEVEN

Semiotics in Learning and Education

ANDREW STABLES AND ALIN OLTEANU

Semiotics has inspired recent contributions to the philosophy and theory of education in a variety of ways. Proposals to overcome simple mind-body dualism, with an inert view of knowledge, via notions of *sign*, often implying an emphasis on process, have been prominent in redefining learning and the rationale of education. The earliest such attempts belong to Cunningham (1987, 1992). There is a shift from construals of *being* as static (fixed) to *being* as transitional, or semiosic. Acknowledgement of this, implicitly or explicitly, is one of the grounds of the broad variety of semiotic approaches to education, spanning from applications in cultural semiotics (e.g. Ojamaa et al. 2019) and social semiotics (e.g. Kress 2003; Joyce and Feez 2018), to language education (Danesi 2000) and to the recent and eclectic edusemiotics framework (Stables and Semetsky 2015). If being is becoming, then education concerns the becoming of individuals and societies (Stables 2012). To study education in terms of meaning is to understand how meaning is transformed through educational processes. This means that education is growth but, while modern philosophy also accepts this general statement, the semiotic view brings a focus on the transformational process itself, instead of outcomes, inputs and standardized methods of yielding the latter from the former. In brief, the concern is not merely what the learner has learnt by the end of a schooling process, in comparison to a supposedly given amount of knowledge, but her transformational journey, which is unique and can only very loosely be evaluated by comparison to formally accepted blocks of knowledge.

This educational paradigm is in a sense egalitarian, in a sense liberal. It encourages individual difference but not at the expense of devaluing certain individuals for their failures according to avowedly objective benchmarks. In economic terms, one might say that the semiotic approach regards the individual person as the ultimate in scarce goods: a recipe for mutual respect as well as personal freedom. This accounts both for the market value of individuals as human resources and for the invaluable existential depth of any human person. The former view without the latter reduces human beings to consumable resources; the latter without the former fails to prescribe educational and professional means of development, which are necessary for human wellbeing and personal fulfilment. Paul Cobley explains that the recent anti-humanist position that some branches of semiotics are taking, by envisaging 'humans within semiosis and within Umwelten' (2017:15) avoids the two polarized views that justify humanities education either, classically, by cultivating normatively fixed values of what is good and beautiful or, in a capitalist fashion, by seeking immediate 'use-value' exclusively. The advocacy that semiotics brings for humanities education, Cobley argues following Sebeok, stems from the evolutionary and cognitive perspective that

> the use-value of aesthetic behaviour consists in not appearing to possess use-value; nevertheless, it serves a long-term purpose for the animal, a purpose which consists of enhancing, extending and embellishing the animal's Umwelt, offering more variation and differentiation of the world and thereby potentially allowing the animal to more efficiently negotiate its environment to avoid predation and more efficaciously seek out sustenance.
>
> (2017: 19)

The semiotic key to reconciling the classic and the extreme utilitarian views is the construal of knowing as inseparable from interpreting. We are all interpreters, consciously and unconsciously, throughout our lives. As Peirce put it, '[a] sign is only a sign *in actu* by virtue of its receiving an interpretation, that is, by virtue of its determining another sign of the same object' (1901: CP 5.569). Replacing the modern philosophical concept of *idea* as the vehicle of knowledge, conceived as a purely mental entity, with the relational concept of *sign* implies more than just accounting for the hermeneutic aspect and fluidity of knowledge. It opens a perspective on the self as *becoming* (Colapietro 1989: 77) which, in turn, construes notions of learning and education accordingly. It can be argued that the necessity of this perspective is growing with the reconfiguration of social awareness that the accelerating development of media and technology is causing. In times when constant change has become the *status quo* of society, interpretative competences appear more clearly than before to facilitate adaptive strategies (Gough and Stables 2012). In this spirit, work in new technologies and digital media strongly informs semiotic educational theory, as explained more fully below.

Before proceeding further, let us give an operational definition of one of our key terms: education. Precise definitions of education vary but, for present purposes, we can adopt the following broad but simple definition. Education concerns the processes of personal, social and environmental becoming, involving institutions prominent among which are schools, colleges and universities. The study of education therefore explores activities recognized as teaching and learning from a broad range of disciplinary perspectives, including philosophy, psychology, sociology and cultural theory. Semiotic perspectives can influence all these fields and, indeed, can often dissolve the boundaries between them, as it can inform German 'stand-alone' educational theory, with its purely educational constructs such as *Bildung, didaktik* and *pedagogik*. (See, for example, the discussion of learning below and in Stableset al. 2018.)

LITERACIES AND MODALITIES: PRINT, DIGITAL AND 'NEW'

The institutionalization of learning into education has been a long historical process, wherein a critical and major achievement has been the universalization of literacy in the modern age. This is a core ideal of Enlightenment, when a social awareness of the importance of public education first arose. The revolution of modernity, the awareness of civil rights and responsibilities, was implemented through the mainstreaming of literacy. This was possible, first of all, due to a media shift (Anderson [1983] 2006: 77–8; McLuhan [1970] 1995: 55), although it took a few centuries for print technology to reach its potential and become an indispensable aspect of everyday life. To understand the phenomenon of literacy therefore implies understanding the semiotic effects of print mediality.

The completion of Augustine of Hippo's *De Doctrina Christiana*, in the early fifth century ([397–426] 1997), is a landmark moment for the vernacularizing of literacy, long predating print. During the first centuries of Christianity, the skill of reading gained prominence in the Mediterranean space because of the importance of Scripture for this new religion. Setting out to write a book that would help Christians not merely to read but also to interpret Scripture on their own, Augustine started by developing and explaining a theory of signs. By doing so, *De Doctrina Christiana* became the major reference for both liberal education and (medieval) logic, understood as the *doctrine of signs* (Deely 2001; Marmo 2010). This proves an intimate connection between literacy, as an empowering set of competences and semiotic theory (Olteanu 2014, 2018).

Much later, the mainstreaming of print not only bestowed upon language even more power but also transformed written language (script) from a codified language of the élites into the new vernacular. These effects of print made the modern world possible, where public education has helped to undermine the pre-established medieval layers of social stratification. These same effects, however, also generated some of the loopholes of modern philosophy, such as anthropocentrism and monolingualism. By monolingualism we mean the supposition that it is possible for there to be no linguistic variation over vast territories, comprising several communities. This supposition became conceivable because print made it possible for populations spanning over vast territories to literally see (and read) a language (as printed) and begat the impression that their spoken languages were all the same, without great variations of idiolects, accents and dialects (Anderson [1983] 2006: 80). Also, print made a different language seem all the more alien, as codified in a way that seemed entirely arbitrary to the known language.

Simultaneously with the spread of the ideal of citizenship, monolingualism became the ideal of academic language (*la langue littéraire*) in modernity: people can co-operate as citizens of a nation-state because they share the same academic language, which, besides being a common code, is supposed to best accommodate education and scientific research. An emblematic example of this merging of citizenship and monolingualism is observed in the constitution of the French Academy (Académie Française [1635, 1752, 1816] 1995, *Status et règlements, article* 24). Having come to embody the principles of Enlightenment, the French Academy served as a model for the organization of education and research in modern political states, in general. In hindsight, we can now observe, as Lähteenmäki (2010: 18) does in inspiration of the Bakhtinian ([1963] 1984) notion of *heteroglossia*, that:

> While [...] all societies are factually multilingual, they may see themselves as monolingual. Such societies are dominated by the ideology of monolingualism and monoculturalism, which is reflected most explicitly in the language policy of a particular society. The ideology of monolingualism assumes that the unity of a linguistic community is based on the existence of a unified language shared by the members of the community.

Connected with monolingualism, print also evoked anthropocentrism. Spoken, articulated language already gives humans a great organizational advantage with respect to other animals, which writing greatly enhances, as particularly put to use educationally. For a long time, this has fuelled the belief that humans are defined by their ability to articulate language, which, supposedly, is intimately connected with a specifically human learning capacity (e.g. Humboldt [1836] 1999). This capacity, as supposed in contractualism (e.g. Hobbes [1651] 1909; Locke [1693] 1889; Rousseau [1762] 1911; see Stables et al. 2018: 119), is the potential to undergo education. However, according to alternative accounts, the physiomotor capability to articulate language is accidental and the adoption of verbal communication is an exaptation (Gould and Vrba 1982) of a physiological feature that evolved for different functions (MacLarnon 2012). This realization implies that the human/non-human animal distinction is subtler (and more complex) than thought of in modern philosophy. Among the humanities, semiotics has been particularly keen in adopting this evolutionary biological discovery about human verbal language, in the form of biosemiotics (Sebeok 1991, 2001). Thomas Sebeok's biosemiotics rests on the hypothesis that humans developed spoken language to more efficiently model the surrounding environment and communicate these models. In this vein, specifically human features are sought from a modelling perspective, at the meeting point of meaning and cognition (e.g. Stjernfelt 2014; Hoffmeyer and Stjernfelt 2016), and are not necessarily a matter of quantifiable *intelligence*.

As written language greatly facilitated carrying out scholarship and enjoying its social benefits, modern philosophy tended to construe language, reading and writing as the essentially defining characteristics of humanity. From this point of view, a process of becoming is also supposed, but with a clear, fixed and finite goal: one fulfils the potential of being human (or citizen) by acquiring reading and writing skills, which, together with arithmetic, came to form the fixed literacy norm. Education, hence, has the goal to pull humanity out of animality by equipping humans with reading, writing and arithmetic skills so that they can perform their duties as citizens. On this account, education is meant to deliver competences of interacting with written codes of letters (symbols), hence the term *literacy*. From the Enlightenment perspective, literacy is necessary for understanding the *social contract* by which humans give up some natural rights in favour of protection and some other rights, such as owning private property, by virtue of which they can live in a society (e.g. Hobbes [1651] 1909). Consequently, by construing the rationale of education as the cultivation of competences of manipulating symbolic codes, modernity framed education as distinctively human. Practically, this assumption is seriously challenged by the complexity of educational issues in the current age of social change. Semiotics recently drew the attention of education research because, as we explain here, it can offer comprehensive theoretical answers to these challenges (e.g. Kress 2003; Stables 2005, 2012). Certainly, between the age of philosophical contractualism and present day semiotics, critical developments were made in educational philosophy, theory and pedagogy (Dewey 1916; Piaget [1924] 1929; Vygotsky [1930–1966] 1978; Bruner 1960; Dearden, Hirst, and Peters 1972, to name a few landmarks). However, while many assumptions have been corrected or adjusted, educational policy still often draws on substantialist and anthropocentric learning theories and educational philosophy still has not fully shaken off substantialism and mind/body dualism. The recent surge of semiotic educational research displays innovative ways out of these loopholes, while often relying on the major educational theories of the past century, informed by state-of-the-art findings.

The great achievements of modernity, including public education, are evoked by the same innovation that inculcated modernity's developmental obstructions, namely literacy in print mediality. Print literacy simultaneously meliorated human life invaluably, made world wars possible, under ideological banners, and allowed for the exploitation of the natural environment to the extent of potentially catastrophic climate crisis. As Stables noted (2012: 47):

> It is an important truth little acknowledged in educational theory that that which makes knowledge and understanding possible – our interpretive frameworks including our assumptions and prejudices – is also that which limits them.

Herein lies the core insight of semiotics for education: learning is hermeneutical. As such, circumstances both evoke and restrict learning possibilities. This acknowledgement reveals that print technology and mediality do not support every possible type of scientific reasoning, infinitely and indefinitely. Rather, medialities have affordances, as this can be optimally expressed in Gibson's (1979) celebrated term. The linear monomodality of the alphabet, of visually represented language, afforded the mainstreaming of literacy, which means that it also limits certain educational possibilities. Hence, a semiotic perspective raises the questions of how to navigate available affordances sustainably and how to design environments that evoke new learning possibilities.

As humanity is currently undergoing a time of fast mediatic and social change, Enlightenment education is a severely challenged practice. The old notion of literacy does not correspond any more to the quickly and unpredictably changing sets of competences that enable a thriving life in contemporary societies. Instead of focusing on delivering a fixed set of literacy skills, the concern has shifted to a plurality of changing *new literacies* (Lankshear and Knobel 2003; Mills 2010). For this reason, as well, a semiotic shift can be observed in recent literacy studies (Kress 2003; Gaines 2010). As the notion of *text*, referring to an interpretable artefact, expanded to encompass a variety of representation modalities, several traditional objects of linguistics, such as translation and literacy, attracted a semiotic approach. This can be seen in the evolution of systemic functional linguistics (Halliday and Webster 2009) into social semiotics (Kress and van Leeuwen 2001), through the introduction of the concept of multimodality (see Jewitt, Bezemer and O'Halloran 2016). Traditional philology no longer suffices as a framework for equipping pupils with competences necessary for thriving in contemporary society. For this reason, we argue, much more than identifying new literacies and cultivating them, the concern must be that of supporting and empowering learners to discover unique and innovative sets of skills that do not correspond to sets of literacies that can be anticipated. This is what we mean by claiming that education is personal (which is different from individual). It has been semiotic approaches, of various forms, that recently unblocked this understanding. Since knowledge consists in meaning, which is subjective, learning is a unique, unrepeatable experience.

THE SCOPE OF EDUSEMIOTICS

While many – the present writers included – would argue that personal and social becoming cannot be seen as distinct from our relationships with non-human nature (Olteanu and Stables 2018), this argument for an ecologically respectful posthumanism (Stables, in press) is not either implicitly or explicitly shared by most contributors to the broad edusemiotic field.

While there may not be universal agreement about the scope of edusemiotics, there is broad agreement about its foci. In the broad sense, edusemiotics is the study of processes of growth and becoming associated particularly with concepts such as childhood, socialization (*Bildung* in the German tradition), teaching and social support structures and institutions. Beyond that, it is a flexible construct, though some commentators adopt a more purist stance than others. Semetsky is representative for a group of thinkers who are very keen to stress the characteristics of edusemiotics as a distinct theoretical subdiscipline that is distinct from applied semiotics of education in its insistence on, particularly, the law of the included middle. Although it is out of Semetsky's work that the term 'edusemiotics' came (Semetsky 2010), operationally the concept is necessarily vague and encompasses a range of theoretical perspectives as its own handbook suggests (Semetsky 2017). For example, Semetsky herself takes a psychoanalytic perspective on the Unconscious as (Peircean) Firstness, while other contributors to the field oppose such strong psychologism or are indifferent to empirically non-verifiable concepts such as conscious/unconscious.

Educational semiotics, or semiotics of education, or edusemiotics is therefore a broad field, and this raises the question of what the term 'semiotics' here actually offers. After all, there have been powerful battles over the last century between educational philosophies and theories; between top-down and bottom-up approaches, between didacticism and active learning, between socialization and personal growth and so on. In this context, what does 'semiotics' offer that is new and distinctive?

Perhaps the first point to stress is that semiotics, as a discipline, is neither psychology nor sociology, as these are the two paradigms that have dominated educational theory (Cunningham 1992; Stables et al. 2018). The former takes the individual mind as its ground; the latter the social structure. Much educational theory has drawn on one or other of these, and often educational debates have been between the two. Semiotics only has semiosis (1907: CP 5.484) as its ground and sees neither the individual mind (whatever that may be) or the social structure as either fixed or prior to any thinking about education. Semiotics is primarily interested in how sense and meaning develop, and questions relating to, for example, individual intelligence or social equality must be addressed at a secondary level. In effect, both psychology and sociology attempt to shoehorn educators into doing things that fit their own primarily psychological and sociological perspectives.

Related to this is the whole idea of relationality itself. Semiosis operates through sociocultural, environmental and interpersonal communicative processes. It is not about either pre-made people or a pre-fixed society determining how people interact, for the persons and the society are co-evolving all the time. In that sense, education both is learner-centred and is not learner-centred, because the child (or learner, subjective self, in general) is never completed but is always a work in progress. Similarly, 'learning' itself is not merely a product of either an individual brain developing or of top-down socialization, but is rather a term we use to discuss events and changes in lives and institutions that have proved significant (Stables et al. 2018). The very pursuit of strictly empirically observable phenomena reveals that, despite much shared optimism, learning is a very subtle phenomenon to observe. When is it justified to claim that someone learned something?

Beyond this, many edusemiotic writers, including Semetsky and the present authors, would argue that semiotic approaches take us away from a series of sterile dualisms that, directly or indirectly, can be attributed to the Cartesian foundations of modernist philosophical thinking, and specifically to Descartes' and others' views of mind as a distinct substance from body (e.g. Stables and Semetsky 2015; Olteanu and Campbell 2018). Instead of seeing people as 'mind' or 'body', or even as 'mind and body', theoretical semiotics often argues for the both and approach of seeing people as 'body-mind' or 'body-and-mind' where the two are never completely separable. (On a day to day level, of course, we can still operationally distinguish mental acts such as thinking from physical acts such as coughing, but if we look closely at how such acts arise, we realize that the sharp theoretical distinction is invalid.) In this regard, the biosemiotic concept of the body can be particularly insightful (Stjernfelt 2006; Hoffmeyer 2008), as we discussed previously (Olteanu and Stables 2018). This Cartesian legacy is evident in the traditional twentieth-century debate about learning, where cognitive learning theories concentrated on concept formation as paramount, while behaviourist theories concentrated on biophysical stimulus-response mechanisms such as reinforcement and punishment. John Dewey began an effective theoretical dismantling of this position in his 'reflex arc' paper of 1896. Semiotics can develop Dewey's cause: neither stimulus and response, nor mental and physical response can be neatly separated, for the question is always about how meaning, sense, knowledge and understanding develop in complex contexts (see Pesce 2020). In this possibility of Deweyan educational philosophy one can recognize Peirce's influence, as part of the broader development of a pragmatist philosophical project. Dewey's rejection of simplistic approaches to behaviour in terms of stimulus and response carries the essence of Peirce's notions of semiosis and sign as triadic. The underlying idea is that understanding, what Peirce termed Interpretant, is not a (mechanical) response to a distinctive input. Knowing involves interpreting, which means that it is subjective, situated and immersed in context. From this perspective, knowledge cannot consist in pure, objective data, regardless of the knower's positioning. If what we know is subjective and viewpointed it does not mean that knowledge is unreliable and that our existence is solipsistic. Rather, starting with Dewey, pragmatic philosophy of education raised awareness that learning cannot be separated from the complexities of human life, starting from mood, experience and personality to social, economic and cultural contexts. Moreover, Dewey's problematization of the reductivist distinction between stimulus and response also parallels the biosemiotic notion of environment (*Umwelt*) as shaped through loops of co-dependent perception- and action-signs (Uexküll 1926). This direction for research was only recently noted by Innis (2009: 94) and Kull (2019: 227), but not explored in an educational scope.

Given that modern science, and indeed analytic philosophy, has specialized in creating increasing fine distinctions between things, the tendency of semiotics to investigate the relational aspects of growth and becoming is a necessary antidote against extreme and unalloyed differentiation. Sound semiotic theory always takes as full account as it can of context.

As mentioned above, modern philosophy manifests a strong Cartesian legacy, evident in the classical debate between rationalism and empiricism. This debate has strongly influenced how we conceive of knowledge, understanding, perception and apperception. In the rationalist tradition the emphasis is always on the concept; in classical empiricism, on sense data. Although few writers about semiotics and education address these issues directly, the adoption of any semiotic perspective at least implies critique of either or both of these traditions. At the most basic level, a view of knowledge as interpretation poses challenges to both rationalism and empiricism. One of the present authors has argued that a strongly semiotic position implies a view of knowledge as 'recognition-as' (as opposed to recognition-of), a view that always acknowledges the importance of habits of perceiving and responding (Stables 2019). On this account, the learning journey is always a story of how one gets to a certain kind of understanding: a narrative rather than a purely logical process of concept development or even a simple process of socialization into recognition of the inherent qualities of objects as entities, led by sense data.

In short, there currently is a group of writers who are directly concerned with the theoretical and philosophical issues that thinking about semiotics and education together throw up (e.g. Cunningham 1987, 1992; Semetsky 2010; Midtgarden 2013; Stables et al. 2018; Campbell 2018b), while there is a much larger group of scholars whose work applies various semiotic perspectives to educational problems (e.g. Lemke 1987; Mittelberg 2002; Radford, Schubring and Seeger 2008; Unsworth 2008; O'Halloran 2011; Campbell 2018a; Milyakina 2018; Kull 2018; Pelkey 2018; Tredinnick-Rowe 2018; Ojamaa et al. 2019).[1] Even the latter offer implicit contributions to ontological and epistemological debates via their assumptions, methods and modes of analysis.

In terms of specific influences on edusemiotic work, C. S. Peirce is by far the most influential (e.g. Nöth in Stables et al. 2018), though there remain a number of writers who are either sceptical about the extent of this influence (e.g. Stables 2012) or take their major inspirations from other schools of semiotics, such as Saussrean-inspired postructuralism or Greimas (e.g. Kukkola and Pikkarainen 2016). Recently, a small group of writers has begun to ground educational thinking in biosemiotics, drawing on von Uexküll and Sebeok as well as a range of more recent thinkers (Pikkarainen 2016, 2018; Campbell 2016; Olteanu and Stables 2018). It is noteworthy that, among other compatibilities and fertile crossovers, biosemiotics re-delivers the old instructional concept of scaffolding (Bruner 1960) to educational research (see Olteanu and Campbell 2018), this time on an evolutionary and embodiment account (Hoffmeyer 2006).

HOW PEIRCE HAS BEEN/IS BEING USED

Peirce's concepts of sign and semiosis have proven particularly revealing for eschewing substantialism and mind/body dualism in learning theory. As such, a broad range of semiotics and education scholars have recently found inspiration in Peirce's semiotics. A thorough treatment of state-of-the-art of Peircean educational thought, inclusive of all existing literature, deserves a volume of its own. Peirce's semiotics has found diverse uses in educational philosophy and theory also because, as Cobley (2020: 31) explains, biographically 'there are many Peirces', as displayed by the still incomplete and dispersed state of his publications. It would be impossible to capture this scholarship in its entirety here but, nevertheless, we hope to delineate the general directions and the most influential studies.

One of the main reasons for the recent popularity of a Peircean approach to education has to do with the processual, or transitional, concept of knowledge that Peirce's semiotics involves, as explained at the beginning of this paper. Strand and Legg explain that (2019: 1), rooted in a pragmati(ci)st and phenomenological philosophy, 'Peirce's most valuable contribution to education [is] his semiotics – a study of the meaning and development of signs – which enables us to conceptualize and explore all communicative processes in terms of sign relations and sign actions.'

Another equally important reason, intimately linked with the first one, is that it does not require language-centrism. Peirce's notion of sign allows discussing learning in a way that avoids the Saussurean notion of meaning as a fixed and arbitrary articulation. From this perspective, more resources than merely articulated language are involved in learning (e.g. Strand 2014a; Olteanu and Stables 2018). What we know is not limited to linguistic competence, in the Chomskyan sense. Knowledge and learning are not restricted within Saussurean *langue*. Overall, a Peircean approach opens the perspective on education as semiosis, which shifts the focus from psychological processes to a more comprehensive notion of learning as knowledge production (Strand 2014b) or discovery (Olteanu 2015). As Nöth (2014: 456) remarks, '[a]t the root of learning and teaching, we are faced with the roots of processes of semiosis in general.'

This approach challenges conventionalist and strongly constructivist perspectives on learning and education as acculturation in favour of a pragmatic notion of knowledge as relying on *critical common sense* (e.g. Olteanu 2015). It eagerly recognizes learning as a rhetoric and dialogical phenomenon proceeding in communication and social engagement in general (see Bergman 2013; Colapietro 2013; Lizska 2013; Pesce 2013), not only in educational contexts. This brings a fresh perspective on education as justified by the pursuit of the greater rationale of learning (Olteanu and Campbell 2019), in contrast to the tendency in modern educational philosophy to define learning as confined by educational goals. Arguably compatible with the notion of *Bildung* (Strand 2005), Peirce's pragmatism brings to the surface the driving role of desire in learning (Seif 2017; Pelkey 2018), to the point that, arguably, learning can be investigated as *agapism* (Olteanu 2015) or, simply, as the love between persons evoked by the sharing of knowledge.

The Peircean concept of sign is not bound to one modality of representation, while not implying idealist claims of concepts as amodal. This is particularly clearly expressed in Peirce's notion of iconicity, which addresses the degree of adequacy between a logical operation and its representation (1905: CP 4.561; see Stjernfelt 2015: 36). Peirce considered that a representation of an inference must display a parallelism of syntax with the logical operation itself. Arguably a conceptualization of (instances of) *common sensism*, this principle led him to develop the system of logical notations which he termed Existential Graphs (1903: CP 4.412–4.418). Aside from the system of Existential Graphs, the underpinning notion of iconicity proves currently particularly useful for detaching learning from language-centrism and, consequently, from anthropocentrism. It is insightful in accounting for the efficiency of pictures, metaphors and, in general, non-formal representations in learning. Existential Graphs are schematic; they have the form diagrams, which means that logic itself is schematic. This corresponds to more recent theories that acknowledge the central role that nonverbal modelling (Sebeok 1991, 2001), embodied schemata (Lakoff and Johnson 1999) and multimodal representations (Kress 2003) have for knowing. Nonverbal modelling, as developed by Sebeok in direct inspiration of Peirce, has been essential to the development of biosemiotics. The recent development of cognitive semiotics (e.g. Brandt 2003, 2011, Paolucci 2020) on the basis of cognitive linguistics relies, as well, to a large extent on Peircean semiotic notions. Through his semiotic understanding of experience, Peirce's theory arguably foreshadowed contemporary philosophy of the body. Strand and Legg (2019: 1) note that, from a Peircean perspective, learning is 'inescapably rooted in […] situated experience'.

While explicitly a semiotic paradigm and often addressing learning and education (e.g. Kress 2003; Bezemer and Kress 2008), the multimodality framework has not explicitly built upon Peircean semiotics, apart from some few and recent instances (Lacković 2018, 2019). This is particularly surprising since the rationale of the theory is to understand the modal complexity of (human) meaning-making and it does so by starting with a criticism of the linguistic double articulation concept (Kress and van Leeuwen 2001: 4).

In light of the criticism of substance dualism and language-centrism that it entails, Peirce's semiotics opened perspectives on education in light of a schematic and implicitly multimodal notion of learning (Olteanu 2015). It questions and relativizes the role of language and, even more so, of pre-given formal languages, such as symbolic calculus, in learning (Olteanu, Kambouri and Stables 2016). It offers strong arguments against the evaluation of educational learning in relation to predefined and supposedly 'proper' scientific language. Arguably, this has constituted one of the backbones of edusemiotics, in general. We consider that bridging this particularly Peircean line of educational research with the multimodality perspective on education will prove a fertile way of developing semiotic theory. In light of the recent iconic turn in the humanities and social sciences (Boehm and Mitchell 2009) and the digitalization of educational practice, as well as of society in general, this semiotic approach, detached from language-centrism and psychologism, has a good chance at becoming a major organizing theory for education.

GREIMASSIAN/STRUCTURALIST INFLUENCES

The most developed educational theory drawing on Greimas as a major influence is that of Pikkarainen, developed over a number of years and summarized in Chapters 13–15 of Stables, Olteanu, Nöth, Pesce and Pikkarainen 2018. Pikkarainen's 'action theoretical semiotics' (2018: 191) focuses on learning as changes in competences of the subject. Drawing particularly on Greimas and Courtes (1982), meaning is construed as the main concern of semiotics, and the 'meaning effect […] is the effect of the discourse to the action of the subject' (Pikkarainen 2018: 192). Actions comprise events and result from interactions between the subject and its environment. Consequently, communication is 'action which causes (intentionally or not) meaning effects' (Pikkarainen 2018: 195).

Pikkarainen argues that approaches to learning based on conditioning and habit do not do enough to explain the particular actions of an individual. For this, it is helpful to invoke the Greimassian concept of competence (the relevance of which, for the development of a semiotic concept of competence, we also mentioned in Olteanu and Stables 2018: 425), defined as 'a special property of the subject which makes it possible for it to act in the way it does' (Pikkarainen 2018: 195; drawing on Greimas and Courtes 1982: 44–6). In effect, a competence is a disposition to act in a certain way. Competences can be descriptive (I can ride a bicycle, for example) or modal: competences of 'want, can, know (how) and must' (Pikkarainen 2018: 197). Pikkarainen continues: 'In every action, it is assumed that there must be functioning in the subject a total competence which is the descriptive competence modalised by all these modal competences' (2018: 197).

Pikkarainen notes that a certain paradox emerges from this theory. In order to learn a new competence, the actor must do something different from merely habitual actions: to some degree, every new competence is learnt by doing something else. This challenge to established models of teaching and learning suggests a view of teaching as (careful) identity disruption.

Further developing his argument, Pikkarainen defines a 'causal event' as 'an encounter between objects so that their properties reciprocally cause them to manifest some qualities (and, as a consequence, possibly some dispositions change also)' (2018: 204). For example, the dispositions of the solubility of salt and the solubility of water cause salt to dissolve in the context of water. This insight has important implications for *inter alia* medical science as well as education. The human organism has a tendency to homeostasis and will adapt through reorganization as best it can in response to challenging circumstances. In the context of education, this puts the emphasis on teachers and the curriculum to offer challenges significant enough to prompt reorganization but not so extreme as to simply destroy the ever-shifting integrity of self.

Pikkarainen situates his action theoretical semiotics within the broader tradition of *Bildung*. In this spirit, the question of which competences should be developed always has a social and cultural dimension so calls for responsibility on the part of the both teacher and student. This leads him to conclude with suggesting a principle that seems to bridge the Kantian and the pragmatic: 'act always so that the wanted consequences and unwanted side effects of your doings help as much as possible and harm as little as possible the actions of other acting subjects' (2018: 225).

LATEST ISSUES OF CONCERN, AND THE CURRENT 'BIG QUESTIONS'

Edusemiotic theory presents a number of significant challenges to established policies and practices in formal education. As indicated above, these relate to:

1. A semiosic conception of being as becoming,
2. An avoidance of strong mind-body dualism,
3. The nature of learning in general, and
4. The particular role of literacy in learning (and literacy's correlates: literature, text, reading and writing, and multimodal expression).

These concerns relate to education generally. In addition, there are many issues relating to the teaching and learning of particular subjects: that is, issues in science education, mathematics education and so on, though it is beyond the scope of this chapter to offer an extensive account of work in these particular sub-fields.

Being as becoming: Implications for policy and practice

Accountability in education is a double-edged sword. Of course, both policymakers and the public expect resources to be used efficiently. This is generally taken to require performative markers, or performance indicators, as they are more commonly known. Measurable and comparable outcomes include examination results and more complex measures of 'value-addedness', for instance tracking students' progress in relation to supposedly objective measures of intelligence. From outcomes flow benchmarks, targets and a whole panoply of monitoring and surveillance techniques.

Lyotard effectively argued (e.g. Lyotard 1984) that reliance on crudely performative measures is the inevitable outcome of postmodern proliferation and dismantling of value systems or 'grand narratives': that is, the less we can agree on the ends and means of education, the more we reduce our conception of it to a series of input-output mechanisms.

This way of thinking is also strongly essentialist. It assumes a high level of stability and predictability within the human organism (both student and teacher), the subject matter and the effective means of 'delivering' it. It assumes that the teacher, a reliable, stable individual, 'delivers' content, which itself is unarguable, fixed and reliable, by accepted means, to the student, who is a person whose individuality can be satisfactorily accounted for according to accepted psychological methods and structural social analysis. We argue, on the other hand, that both teacher and student are works-in-progress, that content knowledge is always context dependent and open to interpretation, and that what works in teaching is extremely varied and hard to predict or police. The differences between the essentialist/substantivist and semiotic views of the teaching process can be summarized as follows.

In traditional educational practice, the 'sign' (word, symbol, number and so on) relates to either a material entity, a conceptual entity or a conceptual entity implying certain material entities. It has reality in and of itself, though it may depend on other entities for its utility. It can therefore be understood or misunderstood. Meanwhile, that which is to be learnt has considerable stability and enduring value and can be learnt and taught about more or less in isolation. On this account, both student and teacher are substantive entities, can be understood primarily as persons in their own right, and can both be understood and misunderstood, and understand or misunderstand that which is to be learnt.

From a semiotic perspective, teaching and learning can be regarded as much more fully relational, on a number of levels. On this account, the sign only makes sense in relation to its spatiotemporal context. It has no firm reality in itself other than experienced. It can therefore never be fully understood nor misunderstood. (The student's context can never be exactly the same as the teacher's, for example.) That which is to be learnt therefore gains its salience from its context, is always open to interpretation, and can never be taught or learnt in isolation. (Even if teachers think they are doing this, students will associate what they hear with their own experience.) Furthermore, both teacher and student as persons are in transition, are themselves relational, and can never have either full understanding or no understanding of that which is to be learnt (for a detailed treatment of this distinction see et al. 2018).

To move educational policy, and the practice that derives from it, from the dominant first approach to the radically semiotic second is an extremely challenging task. The present authors, among others, have discussed these ideas with people of influence in education, but there is a huge gap between sympathetic acknowledgement of the validity of the argument and serious policy change in response to it. The argument can come over to policymakers as support for a return to a somewhat anarchic, radically child-centred approach they associate with a romanticized, unaccountable and above all inefficient past.

The semiotic approach is not, however, child centred in the Romantic sense, nor is it content or teacher centred, for all of these concepts are understood as being in constant flux. Rather, it is a process approach that offers infinite possibilities for progress rather than constrained improvement of standardized output measures. It is an approach to education that is vastly more promising than that of reductive performativity, an approach that prioritizes endless development, with the unpredictability of outcomes that this implies.

Real change in a social policy field such as education is always likely to prove slow. However, the more policymakers and teachers grow to see learning as semiosis rather than as memorization or mechanical skill development, the more they will modify their criteria for success, at the very least by looking beyond the narrow measures of school effectiveness that have dominated the policy landscape of many countries since the new managerialism of the 1980s.

Avoiding strong mind-body dualism

Notwithstanding the influence of Dewey, most formal education relies on young people putting their bodies to sleep, as it were, while they sit quietly at tables and use their (disembodied) minds. The hands (writing, mainly) and the eyes have important roles to play, but in general 'learning' is deemed to require the purely cerebral functions of remembering and understanding.

However, these are not purely cerebral functions. No avowedly mental function can be carried out other than through the mechanisms (as we tend to refer to them) of the body. It is through the body that we sense and through electrical impulses and pathways in the physical brain that we think and remember. Both our interpretations of new events and our memories are affected by the habits of response that we have previously developed. In broad terms, outcomes result from habits encountering new contexts, so that social and individual change is the result of semiotic responses continually modified by signs appearing in new combinations. This view is implicit in Peirce's semiotics, according to which, as Fabbrichesi explains (2020: 341), interpretation 'is no merely intellectual or processual process, but finds its explication in the emergence of a habit understood as a disposition to respond, resolution to act, or tendency toward a reiterated behaviour'. A new encounter calls forth a response by which we seek, largely unconsciously, resonances between the new context and previous responses and select from our repertoires of responses what seems most appropriate to the new situation; thus our responses evolve over time. In general, predictability reinforces habitual responses while problematic situations can modify them – and these responses do not manifest simply as thoughts and emotions but in bodily ways that can be described biochemically (Stables et al. 2018).

A century after Dewey, it is both interesting and frustrating that the simple acknowledgment of the inseparability of mind from body has not been more comprehensively enshrined in education. There have been sporadic movements, such as those towards 'active' and 'discovery' learning, yet somehow the system has tended to retain its emphasis on studying while sitting still, perhaps in part because it makes management of students easier and reduces certain risks. Similarly, despite a wealth of literature on child-centred approaches, education has not moved comprehensively towards an acknowledgement that students will respond to new stimuli in the context of their prior experiences, in this case partly because of the performative criteria by which teachers and schools are judged, as discussed above.

There is, therefore, vast potential for more interplay between edusemiotics and biosemiotics (Campbell 2018a) in studying how the human organism changes and responds to change, along the lines of the contributions to a special issue of *Sign System Studies* on the relationship between the psychological concept of learning and the biological concept of adaptation (Campbell 2018b; Kull 2018; Olteanu and Stables 2018; Pelkey 2018; Pikkarainen 2018; Tredinnick-Rowe 2018). Reminiscent of the discussions on learning in edusemiotics in general, Hoffmeyer (2018) has pointed out that the biosemiotic construal of knowledge as something bodily implies that to understand any piece of information, we unavoidably (re-)contextualize it. The stress on learning as a situated modelling process should be pursued in the future, at the overlap of biosemiotics and edusemiotics. Other early explorations in this area include Olteanu's discussion of the importance of skin (Olteanu in Stables et al. 2017), as an instrumental concept for a biosemiotic construal of the body (Hoffmeyer 2006).

The nature of learning in general

All these debates bear on the debate around the concept of learning in general. Traditionally, learning theory has bifurcated between behaviourist and cognitivist approaches, as alluded to above. Both these traditions carry an implicit Cartesian legacy: according to behaviourism, 'mind' really has nothing to do with the matter, while 'body' has no role in cognitivist accounts of learning. Dewey argued against the limitations of this position as early as 1896 in his paper *The Reflex Arc Concept in Psychology* (Dewey 1896), showing that a stimulus is a response and *vice-versa,* and went on to develop a conative theory of learning grounded in the overall attitude (physical as well as mental) of the learner (e.g. Dewey 1916).

Dewey marks a development in pragmatism which, like all such developments, owes a great deal to Peirce's pragmaticism, though Peirce avoided discussion of semiosis in terms of personal agency so did not directly address issues relating to the individual psychology of the student.

The volume *Semiotic Theory of Learning* (Stables et al. 2018) comprises a range of perspectives on learning from a semiotic, as opposed to a standard psychological or sociological perspective. All such perspectives share a disavowal of inflexible definitions of learning that effectively evaluate education on the grounds of the pre-specified skills and content knowledge that students seem to possess under standardized testing conditions. Not only is learning not the be-all and end-all of education (see Biesta 2006, who argues that democracy should be a higher priority for education than mere learning); it is also not ultimately possible for an observer or evaluator to assess accurately what someone has learnt (indeed, one may only be partly conscious of this oneself), nor is it valid to assess education purely on measures of what students (appear to) have learnt.

One radical perspective is that learning is no more or less than a retrospective judgement on events that prove to have some significance in terms of affecting an individual's life course (Stables 2005). On this account, learning is not something that simply 'happens': like making a decision, it is something that is regarded as having happened in retrospect ('I have made a decision'; 'I learnt something today'). Furthermore, learning is not always pleasant nor evidently positive, and can be highly disruptive. One research agenda that is as yet little developed is that of how to teach in such a way that teaching embraces identity disruption whilst motivating students. In general we may say that on this account of learning as deferred, the emphasis in educational practice shifts from either learner-centredness, grounded in psychological stage theories, or content-centredness, grounded in memorization and simple skill development, towards process: that is, good teaching involves awareness of students' dispositions and experience in order to devise challenging activities for them that aim to disrupt assumptions to some extent while not simply quashing motivation and commitment.

Literacies

'Literacy' is now too narrow a term, while 'semiosy' may be too broad an umbrella concept to have obvious pedagogical implications. With the expansion of media and forms of literacy beyond print, the term 'literacy' has been applied with almost random imprecision to a vast range of areas from 'emotional literacy' to 'computer literacy' to 'environmental literacy', in each case referring in a general way to the ability to understand what is going on and act in relation to it to some extent. Of course, in some cases these collocated forms of literacy have been subject to rigorous development and debate. However, 'literacy' itself has been spread so thinly across this debate as to almost lose any specific meaning that might have been attached to it. Meanwhile, all action is semiosic, so 'semiosy' would refer to all knowledge, skills and understanding without differentiation.

Clearly education can no longer ground itself almost entirely in print literacy, but at the same time, referring to all skills and knowledge as forms of literacy diverts us from the particular educational challenges associated with the areas into which print literacy has spread and developed, particularly with respect to new digital technologies. A growing body of work in semiotics, usually drawing on Peirce, has therefore begun to devote itself to such issues, infiltrating under the broad heading of the 'digital humanities' (Ciula and Marras 2016, 2019; Ciula and Eide 2017). Most of this work does not address educational issues but it opens yet unexplored research avenues for media and digital literacy, where semiotics already is an acknowledged distinctive approach (Gaines 2010; Mills 2016; O'Halloran et al. 2017; Campbell et al. 2021).

Future research in this area could usefully focus on how the parameters of literacy can be redrawn without the term becoming a catch-all. In the contemporary world, how should we understand literacy as a subset of education, given that education is all essentially semiosic? This is one educational area in which philosophical clarity could usefully inform edusemiotics. Empirical work will likely continue into how technologies impact on modelling. This work is important for the future of education and deserves wider dissemination in specifically education circles.

CONCLUSION

Summing up, we have argued that the main starting point for a semiotics of learning and education consists in the reconsideration of essentialism in learning and education and its implied dualism. While the body of semiotic approaches to education is as heterogeneous as the spectrum of semiotic theories, we observed a distinction in literature, however generalized, between a direct concern for theoretical and philosophical questions stemming from joining semiotics and educational theory and the application of various, specific semiotic perspectives to educational problems. Recent semiotic approaches to learning and education converge on a notion of learning as embodied. These are intrinsic to a view on knowledge as subjective but that does not fall into (hard) epistemological relativism. From this perspective learning is an interpretative process.

Eschewing strong mind-body dualism means also eschewing notions of meaning that polarize form and content. That everything is relational and in process implies that a theory of learning must avoid the dichotomy of stimulus and response. Rather, learning is environmental and the environment is constructed by knowing subjects, according to affordances between form and content (van Leeuwen 2005). Affordances are linked to embodiment, experiential situatedness and the semiotic history of the knowing subject.

Another dualism that semiotics can resolve for learning and educational theory is that between natural environment and technological medium. Collapsing this dichotomy has consequences for the notion of literacy and, consequently, learning and education. As such, learning is always medial. Because literacy has generally been understood as consisting in medium-specific competences, by adopting the media ecology perspective of studying media as environments (Scolari 2012), semiotics offers an insightful view on learning as dependent on medial affordances.

NOTE

1 Note the inclusion of Cary Campbell in both groups.

REFERENCES

Académie Française ([1635, 1752, 1816] 1995), *Status et règlements (Statutes and Reglementations)*. http://www.academie-francaise.fr/sites/academie-francaise.fr/files/statuts_af_0.pdf.

Anderson, B. ([1983] 2006), *Imagined Communities: Reflections on the Origin and Spread of Nationalism*, New York: Verso.

Augustine, O. H. ([397–426] 1997), *On Christian Teaching (De Doctrina Christiana)*, trans. R. P. H. Green. Oxford: Oxford University Press.

Bakhtin, M. M. ([1963] 1984), *Problems of Dostoevsky's Poetics*, Minneapolis, London: University of Minnesota Press.

Bergman, M. (2013), 'Fields of Rhetoric: Inquiry, Communication, and Learning', *Educational Philosophy and Theory*, 45 (5): 737–54.

Bezemer, J. and G. Kress (2008), 'Writing in Multimodal Texts: A Social Semiotic Account of Designs for Learning', *Written Communication*, 25 (2): 166–95.

Biesta, G. (2006), *Beyond Learning: Democratic Education for a Human Future*, New York: Routledge.

Brandt, P. A. (2003), 'Towards a Cognitive Semiotics', *Recherches en communication*, 19 (19): 21–34.

Brandt, P. A. (2011), 'What Is Cognitive Semiotics? A New Paradigm in the Study of Meaning', *Signata Annales des sémiotiques/Annals of Semiotics*, 2: 49–60.

Bruner, J. S. (1960), *The Process of Education*, Cambridge: Harvard University Press.

Boehm, G. and W. J. T. Mitchell (2009), 'Pictorial versus Iconic Turn: Two Letters', *Culture, Theory and Critique*, 50 (2–3): 103–21.

Campbell, C. (2016), 'Indexical Ways of Knowing: An Inquiry into the Indexical Sign and How to Educate for Novelty', *Philosophical Inquiry in Education*, 24 (1): 15–36.

Campbell, C. (2018a), 'Returning "Learning" to Education: Toward an Ecological Conception of Learning and Teaching', *Sign Systems Studies*, 48 (4): 538–68.

Campbell, C. (2018b), 'Educating Semiosis: Foundational Concepts for an Ecological Edusemiotics', *Studies in Philosophy and Education*, 38 (3): 373–87.

Campbell, C., N. Lackovic and A. Olteanu (2021), 'A "Strong" Approach to Sustainability Literacy: Embodied Ecology and Media', *Philosophies*, 6 (1.14): 1–20.

Ciula, A. and C. Marras (2016), 'Circling around Text and Language: Towards "Pragmatic Modelling" in Digital Humanities', *Digital Humanities Quarterly*, 10 (3): 17–29.

Ciula, A. and C. Marras (2019), 'Exploring a Semiotic Conceptualisation of Modelling in Digital Humanities Practices', in A. Olteanu, A. Stables and D. Borțun (eds), *Meanings & Co.: The Interdisciplinarity of Communication, Semiotics and Multimodality*, 33–52, Cham: Springer.

Ciula, A. and Ø. Eide (2017), 'Modelling in Digital Humanities: Signs in Context', *Digital Scholarship in the Humanities*, 32 (1): i33–i46.

Cobley, P. (2017), 'What the Humanities Are for – a Semiotic Perspective', in K. Bankov and P. Cobley (eds), *Semiotics and Its Masters: Volume 1*, 3–23, Berlin: De Gruyter Mouton.

Cobley, P. (2020), 'Peirce in Contemporary Semiotics', in T. Jappy (ed.), *The Bloomsbury Companion to Contemporary Peircean Semiotics*, 31–72, London: Bloomsbury.

Colapietro, V. (1989), *Peirce's Approach to the Self: A Semiotic Perspective on Human Subjectivity*, New York: State University of New York Press.

Colapietro, V. (2013), 'Neglected Facets of Peirce's "Speculative" Rhetoric', *Educational Philosophy and Theory*, 45 (5): 712–36.

Cunningham, D. (1987), 'Outline of an Education Semiotic', *The American Journal of Semiotics*, 5 (2): 201–16.

Cunningham, D. (1992), 'Beyond Educational Psychology: Steps toward an Educational Semiotic', *Educational Psychology Review*, 4 (2): 165–94.

Danesi, M. (2000), *Semiotics in Language Education*, Berlin: de Gruyter Mouton.

Dearden, R. F., P. Hirst and R. S. Peters, eds (1972), *Education and the Development of Reason*, London: Routledge & Kegan Paul.

Deely, J. (2001), *Four Ages of Understanding: The First Postmodern Survey of Philosophy from Ancient Times to the Turn of the Twenty-first Century*, Toronto: University of Toronto Press.

Dewey, J. (1896), 'The Reflex Arc Concept in Psychology', *Psychological Review*, 3: 357–70.

Dewey, J. (1916), *Democracy and Education*, New York: The Macmillan Company.

Fabbrichesi, R. (2020), 'From Gestures to Habits: A Link between Semiotics and Pragmatism', in T. Jappy (ed.), *The Bloomsbury Companion to Contemporary Peircean Semiotics*, 339–58, London and New York: Bloomsbury.

Gaines, E. (2010), *Media Literacy and Semiotics*, New York: Palgrave Macmillan.

Gibson, J. (1979), *The Ecological Approach to Visual Perception*, Boston: Houghton Mifflin.

Gough, S. and A. Stables (2012), 'Interpretation as Adaptation Education for Survival in Uncertain Times', *Curriculum Inquiry*, 42 (3): 368–85.

Gould, S. J. and E. S. Vrba (1982), 'Exaptation – A Missing Term in the Science of Form', *Paleobiology*, 8 (1): 4–15.

Greimas, A. J. and J. Courtes (1982), *Semiotics and Language: An Analytical Dictionary*, Bloomington: Indiana University Press.

Halliday, M. A. K. and J. J. Webster, eds (2009), *Continuum Companion to Systemic Functional Linguistics*, New York: Continuum.

Hobbes, T. ([1651] 1909), *Leviathan*, London: Oxford University Press.

Hoffmeyer, J. (2006), 'Semiotic Scaffolding of Living Systems', in M. Barbieri (ed.), *Introduction to Biosemiotics: The New Biological Synthesis*, 149–66, Dordrecht: Springer.

Hoffmeyer, J. (2008), 'The Biosemiotic Body', *Biosemiotics*, 1: 169–90.

Hoffmeyer, J. (2018), 'Knowledge Is Never Just There', *Biosemiotics*, 11 (1): 1–5.

Hoffmeyer, J. and F. Stjernfelt (2016), 'The Great Chain of Semiosis: Investigating the Steps in the Evolution of Semiotic Competence', *Biosemiotics*, 9: 7–29.

Humboldt, W. von ([1836] 1999), *On Language: On the Diversity of Human Language Construction and Its Influence on the Mental Development of the Human Species*, ed. M. Losonsky, trans. P. Heath, Cambridge: Cambridge University Press.

Innis, Robert E. (2009) 'My Way through Signs', in P. Bundgaard and F. Stjernfelt (eds), *Signs and Meaning: 5 Questions*, 87–99, New York: Automatic Press/VI.

Jewitt, C., J. Bezemer and K. O'Halloran (2016), *Introducing Multimodality*, London: Routledge.

Joyce, H. de Silva and S. Feez, eds (2018), *Multimodality across Classrooms: Learning about and through Different Modalities*, New York: Routledge.

Kress, G. (2003), *Literacy in the New Media Age*, London: Routledge.

Kress, G. and T. van Leeuwen (2001), *Multimodal Discourse: The Modes and Media of Contemporary Communication*, London: Arnold.

Kukkola, J. and E. Pikkarainen (2016), 'Edusemiotics of Meaningful Learning Experience: Revisiting Kant's Pedagogical Paradox and Greimas' Semiotic Square', *Semiotica*, 212: 199–217.

Kull, K. (2018), 'Choosing and Learning: Semiosis Means Choice', *Sign Systems Studies*, 48 (4): 452–66.
Kull, K. (2019), 'Jakob von Uexküll and the Study of Primary Meaning-making', in F. Michellini and K. Köchy (eds), *Jakob von Uexküll and Philosophy*, 220–37, London: Routledge.
Lacković, N. (2018), 'Analysing Videos in Educational Research: An "Inquiry Graphics" Approach for Multimodal, Peircean Semiotic Coding of Video Data', *Video Journal of Education and Pedagogy*, 3 (6): 1–23.
Lacković, N. (2019), 'Re-imagining Graduate Employability (GE) Paradigm or Finding a New One? An Integrated Three-layered Approach towards Greater Social and Techno-ecological Relatedness of Graduates' Employment Futures', in M. A. Peters, P. Jandrić and A. J. Means (eds), *Education and Technological Unemployment*, 193–212, Singapore: Springer.
Lähteenmäki, M. (2010), 'Heteroglossia and Voice: Conceptualizing Linguistic Diversity from a Bakhtinian Perspective', in M. Lähteenmäki and M. Vanhala-Aniszewski (eds.), *Language Ideologies in Transition: Multilingualism in Russia and Finland*, 17–34, Frankfurt am Main: Peter Lang.
Lakoff, G. and M. Johnson (1999), *Philosophy in the Flesh: The Embodied Mind and Its Challenge to Western thought*, New York: Basic Books.
Lankshear, C. and M. Knobel (2003), *New Literacies: Changing Knowledge and Classroom Learning*, Buckingham: Open University Press.
Leeuwen, T. van (2005), *Introducing Social Semiotics*, London: Routledge.
Lemke, J. L. (1987), 'Social Semiotics and Science Education', *The American Journal of Semiotics*, 5 (2): 217–32.
Lizska, J. (2013), 'Charles Peirce's Rhetoric and the Pedagogy of Active Learning', *Educational Philosohy and Theory*, 45 (7): 781–8.
Locke, J. ([1693] 1889), *Some thoughts Concerning Education*, London: C. J. Clay and Sons, Cambridge University Press Warehouse.
Lyotard, J. F. (1984), *The Postmodern Condition: A Report on knowledge*, trans. G. Bennington and B. Massumi, Minneapolis: University of Minneapolis Press.
MacLarnon, A. (2012), 'The Anatomical and Physiological Basis of Human Speech Production: Adaptations and Exaptations', in K. R. Gibson and M. Tallerman (eds), *The Oxford Handbook of Language Evolution*, 224–35, Oxford: Oxford University Press.
Marmo, C. (2010), *La semiotica del XIII secolo: tra arti liberali e teologia* [*The Semiotics of the Thirteenth Century: In-between Liberal Arts and Theology*], Milan: Bompiani.
McLuhan, M. ([1970] 1995), 'Culture Is Our Business', in E. McLuhan and F. Zigrone (eds), *The Essential McLuhan*, 35–59, London: Routledge.
Midtgarden, T. (2013), 'On the Prospects of a Semiotic Theory of Learning', *Educational Philosophy and Theory*, 37 (2): 239–52.
Mills, K. A. (2010), 'A Review of the "Digital Turn" in the New Literacy Studies', *Review of Educational Research*, 80 (2): 246–71.
Mills, K. A. (2016), *Literacy Theories of the Digital Age: Social, Critical, Multimodal, Spatial Material and Sensory Lenses*, Bristol: Multilingual Matters.
Milyakina, A. (2018), 'Rethinking Literary Education in the Digital Age', *Sign Systems Studies*, 46 (4): 569–89.
Mittelberg, I. (2002), 'The Visual Memory of Grammar: Iconographical and Metaphorical Insights', *Metaphorik*, 2: 69–88.
Nöth, W. (2014), 'The Semiotics of Learning New Words', *Journal of Philosophy of Education*, 48 (3): 446–56.

O'Halloran, K. L. (2011), 'The Semantic Hyperspace: Accumulating Mathematical Knowledge across Semiotic Resources and Modalities', in C. France and K. Maton (eds), *Disciplinarity: Functional Linguistic and Sociological Perspectives*, 217–36, London, New York: Continuum.

O'Halloran, K. L., S. Tan and K. L. E. Marissa (2017), 'Multimodal Analysis for Critical Thinking', *Learning, Media and Technology*, 42 (2): 147–70.

Ojamaa, M., P. Torop, A. Fadeev, A. Milyakina, T. Pilipovec, and M. Rickberg (2019), 'Culture as Education: From Transmediality to Transdisciplinary Pedagogy', *Sign Systems Studies*, 47 (1/2): 152–76.

Olteanu, A. (2014), 'The Semiosic Evolution of Education', *Journal of Philosophy of Education*, 48 (3): 457–73.

Olteanu, A. (2015), *Philosophy of Education in the Semiotics of Charles Peirce: A Cosmology of Learning and Loving*, Oxford: Peter Lang.

Olteanu, A. (2018), 'Semiotics as a Proposal for a Numanistic Educational Programme', in A. Oana and A. Olteanu (eds), *Readings in Numanities*, 3–17, Cham: Springer.

Olteanu, A. and A. Stables (2018), 'Learning and Adaptation from a Semiotic Perspective', *Sign Systems Studies*, 46 (4): 409–34.

Olteanu, A. and C. Campbell (2018), 'A Short Introduction to Edusemiotics', *Chinese System Studies*, 14 (2): 245–60.

Olteanu, A. and C. Campbell (2019), 'Education, Signs and the History of Ideas: An Interview with Alin Olteanu', *Chinese Semiotic Studies*, 15 (2): 275–88.

Olteanu, A., M. Kambouri, and A. Stables (2016), 'Predicating from an Early Age: Edusemiotics and the Potential of Children's Preconceptions', *Studies in Philosophy of Education*, 35 (6): 621–40.

Paolucci, Claudio (2020), *Cognitive Semiotics: Integrating Signs, Minds, Meaning and Cognition*, Cham: Springer.

Peirce, Charles Sanders ([1866–1913] 1931–58), *The Collected Papers of Charles Sanders Peirce*, vols. 1–6, ed. C. Hartshorne and P. Weiss, vols. 7–8, ed. A. Burks, Cambridge: Harvard University Press.

Pelkey, J. (2018), 'Emptiness and Desire in the First Rule of Logic', *Sign Systems Studies*, 46 (4): 467–90.

Pesce, S. (2013), 'From Peirce's Speculative Rhetoric to Educational Rhetoric', *Educational Philosophy and Theory*, 45 (7): 755–80.

Pesce, S. (2020), 'From Analogical to Analytical Thinking and Back: The Adaptation of Teachers' Reasoning to Complex Situations', in H. Yama and V. Salvano-Pardieu (eds), *Adapting Human Thinking and Moral Reasoning in Contemporary Society*, 223–44, Hershey: IGI-Global.

Piaget, J. ([1924] 1929), *The Child's Conception of the World*, New York and London: K. Paul, Trench, Trubner & Co.

Pikkarainen, E. (2016), 'Signs as Functions: Edusemiotic and Ontological Foundations for a Semiotic Concept of a Sign', *Semiotica*, 212: 27–44.

Pikkarainen, E. (2018), 'Adaptation, Learning, *Bildung*: Discussion with Edu- and Biosemiotics', *Sign Systems Studies*, 48 (4): 435–51.

Radford, L., G. Schubring and F. Seeger, eds (2008), *Semiotics in Mathematics Education: Epistemology, History, Classroom, and Culture*, Rotterdam, Taipei: Sense Publishers.

Rousseau, J. J. ([1762] 1911), *Émile or on Education*, trans. B. Foxley, London: Dent.

Scolari, C. A. (2012), 'Media Ecology: Exploring the Metaphor to Expand the Theory', *Communication Theory*, 22: 204–25.

Sebeok, T. (1991), *A Sign Is Just a Sign: Advances in Semiotics*, Indianapolis: Indiana University Press.
Sebeok, T. ([1994] 2001), *Signs: An Introduction to Semiotics*, Toronto: University of Toronto Press.
Seif, F. Y. (2017) 'Erotica and Semiotica: What's Love Got to Do with Edusemiotics', in I. Semetsky (ed.), *Edusemiotics – A Handbook*, 263–75, Singapore: Springer.
Semetsky, I., ed. (2010), *Semiotics, Education, Experience*, Rotterdam: Sense Publishers.
Semetsky, I., ed. (2017), *Edusemiotics – A Handbook*, Singapore: Springer.
Stables, A. (2005), *Living and Learning as Semiotic Engagement: A New Theory of Education*, Lewiston: Edwin Mellen Press.
Stables, A. (2012), *Be(com)ing Human: Semiosis and the Myth of Reason*, Rotterdam: Sense.
Stables, A., ed. (2017), *Education and Epistemology*, Special Issue of *Education Sciences*, 7 (2).
Stables, A. (2019), *New Localism: Living in the Here and Now*, Dordrecht: Springer.
Stables, A. (2020), 'Environmental Ethics and Ontologies: Humanist or Posthumanist? The Case for Constrained Pluralism', *Journal of Philosophy of Education*, 54 (4): 888–99.
Stables, A. and I. Semetsky (2015), *Edusemiotics: Semiotic Philosophy as Educational Foundation*, New York: Routledge.
Stables, A., W. Nöth, A. Olteanu, S. Pesce and E. Pikkarainen (2018), *Semiotic Learning Theory: New Perspectives in the Philosophy of Education*, New York: Routledge.
Stjernfelt, F. (2006), 'The Semiotic Body. A Semiotic Concept of Embodiment?', in W. Nöth (ed.), *Semiotic Bodies, Aesthetic Embodiments and Cyberbodies*, 13–48, Kassel: Kassel University Press.
Stjernfelt, F. (2014), *Natural Propositions: The Actuality of Peirce's Doctrine of Dicisigns*, Boston: Docent Press.
Stjernfelt, F. (2015), 'Iconicity of Logic – and the Roots of the "Iconicity" Concept', in M. K. Hiraga, W. J. Herlofsky, K. Shinohara and K. Akita (eds), *Iconicity: East meets West*, 35–53, Amsterdam: John Benjamins.
Strand, T. (2005), 'Peirce on Education: Nurturing the First Rule of Reason', *Studies in Philosophy and Education*, 24 (3–4): 309–16.
Strand, T. (2014a), 'Peirce's Rhetorical Turn: Conceptualizing Education as Semiosis', *Educational Philosophy and Theory*, 45 (7): 789–803.
Strand, T. (2014b), '"Experience Is Our Great and Only Teacher": A Peircean Reading of Wim Wenders' Wings of Desire', *Journal of Philosophy of Education*, 48 (3): 433–45.
Strand, T. and C. W. Legg (2019), 'Peirce and Education, an Overview', in M. Peters (ed.), *Encyclopedia of Educational Philosophy and Theory*, 1–6, Singapore: Springer.
Tredinnick-Rowe, J. (2018), 'Can Semiotics Be Used to Drive Paradigm Changes in Medical Education', *Sign Systems Studies*, 48 (4): 491–516.
Unsworth, L., ed. (2008), *Multimodal Semiotics: Functional Analysis in Contexts of Education*, New York: Continuum.
Vygotsky, L. ([1930–66] 1978), *Mind in Society*, Cambridge, MA: Harvard University Press.

CHAPTER EIGHT

Semiotics in Picture and Image Studies

SARA LENNINGER AND GÖRAN SONESSON

According to a perfunctory scenario, pictures were used during earlier millennia mainly to maintain contact with gods and other spiritual creatures; then, in early modern times, they were predominantly treated as objects of art, tailored to offer pleasure to the viewer; and finally, perhaps starting with early broadsheets and reaching an apogee in our time, their principal employment consists in conveying news and, more particularly, inducements to buy certain products. If so, anthropology is marginally involved with the first kinds of uses; art history was created to take care of the second one; while marketing, and largely also more recent domains such as image and visual studies, was designed to analyse the third type of usage. These are all legitimate ways of scrutinizing pictures, but they lack the kind of generalizing approach which semiotics can offer.

In reality, pictures have always been produced and used in many ways, and for many different purposes that affect how they are understood. Since the early eighties of the last century, some art historians, of which the most well-known is no doubt W. J. T. Mitchell (1986; 2015), and even some historians of literature, have taken an increasing interest in other uses of pictures than those connected to the arts, particularly those intervening in the modern media. The result of this 'pictorial turn', to use Mitchell's term, has gone under different labels, such as image theory, visual studies and visual culture. Like in traditional art history, the epistemological viewpoint remains that of the single picture or the pictorial genres, though many exponents make use of a postmodernist jargon. The German *Bildwissenschaft* seems to be very different, because it embraces all conceivable disciplinary approaches to the pictorial artefact. Thus, in the anthology edited by Klaus Sachs-Hombach and Jörg Schirra (2013), there are contributions written by anthropologists, archaeologists, art historians, folklorists, historians, linguists, philosophers, psychologists, students of media, and even a semiotician (Göran Sonesson). In fact, Sachs-Hombach's (2003) own work is clearly meant as a scholarly synthesis of all these scholarly approaches to the picture artefact. In this sense, *Bildwissenschaft* can hardly be distinguished from contemporary pictorial semiotics, as opposed to the much narrower structuralist variant.

Pictorial semiotics is the science of all pictures and all picture types. As a part of general semiotics, its primary aim is to investigate how pictures differ from other signs and other meanings, and in what ways they are similar to them. At the same time, however, it is involved with explaining the ways in which signs which are pictures may differ from each other. Pictorial semiotics is not uninterested in pictures classified as art, but it does in no way attribute any privilege to them: art is simply one of several categories of pictures defined by the social use to which they a commonly put. Instead, we are involved with pictures as the result of a particular cognitive operation, which is, more specifically, a semiotic operation, a subclass which also includes such things as verbal language, gestures, and much more. It should be added, as a caveat, that this also applies *mutatis mutandis* to religious pictures, publicity pictures, and all other kinds of pictures.

After first exploring the nature of pictorial semiotics, as it can be derived from the specificity of semiotics generally, we will have a summary look at its history, divided into approaches which start out from individual pictures, those that rely on more or less closely examined intuitions of the picture user, and the mostly more recent attempts to design an experimental approach. We will consider some current issues, which have resulted from the semiotic approach: the different natures of the pictorial and plastic layers of pictures, the paradoxical nature of pictures which do not depict, and the relation to the wider domain of visual meaning-making. We will then be concerned with some domains of research within pictorial semiotics which deserve to be prioritized in the near future: the categories into which pictures may be divided using different criteria; the close study of such categories, exemplified by the case of photography, where semioticians have been particularly active; the part played by pictures in contemporary society, beyond the easy stereotype of 'the picture society'; and the possible origin of the picture as a semiotic resource among others in early human society.[1]

PICTORIAL SEMIOTICS AS A PARTICULAR DOMAIN OF STUDY

Since the middle of the last century, when semiotics became fashionable anew, there have been many ways to conceive of pictorial semiotics. While we are referring to instances of several of these approaches in the next section, we will, in the rest of the chapter, opt for one particular interpretation, which relies on the fact that pictorial semiotics is a kind of semiotics. Peirce and Saussure may not be the sole pioneers of semiotics, and they are different on many counts, but both clearly think of semiotics as a domain of study concerned with generalities, generalizing, respectively, from philosophy and linguistics.

In line with these scholars, we will consider semiotics, for the purpose of this chapter, to be a domain of study concerned to delineate the different ways in which meaning is created, conveyed and experienced. In other words, semiotics is concerned with the different forms and conformations given to the means through which humankind and other animate beings have access to the world of our experience. It tries to emulate the workings of such operative, albeit often tacit, knowledge which underlies the behaviour constitutive of any system or resource of signification. Moreover, semiotics is devoted to these phenomena considered in their qualitative aspects rather than the quantitative ones, and it is geared to rules and regularities, instead of unique objects. It is not restricted to any single method, and it is certainly not dependant on a model taken over from linguistics, but it is a peculiarity of the approach that it tends to construct models which are then applied to the objects analysed. Since semiotics does not favour any particular method, it certainly employs quantitative methods, at least in the sense of statistics, but this should not occult the fact that the results it hopes to establish are qualitative, that is, categorical. In terms we have used elsewhere (see Sonesson 2014a), it is a *nomothetic* and *qualitative* kind of study: that is, it aims to establish general facts, but those facts, as such, are meanings rather than numbers.

Since pictorial semiotics is a particular application of semiotics, which is concerned with the kind of Lifeworld objects that are colloquially identified by the term 'picture', its goal is to establish the categories of relevance to pictorial meaning, and to formulate the rules and regularities brought to bear on these categories. Thus, the assignments of such a speciality must involve, at the very least, a demonstration of the semiotic character of pictures, as well as a study of the peculiarities which differentiate pictorial meanings from other kinds of signification, and an assessment of the ways (from some or other point of view) in which pictorial meanings are apt to differ from each other while still remaining pictorial.

Being nomothetic and qualitative, pictorial semiotics has as its principal theme a category that may be termed pictoriality, or picturehood, which is not simply the same thing as iconicity (see the chapter on iconicity). To enjoin this parallel to linguistics is not the same thing as embracing the so-called linguistic model, which consists in transposing concepts and terms derived from the (structural) study of language to the analysis of pictures. It is important to distinguish the parallelism in the goal of study, on one hand, and a difference in the terms of adequate analysis, on the other hand.

A SHORT HISTORY OF METHODS AND MODELS IN PICTORIAL SEMIOTICS[2]

Although the history of semiotics goes far back in time, at least to Greek antiquity, there doesn't seem to have been any serious attempt to consider the specific way meaning is conveyed by pictures until the middle of the last century, if we except the pioneering work on 'pictorial consciousness', around the turn of the nineteenth century, of the philosopher Edmund Husserl and those of the philosophers Richard Wollheim and Nelson Goodman, more or less contemporaneous with the first explicit attempts to develop an approach to pictorial semiotics (see the chapter 'Iconicity and semiosis' in Volume 1). Perhaps this late start was prompted by the increasing dissemination of pictures in modern society, itself dependant on the possibilities of their reproduction (see the section on 'The densification of pictures in society' below).

In the following, we will make a distinction between pictures conceived as 'texts' and as 'systems'. This terminology should not be seen as endorsing the structuralist analogy between language and pictures which these terms was used to convey at the time. A less fraught distinction might be that between tokens and types. In this short overview, we cannot address the question whether pictures can be said in any sense to be similar to language, notably in their capacity for conveying propositions. The classical view is that propositions, and thus arguments, can only be expressed in verbal form. Frederik Stjernfelt (2014) has observed that Peirce's notion of proposition, the 'dicisign', supposes that arguments can be formulated using any kind of semiotic resource, including pictures. Anthony Blair (2012: 205–23, 261–79), attending closely to the nature of pictures and language, has claimed that they are not very different from the point of view of argumentation, because in both cases, vagueness can be remedied by other means; but he goes on to claim that there are very few examples of visual arguments within the most abundant contemporary source domain of pictures, publicity. In their recent paper, Marc Champagne and Ahti-Veikko Pietarinen (2020) seem to be headed for a more classical thesis; but, in the end, they make an exception for 'moving images', which allow for the separation of the different stages of an argument. On the basis of the distinction between pre-predicative and predicative meanings, made within phenomenology by Edmund

Husserl, Sonesson (2012; 2014b) contends that there is a sense in which a propositional structure is present also in pictures, and even in perception, and thus can be realized in certain circumstances, only one of which would be the cinema. Nothing below hinges on what stand is taken on these issues.

Pictures as 'texts' or tokens

There is no escaping the mention of the Panzani advertisement as analysed by Roland Barthes (1964) as being the pioneering contribution to pictorial semiotics, although, in the end, it fails to comply with the criteria we have announced above: it is not nomothetic, in spite of using a nomothetic terminology, inherited from Saussure and Hjelmslev, not only because it is only concerned with one particular picture, but mainly because it does not offer any generalizable characterizations of these terms as applied to pictures; and it is not qualitative in the sense of establishing categories. Although Barthes uses the terms wrongly, he still may be taken to suggest two fundamental meanings in pictures which both have bearings on the special way in which pictures carry meaning. 'Denotation' (the visual labelling of the object in the picture) is clearly about the mapping between the picture and the visual world it depicts, while 'connotation', on the other hand, involves adding values to that which is depicted. Barthes fails to notice that these values may be values engaged in the lived world depicted, rather than being construed by pictorial features. As he goes on to argue that the relation between expression and content in the photograph is 'tautologous', this is, in the end, natural. But this leaves no space for 'the rhetoric of the picture', as the title of his essay reads.

Barthes' terminology is still used by many scholars, most notably by Gunter Kress and Theo van Leeuwen and their numerous followers, as well as being applied to artistic pictures by such early 'structuralists' as Louis Marin. More importantly, however, serious work on erecting a model for pictorial semiotics begun, more or less independently, as a critique of Barthes' work, in the three most creative traditions within pictorial semiotics, that of the Greimas school, the μ-group, and the Quebec school – and also independently of all but the first critique, in the work of the second author of this presentation. There is no space to elaborate here on the different points of the critique voiced by these critics. Suffice-it to say that they all clamoured for a definition of terms which was sufficiently general to constitute a model that was transposable to all kinds of pictures.

The Greimasean model preserves the structuralist heritage of binary oppositions (see Greimas and Courtés 1979–86). According to Jean-Marie Floch, all pictures can primarily be separated into two parts (the left and right part, but not necessarily divided at the middle, or else perhaps the upper or lower part, or the central and the marginal part), and sometimes one or both of these parts can be further separated into two subparts. The separation is supported by a series of binary oppositions, specified for each one of the picture parts. For instance, there may be vertical lines and dark colours in one of the parts, and the opposite in the other part. Such a division can be realized both at the so-called iconic level (in the very narrow sense of the one on which depiction takes place; see section on 'Plastic and pictorial layers of the picture') and at the plastic level, that is, the level at which any picture can be seen as a configuration of shapes and colours, or, as Floch (1984, 1986) puts it, where any picture is treated as a 'abstract' work of art. At a later stage, each of these oppositions may be put in opposition to others, forming the Greimasean Square. We may end up with continuity opposed to discontinuity, both opposed to non-discontinuity and non-continuity.

Félix Thürlemann (e.g. 1982) took the Greimasean tradition in a somewhat different direction, more interested in elementary plastic units, and later on other scholars of a Greimasean persuasion, notably Jacques Fontanille (1995), pursued the model initiated by Floch. In any of these instantiations, the Greimasean model comes much closer to being nomothetic than that of Barthes, but its generalizability is still problematic, in particular since the original division is at least not explicitly justified. The mathematical theory of catastrophes, first conceived by René Thom, inspired many members of the Greimas school, through the intermediary of Jean Petitot, who collaborated with both. This is a model used in the study of pictures, by Maria Giulia Dondero (2020), and apparently without any Greimasean connection, by Wolfgang Wildgen (2013).

The μ-group (1992) started out as a group consisting of many scholars, but, for the last decades, Jean-Marie Klinkenberg and Francis Edeline have been the sole members. Their model for a semiotically inspired renewal of classical rhetoric was first applied to language but has for a long time now concentrated on the study of pictures. Since it is rhetorical, the model is concerned to distinguish different ways in which pictures may deviate from what is taken for granted, that is, the norm. Thus, for instance, if Captain Haddock is depicted as having bottles instead of pupils in his eyes, there is a presence of bottles that is not expected in the context of eyes, and the bottle is somehow amalgamated with a human body. Or, contrary to what we would expect in the Lifeworld, one and the same figure contains parts which are normally part of a cat, and parts which are normally parts of a coffee pot (a work by Julien Key). According to this model, pictures can be analysed, on the one hand, in terms of whether they diverge from what we expect to be absent or present, and whether that element is conjoint or disjoint.

Again, this is a model which comes closer to attaining nomothetic status than that of Barthes, but its generalizability remains problematic already within pictorial semiotics, because what is unexpected is not necessarily only the presence or absence of an element, but often both at the same time; and in between conjoint and disjoint elements, there clearly are a whole series of intermediary cases. There is also a more general problem of generalizability, since the way pictorial figures are analysed by the μ-group is quite different from that of linguistic figures, without this being addressed as a possible difference between pictorial and linguistic semiosis. Moreover, as is the case with all rhetorical models, the concept of norm is fundamental for the outcome of the analyses, but, although there is a distinction between the *local norm* (established within the picture) and the *general norm* (a cultural expectation extrinsic to the picture), no clear presentation on the mechanisms of *norms* is given by the authors. To account for the notion of general norms, both a (human) ontology and a sociology seem to be required.

Fernande Saint-Martin's (1987) model is based on the forms discerned by Gestalt psychology as well as the shapes defined by mathematical topology (neighbourhood, closure, seriation, etc.). She and her followers, such as, notably, Marie Carani (1987, 1988), divide the canvas into many squares and count the figures and colour spots filling in each of the squares. She also takes note of the placement of figures in relation to the two diagonals, which can be construed on each picture. In fact, Saint-Martin's model is a series of different tools that may be applied to pictures. It gives more the impression of being a varied toolbox than a model with a specific research interest. However, all the parts of her model are clearly geared to the perceptual appearance of the pictures. It is probably no accident that the pictures analysed by her and by her followers all seem to be abstract paintings. From the point of view of contemporary semiotics, the closeness to perception is something to be appreciated in this approach, but the toolkit character of the proposal makes generalizability difficult.

Another model starts from 'the functions of language' distinguished by Michael Halliday (1985), which, in spite of the label, characterize all kinds of semiosis: they are instrumental, regulatory, interactional, personal, heuristic, imaginative and representational. These functions have not only been applied to pictures in the so-called social semiotics of Kress and Van Leeuwen (1996), but, also, in a more rigorously argued way, by Michael O'Toole (1994), whose interest is more in the direction of fine art. This explains that, in order to create a cross-classification, O'Toole combines the Hallidayan categories with some traditional art historical terms, which means that, like the latter, his categories are not apt to be applied to pictures in any systematic way.

All these approaches started out from singular pictures, or else a series of pictures by the same artist, trying to make sense of them using terms derived from generalizing sciences such as linguistics and psychology, but applying the resulting models in ways which made it hazardous to compare the proceeds of one picture analysis with another. In the jargon of the times, this consisted in studying the picture as 'text' (i.e. as a singular manifestation of the 'system').

Pictures as 'systems' or types

Another approach tried out at the time was parallel in principle to the recourse to the users' intuitions, which has always been essential to linguistics, but which was institutionalized with the grammaticality judgement of generative grammar. This could be considered as a way of approaching 'the system' behind pictures directly. At least when it is taken beyond first impressions, this *modus operandi* is similar to philosophical discourse, as it is conducted within phenomenology and, to some extent, ordinary language philosophy. In spite of such precursors as Husserl and Wollheim, there has hardly been any discussion of the specific nature of pictures from this point of view within semiotics. There has, however, been an extended discussion of iconic signs, in the sense of Charles Sanders Peirce, where the latter was, not always officially, but in practice, identified with pictures. This led to the great iconicity debate, which loomed large during the last half-century of the twentieth century (see the chapter on iconicity). It was also the fundamental approach employed in the study of the particular pictorial category of photography, in which case semiotics seems to have been able to further a deeper understanding (see the section on 'Photography as index and icon' below).

Peircean semiotics is clearly another kind of 'system approach', the application of which to pictures was pioneered by Gérard Deledalle (1976) and later pursued, notably by, Anthony Jappy (2013). The problem with this approach is the opposite of that we have found with the other approaches: the Peircean categories of semiosis are generic to such a point that, while they may tell us something about the nature of pictures, it does so while including in this categorization a great number of other phenomena. This means that, even if the classification as such is enlightening, it is unable to tell us how pictures are different from other 'sign types' falling within the same Peircean category.

Sonesson's (1989a, 1989b) approach consists less in a finished model than in a series of epistemological and methodological observations on the aforementioned models. It recognizes the limited, but real, value of structuralist models, but is based on perceptual and cognitive psychology more generally. This amounts to a rejection of the autonomy postulate, explicitly embraced at least by the Greimas school, according to which semiotics, like Saussurean linguistics, should create its models without taking into account knowledge gathered within other sciences. Insights resulting from, for instance, the cognitive sciences can be used and further verified in the application of semiotic models. The systematic implementation of this idea is cognitive semiotics. Another important point, is that a 'textual' approach which can fulfil the aims of semiotics in being nomothetic and qualitative, needs to scrutinize a representative corpus of pictures, not only a single picture, or the pictures of a particular creator, but either a numerous and varied assembly of pictures, or pictures pertaining to a particular picture category. If, as Sonesson (1988) suggested, different divisions of the pictures are put to the test, which are not necessarily only binary ones, and all the possible relations between these division blocks, in terms of graphic features, are examined, then text analysis amounts to a kind of experimentation. There can be no doubt that this is a Herculean task, which is why it has been suggested, by Reyes and Sonesson (2019), that it might better be implemented using computer algorithms. Even in that case, however, phenomenology is necessary before even elaborating the algorithms.

Experimental approaches

To the extent that the semiotics of pictures is concerned with the seams and joints of meaning-making using pictures, studies of perceivers' understanding and production of pictures should be a part of what belongs to the semiotic of pictures. In fact, the way pictures are handed, deployed and understood does not only say something about the user and the context; it also tells us something about the picture as a communicative resource. From this point of view, experimental and other empirical studies on picture perception in young children and some animals are relevant from a semiotic point of view. For the time being, most relevant studies emanate from psychology and cognitive science, and only a few are the work of semioticians. There are some exceptions, however, such as the work of Martin Krampen (1991) and his collaborators, as well as the early studies by René Lindekens (1971). Nevertheless, it is only in the last few decades that studies have been realized which applies an explicit semiotic point of view to the experimental studies.

Some studies within psychology and cognitive science have examined emergent picture understanding among young children, while others have looked at picture perception in different animals. From a semiotic point of view, these studies support the point that iconicity is fundamental in picture perception. Emphasizing semiotically informed questions on pictorial meanings, however, also serves to bring other questions on the table. These are primarily questions linked to the understanding of pictures as communicative resources and as sign expressions. After a short background on studies of infants' picture perception in cognitive and psychology studies, this section presents some early attempts to develop empirical studies within cognitive semiotics. The first studies were designed as replication of kindred studies in psychology and cognitive science although pushing the semiotic perspective. Soon, however, original studies were designed to trace specifically semiotic questions on pictorial meaning-making.

A frequently cited observation by Julian Hochberg and Virginia Brooks (1962) documents a nineteen-month-old boy's ability to identify and correctly label familiar solid objects from line drawings and photographs, without prior training on using pictures or sharing pictorial meaning. According to the researchers, the child's environment (home) was deprived of pictures, but, on the other hand, the child was used to communication games naming objects (i.e. objects that were not pictures). There were, nevertheless, a few pictures present in his surroundings: framed on the wall or stencilled on the back of his highchair; but his parents had made no attempt to comment on them. Suddenly at nineteen months, the boy began actively seeking out pictures, pointing at them and labelling them e.g. 'baby' or 'dog'. Primary iconic relations were enough for the boy to experience a visual meaning, but also to differentiate its meaning as special. One way of understanding what went on, as suggested by Lenninger (2012), is that the child recognized pictures and brought them into the labelling game he was used to playing with his parents: i.e. he brought the pictures into a communicative context on his own initiative.[3]

Later and more controlled studies support Hochberg and Brooks' observations on young children's ability to identify depicted objects, and to use pictures in label games. Preissler and Cary (2004) showed that at the age of eighteen months children can be taught new labels for unfamiliar objects on the basis of perceiving these objects in pictures. Children as young as fifteen-months have been shown to learn new labels from pictures (Ganea et al. 2008), when enhancing similarity relation between the picture and its object (i.e. photographs vs line drawings).

The ability to recognize depicted objects and to learn new labels by using pictures of unfamiliar objects is only part of what is expected from communication with pictures. Pictures are apt to show something about a real-world-situation. As noted by Judy DeLoache in a series of object retrieval tests, the ability to use pictorial information (in a given context) to find a hidden object here-and-now in the 'real world' could indicate the ability to use the picture as a sign. Interestingly, DeLoache's studies reveal that although children can perceive adequate meanings in pictures at a much earlier age, they cannot be expected to use a picture as a source of information to find a hidden toy in the real room until about two and a half years old. Children six months younger, though, found the hidden toy when given verbal information only. The object retrieval game with pictures has been replicated and altered in different ways to push back the age when children can find the toy to younger ages but the result still seems to be quite robust. Thus, for instance, Lenninger (2012) replicated DeLoache and Burn's (1994) study with some crucial alterations. First, the game was run at the children's pre-school instead of in a laboratory environment; second, the 'hidden toy' was exposed in plain view and not hidden under a cushion or in a wastebasket. Hence, if the child (guided by the pictorial information) entered the correct part of the pre-school locations, the object could be seen without searching for it. Of course, the first alteration made possible the second one, since the children could recognize a familiar environment from the pictures (and they all did). The next step, though, to use the pictorial information to find the toy at the actual place remained difficult for children younger than thirty months even after repeated trials. Thus, the (perhaps) lessened burden of running the game in a familiar environment (where adults often give children 'tasks'), and by avoiding the difficulty to 'search for' the toy, did not help the children to make use of the pictorial information in this task.

From a semiotic point of view, it is interesting to compare the use of pictures with alternative primary iconic resources, such as replicas and film. Although pictures did not help the children to find the object until the age of two and a half years, information from still pictures nevertheless seem to help the children better than the same game played with three-dimensional replicas showing the hiding places. Hence, in this game, the pictorial information was 'easier' to make out than that pertaining to three-dimensional objects (i.e. realistic mini-models of the room and its furniture). When information was given through video, however, children perform in the same way as when using pictures; they can be expected to find the hidden toy from about the age of two and a half years old, but not at the age of two. Moreover, also in a less complex object-choice game – in which the children were given only three options (three different-looking boxes) to choose from in order to find a hidden object, the children indicated difficulties to use pictorial information. The game was designed to study precursors to sign use by looking at children's understanding of helpful 'others', who indicated the correct box either by pointing at it, putting a mark on it (a sticky note), or showing a picture or a three-dimensional replica of the correct choice. This study (Zlatev et al. 2013), which was an extended and semiotically informed version of the experimental paradigm of Tomasello, Call and Gluckman (1997), demonstrated that iconic meanings, as in the picture and the replica (as opposed to indexical ones), could only be mastered by children at the age of two-and-a-half years. Still, the children were more successful than the apes, who only succeeded with the indexical meanings.

Another study involving the difference between information conveyed by different kinds of pictorial media, in the broad sense, that is, static pictures, which were either photographs or drawings, and video clips, compared to direct perception, was only realized with a single enculturated ape, and no human beings, but it remains suggestive. Hribar, Sonesson and Call (2014) showed that a chimpanzee that had learned to repeat certain actions from seeing them performed in direct perception, could repeat those actions with equal success after seeing them on a video and also, more surprisingly, when seeing only static phases of the action on pictures.

In the studies discussed above, variations in iconicity, contextuality and in adults' scaffolding in the communicative situations were altered respectively in order to support children making use of pictorial information to solve a problem in the real world. Interestingly, the difficulty to make sense of the picture as a sign seems to remain. A later study designed within cognitive semiotics instead enhanced the factor of indexicality in picture perception. Two-year-old children were informed about where to find a hidden object by means of watching the hiding either by means of direct perception, from a pre-recorded video, a live video or by means of mirror images (Lenninger et al. 2020). Although, the visual information was the same in all tested conditions (i.e. all conditions deployed the same procedure and image section of the hiding event), children made significantly more correct choices after watching the hiding from live video and direct perception compared to that of pre-recorded video and the mirror condition. An interpretation of the success of live video compared to other media is that, although also live video is perceived on a screen in exactly the same way as the pre-recorded video, live video elicited more continuity information than was the case in the other tested conditions, and this factor is helpful to make use of the images. For the mirror condition, on the other hand, the continuity was perhaps blurred by the difficulty of using the enantiomorphic information.

CURRENT ISSUES IN PICTORIAL SEMIOTICS

By now, pictures can be taken to be established as being signs, in the narrow sense of their parts being differentiated, and one of these parts being immediately perceived, while the other is the focus of the experience. In the same way, in spite of the arguments to the contrary during the last half-century, there is no denying that pictures are essentially motivated by iconicity and that they are essentially resolvable into features, but not of the binary kind known from linguistics (see 'Iconicity and semiosis' chapter in Volume 1). Nevertheless, there are some issues pertaining particularly to pictures on which some preliminary result can be reported. They mostly stem from phenomenological analysis, although some of them have been experimentally supported.

Plastic and pictorial layers of the picture

There is presently a kind of consensus for distinguishing the plastic and iconic layers of the picture. Earlier made in other terms by Lindekens, the distinction is now incorporated into two of the current models, that of the Greimas school and that of the μ-group. Yet it is in fact problematic, in a number of ways, only one of which will be discussed here. According to this conception, roughly, the picture stands, on the iconic level, for some object recognizable from the ordinary perceptual Lifeworld; whereas, on the plastic level, the expression is conveyed by simple qualities of the picture thing itself, which tend to correspond to increasingly abstract concepts. As used in semiotics, on the other hand, iconicity is unavoidably connected, in some way or other, with Peirce's concept of icon, even when, as in the Greimas school approach, it has been redefined to mean something like the illusion of reality, or to correspond to verisimilitude, as it is also found in literature. But the iconicity of the iconic layer is not the same at that of the general sign theory formulated by Peirce: notably, plastic features, in the sense of the μ- and Greimas models, may well be iconic in Peirce's sense. This is why it is better to distinguish the plastic and pictorial layer of the picture.

To illustrate, if the circle is seen to convey softness, and the rectangle signifies hardness, to pick up some of the results obtained by Lindekens (1971) in one of his experiments, then there must be some properties mediating synaesthetically between the visual and tactile sense modalities. Very much in the spirit of Gestalt psychology, but at the same time anticipating the popularity of embodied meanings, Sonesson (1989a, 96 ff., 173 ff.; 2013) speculated on the possibility of there being a small number of topological, bodily anchored, properties, which predominates in such plastic interpretations. Saint-Martin (1987) approached the problem of topology in a more systematic manner. Recently, when such synaesthetically conveyed meanings have turned out to be relevant in linguistics, notably in the discussion of so-called sound symbolism (e.g. Ahlner and Zlatev (2010)), it is worthwhile taking this more seriously in pictorial semiotics. When, in Lindekens' study, the circle is declared to be feminine, and when the triangle is said to be calculating, and the rectangle mathematical, it seems clear that whatever Gestalt properties there are, they have been reinterpreted from a specific cultural point of view.

Pictures that do not depict

A curious problem is the existence of pictures containing no depictions, that is to say, pictorial signs apparently deprived of any pictorial layer. In order to make such pictures accessible to semiotic analysis, Floch interpreted one of Kandinsky's non-figurative paintings, 'Composition IV', by means of a comparison with other, more nearly figurative works by the same painter. In spite of Floch's perspicacity, this procedure is unsatisfactory, as least as a generalizable procedure, because it takes for granted that the plastic layer is redundant in relation to the pictorial one: that is to say, if it is always true that plastic language only repeats (though perhaps on a more abstract, and thus partial, level) that which is already conveyed by the pictorial layer.

'Plastic language', according to Floch's (1986: 169) definition, is a system, which is visual and secondary in nature. There are at least two different senses in which this secondarity could be understood. In a figurative picture, the plastic layer is secondary because, by its very nature, a picture is a picture of something, i.e. a sign of some object in the world, and it will be apprehended plastically, once it's being also a thing in its own right, a self, is attended to. But it does not follow that the plastic layer must be secondary in the sense of being limited to repeating part of the meaning already contained in pictorial layer. If, instead, we suppose there to be an autonomous plastic layer, then there are at least two problems. First, we need to discover what kinds of meanings could be conveyed by the spatial configurations and colours, which are potentially infinite in number (see the section 'Plastic and pictorial layers of the picture' above).

Nevertheless, nonfigurative pictures also pose a second problem, which concerns the sense in which they may be termed pictures. From the point of view of present-day, occidental culture, Yves Klein blue, Pollock's drippings, and even the rugged, coloured surfaces, containing nails, hinges and other debris, are not equivalent to painted walls or fences, no matter how similar the patterns and textures may be, simply because the latter, but not the former, are supposed to have a sense. It is not sufficient to show that the notion of the picture must be a prototype concept, defined by the best instances of its type. There can be no access to the present-day artistic idea of the picture other than by following the historical divagations of the occidental picture concept from its age-old prototype onto the different strands of modernism and postmodernism, and so on. To do that, we need to make our way into the semiotics of culture.

Pictures and other visual signs

One may oppose pictures to other visual signs. Since iconicity is not necessarily visually manifested, and since signs (and more, broadly, meanings) may be visually conveyed, without making use of an iconic ground (see 'Iconicity and semiosis' chapter in Volume 1), this is quite a different question, although scholars have tended to confuse the issues. More explicitly, Donald Preziosi (1983), and more recently Wolfgang Wildgen (2013), has conceived of architecture as a kind of visual semiotics, which is no doubt at least correct, even though architecture clearly may address other sense modalities. We could easily add other visual signs, such as gestures, some aspects of theatre communication, sculptures, ready-mades, objects, writing and much more. Saint-Martin (1987) has made an interesting attempt to impose different constraints on the visual variables appearing in the pictorial picture plane, and inside the virtual cube characterizing sculpture. More recently, there have been bids to analyse semiotically such specific, predominantly visual, phenomena as monuments, tools and design objects (see Niño (2015); Beyaert-Geslin at al. (2020)). Many of these phenomena are visual without being iconic – at least if we take iconic to involve, not the primary impression (Firstness) of Peirce, but the iconic ground.

From the point of view of Hjelmslevean semiotics, no doubt, we should not expect visuality, being a mere substance, to determine any relevant categorizations of semiotic means (Groupe μ (1992)); but the psychology of perception certainly seems to suggest the existence of some common organization which singles out all or most visually conveyed meanings. Nevertheless, before we can even analyse how different visual phenomena differ from each other, we need to know what, if anything, they have in common. Suggestions can no doubt be gathered from the psychology and phenomenology of perception, but as far as the authors of this chapter know, there does not appear to have been any serious effort along these lines.

PRIORITIES IN CURRENT RESEARCH

One may argue that the principal advantage of a semiotic approach is to relate the object of study to other kinds of meaning, not only as to their similarities and differences, but also with respect to the way they may be transferred, with more or less loss of meaning, to another semiotic kind (from picture to language, gesture, music, etc. or vice versa), and, most importantly, how pictorial meaning interacts with other kinds of meaning in the context in which it is experienced. To human beings (and to many other living beings), context is social, that is, dependant on relations to other human beings and the institutions they have brought into being. From the categorical point view, very little has been done in this domain, with the exception of the particular case of photography. However, we do have very suggestive scenarios concerning the 'densification' of picture use in historical time. This, however, brings us to the ultimate social context: the emergence of picture-making out of primordial semiosis, as can be gathered from the admittedly speculative, scenarios proposed by recent, more or less semiotically informed, exponents of evolutionary theory.

Four kinds of pictorial kinds

Once something has been said about the specificity of the picture, in relation to broader categories of which it is a member, whether that of iconic or visual signs, pictorial semiotics also has to account for the subcategories contained in the category of pictorial signs. Since very little has been done so far in this domain, we will only try to sketch a general framework for distinguishing the different ways of dividing pictures into categories (see Sonesson 1992).

First of all, we may differentiate pictorial kinds from the point of view of their rules of construction, that is, the rules specifying which traits of the expression plane are relevant for conveying the content, and vice versa. From this point of view, a photograph differs from a painting and a cut-out; and a linear drawing, to use traditional art historical terms, is different from a painterly one. This could be termed *construction categories*.

Then we may also distinguish categories of pictures according to the effects which they are intended to produce (not the actual effects, which may vary, and which cannot really be known). Thus, publicity pictures are expected (among other things) to sell commodities, pornographic pictures are thought to stimulate sexual imagination, and caricatures supposedly hold the depicted person up to ridicule. Very much less well defined is the intended effect of fine art. We will call this *social purpose categories*.

Third, pictorial categories may be differentiated on the basis of the channels through which pictures circulate. The picture post card, for instance, follows another trajectory to reach the receiver than a publicity poster, a wall painting, a television picture or the illustration of a weekly review. These are *circulation categories*.

There is an additional, very different way of distinguishing picture categories, which depends on the nature of the configuration occupying the expression plane of the picture. Ordinary language does not possess any terms for differentiating pictures in this way, but the existence of such a classification, however tacit, is suggested by the fact that some text analytical models which are very productive when applied to some pictures fail to yield any result when transposed to other pictorial texts. This is the kind of result which might be expected from the 'text analytic' approach, but, which, so far, has hardly been forthcoming (see the section on 'Pictures as "texts" or tokens'). One exception is Jamin Pelkey's (2020) recent report which, starting out from a comparison between traditional visual content analysis and a semiotic approach, suggests a method informed by the Peircean notions of abduction, deduction and induction, and illustrates the latter approach with the help of two case studies involving, in the first case, brand mark logos based on the X-figure, and, in the second case, images depicting the Tibetan Wheel of Life and Yama the monster of death.

The picture which Barthes analysed in his famous Panzani article is, from the point of view of construction, a photograph; according to intended effects, a publicity picture; and as far as its channel of circulation is concerned, an illustration appearing in a weekly review. It should be interesting to investigate which combinations of categories ascribed on the basis of construction, intended effects, channels and configurations, tend to co-occur most frequently in a given society. Another complication of the distinctions suggested above has become manifest in recent decades thanks to the prevalence of the Internet. It is clearly a specific channel of circulation, and yet it serves to convey all manner of construction, social-purpose, circulation and configuration categories. This is testified by such special instances as Instagram, Pinterest, YouTube and, of course, Google Images.

Photography as index and icon

A lot of pictorial text analyses have been concerned with publicity pictures; a fair amount has been devoted to paintings. With few, and minor, exceptions, however, publicity pictures, paintings and so on, are simply occasions giving rise to identical analyses; very rarely is their *differentia specifica* attended to. The only real exception is the case of photography, the specificity of which has been widely discussed.

Most scholars applying semiotics to the study of photography have ended up with the idea that it is characterized by indexicality. Henri Van Lier's (1983) notion of indexicality (split into the untranslatable opposition between 'indice' and 'index') is not really derived from Peirce; indeed, his 'indice' is, in the most literal sense, a mere trace, of which he offers some very useful descriptions. Contrary to Van Lier, Philippe Dubois (1983) has recourse to the Peircean tradition, though he may not be all that immersed in its ambience. Jean-Marie Schaeffer (1987) takes a less extreme stand, arguing that the photograph is an indexical icon, or, in other cases, an iconic index. His Peirce-reception is more faithful than that of Dubois, at least in the sense that he allows for a sign being both iconic and indexical (but see Sonesson 1989b; 2015b).

But even Schaeffer's conception is too absolute. There can be no doubt that, first and foremost, the photograph is an iconic sign, since its surface creates the illusion of a semblance with its object. Moreover, very little is said and done when a sign is classified as being an index. Consider the difference between a hoof print and a photograph: while both the photograph and the trace stand for a referent which has vanished from the scene, the signifier of the hoof print continues to occupy the place that was that of the animal, i.e. the referent, and it still remains temporally dated, whereas the photographic signifier, like that of the verbal sign, is omnitemporal and omnispatial. This means that the photograph can be instantiated at any time and place (although only after the referential event). This may be contested nowadays, since digital photos contain a time and in cell phones also a place stamp, but this is an information which is not conveyed by pictorial means. Thus, if, for the sake of simplicity, we attend merely to the temporal aspects, the following table can be constructed (Table 8.1).

TABLE 8.1 Indexicality of footsteps and photographs (adapted from Sonesson, 1988).

		Expression	
		Time-dependant	Omni-temporal
Content	Time-dependant	Footsteps	Photograph
	Omni-temporal	?	Verbal sign

At this point, it may seem that we could say that, whereas the hoof print is first and foremost an index, the photograph must originally be seen as an icon, before its indexical properties can be discovered. In fact, however, things may be still more complicated. Schaeffer is, of course, right in pointing out, against Peirce, that not all indices involve some iconic aspect, but it so happens that the hoof prints, just like all other imprints and traces, in the narrow sense of these terms, also convey a partial similarity with the objects for which they stand. We have to recognize the hoof print as such, that is, differentiate it from the traces of a human foot, or of a donkey, as well as from fake hoof prints, and from accidental formations worked by the wind in the sand. Only then can we interpret the hoof prints indexically. It remains true, however, the essential meanings of the hoof prints are embodied in indexicality: they tell us the whereabouts of the animal.

In the case of a photograph, on the other hand, we do not need to conceive of it indexically to be able to grasp its pictorial meaning. It will continue to convey significations to us, whether we are certain that it is a photograph or not. Indexicality, in photographs, really is a question of second thoughts and peculiar circumstances. Therefore, we may conclude that indexicality cannot be the primary sign relation of photographs, although it is an open potentiality present in their constitution and exploited in certain cases, such as spy photography or medical photography to track changes in the course of a medical treatment. In all, the potentiality to also carry indexical meaning gives a distinct import to photography among other pictures, while it nevertheless remains iconic as to its basic way of meaning-making (for a more strict Peircean interpretation, see Nöth 2020).

The densification of pictures in society

It is often said, nowadays, that we live in a society dominated by pictures. No doubt, pictures should here be taken in a wider sense than the one we have employed in the present chapter, including television, home video, emoji, YouTube, Instagram and the like. In any of its variants, this pronouncement merely serves to set a problem: for if our culture is a predominantly pictorial one, its way of being so could hardly be the same as that prevalent before the emergence of language (which is a mythical antecedent) and before the invention of writing and printing. It is also often said that we live in a society dominated by visual communication. But this is quite a different question (see above: 'Pictures and other visual signs').

It is possible, following Juan Ramírez (1981: 17ff), to conceive of the development of a pictorial culture as a progressive iconographical densification, that is to say, an augmentation of pictures per inhabitant on the globe. One may, however, distinguish several processes accounting for this state of densification (see Sonesson 1993):

1. That, the production of pictures having been made less costly, in particular in terms of what Abraham Moles would have called the time budget, the number of pictures-type (or originals) has been increased;

2. That since the means of reproduction have been perfected, more, and more adequate picture tokens (or copies) are made from each picturetype (as demonstrated by William Ivins and Walter Benjamin);
3. That the categories of pictures multiply, as pictures turn out to be useful for a number of purposes, including propaganda and entertainment;
4. That pictures, which were at other times only accessible in a small number of spaces, such as churches and palaces, where most people could not be present most of the time, are now circulated widely;
5. That, by means of such channels as television, journals and, in particular, the internet, pictures may nowadays be more actively circulated, issued more explicitly as directed messages, at particular moments and places, as presupposed in the communication model familiar from information theory.

A sixth process which was less apparent when the list was first made can be added:

6. That, thanks to the technical accessibility offered by the internet, in combination with the widespread available of smartphones and iPads, an increasing number of senders having more different background, age, context and so on are able to produce pictures and to put them into circulation.

The semiotics of pictorial culture remains to be made. Its place, however, as Saussure would have said, is determined beforehand. All existing societies have been societies of information (and disinformation); but contemporary society no doubt possesses its peculiar mode of information. In the world dominated by the internet and its social media, it is much more difficult to separate pictures from all kinds of more or less similar artefacts, such as diagrams, video clips, GIFs, emojis, games, animations and presentation software, which also form different hybrids. While semioticians have looked at instances of these different vehicles of meaning, we are aware of no analysis of the difference made in the social world of their combined impact.

It was suggested by Sonesson (2020), nevertheless, that the use of pictures and different hybridized forms which includes them in the Internet tends to conform much more to the idea of a message sent from one subject to another than is the case with the notion of pictures serving aesthetic contemplation which has predominated in most societies for the reckonable past.[4] If this is a correct observation, it seems to make our present use of pictures more similar to the ones found in some earlier cultures. Thus, for instance, Moctezuma knew about all the actions of Cortes and his men since they first came ashore, thanks to pictures sent to him by his spies. Indeed, Aztec pictures are really conceived to convey simple messages such as 'here mountain', rather than spelling out the specific properties of the mountain for easy contemplation (see Sonesson 2020). Something similar would seem to apply to the instrumental use of sand drawings by speakers of Arandic languages in Australia (Green 2014) and the speakers of Paama in Vanuatu (Devylder 2019).

The picture in deep prehistory

The search for the evolutionary origin of language, more or less explicitly proscribed since the Enlightenment, has again become a widespread preoccupation in recent decades. Many studies are also concerned with the origin of gestures, and, as during the Enlightenment, with the question of whether gestures or language came first as a distinctive mark of human beings. On the contrary, the question of the origin of pictures is rarely asked. An exception is the book by William Noble and Iain Davidson (1996), where they muse that the first signs must have been pictures, since this is the only type of sign which serves to congeal perceptual experience. Nevertheless, it is not clear why such a function could also not be fulfilled by gesture.

In several books and papers, Merlin Donald (1991) has suggested an evolutionary scheme, which includes, at the very end, the emergence of pictures. According to Donald, human beings share episodic memory, in which the present experience is explicitly situated in between a past and a future, with many animals; they also share, at least with other primates and with the precursor species of human beings, at least some kind of mimetic skills, which implies the ability to employ gesture, to imitate others and to use tools. Still, human beings differ from other animals, not only thanks to the third stage, which involves the use of language, but also because of the fourth stage, the emergence of exograms, that is, ways of conserving meaning separately from the human organism, which is the case with pictures, writing, and theory.

Even if we accept the implication that exograms can only be created after language has emerged, it does not necessarily follow that pictures can only appear at this stage (Lenninger 2016). We know of several cultures, some still existing (see Green 2014), where pictures are made in the sand, and almost directly erased, once they have fulfilled their function, which is to convey a message within the framework of a communicative game. The pictorial exogram may really be a product of a particular use of pictures, that of aesthetic experience.

As can be seen from the proposal discussed above, this kind of study does not allow for any direct sources. It is mostly a kind of phenomenological analysis, which may build on historical, anthropological and archaeological facts, as well as comparisons with what we can learn about other animals. It still remains a fascinating preoccupation.

CONCLUSIONS

The international association of visual semiotics (AISV-IAVS) was founded in Blois in 1989, and it has since then held twelve international conferences, the most recent one of which took place in Lund in 2019. The thirteenth conference was scheduled to take place in 2021, but has been adjourned because of the Covid-19 pandemic.[5] It is an association which brings together scholars, some of whom identify with the definition of pictorial semiotics offered above, and some who may rather favour an approach less different from traditional humanities. Textual analyses are still being realized, as are system analyses, but no new models for these analyses have been proposed since the end of the last century. Meanwhile, we have learned a lot about the specificity of pictorial meaning, and even, at least in the case of photography, about subcategories of pictures. Other tasks for pictorial semiotics can at least be defined, even if we are only at the beginning of offering any answers. Contrary to text and system analyses, experimental approaches have recently come to the fore, partly inspired by studies in psychology and cognitive science, but highlighting specifically semiotic issues, and these attempts even seems to have had repercussions in studies by psychologists. A promising approach in pictorial semiotics in the future thus seems to lay in experimental studies. The preponderance of text analysis may have been a blind alley. But we should never forget that, since we are concerned with meaning, there is no avoiding phenomenology.

NOTES

1. In the following, we will refer to the artefact described in English by the terms 'picture' and 'image' exclusively by means of the former term. Although some dictionaries make a difference between the meanings of these terms, they seem to be used interchangeably in everyday language; and other languages do not have the means to make any distinction. For our purpose, the term 'image' will be reserved for referring to Peirce's notion of First Firstness which clearly cannot account for the meaning conveyed by pictures (see the chapter 'Iconicity and semiosis' in Volume 1).
2. For a more detailed history, and all the references to works not given here, see Sonesson (2015a).
3. In this context, and in the following, we prefer to use the word 'game' instead of 'test'. This is because in designing the procedures, and from the point of view of the child, the participants are part of a joyful activity together with others that follows a setup of local 'rules' but that also can be ended at any time the child chooses. Thus, it is a structured activity that involves local establishments of norms.
4. Somewhat similar comparisons between contemporary media and oral culture were independently made by Alin Olteanu (2020).
5. For news of this and other things concerning the association, see https://aisviavs.wordpress.com.

REFERENCES

Ahlner, F. and J. Zlatev (2010), 'Cross-modal Iconicity: A Cognitive Semiotic Approach to Sound Symbolism', *Sign Systems `Studies*, 38 (1/4): 298–346.

Barthes, R. (1964), 'Rhétorique de l'image', *Communications*, 4: 40–51.

Beyaert-Geslin, A., L. Chatenet and F. Okala, eds (2020), *Monuments, (de)monumentalisation: approches sémiotiques*, Limoges: P.U.L.I.M.

Blair, J. A. (2012). *Groundwork in the Theory of Argumentation: Selected Papers of J. Anthony Blair*, Springer: Netherlands.

Carani, M. (1987), 'Sémiotique de l'abstraction picturale', *Semiotica*, 67 (12): 1–38.

Carani, M. (1988), 'Sémiotique de la perspective picturale', *Protée*, 16 (1–2): 171–81.

Champagne, M. and A.-V. Pietarinen (2020), 'Why Images Cannot Be Arguments, but Moving Ones Might', 34 (2): 207–36. https://doi.org/10.1007/s10503-019-09484-0.

DeLoache, J. and N. Burns (1994), 'Early Understanding of the Representational Function of Pictures', *Cognition*, 51 (2): 83–110.

Deledalle, G. (1976), 'La Joconde. Théorie de l'analyse sémiotique appliquée à un portrait', *Semiosis*, 4: 25–31.

Devylder, S. (2019), *Paamese Sand Drawings – Polysemiotic Communication and Revitalization Efforts of an Endangered Practice*, Paper presented at the 15th International Cognitive Linguistic Conference, Nishinomiya, Japan, August 2019.

Donald, M. (1991), *Origins of the Modern Mind: Three Stages in the Evolution of Culture and Cognition*, Cambridge: Harvard University Press.

Dondero, M. G. (2020), *The Language of Images: The Forms and the Forces*, Cham: Springer.

Dubois, P. (1983), *L'acte photographique*, Paris: Nathan/Labor.

Floch, J-M. (1984), *Petites mythologies de l'œil et l'esprit*, Paris: Hadès.

Floch, J.-M. (1986), *Les formes de l'empreinte*, Périgueux: Pierre Fanlac.

Fontanille, J. (1995), *Sémiotique du visible*, Paris: Presses Universitaires de France.
Ganea, P., M. Bloom Pickard and J. DeLoache (2008), 'Transfer between Picture Books and the Real World by Very Young Children', *Journal of Cognition and Development*, 9: 46–66.
Green, J. (2014), *Drawn from the Ground: Sound, Sign and Inscription in Central Australian Sand Stories*, Cambridge: Cambridge University Press.
Greimas, A. J. and J. Courtés ([1979] 1986), *Sémiotique. Dictionnaire raisonné de la théorie du langage*, 1–2, Paris: Hachette.
Groupe μ (Dubois, J., Ph. Dubois, Fr. Edeline, J. M. Klinkenberg, Ph. Minguet, Fr. Pire and H. Trinon) (1992), *Traité du signe visuel, Pour une rhétorique de l'image*, Paris: Seuil.
Halliday, M. A. K. (1985), *An Introduction to Functional Grammar*, London: Edward Arnold.
Hochberg, J. and V. Brooks (1962), 'Pictorial Recognition as an Unlearned Ability: A Study of One Child's Performance', *The American Journal of Psychology*, 75 (4): 624–8.
Hribar, A., G. Sonesson and J. Call (2014), 'From Sign to Action: Studies in Chimpanzee Pictorial Competence', *Semiotica*, 198: 205–40.
Jappy, T. (2013), *Introduction to Peircean Visual Semiotics*, London: Bloomsbury.
Krampen, M (1991), *Children's Drawings: Iconic Coding of the Environment*, New York: Plenum Press.
Kress, G. and T. Van Leeuwen (1996), *Reading Images: The Grammar of Visual Design*, London: Routledge.
Lenninger, S. (2012), *When Similarity Qualifies as a Sign: A Study in Picture Understanding and Semiotic Development in Young Children*, Lund: Lund University.
Lenninger, S. (2016), 'Pictures: Perception of realism in the service of communication', in D. Dunér and G. Sonesson (eds.), *Human Life World: The Cognitive Semiotics of cultural evolution*, 97–121, Frankfurt am Main: Peter Lang.
Lenninger, S., T. Persson, J. van de Weijer and G. Sonesson (2020), 'Mirror, Peephole and Video: The Role of Contiguity in Children's Perception of Reference in Iconic Signs', *Frontiers in Psychology*, 11 (1622), doi: 10.3389/fpsyg.2020.01622.
Lindekens, R. (1971), *Eléments pour une sémiotique de la photographie*, Paris/ Bruxelles: Didier/Aimav.
Niño, D. (2015), *Elementos de Semiótica Agentiva*, Bogota: Universidad Jorge Tadeo Lozano.
Noble, W. and I. Davidson (1996), *Human Evolution, Language and Mind: a Psychological and Archaeological Inquiry*, Cambridge: Cambridge University Press.
Nöth, W. (2020), 'The Iconic, Indexical, and Symbolic in Language: Overlaps, Inclusions, and Exclusions', in P. Perniss, O. Fischer and C. Ljungberg (eds.), *Operationalizing Iconicity* (Iconicity in Language and Literature 17), 308–26, Amsterdam: John Benjamins. https://doi.org/10.1075/ill.17.18not.
Mitchell, W. J. T. (1986), *Iconology: Image, Text, Ideology*, Chicago: Univ. of Chicago Press.
Mitchell, W. J. T. (2015), *Image Science: Iconology, Visual Culture, and Media Aesthetics*, Chicago: The University of Chicago Press.
Olteanu, A. (2020), 'Translation from a Contemporary Media Perspective: Avoiding Culturalism and Monolingualism', *Social Semiotics*, aop: doi.org/10.1080/10350330.2020.1714204.
O'Toole, M. (1994), *The Language of Displayed Art*, London: Leicester University Press.
Pelkey, J. (2020) 'Researching Visual Semiotics Online', *TECCOGS: Revista Digital de Tecnologias Cognitivas*, 21 (1): 116–45. https://doi.org/10.23925/1984-3585.2020i21p116-145
Preissler, M. and S. Cary (2004), 'Do Both Pictures and Words Function as Symbols for 18- and 24-month-old Children?', *Journal of Cognition and Development*, 5 (2): 185–212.

Preziosi, D. (1983), 'Advantages and Limitations of Visual Communication', in M. Krampen (ed.), *Visuelle Kommunikation und/oder verbale Kommunikation*, 1–34, Berlin: Olms Verlag, Hildesheim/Hochschule der Künste.

Ramírez, J.-A. (1981), *Medios de masas e historia del arte*, 2nd edn, Madrid: Ediciones Cátedra.

Reyes, E. and G. Sonesson (2019), 'New Approaches to Plastic Language. Prolegomena to a Computer-aided Approach to Pictorial Semiotics', *Semiotica*, 230: 71–95.

Sachs-Hombach, K. (2003), *Das Bild als kommunikatives Medium. Elemente einer allgemeinen Bildwissenschaft*, Köln: Herbert von Halem Verlag. (3., überarbeitete Neuauflage 2013).

Sachs-Hombach, K. and J. R. J. Schirra, eds (2013). *Origins of Pictures: Anthropological Discourses in Image Science*, Köln: von Halem.

Saint-Martin, F. (1987), *Sémiologie du langage visuel*, Québec: Presse de l'Université du Québec.

Schaeffer, J-M. (1987), *L'image précaire*, Paris: Seuil.

Sonesson, G. (1988), *Methods and Models in Pictorial Semiotics*, Lund: Lund University Semiotics Project.

Sonesson, G. (1989a), *Pictorial Concepts. Inquiries into the Semiotic Heritage and Its Relevance for the Analysis of the Visual World*, Lund: Lund University Press.

Sonesson, G. (1989b), *Semiotics of Photography. On Tracing the Index*, Lund: Lund University Semiotics Project.

Sonesson, G. (1992), *Bildbetydelser*, Lund: Studentlitteratur.

Sonesson, G. (1993), 'Die Semiotik des Bildes. Zum Forschungsstand am Anfang der 90er Jahre', *Zeitschrift für Semiotik*, 15 (1–2): 131–64.

Sonesson, G. (2012), 'The Foundation of Cognitive Semiotics in the Phenomenology of Signs and Meanings', *Intellectica*, 2 (58): 207–39.

Sonesson, G. (2014a), 'The Cognitive Semiotics of the Picture Sign', in D. Machin (ed.), *Handbook of Visual Communication*, 23–50, Berlin: DeGruyter.

Sonesson, G. (2014b), 'Still Do Not Block the Line of Inquiry. On the Peircean Way to Cognitive Semiotics', *Cognitive Semiotics*, 7 (2): 281–96.

Sonesson, G. (2013), 'Aspects of "Physiognomic Depiction" in Pictures: From Macchia to Microgenesis', *Culture & Psychology*, 19 (4): 533–47.

Sonesson, G. (2015a), 'Pictorial Semiotics', in T. Sebeok and M. Danesi (eds), *Encyclopedic Dictionary of Semiotics*, 3rd revised edn, Berlin: De Gruyter Mouton. https://www.degruyter.com/document/database/EDS/entry/pictorial_semiotics/html.

Sonesson, G. (2015b), 'Semiotics of Photography: The State of the Art', in P. Trifonas (ed.), *International Handbook of Semiotics*, 417–83, Berlin: Springer.

Sonesson, G. (2020), 'Translation as Culture: The Example of Pictorial-verbal Transposition in Sahagún's primeros memoriales and codex florentino', *Semiotica*, 232: 5–39.

Stjernfelt, F. (2014), *Natural Propositions: The Actuality of Peirce's Doctrine of Dicisigns*, Boston: Docent Press.

Thürlemann, F. (1982), *Paul Klee. Analyse sémiotique de trois peintures*, Lausanne: L'Age d'Hommes.

Tomasello, M., J. Call and A. Gluckman (1997), 'Comprehension of Novel Communicative Signs by Apes and Human Children', *Child Development*, 68 (6): 1067–80.

Van Lier, H. (1983), *Philosophie de la photographie*, Laplume: Les cahiers de la photographie.

Wildgen, W. (2013), *Visuelle Semiotik. Die Entfaltung des Sichtbaren. Vom Höhlenbild bis zur modernen Stadt*, Bielefeld: Transcript-Verlag.

Zlatev, J., E. Alenkaer Madsen, S. Lenninger, T. Persson, S. Sayehli, G. Sonesson and J. van de Weijer (2013), 'Understanding Communicative Intentions and Semiotic Vehicles by Children and Chimpanzees', *Cognitive Development*, 28: 312–29.

CHAPTER NINE

Semiotics in Film and Video Studies

PIERO POLIDORO AND ADRIANO D'ALOIA

One of the foundational moments in the birth of contemporary semiotics took place in 1964 with the publication of the fourth issue of the French journal *Communications*, dedicated to 'Recherches sémiologiques'. The volume hosted an essay by Claude Bremond on narrative message, another by Tzvetan Todorov on literature, and two important writings by Roland Barthes: the analysis of the Panzani pasta advertisement, which inaugurated the study of visual semiotics, and his 'Elements of Semiology', which for many years was one of the main theoretical references of the discipline. Rounding out the volume, alongside the two works by Barthes, was an essay by Christian Metz entitled 'Le cinéma: langue ou langage?' Since its moment of birth, then, contemporary semiotics has concerned itself with the audiovisual in its efforts – unique at the time – to bring together various forms of arts and communication (from literature to advertising, from myth to cinema) and seek shared structures and local variations among them.

In this chapter we[1] seek to reconstruct the contribution that semiotics has made and can make today to the study of the audiovisual. By the term 'audiovisual', we mean a domain defined by certain expressive materials or, better, by specific modalities of sensory apprehension, at once aural and visual. Multiple different languages are used within this realm, some of which exceed its boundaries, such as verbal, musical or pictorial ones (suffice it to think of the influence of traditional iconography upon cinema); others, however, are more specific, even if not always exclusive to audiovisual media (for example, the montage).

This subject requires a discussion, and not only for historical reasons, of the approach that semiotics took in respect to the two main audiovisual media that accompanied its birth and its development over the course of the second half of the twentieth century: cinema and television. We will begin with an analysis of the origin and evolution of the semiotics of cinema, which laid the bases for the analysis of the audiovisual text in general. We will then move to semiotic studies of television and its more specific aspects. This will then bring us to the developments that have, in the last few decades and with the arrival of digital media, profoundly transformed the media system, bringing about new forms and phenomena and overcoming several classical divisions through growing convergence and transmediality. In this context, semiotics (no longer simply considered as the 'semiotics of cinema' or the 'semiotics of television') once again offers fundamental tools for describing and mapping these phenomena and their mechanisms, opening onto previously little-explored fields – for example, that of perception, to which we will turn at the end of this chapter.

SEMIOTICS AND CINEMA

Because a film, or more broadly any audiovisual text, is a cultural object that results from a complex linguistic assemblage, it is one of the most interesting semiotic objects within modern human experience. The subjects – abstract and concrete – that animate the communicative and signifying dynamics of the audiovisual are involved in an intense process of communicative prefiguration (on the part of the author) and interpretation (on the part of the user) at multiple levels of intentionality and awareness in respect to both the represented contents and the formal modalities used to represent them.

The different phases of the semiotics of cinema that have unfolded from the 1960s until today placed an emphasis either on issues related to the constitution of the film (a text made up of signs and codes, inhabited and activated by abstract and disincarnate entities), or on the cognitive aspects of its reception (the interpretative activity carried out by the spectator in order to understand it). In the following pages we will first retrace the fundamental steps of the cine-semiological adventure, and then return to this topic at the end of the chapter, where we will focus on the present state of the semiotics of cinema and the audiovisual in general, and their conditions of existence (and resistance), in particular as a function of their dialogue – only seemingly impossible – with cognitive and neurocognitive sciences.

As we noted in the introduction, the semiotics of cinema was born in the 1960s through the influence of Christian Metz's essay 'Le cinéma: langue ou langage?' (1974a), and soon positioned itself in opposition to psychological and sociological approaches that were dominant in the second post-war period, above all through the adoption of a methodological approach more rigorous than those of the preceding paradigms. As Francesco Casetti emphasizes,

> The semiotic approach created fractures, aggregations, resistances; its presence both accented and realigned other theoretical formations. This occurred because semiotics, more than other disciplines, tended to highlight certain fundamental points: on the one hand, the dissatisfaction with discourses that are too general, with impressionistic observations, with the search for essences; on the other hand, the need to define its own interests, to deploy rigorous analytical procedures, to make use of well-defined categories.
>
> (Casetti 1999: 132)

It is not by chance, then, that the principal concern of the early years of the cine-semiological adventure was above all one of foundations. The new discipline sought to affirm its *raison d'être* and its specific role in light of a 'translinguistic' proposition, namely the possibility of applying the semiotic method derived from linguistics (and thus primarily Saussurean) to systems of signification beyond verbal language. The process of adapting concepts from linguistics to cinema was anything but peaceful. The fundamental question posed by Metz beginning from the title of his essay is clear: is it possible to conceive of cinema as a system of *signs* like a language, possessing double articulation in minimal unities like phonemes (sounds, without signification in themselves) and morphemes (words formed by the combination of sounds, imbued with meaning), which can be combined with one another and thus signify through differential logic? Metz first responds negatively: the cinema is, if anything, a spontaneous and self-regulated language since, for example, the shots and the framings have meanings even without being combined together. The cinema does not have a 'dictionary' that can be constructed in the abstract, made up of terms that take on meaning through reciprocal difference; the images are not assimilable or reducible to signs in the strict sense because they are expressive materials that imply an act of enunciation, that is, the showing of something that has already taken place and is directed towards the spectator.

On one hand, Metz's provocation brought about a complex debate in which numerous intellectuals – in particular Italian ones – participated, such as Pier Paolo Pasolini (1988), Umberto Eco (1976), Emilio Garroni (1968) and Gianfranco Bettetini (1973). On the other hand, thanks to the English translation of his article, the 'Grande Syntagamatique' (1974a), which poses the problem of *langue/langage* in terms of 'narrative discourse', achieved international notoriety. Metz draws a series of analogies between cinema and language based on the ways in which cinematographic montage combines space and time (in other words, syntagmas). In a second volume translated into English the same year (1974b) Metz had already moved on to the identification of a series of specific (exclusive to cinema) and non-specific (shared with other media) codes and subcodes (the specifications of codes), and to the development of the concept of the 'textual system', that is to say, the analyst's (de)construction of the codes whose combination constitutes the film as 'singular totality'.

Metz's (1974b) idea that cinema is a form of the narrative organization of images (above all through montage) resulted in the following phase of the cine-semiological enterprise paying particular attention to the narrative dynamics of the film story. This intuition developed above all through the recuperation and redevelopment in filmic terms of the literary theory developed by the Russian formalists in the 1930s. The so-called narratology of cinema was driven by the formalist distinction between *fabula* and plot (*syuzhet*), that is, between the immanent structure or 'raw materiality' ideally existing in logical and chronological order and the expressive modalities according to which this is organized and presented to the spectator, setting in motion processes of comprehension intended precisely to allow for the reconstitution of this structure. The influence of formalism (particularly the morphology of the folktale developed by Vladimir Propp ([1928] 1968) in the late 1920s, then re-popularized in the 1960s through its translation into Western languages (1968) and redeveloped in a modern semiotic key by Algirdas J. Greimas ([1983]), along with the structural theories of Claude Lévi-Strauss (1963) and the systematization of Roland Barthes (1975), made a significant contribution to the narratology of cinema, in particular in respect to the analysis of the deeply typical (and archetypical) structures that underlie the surface of the film. The culmination of semiotic reflection in a narratological vein, finally, was represented by the work of Seymour Chatman (1978).

The narratological approach to film narrative also borrowed from literary theory (in particular from Gerard Genette 1980) a distinct attention towards the multiple determination of point of view (optical, cognitive and epistemic), with particular regard to the concept of *focalization*, that is, the point of view constructed within the story and determined by the level of symmetry or asymmetry between the narrator and the reader. Starting from this point, it was possible to identify different types of narrators and new ways of understanding point of view, such as the *ocularization* theorized by François Jost (1989).

Narratology led to a deeper understanding of the nature and filmic version of another linguistic category, namely enunciation, which as defined by Émile Benveniste (1971), designates the presence in the discourse of the traces of its production. The enunciator is always implicitly present in filmic communication, often – as in classical 'canonical' cinema – hiding its traces, but sometimes – as in avant-garde or modern cinema – deliberately revealing itself. The study of forms of filmic enunciation would be given further depth in particular by the 'Scuola di Milano', represented by Bettetini (1984) and Casetti (1998). The latter in particular encouraged a further progress in semiotics, and more incisively attended to the position attributed by the film to the spectator, who was no longer considered a simple 'decoder', but rather a subject who actively converses with filmic texts. Already taking a step towards spectatorship theory, Casetti stressed the relevance of the enunciative apparatus as an interface between the body of the film and the body of the spectator, anticipating the next phase of semiotic studies which we will discuss further below.

As noted, the passage from the foundational phases to that of its narratological and enunciational consolidation corresponds to the shift of cine-semiology's attention from the concept of the sign to that of the *text*. A further development of this trajectory emerges in the 1980s through a move from the textual nucleus to the social and cultural surroundings in which processes of filmic communication and signification take place, that is, to their *context*. One example of this is Rick Altman's study (1984) on film genres as defined not by the text operating 'top-down', but rather from the use that spectators make of it, hence 'bottom-up'. The prevalence of the *pragmatic* dimension of the semantic and syntactical one brings Roger Odin (1995) to formulate a semio-pragmatics concerned with the way in which texts are constructed and on the effects (also pathemic and affective ones) of such a construction upon the spectator: meaning, even if it is not produced independently of the text, is produced outside of it.

SEMIOTICS AND TELEVISION

Semiotic studies of television have undoubtedly benefited from work done within the context of film semiotics. The fundamental categories and instruments of analysis of montage and other textual properties shared by these two audiovisual media are, in fact, largely the same. Even so, semiotics has also attended to other aspects of the televisual text, starting with its ideological content. This could not have been otherwise, given that television is clearly seen as the dominant medium in the period of the expansion of contemporary semiotics.

Studying television (and any medium in general) from an ideological point of view means – according to the lessons of Roland Barthes (1964, 1994) – considering it as a vehicle for the construction and diffusion of a specific way of conceiving of reality, whether this is seen as hegemonic (as in the case of the bourgeois ideology analysed by Barthes), or simply in competition with other ideological systems.

To understand the efficacy of the ideological messages conveyed by the media, we can take from Eric Landowski (1989) the image of the *reflected society*. Media (and therefore television) have a dual relationship with the social system in which they circulate: on one hand they are produced by it and represent it, or better, represent a particular point of view and a particular reconstruction of it; on the other they are consumed by a public that belongs to that same social system, and appropriates schemas and representations, making them their own and recognizing them as the 'real' representation of the reality in which they live. In a kind of prophetic self-fulfilment, society produces images of itself that it presents to itself, and adapts itself to them.

It is not necessary, however, that these images be presented as non-fictional, or even realistic, representations of society. It is sufficient that they construct possible worlds analogous to it. The concept of the possible world derives from logic, and was extensively studied by Jakko Hintikka (1967, 1969), and later introduced into semiotics by Umberto Eco (1979, 1991) and further developed by Lubomir Doležel (2010). What concerns us here is not so much the logic and formal aspects of the idea, but simply its status as a fictional representation of a state of affairs containing propositions about individual properties or actions and sometimes governed by a set of rules. Thus, a television series or an advertisement both construct possible worlds, which on the surface may be very distant from the real one in which we live, but can be linked to it through deep analogies and thus represents, explicitly or more often implicitly, a metaphor for it. For example, even if the possible world of the classic series *Star Trek* (1966–9) is clearly different than ours and perhaps governed by different physical laws (ones that would allow for long-distance space travel), it incarnates an optimistic image of society compatible with the Western point of view of the second half of the 1960s. The adventures of the crew of the Enterprise, in fact, take place, at least from a certain point onward, within the context of a peaceful United Federation of Planets. Furthermore, the ship's crew is cosmopolitan: several of its important members have different national origins (the Russian Chekov, the Japanese or generically Asian Sulu, the Scottish Scott), while others are people of colour (Uhura was one of the first female characters of colour to appear in a prime-time television series), and even extra-terrestrials (Spock), even if the commander – Captain Kirk – is clearly American. The classic series thus describes a possible world that is in many ways different from the one we live in, but that clearly represents the ideal of a prosperous, peaceful and progressive alliance between evolved nations (NATO or the UN), under American leadership. Another much-studied example (Baena and Byker 2014; Byrne 2014; Polidoro 2016a; Niemeyer 2014; Czarniawska 2018) could be that of the so-called *nostalgia drama*, a typically British genre that nonetheless has equivalents in other countries. In these series, a past world is represented, usually that of the golden age of a specific culture. The nostalgia drama proper (that is, the British one) is for this reason usually set during the Victorian or Edwardian era, between the second half of the 1800s and the First World War; but *Happy Days*, which represents the golden age of the 1950s and 1960s in the United States, could also be considered a form of this genre. The ideological content of the nostalgia drama is usually conservative, conservative being understood not as a political orientation (i.e. 'on the right') but literally, as the desire to conserve social forms as they are, or to restore a previous order, more familiar or perceived as more reassuring.

A semiotic analysis of the ideological content of television texts can lead to multiple levels. One can certainly concentrate on the most superficial levels, identifiable with what Greimas (1987b; Greimas and Courtés 1982) calls *discursive structures*. From this point of view, the *themes* dealt with indicate the priorities of a particular ideological vision, the *figures* can be studied for their connotative value, and the *thematic roles* for the stereotypes that they construct or consolidate. But while this approach may seem similar to that of other disciplines dealing with the ideological analysis of media (and of television in particular), the specific approach of semiotics can extend its type of analysis to deeper levels. In particular, once again taking up Greimas's terminology, the analysis of the *surface semio-narrative structures* can illuminate systems of roles and relations of power that operate at deeper levels and can thus transmit, in a less explicit way, models and schemas that are then adopted by the public and thus become the basis for further interpretative practices.

This mechanism of ideological transmission is further amplified in television series through the way they are viewed. In television broadcasting the watching of series is enhanced through periodicity (transmission at regular intervals, for example, weekly) and by extension over a long period of time (up to many years in the case of the most successful series). In the modalities characteristic of streaming on-demand platforms, the loss of periodicity and extension are compensated for through *binge watching*, that is, the possibility of watching multiple episodes in a single session; what is lost in extension is thus made up for through the intensity of the experience. In both cases, more than with other media and audiovisual formats, television series make possible an intensification of the exposure to the ideological content of the text.

The semiotic approach to the television text, of course, cannot be reduced to ideological analysis. The variety of types of semiotic reflection on this medium, but also its evolution in time along with that of television language, is evident if one considers Umberto Eco's work on television. Eco indeed dedicated much of his theoretical work and analyses to TV, examining it from its beginnings. His first writings on the topic go back to 1956, and it is worth recalling that television only began to be broadcast in Italy in 1954. It is also important to remember that Eco had a direct knowledge of the television world, having worked – shortly after finishing his degree – in the newborn Italian public television in the mid-1950s.

Eco's writings on television were recently collected in an Italian volume edited by Gianfranco Marrone (2018). In his post-face, Marrone identifies six phases in Eco's thinking about television, which at least in part reflect the parallel evolution of semiotic reflection on the topic. According to Marrone, the six phases, albeit with the limits of such a schematization, can be summarized as follows:

1. 1956–64: in this phase attention is dedicated above all to the effects and aesthetic meaning of live television.
2. 1965–8: working in a full-scale interpretative mode, Eco poses the problem of how the public receives the television message; he stresses the multiplicity of codes that constitute the television text and the fact that different groups can interpret them in different ways. From a theoretical and methodological point of view this is the moment in which Eco, unsatisfied with the instruments offered by aesthetics and sociology, moves towards semiotics.
3. 1968–73: attention is focused on ideological analysis and the strategies that the spectator, now considered an active interpreter, can carry out in order to take a critical approach to the television message.
4. 1973–84: with the political and critical impetus of the early 1970s exhausted, Eco's attention turns to the textual mechanisms of television.
5. 1985–2000: during these years Eco dedicates himself less systematically to television and focuses most of all on its new tendencies, such as reality TV (for example, court shows), demonstrating the progressive overlapping of television and reality.
6. 2000–15: in the last phase of his activity, Eco concerns himself more with digital media and less with television, even if a continuity emerges in this shift: the insistence on a tendency towards subjectivity, immediacy and post-mediality, understood as the end of the function of mediation that the media had carried out up to that point, which was replaced by the emergence of a seeming spontaneity and lack of intermediaries.

In this intense activity that covered more than half a century, we can isolate two particularly relevant contributions to the application of semiotics to television.

The first goes back to the dawn of the television medium and thus to the mid-1950s. In this period Eco dedicated himself above all to the problem of live transmission, which he considers – in the theoretical style of the time – to be the truly 'specific' quality of television, just as montage can be considered that of the cinema. It is clear that television is always, however, staged, and that even the simple positioning of the television camera represents a selection and intervention by the director into reality. To this, montage is added, with the choice of lenses and the sequence of shots. What distinguishes this montage from that of cinema is that it takes place live, and not in post-production, which changes things considerably, at least in early television. Before the indeterminacy of the real (for example, a football match broadcast live), the specificity of the intervention of the television director lies in the way he seeks to place this indeterminacy within the framework of traditional narrative schemas. Eco argues that this is also, if one looks closely, a movement in opposition with that attempted by cinema during those years (for example, that of Michelangelo Antonioni), which sought, within the fabric of a structured story, to represent the indeterminacy and the meaninglessness of daily life.

Another important and influential contribution by Eco concerns the evolution of television between the end of the 1970s and the beginning of the 1980s. To demonstrate the difference between two historically different modes of making television, Eco coins the terms 'Paleo-TV' and 'Neo-TV'. The increase in the number of television channels (which comes about in Europe with the addition of the first private television channels alongside those of public television) and the natural evolution of television language profoundly alter the semiotic characteristics of the medium. The difference between informational and fiction programs progressively decreases: reality TV is in fact the realization of a new format in which it is difficult to understand where the information ends and the fictional aspects begin. This is part of a broader transformation in which television gradually comes to occupy centre stage: whereas earlier it had been a medium that served to represent reality (or versions of it), now television itself, with its forms, characters and dynamics, is the centre of attention. This is the era of the self-referentiality of television, which emerges from characteristics such as the dominance of the phatic function over the referential one, the intervention of the public from home, and the construction of events specifically for television broadcast (exemplified by the contrast between the marriage of Prince Rainier of Monaco and Grace Kelly in 1956 and the Royal Wedding of Charles and Diana in 1981). From a semiotic point of view, one of the clearest novelties is the change in enunciative strategies. Eco stresses how usually on television, the person who is looking into the camera (e.g. the anchor of a news show, a comic delivering a monologue) speaks for themselves, while the one who speaks without looking into the camera (the actor playing a role a fiction) represents someone else. Not looking into the camera indicates that what is being represented occurs independently of television, while looking into the camera means recognizing the presence and the necessity of television. For this reason, Neo-TV makes extensive use of the look into the camera and, most importantly does not erase, as Paleo-TV rigorously did, the traces of enunciation. At this point, in fact, television enunciation becomes significant in itself, independently of what is being enunciated.

TELEVISION AND ENUNCIATION

Eco's reflections on Neo-TV demonstrate the centrality of the question of enunciation (which we have already encountered in the semiotics of cinema) in the evolution of television and in the field of the audiovisual in general. At the moment in which the medium itself becomes the centre of attention, it is its way of constructing a relationship with the spectator that becomes fundamental, and this involves, from a semiotic point of view, the dimension of enunciation.

Other authors, with different tools and terms, have dealt with the question. In the extra-semiotic field, for example, Bolter and Grusin's (1999) work on *remediation* and other significatory mechanisms of contemporary media, is fundamental. Bolter and Grusin, however, do not focus solely on remediation (the process through which each new medium takes up communicative characteristics from its predecessors, for example when the television of the 1950s remediated theatre and radio, before fully and consciously developing its own language) but also on *immediacy* and *hypermediacy*. The first is a search for a reality effect and authenticity which comes about through the removal of traces of enunciation. The second is even more interesting from our point of view: hypermediation is a style that favours fragmentation and heterogeneity, and makes the process of the communicative performance evident. In other words, it consists of placing the 'mediated' character of a given text in the foreground. Bolter and Grusin then discuss a further aspect of hypermediation, which is illustrated with the example of television, namely the 'CNN look'. They show how as television news programs attempt to offer the greatest number of stories in the minimum possible time, they adopt a style using numerous windows (one for the anchor, one for the guest, one for a camera on the scene where the events are taking place) and writing superimposed over other news items. This underscores the medium's capacity to capture events and give the spectator the complexity and dynamic quality of reality.

This is, however, a tendency that is not limited to television, but which extends across the audiovisual in general as well as to other media. It is present, for example, in cinema, in which – at least in spy and war films – we have recently seen a multiplication of screens, infographics, tracking devices and many other traces or metaphors of enunciation (Polidoro 2016b). It of course happens on the web as well, so much so that already at the time when Bolter and Grusin were writing it was difficult to tell whether it was television that was influencing web sites (which had 'remediated' it) or the opposite.

Questions concerning remediation, and most of all, immediacy and hypermediation, are clearly of great pertinence to semiotics. Semiotics, unlike other disciplines, already has at its disposal concepts and analytical instruments suited to identify and describe the mechanisms through which these strategies are carried out. The immediacy/hypermediation dyad, for example, can be traced back – with the necessary precautions – to the transparency/opacity opposition studied by Louis Marin (2002) in painting. According to Marin, in an image we must recognize two aspects: *transitivity* or *transparency*, through which the image represents something, and *reflexivity* or *opacity*, through which it presents itself as representing something. This means that an image (but also any sign in general) not only represents something (and thus in a certain sense refers us back to that thing), but also 'says' it is an image, and stresses its nature as an artificial sign (insofar as it is produced by human beings). We should also recall the work of Victor Stoichita (1993), an art historian very close to semiotics, on the birth of the 'frame' form and the numerous figures of enunciation that can be found in painting, as well as the observations of Landowski (1989) concerning the relationship between the gazes of the represented subjects and the spectators. Landowski, furthermore, contributed several works (albeit not dealing with the audiovisual) on how enunciative strategies can be employed in the construction of a relationship with the reader/listener/spectator.

NEW TENDENCIES: SERIALITY AND TRANSMEDIALITY

With the advent of digital media, and in particular beginning in the early 2000s, the panorama of traditional media was revolutionized, and this of course impacted television as well. The borders between media became blurrier, and intermedial exchanges more frequent; new formats also arose, better adapted to use on devices other than traditional televisions, and in different circumstances (for example, while riding on public transportation). Two new phenomena in particular had a significant impact on television and the audiovisual: the evolution of seriality and transmedial convergence.

Seriality is of course nothing new, and was already present even in pre-modern sagas. Contemporary seriality, however, begins at the dawn of mass culture. It is in the first half of the 1800s that the first narratives began to appear, divided into instalments and presenting recurring characters, settings and narrative patterns. Charles Dickens's *Pickwick Papers* (1836–7) is one example, and heralded the publication, in the following decade, of several masterpieces of the French *feuilleton*, such as *The Mysteries of Paris* by Eugène Sue (1842–3), and *The Three Musketeers* (1844) and *The Count of Monte Cristo* (1845), both by Alexandre Dumas.

In the second half of the 1900s, television was undoubtedly the privileged site for seriality. Television historian Robert J. Thompson (1997) identified at least two golden ages of the television series; the first spanned from the end of the 1940s through all of the 1950s, and saw the birth and consolidation of various genres and serial schemas. The second took place during the 1980s, with the maturation of serial television forms and the increasing presence of multiple storylines taking place over a long period (a gradual passage, following a traditional opposition, from the *series* to the *serial*). Beginning in the early 2000s, it is possible to identify a third golden age of the television series, owing to the intense competition in quality products hosted on subscription platforms (Netflix, HBO, Amazon Prime Video) characterized by well-structured and careful narratives, the adoption of cinematic techniques and styles, and the involvement of famous actors.

Seriality poses interesting questions for semiotics. In addition to the approaches to the audiovisual that we have already analysed, there is also the possibility of studying the construction of this kind of seriality, which is always the establishment of a repetition (of actors, schemas, situations) within a variation. A complex and articulated taxonomy of serial genres (Grignaffini 2016) can be based on many factors: for instance, the kind of seriality (in *series* each episode tells a self-concluding story, while in *serials* one or more narrative lines span across the arc of a season or of the entire work); the tone (dramatic or comedic); the subject (crime, romance, adventure, medical, etc.). From the combination of these elements develops a very rich system that can be studied either synchronically or diachronically, and whose most interesting nodes concern the exchange and hybridization that have become more frequent in recent years.

The characteristically semiotic question of genre – which of course is not limited to television series (it suffices to think, remaining within the audiovisual, of cinematic genres), but finds a particularly fertile and innovative terrain there – gained further prominence through the progressive expansion of television seriality from the traditional channels to streaming on-demanding platforms and finally, to the web (with the web-series), a transformation that brings about the adoption of new formats (suffice it to think of the progressive abandonment of the binary division between episodes of little more than 20 minutes – characteristic of the sitcom – and of around 50 minutes – characteristics of other series). This last change exemplifies another phenomenon which, in recent years, has profoundly transformed the audiovisual, and hence, its study: transmediality.

Beginning in the 2000s, the world of the audiovisual and of media culture in general was increasingly populated by the concepts of *convergence* and *transmedia* (or its variation *crossmedia*, which some consider a synonym, and others a phenomenon at least in part different and more oriented towards interactivity). The author of reference in this case is certainly Henry Jenkins (2003; 2006; 2011). Jenkins had the merit of being one of the first to describe certain phenomena that, although they had existed for some time, emerged overwhelmingly with the spread of digital media. For Jenkins, convergence does not consist in the substitution of traditional media by digital media, but rather the continual overlap and exchange between media. Transmediality is, however, something more than the presence of narrative elements spread across multiple media: this would not be anything new, since *adaptations*, that is, the transposition of the same story from one medium to another, have always existed. Jenkins, instead, deals with 'transmedia storytelling', in which there is an actual *extension*, that is, when a story is enriched or developed in its passage from one medium to another. This extension may have a centre and spread out to other media, as when a film spawns a mini-series, videogames, comic books, etc. Or, increasingly often, it may be a strategy conceived of as transmedial from the very beginning, with the different media taking on different functions. *Transmedia storytelling* can be directed from above, or it can arise from or be fed from the bottom, namely the fans. In this sense, we can see how digital media did not invent these mechanisms, but certainly served as catalysts for them: *fanfiction*, stories written by fans on the basis of an official canon, has existed for a long time, but the internet has made its creation (at least in the case of audiovisual texts) and distribution, and in some cases its collaborative creation, much easier.

Convergence and transmedia storytelling thus advance parallel with the spread of the bottom-up content, with new forms like the *remix* and the *mashup* taking their places alongside the traditional forms of extension of a text (we might think, within the cinematic context, of the *remake*, *sequel*, *prequel* and *spin-off*).

Here too, semiotics has tools well suited to intercept these phenomena, to map them in a coherent way and understand their mechanisms. Multiple semiotic approaches are involved. First of all, we need to consider studies on translation, which begin from the Jakobsonian distinction between *intralinguistic*, *interlinguistic* and *intersemiotic* translation (Jakobson 1958). An adaptation of a novel into a film, then, would be a typical example of intersemiotic translation. But of course the recognition of this type of translation is only a first step, preliminary to a more systematic investigation that can be carried out at every semiotic level: in this process of translation, which elements are maintained, which are modified and which must be modified due to the differences between expressive material or media? Also, at what level have the modifications taken place: the expressive level (linked to the material), the discursive level (actors, figures, spatialization and temporalization), the level of narrative structure (variation of actantial roles, suppression or addition of narrative programs)? Remaining on the subject of semiotics and translation, one cannot neglect the semiotics of culture approach, and in particular the school of Yuri Lotman, which already ventured into this field (Saldre and Torop 2012).

The other important semiotic thread here is the aforementioned narratology of Genette (1997), who already in *Palimpsestes* had classified different types of intertextual relationships, composing a grid that can, with the necessary modifications, be adapted to a transmedial reality. One example of this is an Italian collection that had the merit, already in 2006, of approaching questions related to the remix, the remake and other emerging forms of textual transformation from a semiotic viewpoint (Dusi and Spaziante 2006).

The question of transmediality shows how the traditional schemas of media studies and the application of semiotics to specific fields need to be updated. Traditional textual semiotics can continue to use its old instruments and also develop new ones in order to map, describe and trace a reality that seems much more fluid than before but in which, nonetheless, the audiovisual still shows regularity and structures that can be investigated. But the textual approach is not the only future of semiotics, which as we will see in the next paragraph, has for a number of years begun to follow completely new pathways.

FROM PASSIONS TO EXPERIENCE

As we saw at the end of the first section, the maturation of the semiotics of cinema brings it progressively towards narratology. In the anglophone context, a reaction to this tendency begins in the 1980s, bringing forth the cognitivist approach to film studies, which criticizes the abstractness of semiotic constructs derived from linguistics and takes a position that is indeed anti-semiotics. For cognitivists, the spectator is not an ideological or abstract subject, but one that actively intervenes through their own rational activity. Despite the attempt at mediation between semiotics and cognitivism offered by Warren Buckland (2000), the two approaches remain substantially distant from one another, also due to a mutual ignorance, despite the circulation in English of important studies by Casetti (1998) and Eco (2000).

The enunciational conception of narration based in linguistics and developed by film semiotics in the early stages of its history gives way to a more phenomenological dimension. The abstraction of textual instances progressively begins to be replaced by the concreteness of the spectator, with their psychology and their emotions; a 'semiotics of experience' takes the place of the semiotics of the text, and places the *body* at the centre of its inquiries. Greimas (1987a, 1987b) had already shown the importance of the study of the 'aesthetic apprehension' of experience, focusing his analyses on affectivity, emotion, thymic investment and *tensivity*, understood as processes of the production and reception of meaning. The 'semiotics of passions' (Greimas and Fontanille 1993) finds in corporeal sensibility the site within which the signification process originates and plays out. In accord with the philosophical approach of Maurice Merleau-Ponty (2002), Jacques Fontanille (2004) conceives of the body as a terrain co-inhabited by the intentions of two subjects on the basis of a process of simulation, an imitative movement that connects the external perceptual *frame* and the internal emotional *frame*. This process, carried out by the actant as a 'incarnated' operator, takes pace on two corporeal levels (whose differentiation in a sense follows the Husserlian distinction between *Körper* and *Leib*). At its base, it occurs at a sensorimotor level, affecting the body as flesh or material body; then, the body understood as lived-body is the site of the construction of identity. In Fontanille's 'figures of the body', the passions are inscribed through a process of 'hypoiconic adaptation' carried out on the *shell* of the body, that is to say the interface or the surface of mediation between interoception (expression) and exteroception (content), leaving upon it the imprint of variations and changes (on the skin, in muscle tone, in posture) involved in intersubjective relations. Interpretation entails searching for the experience that has left its trace on the surface. In such research meaning is *felt* rather than generalized or conceptualized.

Similarly, in the socio-semiotic context, Landowski argues that meaning is grasped not through categorization or codification, but rather in the process of its making, and is *felt* before it is understood. The subject, situated before another subject (copresence of actants), does not carry out a decodification of the 'symptoms' of the passions, but instead is 'infected' by them and reproduces them in his/her own subjectivity, as though they inhabited his/her own body, making use of a simulacral substitution (Landowski 2004). This imaginative simulation, referred to by Landowski as contagion, corresponds to an operation of *débrayage* (the projection of a subjectivity different from that of the enunciation), which follows an *embrayage*, the moment of recognition and attribution of an affective state to the observed subject, or to oneself in virtue of somatic contagion. Involving this enunciational operation, contagion is the means through which the meaning of the interaction is interpreted. Landowski's approach thus fully embraces the assumptions of the theory of 'embodied' experience, aimed at the overcoming of the dualism of mind and body, and between the intelligible and the sensible – a dualism that corresponds to two tendencies that have long remained irreconcilable: the 'desemanticization of the body' in the natural sciences, and the 'disincarnation of meaning' in the human sciences (Landowski 2001). Hence the importance of broadening the investigative domain of the sign-text-context to the wider field of lived experience (*Erlebnis*) and thus to intersubjective experience, the negotiation between living and desiring corporealities. The site of sensoriality, the body is the true medium of experience, at once the support and the space of the discursive unfolding of interactive processes of reading and decodification.

PRE-REFLEXIVE SEMIOTICS

The attention to corporeality and the 'sensible' aspects of perception lies at the basis of a new strand of semiotic studies of media experience. Unlike textual semiotics, the 'cousin' of linguistics, this approach aims to engage with the cognitive neurosciences. The advancements in the field of neuroscience beginning in the 1990s, not only empirical but also philosophical, accelerated the emancipation of cognitive science from classical models, which used a computational metaphor to explain the mechanisms of human comprehension, and began to adopt an *embodied* perspective that takes account of the intimate unity between body and mind and stresses the role of corporeality and the sensible in the perceptual-cognitive-emotive macrosystem of human experience (Varela, Thompson and Rosch 1991; Damasio 1995; Lakoff and Johnson 1999).

One of the most important elements that the semiotics of experience borrow from the neurosciences is the 'mirror system'. Beginning in the mid-1990s, Italian neurophysiologists, exploring the premotor cortex of the brain with the aid of neuroimaging techniques, discovered the existence of 'mirror neurons', cells capable of at once guiding an action and 'thinking' of a potential action. Thanks to the activity of these neurons, the subject understands the meaning of the received stimulus through an implicit recognition, based on the unintentional 'recuperation' of the observed action within one's own motor domain. When we see a finalized action carried out by another subject, a motor representation of this action is generated in our brains, as though we were executing it (Rizzolatti and Sinigaglia 2007). The first and fundamental application of this discovery concerns the motor aspects of corporeal imitation and explains in neurological terms, for example, the phenomena of facial feedback and corporeal synchronization in respect to the movements of characters in a film. The second is that the mirror neurons constitute the neural correlate of the processes of simulation necessary for the comprehension of the minds of others, furnishing the bases for learning how to empathize with the other (Gallese and Goldman 1998). The mirror mechanism is capable of codifying sensorial experience not through cognitive processes of an inferential or associative type, but directly and implicitly in pre-cognitive terms. Third, at a deeper and more complex level, the activity of the motor neurons provides the basis for the recognition of the emotions of others. For example, to observe a face that expresses an emotion (including that of a character in a film) stimulates in the observer the same cerebral centres that are activated when the observer has an analogous emotional reaction, and can thus lead to empathetic sharing (Gallese 2001).

The domain of application of these discoveries has at its centre intersubjectivity and the processes of mediation and negotiation of meeting on the basis of a corporeal relationship, whether of physical co-presence or in mediated situations such as that of the audiovisual. These neurocognitive discoveries support the assumptions of Simulation Theory, according to which our understanding of the other is based on the ability to simulate what the other is thinking and feeling, without needing to carry out inferential activity or postulate theories to predict their behaviour, as instead is argued by Theory Theory (Gallagher and Zahavi 2007). In semiotic terms, the assumption that the activity of the mirror neurons physiologically 'corporealize' the modality of comprehension that makes up the experience of the other before any conceptual mediation supports the idea that the perceptual-affective dimension constitutes the precondition of signification. Thus there would be a foundational moment of signification, a logically necessary one already present in a pre-categorical and pre-linguistic space. Insofar as the neurons and their combinations cannot be considered in themselves to be semiotic material, they form a minimal structure that activates the process of generation/interpretation of meaning at a proto-semiotic stage. This would empirically verify Greimas's intuition that the visual perceptive level leads to a tactile perceptual level, which in reality lies beneath the first, a deeper stage of sensoriality in which the character of knowledge is gradual, continuous, and modular.

Albeit with some resistance, contemporary semiotics has now fully entered into the heart of this theoretical turn. The intersubjective and thus social dimension of experience and the overcoming of the sensible/intelligible dichotomy through the mediation of the body brings it closer to post-computational cognitive science in its attempt to trace and give a determinative role to the pre-logical basis of meaning situated in corporeality.

Semiotics and the neurosciences both investigate the processes of the sharing of experience; a sharing that springs from the recognition of an analogy that is in the first instance corporeal-material, which develops through corporeal-experiential negotiation but matures and fully realizes itself only as an existential congruity, while not, however, extinguishing the subjectivities involved by reducing each to the structure of the other. The empathic relationship can be understood as a dynamic negotiational process of configuration and interpretation of meaning (and the meaning of the relation itself) through the senses, and not as an invariable program of the automatic determination of meaning on the basis of a somato-corporeal analogy. Recent neurocognitive discoveries have the merit of having rendered research into intersubjectivity in the philosophical and psychological schools less mystical and transcendent, providing empirical explanations for the functioning of the biological and physiological component of sensory experience, and offering contemporary semiotics the concreteness whose lack the cognitivists lament.

There is of course a strong risk that the presumed irrefutability of the neurocognitive method will minimize the significance of lived subjectivity, reducing the qualitative difference of the meaning of the shared experience to a quantitative investigation into the extension of areas of the brain. Furthermore, insofar as the *recognition* of an action/intention/emotion through one's own 'experiential encyclopaedia' also precedes its *simulation*, brain activity represents only the neurophysiological substrate of experience, which is much wider and involves the individual and unique history of each individual, as well as their self-reflexive capacity. While keeping the reductionist risks of this approach in mind, by adopting the insights concerning incorporated simulation, the semiotics of media and the audiovisual has the chance to renew itself by constructing new models of analysis focusing on the perceptual and relational aspects of the media experience (Eugeni 2009), the audiovisual versions of certain embodied rhetorical figures, such as metaphor (Coëgnarts and Kravanja 2015), the experimental verification of the 'embodied semiotics' that lies at the basis of the corporeal nature of film theorized by Vivian Sobchack (1992) (Gallese and Guerra 2019); and the formulation of new epistemological models that seek to reconcile cine-semiology and cognitive neurosciences (D'Aloia and Eugeni 2014).

In each of these cases, the new semiotics of audiovisual media experience is concerned with structures that pre-exist signification, or rather with their conditions of possibility, and no longer with, as at the beginning, the structures underlying textual dynamics (which however remain the legitimate object of other semiotic approaches, as we have seen in the preceding sections), thus indeed going back to a radical pre-semiotics focused on the somatic and pre-categorical aspects of semiosis.

CONCLUSION

As we have seen in this chapter, the interest of contemporary semiotics in cinema, television, and audiovisual media in general starts from the reflections of Christian Metz and other scholars about the semiotic status of these languages: are they similar to or different from verbal language? And does the audiovisual sign have its own specificity?

After this first phase, the attention moved gradually towards more text-oriented approaches. Among them, the most remarkable were the research about narrative dynamics in cinema and the application of the concept of enunciation to audiovisual texts (with the consequent introduction of concepts such as point of view, focalization, etc.). The idea of enunciation also underlies the work of Bolter and Grusin, and their concepts of remediation, immediacy and hypermediation, which span from traditional visual and audiovisual media to digital ones.

Another approach to cinema and television studies has been the focus on context and social meaning of these media and, from a semiotic point of view, of their narrative contents. Cinema, television and other audiovisual media have been considered as ways of spreading or confirming ideological patterns. This has been also the approach to television followed by Umberto Eco in the first part of his work, while between the late Seventies and the Eighties he introduced some relevant reflections about the new emerging forms of television language (once again, focusing also on enunciative aspects). Eco was also an anticipator of the studies about seriality and its forms and of the different ways in which texts and media contaminates each other; this is a field which in recent years received a renewed attention, as a consequence of the commercial success of TV series.

On another side, the enunciational approach, imbued with phenomenology and cognitivism, developed a stronger semiotic attention towards the audiovisual experience. In this frame, concepts such as passion, embodiment and perception intertwined in different ways. These concepts have grown in importance, creating a scientific scenario in which audiovisual semiotics is pushed towards an increasing dialogue with cognitive science, neuroscience and other disciplines.

NOTE

1   This chapter is the product of work carried out in common by two authors, and the result of a single shared process of reflection. As far as the writing of the individual sections of the text is concerned, the introduction and sections "Semiotics and Television", "Television and Enunciation", and "New Tendencies: Seriality and Transmediality" can be attributed to Piero Polidoro, and sections "Semiotics and Cinema", "From Passions to Experience", and "Pre-Reflexive Semiotics" to Adriano D'Aloia.

REFERENCES

Altman, R. (1984), 'A Semantic/Syntactic Approach to Film Genre', *Cinema Journal*, 23: 6–18.
Baena, R. and C. Byker (2014), 'Dialects of Nostalgia: Downton Abbey and English Identity', *National Identities*, 17 (3): 259–69.
Barthes, R. (1964), 'Rhétorique de l'image', *Communications*, 4: 40–51.
Barthes, R. ([1966] 1975), 'An Introduction to the Structural Analysis of Narrative', *New Literary History*, 6 (2): 237–72.
Barthes, R. ([1957] 1994), *Mythologies*, London: Grant & Cutler.
Benveniste, É. ([1966] 1971), *Problems in General Linguistics*, Miami: University of Miami Press.
Bettetini, G. ([1968] 1973), *The Language and Technique of the Film*, Mounton: The Hague.
Bettetini, G. (1984), *La conversazione audiovisiva. Problemi dell'enunciazione filmica e audiovisiva*, Milano: Bompiani.
Bolter, J. D. and R. Grusin (1999), *Remediation: Understanding New Media*, Cambridge: The MIT Press.
Buckland, W. (2000), *The Cognitive Semiotics of Film*, Cambridge: Cambridge University Press.
Byrne, K. (2014), 'Adapting Heritage: Class and Conservatism in Downton Abbey', *Rethinking History: The Journal of Theory and Practice*, 18 (3): 311–27.
Casetti, F. ([1986] 1998), *Inside the Gaze: The Fiction Film and Its Spectator*, Bloomington-Indianapolis: Indiana University Press.
Casetti, F. ([1993] 1999), *Theories of Cinema, 1945–1995*, Austin: University of Texas Press.
Chatman, S. (1978), *Story and Discourse*, Ithaca: Cornell University Press.
Coëgnarts, M. and P. Kravanja (2015), *Embodied Cognition and Cinema*, Leuven: Leuven University Press.
Czarniawska, B. (2018), 'On Retrotopias', *Scandinavian Journal of Management*, 34: 349–53.
D'Aloia, A. and R. Eugeni, eds (2014). *Neurofilmology: Audiovisual Studies and the Challenge of Neuroscience*, Special Issue of *Cinéma&Cie: International Film Studies Journal*, 14: 22–3.
Damasio, A. R. (1994), *Descartes's Error: Emotion, Reason and the Human Brain*, New York: Grosset/Putnam.

Doležel, L. (2010), *Possible Worlds of Fiction and History: The Postmodern Stage*, Baltimore: The Johns Hopkins University Press.
Dusi, N. and L. Spaziante (2006), *Remix-Remake*, Roma: Meltemi.
Eco, U. ([1968] 1976), 'Articulation of the Cinematic Code', in B. Nichols (ed.), *Movies and Methods*, 590–606, Berkeley: University of California Press.
Eco, U. (1979), *The Role of the Reader*, Bloomington: Indiana University Press.
Eco, U. ([1990] 1991), *The Limits of Interpretation*, Bloomington: Indiana University Press.
Eco, U. ([1997] 2000), *Kant and the Platypus*, London: Secker and Warburg.
Eco, U. (2018), *Sulla televisione*, ed. G. Marrone, Milano: La Nave di Teseo.
Eugeni, R. (2009), *Semiotica dei media. Teoria e analisi dell'esperienza mediale*, Roma: Carocci.
Fontanille, J. (2004), *Soma et séma. Figures du corps*, Paris: Maisonneuve et Larose.
Gallagher, S. and D. Zahavi (2007), *The Phenomenological Mind: An Introduction to Philosophy of Mind and Cognitive*, London: Routledge.
Gallese, V. (2001), 'The "Shared Manifold" Hypothesis: From Mirror Neurons to Empathy', *Journal of Consciousness Studies*, 8 (5–7): 33–50.
Gallese, V. and A. Goldman (1998), 'Mirror Neurons and the Simulation Theory of Mind-Reading', *Trends in Cognitive Sciences*, 12: 493–501.
Gallese, V. and M. Guerra ([2015] 2019), *The Empathic Screen: Cinema and Neuroscience*, New York: Oxford University Press.
Garroni, E. (1968), *Semiotica ed estetica*, Bari: Laterza.
Genette, G. ([1972] 1980), *Narrative Discourse: An Essay in Method*, Ithaca: Cornell University Press.
Genette, G. ([1982] 1997), *Palimpsests: Literature in the Second Degree*, Paris: Seuil.
Greimas, A. J. ([1966] 1983), *Structural Semantics: An Attempt at a Method*, Lincoln: University of Nebraska Press.
Greimas, A. J. (1987a), *On Meaning. Selected Writings in Semiotic Theory*, Minneapolis: University of Minnesota Press.
Greimas, A. J. (1987b), *De l'imperfection*, Périgueux: Pierre Fanlac.
Greimas, A. J. and J. Courtés ([1979] 1982), *Semiotics and Language. An Analytical Dictionary*, Bloomington: Indiana University Press.
Greimas, A. J. and J. Fontanille ([1991] 1993), *The Semiotics of Passions: From States of Affairs to States of Feeling*, Minneapolis: University of Minnesota Press.
Grignaffini, G. (2016), 'Generi e rigenerazioni nella serialità Tv americana', *Between*, 6 (11): 1–14.
Hintikka, J. (1967), 'Individuals, Possible Worlds and Epistemic Logic', *Noûs*, 1 (1): 33–62.
Hintikka, J. (1969), *On the Logic of Perception. Models for Modalities*, Dordrecht: Reidel.
Jakobson, R. (1958), 'On Linguistic Aspects of Translation', in R. A. Brower (ed.), *On Translation*, 232–9, Cambridge: Harvard University Press.
Jenkins, H. (2003), 'Transmedia Storytelling', *MIT Technology Review*, January 15. https://www.technologyreview.com/2003/01/15/234540/transmedia-storytelling/.
Jenkins, H. (2006), *Convergence Culture: Where Old and New Media Collide*, New York: New York University Press.
Jenkins, H. (2011), 'Transmedia 202: Further Reflections', 31 July. http://henryjenkins.org/blog/2011/08/defining_transmedia_further_re.html.
Jost, F. (1989), *L'Oeil-Caméra. Entre film et roman*, Lyon: Presses Universitaires de Lyon.
Lakoff, G. and M. Johnson (1999), *Philosophy in the Flesh: The Embodied Mind and Its Challenge to Western Thought*, New York: Basic Books.
Landowski, E. (1989), *La société réfléchie*, Paris: Seuil.

Landowski, E. (2001), 'Fare segno, fare senso: regimi di significazione del corpo', in P. Berretti and G. Manetti (eds), *Forme della testualità. Teorie, modelli storie e prospettive*, 60–75, Torino: Testo & Immagine.

Lévi-Strauss, C. ([1958] 1963), *Structural Anthropology*, New York: Basic Books.

Marin, L. ([1994] 2002), *On Representation*, Redwood City: Stanford University Press.

Merleau-Ponty, M. ([1945] 2002), *Phenomenology of Perception*, London: Routledge.

Metz, C. ([1968] 1974a), *Film Language: A Semiotics of the Cinema*, New York: Oxford University Press.

Metz, C. ([1971] 1974b), *Language and Cinema*, The Hague: Mouton/Paris.

Niemeyer, K., ed. (2014), *Media and Nostalgia: Yearning for the Past, Present and Future*, New York: Palgrave Macmillan.

Odin, Roger ([1983] 1995), 'For a Semiopragmatics of Film', in W. Buckland (ed.), *The Film Spectator. From sign to mind*, 213–26, Amsterdam: Amsterdam University Press.

Pasolini, P. P. ([1972] 1988), *Heretical Empirism*, Bloomington: Indiana University Press.

Polidoro, P. (2016a), 'Serial Sacrifices: A Semiotic Analysis of *Downton Abbey* Ideology', *Between*, 6 (11): 1–27.

Polidoro, P. (2016b), 'Rimediazione, immediatezza e ipermediazione nella rappresentazione della guerra', in T. Migliore (ed.), *Rimediazioni. Immagini interattive*, vol. 2, 279–95, Roma: Aracne.

Propp, V. I. ([1928] 1968), *Morphology of the Folktale*, 2nd edn, Austin: University of Texas Press.

Rizzolatti, G. and C. Sinigaglia (2007), *Mirrors in the Brain: How Our Minds Share Actions, Emotions, and Experience*, trans. F. Anderson, Oxford: Oxford University Press.

Saldre, M. and P. Torop (2012), 'Transmedia Space', in I. Ibrus and C. Scolari (eds), *Crossmedia Innovations: Texts, Markets, Institutions*, 25–6, Frankfurt am Main: Peter Lang.

Sobchack, V. (1992), *The Address of the Eye: A Phenomenology of Film Experience*, Princeton: Princeton University Press.

Stoichita, V. (1993), *L'instauration du tableau*, Paris: Méridiens Klincksieck.

Thompson, R. J. (1997), *Television's Second Golden Age*, Syracuse: Syracuse University Press.

Varela, F. J., E. Thompson and E. Rosch (1991), *The Embodied Mind. Cognitive Science and Human Experience*, Cambridge: The MIT Press.

CHAPTER TEN

Semiotics in Music and Musicology

WILLIAM P. DOUGHERTY AND ESTI SHEINBERG

INTRODUCTION

While surveying the topography of a vast semiotic landscape, Umberto Eco observed that 'the whole of musical science since the Pythagoreans has been an attempt to describe the field of musical communication as a rigorously structured system' (1976: 10). He noted that 'in the last two or three years musical semiotics has been definitely established as a discipline aiming to find its "pedigree" and developing new perspectives' (1976: 10). Only a few years later, Henry Orlov, arguing for a musical semiotics constructed from the primary reality of music as sound, offered the following warning:

> That music may be described in semiotic terms does not necessarily mean that the terminology and theory of semiotics will help us to understand music better. As such attempts have shown, music stubbornly and defiantly conceals even what is already known, and turns out to be a very difficult object to deal with.
>
> (1981: 131)

Striking a balance between both of these assessments – cautious optimism, if you will – concerning the potential value of a full-throated semiotic approach to music was a challenge for the first music semioticians. Emerging at a time when musicology and music theory were dominated by the analysis of musical structure, designs for a semiotics of music were often caught in the struggle to articulate an approach that accounted for the richness and complexity of music signification without an over-reliance on sometimes fashionable, but arcane, semiotic jargon. Questions surrounding whether, and to what degree, appeals to semiotics help us to understand music better, as Orlov aptly put it, typically overshadowed assessments of methodological or epistemological allegiances (e.g. a grounding in structural or transformational-generative linguistics; fidelity to Saussurean or Peircean underpinnings; or a view of music as a primary or secondary modelling system). These early obstacles were, happily, surmounted (otherwise this chapter would not have been written). As musicology opened its doors in the late 1980s and early 1990s to a variety of treatments of musical meaning, music semiotics, with its focus on the intricacies of sign functions, emerged as a powerful tool to address the ways in which music communicates expressive meanings. Musicologists and music theorists explicitly engaged principles developed from general semiotic theory and actively applied them in sophisticated fashions to issues of music signification.

This chapter traces the various principles that have guided music semiotics from its earliest phases to the present day. We have subdivided the chapter into six broad areas reflecting what we take to be common orientations in order to provide a structure, or a filter, for the diffuseness of writings about music semiotics. These subdivisions, as well as the discussions of authors and tendencies within them, are organized in a roughly chronological fashion. The reality is, though, that the categories overlap, much like shingles on a roof. In addition, the work of music semioticians routinely crosses categorical boundaries by drawing on, instersecting with, and contributing to more than one area (as a result, some authors are discussed in more than one of our subdivisions). Nevertheless, we believe that our segmentation of the musico-semiotic continuum permits a sensible and equitable survey of the large number of writers and the breadth of ideas that have shaped the trajectory of semiotics in music and musicology.

DEFINING MUSICAL UNITS

The publication of *Fondements d'une sémiologie de la musique* in 1975 by the French-Canadian musicologist Jean-Jacques Nattiez marked an important milestone on the road to establish a fully formed music semiology.[1] Building on and expanding ideas that had been percolating for many years, particularly in the writings of European theoreticians, and enveloping them in principles derived from Saussurean linguistics and structuralism, *Fondements* offers an over-arching music semiology – one that embraces all musics in all cultures – and weaves theory and analysis into a dense fabric. The principles espoused in *Fondements* received widespread critical discussion (see Subotnik 1976; Dunsby 1977, 1983; Laske 1977; Lidov [1978] 2005; Hatten 1980; Schneider 1980: 164–242; Keiler 1981), and overviews of musical analysis extolled it as the *sine qua non* of a semiological approach to music (e.g. Bent 1980; Cook 1987).[2] Although emendations, clarifications and extensions during subsequent years were common – not the least by Nattiez himself (1990, 2004; see also Dunsby and Goldman 2017), in the main, *Fondements* stands as the definitive exposition of the tenets underlying the semiological enterprise in music.

The theoretical model adopted and developed by Nattiez to address music as a symbolic fact is the tripartition, a model presented earlier by Jean Molino ([1975] 1990). The tripartition consists of three poles:

1. the poietic (*poiétique*), in which analysis focuses on the strategies of a work's production;
2. the esthesic (*esthésique*), in which analysis focuses on the strategies of perception or interpretation; and
3. the neutral level (*niveau neutre*), in which immanent structural and recurring features of the signifier are distributionally analysed and cataloged.

As Nattiez formulates it, the neutral level:

> is a level of analysis at which one does not decide a priori whether the results generated by a specific analytical proceeding are relevant from the esthesic or poietic point of view. The analytic tools used for the delimitation and the classification of phenomena are systematically exploited, until they are exhausted, and are not replaced by substitutes

until a new or new difficulties lead to the proposition of new tools. 'Neutral' means both that the poietic and esthesic dimensions of the object have been 'neutralized', and that one proceeds to the end of a given procedure regardless of the results obtained.

(1990: 13; see also 1975: 54–5)

The neutral level stands as an empirically objective arena wherein the musical text only is treated as an independent semiological system. The results are revealed by applying discovery procedures that are exhaustively carried out without reference to either its mode of production or its mode of perception. The segmented units are classified by virtue of recurring patterns (usually based on melodic segmentations) that are related to one another through repetition or transformation. These segmentations are projected paradigmatically on a vertical axis while temporal continuity is projected syntagmatically on a horizontal axis. This rigorous distributional analysis strives for a clear-cut inventory of units that comprise the material of the message. After the application of these procedures, the combination rules of the units constitute the code. By way of illustration, Ruwet's oft-cited analysis of a fourteenth-century *Geisslerlied* is given in Figure 10.1.

FIGURE 10.1 Ruwet's analysis of a *Geisslerliede* ([1966] 1987: 21).

Although the ontological status of the neutral level and the methodology to identify units on it has been challenged (see, e.g., Keiler 1981), a neutral level of analysis strives to achieve at least four interrelated goals:

1. Insofar as the discovery procedures are applied rigorously following precise criteria, the segmentations and paradigmatic associations they reveal are unambiguous and reproducible; as such, they allow later analysts to ascertain how each decision was made.
2. The metalanguage used to label the segmented units and the hierarchic structure (here 'a', 'b[1]', 'A' and so on) is not encumbered by unclear, *ad hoc*, or ill-defined terminology (e.g. 'cell', 'motive', 'phrase' and so on), and it thus respects the internal organization found in the signifier itself.
3. Analytic procedures are carried out with strict adherence to the immanent structure of the composition, regardless of any input or bias emanating from poietic or esthesic vantage points.[3]
4. Issues involving potential correlations with poietic or esthesic concerns can only be meaningfully addressed after the inductive neutral analysis.

The semiological approach has been applied to analyses of compositions by Brahms (Nattiez 1975a), Debussy (Nattiez 1975b), Xenakis (Naud 1975), Varèse (Nattiez 1982), Boulez (Goldman 2011), and Chopin (Rosato 2018), among others. But the early hegemony enjoyed by proponents of a music semiology has largely been eclipsed by musicologists and theorists preferring other approaches – for instance those developed from Griemas or Peirce – to address the issues surrounding meaning in music.

IDENTIFYING SEMANTIC UNITS IN MUSIC

The ability of music to signal non-musical objects, concepts and subjects has been a traditionally accepted premise that affected the ways in which composers composed and listeners listened. It was only during a relatively short period (*c.* 1890–1960) that ideas of 'absolute music' gained supremacy, and music was looked on as 'pure formations of sounds' with no external meaning. This period was rich in theoretical and aesthetic writings that exerted a major influence on music composition and music education (although they were not embraced by all listeners). It was during the last third of the twentieth century that theoretical writings gradually re-introduced music's traditional role as an art that communicates emotional, psychological and social meanings: music signifies beyond its own immanent units. Terms such as 'semes', 'isotopes', 'intonations', 'tropes' and 'topics' became part and parcel of newly vibrant approaches to musical meaning, and they are now mainstays in the current analytical and musicological vocabulary. The frequent interchangeable synonymy of 'semiotics' and 'semantics' points to the commitment that recent music semiotics has with engaging with the extra-generic nature of music signification.

An early-twentieth-century advocate of musical meaning was Leonard B. Meyer (1956, 1973). While not explicitly invoking semiotic theories, Meyer – who could aptly be called a 'proto-semiotician' – considers musical meaning to arise as a result of the fulfilment or unfulfilment of expectations, based on culturally dependent musical events. He explains the ability of listeners to apprehend musical meanings through a generalized and reconstructable stylistic competence, a notion that would later secure a central position in the semiotic studies (see, especially, Hatten 1982, 1994).

During the 1970s, attempts to implement a semiotic approach to music were launched by Wilson Coker (1972) and David Osmond-Smith (1972, 1973, 1976). Starting from Peirce's trichotomy of icon, index and symbol, as viewed through Charles Morris's behavioural lens (1946), Coker combines musical aesthetics and semiotics with a germinal concept of music as gesture. Coker's semiotic program, though, did not attract a widespread following. Osmond-Smith, who also appealed to Peircean concepts, understood a musical icon in two ways:

1. that music can be iconic of an idea, a concept or a thing – in which case the musical motive (or seme) functions as an icon of some existing entity; and
2. it can be iconic of a gesture – in which case the direction, contour or progress of a musical unit is perceived as an icon of either vocal or bodily motion.

Both Coker and Osmond-Smith are fusing the Peircean conception of the sign with the time-dependent nature of music. Subsequent studies of musical gesture and its relation to bodily motion (see below) manifest both the explanatory power derived from the temporal nature of sound as a sign.

Little known in the West, but significant and influential in certain parts of Europe, East-European theoreticians made remarkable advances in semiotic research and in the application of semiotics to music, much earlier than – and ostensibly with no connection to – American trends in semiotics. For historical, cultural and no less political reasons, Russian musical aesthetics never questioned the relation between music and its meanings in the phenomenal world. The contributions of Boris Asafiev (1947), whose interpretation of the Russian term *intonatsia* incorporates both the definition of a musical sign and its functioning within a musical time-axis, are cardinal. While the term itself is complex, if not vague (Khananov 2018), its application has had an important impact on both Soviet musicology and Soviet music, discussing music in terms of tension and resolution, energy, gravitation and ideological content. When Asafiev's *Music as Form and Process* was translated into English by James Robert Tull (1976), it provided a link by which former centuries' Western perceptions of meaning in music could again be treated as a legitimate component of music semiotics. Despite being available in English, however, Asafiev's ideas were slow in gaining an audience, let alone in gaining popularity. Even among the French and other European musicological communities, who were closer to Russian semiotic writings, this term did not muster many disciples, perhaps because of, among other reasons, Asafiev's political involvement in the Soviet administration during the Cold War.

One of the first to absorb Asafiev's contributions is Eero Tarasti. His *Myth and Music* (1979) examines music's ability to reflect mythical content through associations and symbolisms. Tarasti's pluralistic approach, influenced by the Lithuanian-French theorist Algirdas Julien Greimas, is an important influence on the development of music semiotics. Tarasti applies to music Greimas's concept of *isotopies*, first outlined in *Structural Semantics* ([1966] 1983), coining the term 'musical isotopies'. A musical isotopy is created when learned and conventional connotations of several elements of a musical unit – rhythm, dynamics, timbre, mode, contour, register and so on – coalesce into a coherent and congruent meaning. These units, identified by the repetition of musical elements, are connected, in programmatic and vocal works, to things, ideas and emotions in the extra-musical world.[4] The concept of musical isotopies is further developed by Márta Grabócz (1986), who combined them with Asafiev's notion of *intonatsia*.

Robert Hatten, in his *Musical Meaning in Beethoven* (1994), codified his construal of an *expressive genre*, a concept in some ways similar to Tarasti's notion of isotopies. Building from his treatment of topics and tropes (see below), Hatten describes how an expressive genre subsumes the ways in which oppositional relations at the level of dramatic structure articulate a change of expressive states that are distinct from – and independent of – traditional formal genres (e.g. sonata, rondo, fugue). For example, Hatten tracks a tragic-to-transcendent expressive genre as a type in several specific tokens:

1. a single sonata-form movement (the third movement of Beethoven's Piano Sonata, Op. 106);
2. a fugue (the first movement of Beethoven's String Quartet, Op. 131); and
3. the two movements of a complete sonata (Beethoven's Piano Sonata, Op. 111).

In his quest to identify musical semantic units and their relationships, one of Hatten's most consequential contributions to music semiotics is the application of the concept of *markedness* to music. Initially developed in the Prague Linguistic Circle and subsequently grounded as a species of interpretant by Michael Shapiro (1983), markedness theory posits that the terms of an opposition are asymmetrical: the marked term of an opposition has a narrower referential scope, while the unmarked term is broader. Hatten (1994: 36–8) uses major versus minor to illustrate the distinction. In the Classical style, minor has a smaller distribution and narrower range of meaning than does major. As a result, the minor mode consistently cues the tragic whereas the major mode may encompass not only the comic or buffa, but also the heroic or the pastoral. Moreover, the asymmetry exemplified in the markedness values *correlates* with similar markedness values at the level of meaning. Thus, the minor mode, which occurs with less frequency, carves out a more specific expressive meaning ('tragic') than does the major mode. Hatten demonstrates how new meanings (and thus style change and growth) emerge from the creation of new oppositional relationships in markedness categories (for example, when a previously marked category is subdivided into another marked-unmarked pair).

THE MUSICAL TOPIC

In 1980, Leonard Ratner deployed the term 'topic' to embrace the various subjects of musical discourse that he construed to be vital to the expressive import of Classical music. In fact, the concept had a long history in writings about music, as numerous writers in the eighteenth century explored similar or related notions, albeit in a variety of guises.[5] Wye Jamison Allanbrook asserted that eighteenth-century composers were

> in possession of something we can call an expressive vocabulary, a collection in music of what in the theory of rhetoric are called *topoi*, or topics for formal discourse. [They] held it in common with [their] audience …. This vocabulary, when captured and categorized, provides a tool for analysis which can mediate between the [compositions] and our individual responses to them.
>
> (1983: 2)

By way of illustration, we offer Allanbrook's (1983: 6–8) topical analysis of the opening of Mozart's Piano Sonata in F major, K 332, in Figure 10.2. The first four measures

FIGURE 10.2 Topical analysis (after Allanbrook) of Mozart, Piano Sonata in F Major, K 332; I: 1–24.

exemplify a singing style topic (cued by a diatonic lyrical melody accompanied by a gentle Alberti bass). The melody abruptly breaks off, and measure 5 initiates a reference to (or parody of) the learned style (quasi-fugato writing, imitative counterpoint). Following the cadence in measure 12, Mozart invokes the hunt topic (cueing the hunting horn through the use of the so-called horn fifths). Finally, in measure 23, Mozart summons the *tempesta* or *Sturm und Drang* topic (cued by the abrupt shift to the key of D minor, the wide-spanning arpeggiation, the quicker rhythmic motion and the *forte* dynamic). As will become clear, topic theory is not only concerned with identifying the universe of topics available to composers in a style and their defining musical characteristics, but also how their combination and succession – their interplay – result in an expressive trajectory that demands interpretive consideration.

The concept of musical topics as a repository of a shared stylistic competence that is potentially intersubjectively verifiable launched a multitude of studies. Topic theory, although initially associated with music from the long eighteenth century, cuts across eras and repertoires in the quest to unravel how content is expressed and communicated. Fully aware of the risk of overstatement, we claim that all studies of musical topics are, at their core, semiotic, whether or not an analyst casts them in semiotic terms (many do not). We note, though, that signature advances in topic theory have been made by musicologists who explicitly ground musical topics in a semiotic framework.

In his *Playing with Signs* (1991), Kofi Agawu invokes Jakobson's terminology (1971) – and echoes Coker's distinction between congeneric and extrageneric musical meaning (1972) – to craft a semiotics of music that treats a composition's meaning in terms of interactions between 'introversive semiosis' (essentially, the purely musical elements articulated at various structural levels) and 'extroversive semiosis' (essentially, the flow of musical topics). To address the introversive aspect of musical structure, Agawu relies on the theories and analytic techniques of the Austrian theorist Heinrich Schenker ([1935] 1979). Agawu expands them, though, by positing a beginning-middle-end paradigm to capture the rhetorical strategies realized across middle-ground structural levels. Musical topics become the key element of Agawu's treatment of extroversive semiosis:

> Topics are musical signs. They consist of a signifier (a certain disposition of musical dimensions) and a signified (a conventional stylistic unit, often but not always referential in quality). Signifiers are identified as a relational unit within the dimensions of melody, harmony, rhythm, and so on, while the signified is designated by conventional labels drawn mostly from eighteenth-century historiography (Sturm und Drang, fanfare, learned style, sensibility, and so on).
>
> (Agawu 1991: 41)

Written at a time when, at least in American music theory, structural (i.e. Schenkerian) analyses reigned supreme, Agawu's charge to blend structural analysis with expressive analysis was an important catalyst in launching an openly semiotic engagement with musical meaning.

The quest to apply topic theory to music written outside of the Classical era was keen (see, e.g., Ratner 1992 and Dickensheets 2012, among others). In *Music as Discourse* (2009), Agawu extends his approach to the music of the Romantic period (and beyond) by combining an expanded set of topics (incorporating the work of Grabócz on Liszt [1986] and Bartók [2002]). His beginning-middle-end paradigm now incorporates a treatment of high points or climaxes, periodicity and discontinuity, modes of utterance, and narrativity. In a series of analyses, Agawu projects musical units (segmented by repetition or transformational associations, à la Ruwet and Nattiez) on a paradigmatic axis to determine how their modes of succession and combination can become the basis for an understanding of musical meaning.

Robert Hatten's *Musical Meaning in Beethoven* (1994) uses musical topics, understood as coded stylistic types, within an interpretative system that combines insights from music theory, music history, linguistics and the semiotics of Peirce. Influenced by Rosen (1972) and Meyer (1989), Hatten focuses on expressive meanings and the (reconstructed) stylistic competence they presuppose. He emphasizes that both of these features are inherently musical. Hatten describes his combination of structuralist and hermeneutic components addressing the correlation of sound to meaning as follows:

> A *structuralist* approach ... is concerned with mapping associations (*correlations*) of structures and meaning in a manner that reveals their oppositional organization .... A *hermeneutic* approach is concerned with interpretation beyond the more general oppositional meanings secured by correlations. Although guided by stylistic correlations, hermeneutic inquiry expands the theoretically stable bases of a structuralist modeling to encompass the subtlety, ambiguity, and allusive richness implied by any truly artistic competency.
>
> (1994: 2)

The notion of *trope* is vital to Hatten's construal of musical meaning, and it stands as an important contribution to topic theory. A trope is the combination of two (or more) expressive signs (topics or style types) that create an idiosyncratic meaning resulting from their fusion or collision (e.g. the fanfare topic conjoined with the learned style in the first measures of the Finale of Beethoven's Piano Sonata, Op. 101 [see Hatten 1994: 170]). Conceived as such, the interaction between the signs becomes a nexus of interpretation, and the analyst's task is to abductively ferret out the expressive purport articulated by their juxtaposition. In his conception of troping, Hatten embraces the mergers of correlations of these types to generate complex meanings. When the semantic correlations of tropes interact, the result can be something akin to metaphor. When the correlations, however, tend to contradict, exaggerate or distort each other, the result is irony (see Sheinberg 2000).

Following the publication of his *Linguistics and Semiotics in Music* (1992) – a comprehensive description of the trends in music semiotics at the time – Raymond Monelle's *The Sense of Music* (2000) includes criticism of Ratner's somewhat perfunctory list of eighteenth-century musical topics. He argues that topics, qua signs, are indexes (in the Peircean sense) that correlate to richly relational 'cultural units' (a term from Eco 1976). As a result, their full sense is revealed only after a thorough historical study of the (dynamic) object:

> In describing a musical topic, it is not enough to identify a motive, give it a label, and then move on to the next. Each topic may signify a large semantic world, connected to aspects of contemporary society, literary themes, and older traditions.
> (Monelle 2000: 79)

Monelle's *The Musical Topic* (2006) details the reticular relationships arising from the sign, its object and its interpretant. Focusing on three topics – the hunt, the military and the pastoral – he demonstrates how music semiotics can capture the ways in which music signification accesses and develops cultural and historical categories. A musical topic is recreated and enriched through styles and periods, and thus it is constantly enhanced by historical layers of accumulated meanings. Older connotations never disappear; instead, they continue to perform an active role in the process of semiosis.

As noted earlier, topic theory has spawned a vast literature in musicology, not all of which flies under a semiotic banner. We conclude this survey of musical topics by listing some other formulations of topic theory that are couched in an overtly semiotic context. William Echard (2017) uses topic theory to explore the culture associated with the development of psychedelic popular music; Nicholas McKay (2020, see also 2012) treats the dialogic and intertextual interplay of topics in two neo-classical operas, Stravinsky's *The Rake's Progress* and Britten's *The Turn of the Screw*; William P. Dougherty (1993, 2014) grounds musical topics in an explicit Peircean framework; Yayoi Uno Everett (2020, 2012) traces the signification of the *pianto* topic in contemporary operas by Thomas Adès, Kaija Saariaho and John Adams; and Johanna Frymoyer (2020) tracks the transformations of stylistic register that European topics underwent in their incorporation into Russian operatic contexts in the eighteenth century.

MUSICAL GESTURE AND EMBODIMENT

In his article 'Mind and Body in Music' ([1987] 2005), David Lidov addresses how music, prior to its status as a sign, 'is an action on and of the body' ([1987] 2005: 145). He uses Manfred Clynes's work on 'sentics' (1977) and Peirce's icon-index-symbol trichotomy to explore how 'the interplay between the representation of gesture and its formal contextualization creates discourse – a representation of think*ing* in action' (Lidov [1987] 2005: 138; see also Lidov 2020). For Lidov,

> the transformation of body to mind in music appears as a transcendent process of articulation. The immediate expression of physiological values in sound as performed nuance, is indexical. Where these values are translated into arrangements of formal units, for example, melodic contours, harmonic modulations, and so on, we have iconic signs. The further substitution of formal relations for physiological values (the developmental calculi of fragmentation, inversion, transposition, and so on, which can be but need not be subordinated to images of feeling) carries us toward the symbol.
>
> ([1987] 2005: 149)

Although music is an inherent part of mental life, as well as its product, Lidov sees close correspondences between the details of music and bodily properties, such as gestures, postures and even psychological states including moods and emotions. Lidov's attention to the complexities of the *temporal* link between a sonorous musical motion and its somatic experience is a cornerstone to his understanding of music signification.

Naomi Cumming's *The Sonic Self* (2000) elaborates a theory of musical subjectivity. Drawing on a vast array of thinkers and authors – including Lidov's sentic treatment of melodically embodied gesture – Cumming rethinks how the 'sonic self' is mediated by the patterning of audible musical signs and inner states. Subjectivity and the self, she argues, are positioned between the music and the listener, and it is at precisely this confluence that musical signification arises. Access to this realm is offered through a synthesis of insights gleaned from the performer's perspective, from the listener's perspective and from the careful analysis of the music. In the main, Cumming's entire enterprise is constructed from Peirce's full system of semiotic (with its categories, ten classes of signs, and its pragmaticism) to address how musical sounds are capable of carrying connotations of human subjective qualities in a way that suggests wilfulness. On the one hand, the self makes (performs, listens to, analyses) the music; on the other hand, music makes the self: the nature of the expressive shaping of human movement in musical signs is the entry point for exploring subjectivity and musical meaning.

In *Interpreting Musical Gestures, Topics, and Tropes*, Robert Hatten develops his concepts of stylistic correlation, markedness, topics, tropes and expressive genres, to include a theory of musical gesture as integral to the synthetic nature of meaning in music (2004; see also 1997–9). Hatten understands human gesture broadly, defining it as a significant energetic shaping through time. As he elaborates, though, gestural types may be oppositionally marked and correlated with the oppositions between musical tokens, suggesting a symbolic level of interpretation for gestural content. While both iconic and indexical correlations to gestures in other modalities motivate gestural interpretations, the symbolic level maintains its coherence through its realization in a musical style. Gestures can have different strategic functions in music (he identifies five types), many of which play both a structural and expressive role in the unfolding discourse of a musical composition.

Arnie Cox, in his *Music and Embodied Cognition* (2016), presents a theory of musical meaning based on musical signs that are perceived through embodiment, imitation and metaphorical thinking. This meaning is achieved through the physical or imagined interpretation of musical gestures, of music's motion through time and space, and of the spatial and temporal distribution of the musical elements of a composition. Cox explains that 'according to the mimetic hypothesis, perception of a leap involves feeling something of what it would be like to perform the same or analogous action, and this quasi-first-person experience is part of our relationship with music' (2016: 224). Other musical elements that contribute to the perception, understanding and communication of music's cognitive and emotional (albeit not verbal) content could be, for example, melodic range and contour, musical texture or rhythmic density. Beyond this type of emphatic experience, Cox also identifies conceptual metaphors as cognitive functions activated by acts of musical comprehension (drawing on the theories of Lakoff and Johnson 1980). These metaphors function in a manner similar to the idea of connotations that arise between music and the phenomenal world, only that Cox focuses specifically on bodily and spatial connotations rather than on cultural associations or stylistic competence. The entire range of sound frequencies is conceptualized as a metaphorical space that is rooted in our embodied perceptions. Positional and distributional interpretations, however, are sometimes culture-dependent. His focus on the physical and cognitive-metaphorical level allows Cox to see a listener as imagining moving within musical space and time, actually being able to identify with any element, such as a motif, theme, rhythmic pattern and so on.

MUSICAL NARRATIVITY: SIGNS THROUGH TIME

Narrative studies were introduced into music semiotics by Eero Tarasti. Building on Greimas's *Structural Semantics* (1966), Tarasti examines the ability of music to 'tell a story' (1979: 38). His earliest attempts at describing narrativity in music relate almost exclusively to operas, ballets and symphonic poems, but he soon moved to the narrative aspects of non-programmatic music, adopting from Greimas two basic terms: *actants* and *modalities* (Tarasti 1984, 1987). The actants are the *functions* in a narration. Greimas counts six actants: a *Subject* who desires an *Object*; a *Sender* that sends the object to a *Receiver*; a *Helper* that helps the subject, and an *Opponent* who inhibits the subject's success. Tarasti proposes to see in any musical theme, gesture, or musical isotopy a potential actant in an interpreted musical narration. Tarasti's narrative analysis of Chopin's *Polonaise-Fantaisie*, op. 61 (1984) and Grabócz's studies of Liszt's piano music (1986, 1987; see also 2009) examine musical narrative by detailing the order in which the musical isotopies are presented and by interpreting the trajectory of the relationships that are articulated by the sequential unfolding.

The second concept adopted by Tarasti, and one that is crucial to his conception of musical narrative, is *modalities*, or the states of mind that enhance the action of the plot. Semantic modalities are manifested in modal verbs: those that require additional information (e.g. to want, to know, to be able, to do, to have to, to believe and so on). Tarasti identifies the dynamic elements of music as the modalities of its actants. In his discussions (1985, 1988), Tarasti explains how Greimas's theory of actants and modalities can be combined with both Asafiev's concept of *intonatsia* and the idea of a mimetic musical gesture: the modalities lie in the manner in which the actants are presented and developed in time. This idea is developed in *A Theory of Musical Semiotics*:

> Behind music, speech and gesture lies an unknown factor that is not reducible to the mere syntax of music or speech, or to the external, measurable movements of gesture. [...] Modalities denote all the intentions by which the person who voices (*énonciateur*) an utterance may color his or her 'speech', i.e. modalities convey

evaluative attitudes (such as will, belief, wishes) toward the content of an utterance [...]. Modal articulations also can be considered the proper form-building elements of art, if form is construed as the living tensions inside the external manifestation.

(1994: 38–9)

Through modalities, music presents the attitude and behaviour of its actors in time. This allows an 'actor' (e.g. a theme, musical topic or musical trope – what Grabócz and Tarasti call an 'isotopy' [Grabócz 1986: 120–1; Tarasti 1994: 6]) to change behaviours without changing identity, precisely what would make a still picture, a sculpture or a short lyrical poem to become a story with a plot and action.

After years of disciplinary borrowings from semantics and literary criticism, Byron Almén (2008) shines a semiotic light on issues of musical narrativity by adapting Liszka's concept of *transvaluation*, which was initially developed in connection with a semiotic theory of myth (Liszka 1989). For Almén,

Musical narrative is the process through which the listener perceives and tracks a culturally significant transvaluation of hierarchical relationships within a temporal span. A piece's initial network of hierarchical relationships possesses a certain positive or negative cultural value, and the subsequent changes in these relationships instigate a crisis that will be resolved in a manner either acceptable or nonacceptable to the culturally informed listener.

(Almén 2003: 12, emphasis in original)

Musical narrative, according to Almén, requires a culturally informed listener immersed in a process of transvaluation. The interpretive system that Almén describes results in four types of narrative strategies: Tragedy, Satire/Irony, Romance or Comedy. Foundational to his approach to musical narrative is the inclusion of hierarchic relationships wherein certain musical components (e.g. tonality, or thematic vs nonthematic material) represent a given order by invoking elements relating to listener sympathies. Only listeners armed with these insights are able to identify, or, rather, empathize, with the narrative process.

As might be expected, Hatten's treatment of narrativity is constructed on his decades-long development of a theory of musical meaning, and it relies heavily on his construal of markedness, topics, tropes, gestures and expressive genres in music. His recent work (2018) articulates a theory of virtual agency as a means to account for our ability to attend to, recognize and interpret energetic shaping as significant and to posit an implied agent behind the expressive trajectory that the music projects and embodies. The expressive nature of gestures, complemented by other musical features (e.g. tonal stability, texture, dynamics, articulation and so on) is the means by which music can suggest a virtual agent. For instance, in the first measures of Beethoven's Piano Sonata in F Major, op. 10, no. 2, the opening melodic material is an ascending third in the major mode (suggesting an unmarked euphoric disposition), in a chordal texture (suggesting confidence), marked *piano* (suggesting restraint) and articulated staccato (injecting energy and perhaps some humour) (Figure 10.3). The musical qualities of these two opening chords and their expressive implications, isolated as a unit by rests, suggest the presence of a virtual agent, whose independent existence is supported by the varied repetition of the gestures in the measures immediately following. This virtual

FIGURE 10.3 Beethoven, Piano Sonata No. 6 in F Major, op. 10, no. 2. I: 1–4.

agent presents, as Hatten describes it, 'a relatively spontaneous gesture, injecting an individual energy into a somewhat conventional, galant-style opening gesture, perhaps also alluding to opera buffa' (2018: 16), thus combining iconic, symbolic and topical modes of signalling, which by their markedness (or lack thereof) present a culturally meaningful clear musical profile. The juxtaposition of (and separation from) other virtual agents and their behaviour, enable the musical material to narrate a plot, without the recourse to verbal allusion.

PHILOSOPHICAL UNDERPINNINGS

While most studies in music semiotics are focused on specific musical compositions, types, styles and genres, a number of music semioticians take a purely philosophical view of music as a generally cognitive, social or ethical phenomenon. For instance, Ben Curry (2012) develops Peircean constructs as they apply to music and, more recently (2020), employs the work of the philosopher Wilfrid Sellars to explore the connection between music and reality. Juha Ojala (2009) examines the concept of musical space through a lens developed from the philosophic and semiotic theories of Peirce. Mark Reybrouck (2014, 2017) uses semiotics as a tool in crafting a theory of musical 'sense-making', incorporating insights from a host of fields, including communication theory and research in perception and cognition, among others. Charting a different path, Christine Esclapez (2020) uses Augusto Ponzio and Susan Petrilli's concept of semio-ethics to music listening as a means to tackle issues surrounding how ethical repercussions emphasize a care for life. All of these studies are fertile explorations that are highly relevant in connecting studies in music with studies in the humanities and with folding music semiotics into a broad interdisciplinary dialogue.

Perhaps the most prolific writer on the philosophical aspects of music semiotics is Eero Tarasti. His foundations are grounded in the structuralist approaches of Lévi-Strauss, after which he embraced the structural semiotics of Greimas; and, since the late 1990s, he has incorporated German existentialism. In general, Tarasti's engagement with existentialist ideas blends a pragmatic approach into his semiotic analysis of music.

After detailing his philosophical infrastructure in *Existential Semiotics* (2000), Tarasti applies his approach to specific issues in music semiotics. His system develops a Zemic model that accounts for four aspects of being (in this case – musical being) in which the *Soi* and the *Moi* serve as signs of the ego by reference to itself and to the social context in which it exists. The model adopts, combines and modifies concepts developed

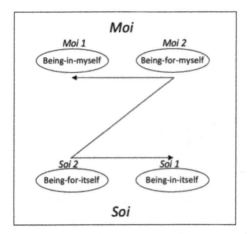 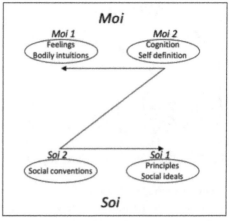

FIGURE 10.4 Tarasti's Zemic model.

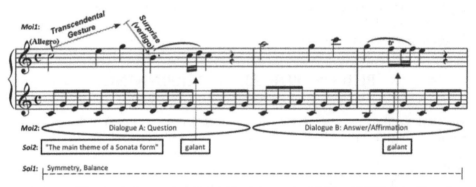

FIGURE 10.5 The Zemic Process in Mozart, Piano Sonata in C Major, K 545, from Tarasti (2020).

by earlier philosophers: one such idea is 'Being-in-myself' and 'Being-for-myself' (after Hegel); another idea is the *moi*, representing the self, and the *soi*, representing all that is outside of self (after Ricoeur and Fontanille). The Zemic model is named after the Z-like configuration drawn through the corners of his quadrangular representation of the relationships (Figure 10.4); in other words, the shape that results from the movement from 'being-in-myself' (top left, *moi* 1) through 'being-for-myself' (top right, *moi* 2) and 'being-for-itself' (bottom left, *soi* 2) to 'being-in-itself' (bottom right, *soi* 1).

The motion can start either at the top left corner (*moi* 1) or at the bottom right corner (*soi* 1). The application of this model to music is demonstrated in Figure 10.5, where the modes of being are expressed by different musical elements: *Moi* 1 is manifested through iconic gestures and their distribution in the musical space; *Moi* 2 is rhetorical, organizing the discourse into discrete units; *Soi* 2 relates to musical conventions and topics; and *Soi* 1 links to the general stylistic ideals of the eighteenth century, symmetry and balance (see Tarasti 2020: 52–3).

The 'being-in-myself' could be related to Peirce's firstness: the first, immediate quality perceived from a musical unit; the 'being-for-myself' would be the aspect that translates the unit to the self in cognitive terms; the 'being-in-itself' is expressed in conventional units (for example, musical topics); and the 'being-in-itself' is represented by transcendental elements in the music.

CONCLUSION

Since the 1980s and early 1990s, when music semiotics was viewed by some with scepticism, this subdiscipline has branched into several research areas and contributed to a notable shift in musicological discourse, engaging with the variety of ways in which music signifies. To a large extent, because of the variety and sophistication of the methods and techniques developed by music semioticians, it is now generally agreed that music teems with intersubjectively communicable units of meaning that result from the manipulation of musical sign functions. Embarking on further studies of communication channels and cognitive processes in music that arise at different levels of competency and in various cultural contexts offers a potentially infinite chain of research projects.

Music semiotics crosses international borders and languages. As a result, finding, tracing and defining the sources of tools that investigate the meanings of music often encounters constellations of political, geographical and linguistic obstacles. Studies in Russian, Hungarian, Slovak and Czech, Polish, Spanish, Portuguese, and even German and French are not always readily available to the English reader. Although there has been, and is, a steady trickle of translations, we still risk missing important advances. We hope that translations of contributions to music semiotics will be undertaken, as we have no doubt that they will prove to be of major importance to the development of the field by expanding both its scope and its universality.

Music semiotics, once a fairly self-contained field, has now entered into a productive and dynamic synergy with other approaches to music signification. Although these approaches have, indeed, resulted in fewer studies exclusively focused on music semiotics, the difficulties associated with subtle and elegant approaches to music signification are currently engaged with openly interdisciplinary perspectives. Many of these perspectives continue to incorporate and develop semiotic insights, even as they bring other fields in the humanities, social sciences and life sciences into the fold. This process of assimilation and growth, coupled with the explanatory power it portends, bodes well for future studies of the expressive power of music.

NOTES

1 Although it is a matter of some contention, we use 'semiology' to refer to approaches that largely owe their allegiance to Saussure; 'semiotics' is used to indicate all other theoretical allegiances.
2 It is odd that no English translation of *Fondements* ever appeared, given its seminal importance in music semiology and given that many foundational works from the Nattiez 'circle' have appeared in translation.
3 Lidov, among others, has challenged the idealism of a strictly neutral analysis by observing that 'inspection of a text for repetition and variation is no more objective a discovery procedure than inspection for phrases and cadences' ([1978] 2005: 96).
4 In this book Tarasti also developed Greimas's concepts of *actors, actants* and *modalities*, which are discussed below.
5 For an informative survey of some of these writings, see Mirka (2014).

REFERENCES

Agawu, V. K. (1991), *Playing with Signs: A Semiotic Interpretation of Classic Music*, Princeton: Princeton University Press.

Agawu, V. K. (2009), *Music as Discourse: Semiotic Adventures in Romantic Music*, New York: Oxford University Press.

Allanbrook, W. J. (1983), *Rhythmic Gesture in Mozart*, Chicago: University of Chicago Press.

Almén, B. (2003), 'Narrative Archetypes: A Critique, Theory, and Method of Narrative Analysis', *Journal of Music Theory*, 47 (1): 1–39.

Almén, B. (2008), *A Theory of Musical Narrative*, Bloomington: Indiana University Press.

Asafiev, B. ([1947] 1976), 'Musical Form as Process', 3 vols, Ph.D. Dissertation, trans. J. R. Tull, The Ohio State University, Columbus.

Bent, I. D. (1980), 'Analysis', in S. Sadie (ed.), *The New Grove Dictionary of Music and Musicians*, vol. 1, 340–88, London: Macmillan.

Clynes, M. (1977), *Sentics: The Touch of Emotions*, New York: Anchor Press.

Coker, W. (1972), *Music and Meaning: A Theoretical Introduction to Musical Aesthetics*, New York: The Free Press.

Cook, N. (1987), *A Guide to Musical Analysis*, New York: George Braziller.

Cox, A. (2016), *Music and Embodied Cognition: Listening, Moving, Feeling, and Thinking*, Bloomington: Indiana University Press.

Cumming, N. (2000), *The Sonic Self: Musical Subjectivity and Signification*, Bloomington: Indiana University Press.

Curry, B. (2012), 'Time, Subjectivity and Contested Signs: Developing Monelle's Application of Peirce's 1903 Typology to Music', in E. Sheinberg (ed.), *Music Semiotics: A Network of Significations – in Honour and Memory of Raymond Monelle*, 149–60, Aldershot: Ashgate.

Curry, B. (2020), 'Music and Reality', in E. Sheinberg and W. P. Dougherty (eds), *The Routledge Handbook of Music Signification*, 33–43, London: Routledge.

Dickensheets, J. (2012), 'The Topical Vocabulary of the Nineteenth Century', *Journal of Musicological Research*, 31 (2–3): 97–137.

Dougherty, W. P. (1993), 'The Play of Interpretants: A Peircean Approach to Beethoven's Lieder', in M. Shapiro (ed.), *The Peirce Seminar Papers: An Annual of Semiotic Analysis*, vol. 1, 67–95, Oxford: Berg.

Dougherty, W. P. (2014), 'What Is a Musical Sign?: A Guess at the Riddle', *Interdisciplinary Studies in Musicology*, 14: 62–81.

Dunsby, J. (1977), 'Review of *Fondements d'une sémiologie de la musique*, by Jean-Jacques Nattiez', *Perspectives of New Music*, 15 (2): 226–33.

Dunsby, J. (1983), 'Music and Semiotics: The Nattiez Phase', *The Musical Quarterly*, 69 (1): 27–43.

Dunsby, J. and J. Goldman, eds (2017), *The Dawn of Music Semiology: Essays in Honor of Jean-Jacques Nattiez*, Suffolk: Boydell and Brewer.

Echard, W. (2017), *Psychedelic Popular Music: A History through Musical Topic Theory*, Bloomington: Indiana University Press.

Eco, U. (1976), *A Theory of Semiotics*, Bloomington: Indiana University Press.

Esclapez, C. (2020), 'From Semio-ethics to a Semiotics of Speech in Music and Musicology: Theoretical (and Utopian) Projections', in E. Sheinberg and W. P. Dougherty (eds), *The Routledge Handbook of Music Signification*, 24–32, London: Routledge.

Everett, Y. U. (2012), '"Counting Down" Time: Musical Topics in John Adams' *Doctor Atomic*', in E. Sheinberg (ed.), *Music Semiotics: A Network of Signification – in Honour and Memory of Raymond Monelle*, 263–74, Aldershot: Ashgate.

Everett, Y. U. (2020), 'Pianto as a Topical Signifier of Grief in Contemporary Operas by John Adams, Thomas Adès, and Kaija Saariaho', in E. Sheinberg and W. P. Dougherty (eds), *The Routledge Handbook of Music Signification*, 333–44, London: Routledge.

Frymoyer, J. (2020), 'Topics and Stylistic Register in Russian Opera, 1775–1800', in E. Sheinberg and W. P. Dougherty (eds), *The Routledge Handbook of Music Signification*, 127–41, London: Routledge.

Goldman, J. (2011), *The Musical Language of Pierre Boulez*, Cambridge: Cambridge University Press.

Grabócz, M. (1986), *Morphologie des oeuvres pour piano de Liszt*, Budapest: MTA Zenetudományi Intézet.

Grabócz, M. (1987), 'La sonate en si mineur de Liszt: une strategie narrative complexe', *Analyse Musicale*, 8: 64–70.

Grabócz, M. (2002), '"Topos et dramaturgie": Analyse des signifiés et de la strategie dans deux mouvements symphoniques de B. Bart[ó]k', *Degrés*, 109–10: j1–j18.

Grabócz, M. (2009), *Musique, narrativité, signification*, Paris: L'Harmattan.

Greimas, A. J. ([1966] 1983), *Structural Semantics*, trans. D. McDowell, R. Schleifer and A. Velie, Lincoln: University of Nebraska Press.

Hatten, R. S. (1982), 'Toward a Semiotic Model of Style in Music: Epistemological and Methodological Bases', Ph.D. Dissertation, University of Indiana, Bloomington.

Hatten, R. S. (1994), *Musical Meaning in Beethoven*, Bloomington: Indiana University Press.

Hatten, R. S. (1997–9), 'Musical Gesture', *Eight Lectures for the Cybersemiotic Institute*. http://projects.chass.utoronto.ca/semiotics/cyber/hatout.html.

Hatten, R. S. (2004), *Interpreting Musical Gestures, Topics, and Tropes: Mozart, Beethoven, Schubert*, Bloomington: Indiana University Press.

Hatten, R. S. (2018), *A Theory of Virtual Agency for Western Art Music*, Bloomington: Indiana University Press.

Keiler, A. (1981), 'Two Views of Musical Semiotics', in W. Steiner (ed.), *The Sign in Music and Literature*, 138–68, Austin: University of Texas Press.

Khananov, I. (2018), 'Boris Asafiev's *Intonatsia* in the Context of Music Theory of the 21st Century', *Rasprave*, 44 (2): 485–501.

Lakoff, G. and M. Johnson (1980), *Metaphors We Live By*, Chicago: University of Chicago Press.

Laske, O. (1977), 'Review of Nattiez, *Fondemenets d'une sémiologie de la musique*', *Perspectives of New Music*, 15 (2): 220–5.

Lidov, D. ([1987] 2005), 'Mind and Body in Music', *Semiotica*, 66 (1–3): 69–98. Reprinted in Lidov 2005, op. cit., 145–64.

Lidov, D. ([1978] 2005), 'Nattiez's Semiotics of Music', *The Canadian Journal of Research in Semiotics*, 5 (2): 13–54. Reprinted as 'Nattiez's *Foundations for Musical Semiotics*' in Lidov 2005, op. cit., 85–103.

Lidov, D. (2005), *Is Language a Music: Writings on Musical Form and Signification*, Bloomington: Indiana University Press.

Lidov, D. (2020), 'Melody as Representation', in E. Sheinberg and W. P. Dougherty (eds), *The Routledge Handbook of Music Signification*, 285–96, London: Routledge.

Liszka, J. J. (1989), *The Semiotic of Myth: A Critical Study of the Symbol*, Bloomington: Indiana University Press.

McKay, N. (2012), 'Dysphoric States: Stravinsky's Topics – Huntsmen, Soldiers and Shepherds', in E. Sheinberg (ed.), *Music Semiotics: A Network of Significations – in Honour and Memory of Raymond Monelle*, 249–62, Aldershot: Ashgate.

McKay, N. (2020), 'Britten and Stravinsky's Neoclassical Operas: Signs, signification, and Subjectivity', in E. Sheinberg and W. P. Dougherty (eds), *The Routledge Handbook of Music Signification*, 78–88, London: Routledge.
Meyer, L. B. (1956), *Emotion and Meaning in Music*, Chicago: University of Chicago Press.
Meyer, L. B. (1973), *Explaining Music: Essays and Explorations*, Chicago: University of Chicago Press.
Meyer, L. B. (1989), *Style and Music: Theory, History, and Ideology*, Philadelphia: University of Pennsylvania Press.
Mirka, D. (2014), 'Introduction', in D. Mirka (ed.), *The Oxford Handbook of Topic Theory*, 1–57, Oxford: Oxford University Press.
Molino, J. (1975), 'Fait musical et sémiologie de la musique', *Musique en jeu*, 17: 37–62. Translated as 'Musical Fact and the Semiology of Music' by J.A. Underwood, introduction by Craig Ayrey. *Music Analysis*, 9 (2) (1990): 105–56.
Monelle, R. (1992), *Linguistics and Semiotics in Music*, Chur: Harwood Academic Publishers.
Monelle, R. (2000), *The Sense of Music: Semiotic Essays*, Princeton: Princeton University Press.
Monelle, R. (2006), *The Musical Topic: Hunt, Military and Pastoral*, Bloomington: Indiana University Press.
Morris, C. (1946), *Signs, Language and Behavior*, New York: Prentice Hall.
Nattiez, J-J. (1975a), *Fondements d'une sémiologie de la musique*, Paris: Union Générale d'Éditions.
Nattiez, J-J. (1975b), 'From Taxonomic Analysis to Stylistic Characterization: Debussy's *Syrinx*', in G. Stefani (ed.), *Proceedings of the 1st International Congress on Semiotics of Music*, 83–110, Pesaro: Centro di Iniziativa Culturale.
Nattiez, J-J. (1982), 'Varese's "Density 21.5": A Study in Semiological Analysis', trans. A. Barry, *Music Analysis*, 1 (3): 243–340.
Nattiez, J-J. (1990), *Music and Discourse: Toward a Semiology of Music*, trans. C. Abbate, New Haven: Yale University Press.
Nattiez, J-J. (2006), *The Battle of Chronos and Orpheus: Essays in Applied Musical Semiology*, trans. J. Dunsby, Oxford: Oxford University Press.
Naud, G. (1975), 'Aperçus d'une analyse sémiologique de *Nomos Alpha*', *Musique en jeu*, 17: 63–72.
Ojala, J. (2009), *Space in Musical Semiosis: An Abductive Theory of the Musical Composition Process*, Imatra: International Semiotics Institute.
Ojala, J. (2020), 'Musical Semiosis as a Process of Learning and Growth', in E. Sheinberg and W. P. Dougherty (eds), *The Routledge Handbook of Music Signification*, 299–309, London: Routledge.
Orlov, H. (1981), 'Toward a Semiotics of Music', in W. Steiner (ed.), *The Sign in Music and Literature*, 131–7, Austin: University of Texas Press.
Osmond-Smith, D. (1972), 'The Iconic Process in Musical Communication', *VS* [Versus]: *Quaderni di studi semiotici*, 3: 31–42.
Osmond-Smith, D. (1973), 'Formal Iconism in Music', *VS* [Versus]: *Quaderni di studi semiotici*, 5: 43–54.
Osmond-Smith, D. (1976), 'The Semantics of Pluralism: A Study of Connotations of Origin and Use in Music', *VS* [Versus]: *Quaderni disStudi semiotici*, 13: 5–10.
Ratner, L. (1980), *Classic Music: Expression, Form, and Style*, New York: Schirmer.
Ratner, L. (1992), *Romantic Music: Sound and Syntax*, New York: Schirmer.
Reybrouck, M. (2014), 'Musical Sense-Making between Experience and Conceptualisation: The Legacy of Peirce, Dewey and James', *Interdisciplinary Studies in Musicology*, 14: 176–205.

Reybrouck, M. (2017), 'Music and Semiotics: An Experiential Approach to Musical Sense-Making', in A. L.-V. Azcárate (ed.), *Interdisciplinary Approaches to Semiotics*, 73–93, London: InTechOpen.

Rosato, P. (2018), 'Modeling Analysis and the Musical Text Generation Process: An Analysis of Chopin's Prelude in B-flat Major, Op. 28, No. 21', *Indiana Theory Review*, 35 (1–2): 161–210.

Rosen, C. (1972), *The Classical Style: Haydn, Mozart, Beethoven*, New York: W.W. Norton.

Ruwet, N. ([1966] 1987), 'Méthodes d'analyse en musicologie', *Revue belge de Musicologie*, 20: 65–90. Translated as 'Methods of Analysis in Musicology' by Mark Everist. *Music Analysis*, 6 (1–2): 3–36.

Schenker, H. ([1935] 1979), *Free Composition [Der freie Satz]*, trans. E. Oster, vols. 1–2, New York: Longman.

Schneider, R. (1980), *Semiotik der Musik: Darstellung und Kritik*, Munich: Wilhelm Fink.

Shapiro, M. (1983), *The Sense of Grammar: Language as Semeiotic*, Bloomington: Indiana University Press.

Sheinberg, E. (2000), *Irony, Satire, Parody and the Grotesque in the Music of Dmitry Shostakovich: A Theory of Incongruities*, London: Routledge.

Sheinberg, E., ed. (2012), *Music Semiotics: A Network of Significations – in Honour and Memory of Raymond Monelle*, Aldershot: Ashgate.

Sheinberg, E. and W. P. Dougherty, eds (2020), *The Routledge Handbook of Music Signification*, London: Routledge.

Subotnik, R. R. (1976), 'Review of *Fondements d'une sémiologie de la musique* by Jean-Jacques Nattiez', *Journal of Aesthetics and Art Criticism*, 35 (2): 239–42.

Tarasti, E. (1979), *Myth and Music: A Semiotic Approach to the Aesthetics of Myth in Music, Especially that of Wagner, Sibelius and Stravinsky*, The Hague: Mouton.

Tarasti, E. (1984), 'Pour une narratologie de Chopin', *International Review of the Aesthetics and Sociology of Music*, 15 (1): 53–75.

Tarasti, E. (1985), 'A la recherche des "modalités musicales"', in H. Parret and H.-G. Ruprecht (eds), *Exigences et perspectives de la sémiotique: Recueil d'hommage pour A.J. Greimas*, 648–69, Amsterdam: Benjamins.

Tarasti, E. (1987), 'Le rôle du temps dans le discours musical', in M. Arrivé and J.-C. Coquet (eds), *Sémiotique en Jeu*, 105–25, Paris: Hades-Benjamins.

Tarasti, E. (1988), 'On the Modalities and Narrativity in Music', in V. Rantala, L. Rowell and E. Tarasti (eds), *Essays in the Philosophy of Music* (Acta Philosophical Fennica 43), 143–55, Helsinki: Societas Philosophica Fennica.

Tarasti, E. (1994), *A Theory of Musical Semiotics*, Bloomington: Indiana University Press.

Tarasti, E. (2000), *Existential Semiotics*, Bloomington: Indiana University Press.

Tarasti, E. (2020), 'From Ursatz to Urzemic: Avenues for Theories and Analyses of Music Signification', in E. Sheinberg and W. P. Dougherty (eds), *The Routledge Handbook of Music Signification*, 44–54, London: Routledge.

CHAPTER ELEVEN

Semiotics in Performance and Dance

NICOLETA POPA BLANARIU

SEMIOTICS AND PERFORMANCE MOVING IN TANDEM: A WORK-IN-PROGRESS

Along with changes in how the performing arts are understood and practised, their semiotic approach also naturally evolves, together with the entire field of performance and dance studies. Prefigured since antiquity (Augustine [426 CE] 2002; Lucian of Samosata [second century CE] 2009), the semiotics of performance is very indebted, especially since the 1930s–40s, to The Prague School Theory of Theatre, and even later, in the 1970s, to the linguistic paradigm of structuralism. This has the great advantage of having changed the perspective on the aesthetic object. However, the semiotics of performance emerges with the awareness of the methodological risk to which it is exposed by some 'tendency to reduce all the problems of sign to language' (Kowzan 1968, Lehmann [1999] 2002, Barba and Savarese [2008] 2012). In fact, performing arts cannot be reduced to a textual component or to one assimilated to the functioning of verbal language. New symptoms of identity crisis arose again later when the nature of the performance and its semiotic approach were equally and insistently called into question. Semiotics then tried to cover the *performative* turn of theatre which debuted in the sixties. In such a context, semiotics was particularly interested in the 'crisis of representation', the 'crisis of the body's mediation' and the crisis of the 'classic textual invariant' (Helbo, Bouko, and Verlinden 2011: 100; Helbo 2016: 342–5), as well as the crisis of 'authoritarian staging' (Pavis 2014: 238). These came together with Kaprow's 'idea of a performance that isn't theatre' ([1976] 2020) and the replacement of the 'dramatic text' with the 'performance text' (Schechner 2011: 25).

However, ideas ingeniously adapted from linguistics and structuralism have become valuable contributions to the semiotics of performance. To illustrate just a few of many possible examples, Erika Fischer-Lichte organizes her *Semiotics of Theatre* (1992) according to the trichotomy '*systema, norma y habla*' from Eugen Coşeriu's 'integral linguistics' ([1952] 1967), and De Marinis ([2008] 2012: 182–5) applies the principle of 'double articulation' to the description of the actor's 'physical actions'. In his turn, Philippe Hamon saw the character as a sign, 'a kind of doubly articulated morpheme, manifested by a discontinuous signifier that refers to a discontinuous signified' (1972: 86–110). In this sense, the character is part of the 'paradigm' that the message builds.

In the 1970s, the idea of the 'possibility of a theatrical semiology' (Pavis 1982: 9) emerged, inspired by the models provided by the language sciences. It was a period of intense theoretical concerns, having as an object a hypothetical 'theatrical language' (which had also fascinated Antonin Artaud in the 1930s). Such preoccupations set the stage (so to speak) for a more pragmatic and versatile semiology, able to contribute to the analysis of some practical aspects: the staging, the scenery, the acting, etc. This direction took shape especially in the 1980s, with the reaction against a 'universal model' of theatrical semiology. Thus was born a 'method of semiological inspiration' allowing reconciliation of semiology with other ways of approaching theatre: aesthetics, chronicle play, dramaturgy, among them (Pavis 1982: 9). In this phase, 'theatrical semiology' develops 'as a descriptive system', 'analysis of the show', rather than as an 'axiological' system, 'analysis of meaning' (De Toro 2011: 80). Hence, theatrical semiology loses its 'radicalism', preferring a federal role of 'epistemologist, of hermeneut, a propaedeutic role' (Pavis 1982: 9; Helbo 2021).

The transformations of artistic practice – the 'avant-garde' after 1960 – imposed an adaptation of theoretical discourse (Elam 1980; Fischer-Lichte 1992; De Marinis 1993; De Toro 1995; Pavis ([1980] 1996); Schechner 2002; Pavis 2007; Féral 2008; Fischer-Lichte 2008, Bouissac 2011; De Marinis 2011; De Toro 2011; Féral 2011; Helbo 2011; Schechner 2011; Pavis 2014; Bouissac 2015; Helbo 2018, Helbo 2021). On the one hand, postmodern creators theorize their own theatrical or choreographic practice; and on the other hand, in their creative activity, they capitalize on theory (including structuralism, such as Kirby). *In extremis*, a 'nonsemiotic performance' may appear (Kirby 1982), which goes along with the 'nontheatrical performance' (Kaprow [1976] 2020). *La sémiologie de la mise en scène* gives way to a *phénoménologie de la performance* (Pavis 2007). The result is an 'experiential semiotics' (Helbo 2016) which seeks a rapprochement between lived experience and its conceptualization. This approach is more appropriate to contemporary performance, with its extreme subjectivization and emphasis on perception; the central role it gives to the body, presence, (unpredictable) spectator-performer interaction; and the dissolution of the old narrative-dramatic structure and classical space-time landmarks. This calls for overcoming the 'cleavages' between production and reception, between the 'immanentist approach to meaning' (concerned with 'the significance of the object to be decrypted') and, respectively, 'a constructivist approach' (related to reception, insofar as 'I build a message, and it builds me according to what I am') (Helbo 2021).

Thus, the theoretical discourse changes with its corpus of analysis, now refractory to the old constraints of elitist aesthetics. In it are found, by their 'spectacular' nature, theatre, dance, dance-theatre, opera, circus, street arts, happening, performance, ritual, folklore. The new semiotics dialogues with performance theory, communication theories, pragmatics and speech act theory, reception studies, reader-response, theatrical anthropology, and cognitive and behavioural neuroscience.

A QUICK OVERVIEW

Towards the end of Greco-Latin Antiquity, Lucian of Samosata ([second century CE] 1983) and Augustine of Hippo (2002) anticipated a semiotics of the performing arts, especially dance (Popa Blanariu 2017). In the opinion of Lucian ([second century CE] 1983: 235–6), the understanding of dance depends on the iconic transparency of the choreographic sign. The movement depicts actions and passions, specifying the meanings of the songs that accompany it. It must have a 'clear' meaning so that the public does not need the help of 'connoisseurs' to understand it. But two centuries later, in Carthage, Augustine ([426 CE] 2002: 165) notes the importance of the hermeneutic function of the herald who reveals the forgotten meanings of the dances on stage. The explanatory role of the herald – which will be continued by the theatre and dance critic, in the modern era – derives from the specificity of choreographic semiosis. The signs are 'similar' to what they designate, but the 'similarity' manifests itself in different ways. Therefore, a 'consensus' must be reached (Augustine [426 CE] 2002: 165). Apparently 'natural', the relationship of the iconic sign with its object is regulated by the 'consensus' of the collectivity (Augustine [426 CE] 2002: 165) – by 'habit' (in Peircean terms) or 'convention' (in Saussurean terms). This idea significantly differentiates Lucian and Augustine's views on dance. Lucian ([second century CE] 1983) praises (iconic) 'clear' dances, while Augustine ([426 CE] 2002: 165) is aware that meanings, including artistic ones, depend on the conventions of each society.

The year 1931 was pivotal for theatre studies. Until then, dramatic poetics 'had made little substantial progress since its Aristotelian origins' (Elam 1980: 4). In 1931, Zich's *Aesthetics of the Art of Drama* and Mukařovský's 'An Attempted Structural Analysis of the Phenomenon of the Actor' inaugurated the body of theatrical theory produced in the 1930s and 1940s by the Prague School structuralists. They were interested in various forms of theatre (Veltruský 1981): the ancient, the avant-garde (Veltruský 1995), the Oriental (Brušák [1938] 1976), folk theatre (Bogatyrev [1938] 1976). The Prague School is essentially influenced by Saussure and the Russian formalists. From a Saussurean perspective, the theatrical performance couples 'thing' and 'aesthetic object' (Mukařovský [1934] 1976: 5): it is a 'sign composed of (1) a perceivable signifier, created by the artist', '(2) a signification' or 'aesthetic object registered in the collective consciousness' and '(3) a relationship with that which is signified, a relationship which refers to the total context of social phenomena' (Mukařovský [1934] 1976: 6). Later, Prague School structuralists saw 'the performance not as a single sign but as a network of semiotic units belonging to different cooperative systems' (Elam 1980: 5). A key principle of the Prague semioticians is that of the 'semiotization of the object' (Elam 1980: 5): 'All that is on the stage is a sign' (Veltruský [1940] 1964: 84). On the stage things 'acquire special features' that they 'do not have in real life' (Bogatyrev [1938] 1976: 35–6). Moreover, the theatrical sign is 'a sign of a sign and not the sign of a material thing' (Bogatyrev [1938] 1976: 33). In fact, Bogatyrev's 'sign of a sign' could be termed as 'connotation' (Elam 1980: 7).

In the 1970s, an 'interpretive semiology' (Helbo 2018: 451–70) was outlined, characterized by 'impersonal enunciation' (Metz 1991), focused on invariants – on the dramatic text first and on the segmentation of the theatrical or choreographic ensemble into minimum units (Helbo 2018: 451–70). This trend is illustrated by Kowzan (1968, 1992), Marcus (1975), Ubersfeld ([1977] 1999), Durand (1975), Zelinger (197 9), among others. What is the problem of this stage of theatrical semiology? What are the difficulties and ways to overcome them? The initial attempt to identify minimum units was eventually abandoned, as long as it 'would only "pulverize" the staging', neglecting the whole stage project (Pavis [1980] 1996: 318–19). Neither the establishment of minimum units nor the specification of a typology of signs was deemed necessary for a semiology of theatre. As it would be far too general, such a typology could not capture the complexity of theatrical phenomena. More useful, it was determined, would be the analysis in terms of 'sign-function' (Eco ([1975] 1982), which presupposes a correlation between the plane of expression and the plane of content. This is not given from the very beginning but is instituted by the 'productive reading of the director' and the 'receptive reading of the spectator' (Pavis [1980] 1996: 319). The interpretation of theatre can also be distorted by the non-nuanced application of the model of communication semiology and by 'code fetishism'. In reality, any show creates its own codes (Pavis [1980] 1996: 319). As far as the relationship between text and representation is concerned, staging is not the transposition of 'textual evidence'; on the contrary, it is precisely the 'enunciation of the dramatic text through a particular staging' that 'gives the text one meaning or another' (Pavis [1980] 1996: 320).

CHALLENGES IN FACING CONTEMPORARY PERFORMANCE: MIMESIS VERSUS PERFORMANCE

Performance is a symptomatic product of postmodernism. It has dominated the performing arts in the twentieth century and annexed much of the social field. Erwing Goffman (1959) studied 'the presentation of self in everyday life'; Richard Schechner (2002) has equated all organized social behaviours with performance. André Helbo (2011) emphasizes the 'complex performative processes' that question the boundary between life and performance. Patrice Pavis (2007: 16–17) recommends the careful use of the word 'theatre', in order not to apply 'a Greek or Western conception to cultural performances' from which the former is very different. The essential characteristic of performance is that some 'action' or 'event' is 'achieved through that very performance' (Pavis, 2007: 17).

As a 'spectacular' genre, postmodern performance rejects the stability of a predetermined form, fixed by repetitions and resumed without significant changes. On the contrary, postmodern performance prefers the flexibility of the creative process, unrepeatable and unpredictable, always open to context and to interaction with the audience. Today, we are witnessing a paradigm shift, a transformation of the aesthetic form that relies on a new 'relational aesthetics' (Bourriaud 1998) which is consistent with the transition from work of art to process, from re-presentation to presentation, from the multipliable theatrical form to the unique event, from 'sense to sensation' (Pavis 2014: 238). In other words, from the 'allograph' language (of the work regulated by creation and execution norms that ensure the accuracy of the transmission) to an 'autograph' language of art as an irreversible configuration, inseparable from its production *hic et nunc* (Goodman 1976). There is also a shift from 'a dramaturgy of meaning' to a (post)dramaturgy 'of the signifier, of the reception and formal analysis of rhythms, gestures or visuals' (Pavis 2014: 239).

Theatrical staging began in the nineteenth century, along with naturalism and the aesthetics of the 'real effect'. As of the 1960s, performance started to leave plausible imitation behind and instead inserted itself into the surrounding nonfiction space. At the moment of the pragmatic turn in philosophy and language sciences, the performing arts especially emphasized the relationship of signs with their 'users', in fact with an entire context from which deeply subjectivized meanings emerge (Popa Blanariu 2017). The postmodern performance brings its spectators on stage or climbs down among them, on the street, in unconventional spaces. Formerly well defended by the classical poetics, the border between the hall and the stage now opens, and everyone is invited to perform: e.g. audience, the sound engineer, the light designer. The roles – of the dancer, of the actor, of the audience – are mixed, and the show merges with the real-life surrounding it.[1] In postmodern performance, the result is a wide range of 'spectacular' hybrid forms: in between drama and (a kind of) reality show, in between *mise en scène* and *mise en perf* or *performise* (Pavis, 2007: 55), in between presence and representation, with elements of 'physical theatre' and 'post-dramatic theatre' (Lehmann [1999] 2002). There is mostly a fusion of dance, drama and multimedia show. Postmodern interactive genres are open art forms, strongly dependent on context and owing much to the presence of the audience, here and now.

Representation involves mediated discourse (which carries out the otherness of the character) and is generally assumed to be fictional. Performance, on the other hand, is nonfictional and subjective. It claims the presence of a performer who manifests him/herself in an unmediated way, through verbalized speech or not, generally autobiographical. It certainly challenges the idea of re-presentation (Pavis 2007: 14–15). Thus, beginning with the 1960s, performance became an alternative to *mimesis*. Moreover, the postmodern performance includes a metafictional and self-referential component of deconstruction and 'dedoxification' (Hutcheon [1989] 2002). It questions artistic codes and languages. Postmodern performance involves the shift from a well-knit and meaningful narrative – which is highly specific to the classical theatre – to an event that often addresses the body, sensation and proprioception of the audience. In contemporary performance, the visual aspect of the (re)presentation is frequently mitigated while emphasizing the 'proprioceptive introspection'. This narrows the 'contemplative distance' (Suquet [2006] 2009) between the audience and the stage, life and fiction, body and its cultural image. Notably the Russian painter and art theorist Wassily Kandinsky (qtd. Suquet [2006] 2009), as early as 1912, saw in this proprioceptive sensitivity *per se* an intimation of the eventual end of traditional dance at some time in the future. All these issues raise the problem of adapting semiotic instruments to a very diverse corpus of phenomena, which the concepts and methods of the first semiology can no longer manage satisfactorily.

WHAT ROUTE TO TAKE? SOME METHODOLOGICAL ISSUES

Towards a framework of a semiotics of dance: Above and beyond structuralism

Birdwhistell (1970) tried to formalize kinesic 'language' using the method of structural linguistics. Within an anthropological approach to dance, Kaeppler (2001: 49–63) adds two other levels of analysis (motifs and choremes) to Birdwhistell's kinemes and morphokines. 'Kinemes are minimal units of movement [...] having no meaning in themselves'; 'morphokines are the smallest units that have meaning as movement in the structure of a movement system', and they 'are organised in a small number of motifs'. 'Motifs choreographed in association with meaningful imagery form a choreme' (Kaeppler 2001: 51–2). However, it is difficult to isolate such elements that are generally valid for dance 'language.' They are only relevant for a certain 'dance tradition or genre' (Kaeppler 2001: 51–2). In dance, we cannot delimit 'an autonomous plan of expression for gestures' and no systematic 'visual phonology'. Therefore, we will consider 'gestural units cut as phonemes and as sememes at the same time' (Greimas [1970] 1975: 99; Zelinger 1979). The choreographic expression is conditioned by the articulatory possibilities of the body and by cultural conventions. Being codified, it remains dependent on a certain co(n)text. No matter how codified they may be, choreographic figures still retain an 'expressive kinship' (Laban [1960] 1994: 124) with the current actions from which they come (Popa Blanariu 2021).

The concept of basic dance has dominated choreographic practice and theory since the first decades of the twentieth century when the alternative to the academic ballet was born. This basic dance is a 'universal', 'primordial' language (Robinson 1981: 22). (Post)modern choreographers look for this first code of gestures or 'first movement' prior to aesthetic codification. Dance is a composite of signal and symptom, but it also acquires symbolic features within sociocultural codes. Dance particularly reveals a process which is specific to semiosis, the 'culturalization' of the natural (Barthes qtd. Greimas and Courtès 1979: 240). This can be described in terms of the phaneroscopic categories theorized by Peirce (Popa Blanariu 2013). Primary emotionality (firstness) is related to the pre-conscious feeling, and can be exteriorized by (quasi-)involuntary gestures (secondness). Kinetic manifestations acquire a symbolic character (thirdness) as a kind of mediating thought. This includes various codes such as choreographic ones. Although conventionalized, the choreographic symbol retains the evoking potential and the motivated character of the index and icon. From this derives the 'translucence' of choreographic symbols (see Bouvet 1997: 91).

Dance allows us to identify a 'gestural *form* behind the gestural *substance*', a semiotic scheme beyond empirical phenomena. Through the process of 'variations of possible gestural contexts', 'substance' is reduced to a 'minimal visual figure' (Greimas, 1975 [1970]: 99). Such 'visual figures' are the 'elementary actions' of classical dance, as Laban calls them ([1960] 1994: 103). A type/token relationship is established between 'elementary' and 'derived' actions (Laban [1960] 1994). The transition from token to type implies a process of 'abstraction' (Robinson 1981: 79). The choreographer modifies 'an experience or an image' 'depending on the applied subjective optics' (Robinson 1981: 79) which is that of an 'interpretive consciousness' (Peirce 1978 [1931–1958]: 120).[2] The choreographic sign is constituted by 'emphatic exploitation' of the appearance of things, which means not reproducing the model but signifying a function or aspect of it (Lévi-Strauss [1964] 1995: 413). Each style has its ways of such 'distortion' (Arnheim 1954: 147, Popa Blanariu 2008, 2013, 2014, 2015, 2021).

Signification and communication in performing arts: Functional *and orchestral models of communication*

The disassociation between the semiology of meaning and that of communication is well known. The latter is intentional and based on a code shared by the sender and the recipient; the former requires only the existence of a recipient capable of interpreting the signs. These are not necessarily intentional. In the opinion of Eco ([1975] 1982: 26–9), it is precisely intentionality that makes it possible to distinguish between communication and signification. However, with the New Communication, a paradigm proposed by the Palo Alto School, communication no longer means only the transmission of explicit and intentional messages, but includes all those processes by which individuals '*influence* each other'. Every action and every event has communicative aspects, as soon as they are perceived by a human being (Bateson and Ruesch [1951] 1988: 6). Ruesch and Bateson focus on the receiver and the perception of those 'impressions' that other individuals, as well as 'himself, the events, the environment' provoke in him (Winkin 2001: 55). The New Communication, also called 'orchestral', depends on a '*hic et nunc* interaction' – it equally integrates an unintentional aspect: by its nature as a 'social animal', man is biologically constrained to communicate (Bateson and Ruesch [1951] 1988: 18–19).

It is this orchestral and unintentional aspect of communication that is often exploited by postmodern performance: the audience intervenes in real time and (co)participates, communicating even more than they would like (Popa Blanariu 2017).[3] This leads to a change in the reception. In classical theatre and dance, the spectator watches from the outside, (s)he does not interfere on the stage; while in performance, the spectator is immersed in the artistic system. 'We cannot not communicate' is the axiom of the New Communication. It occurs both in everyday interaction and in the circumstances of postmodern performance. On and off the stage, the gesture communicates, the body 'speaks' (Sapir 1927), 'silent is eloquent in its own right' (Sheets-Johnstone 2019: 35), space sends messages (Hall 1971), as do the rhythm and the music. An individual 'does not communicate'; he 'takes part' in a communication whose element he becomes (Birdwhistell qtd Winkin 2001: 75).

Implicit, unintentional performativity lies in everyday phenomena: the sound of the rain or breathing, klaxon horns on the street, the radio. John Cage, a key founder of contemporary performing arts, capitalized on these elements in *Imaginary Landscape No. 4* (1951). Similarly, unintentional behaviours of the audience or artists can become 'performative' in the postmodern show. In *Points in Space* (1986), Cage and Cunningham compose music and choreography without any relationship of motivation, in the Saussurean sense. However, the separate elements complement each other as soon as they are placed together, at the time of the meeting with the public. Before Cage, Artaud (1964) had also noticed the 'performative' value of the sound and visual components of a show. The discovery of a 'pre-expressive', unintentional layer in the actor's play is central to theatrical anthropology (Barba and Savarese ([2008] 2012).

The functional model of language – proposed by Bühler and Jakobson, and applied to theatre by Elam (1980: 20–30), among others – derives from a 'telegraphic' view of communication, different from the 'orchestral' model. Jakobson's scheme can serve to systematize the choreographic field (Popa Blanariu 2015). From Lucian of Samosata and Augustine of Hippo to contemporary choreographic practices, from *Kathakali* to *Tanztheatre* and (post)modern dance, from 'abstract ballet' (Ballanchine) to Expressionism, two dance paths can be identified: 'pure' dance (which evades *mimesis*) and 'theatrical' dance (based on iconicity and narrative logic of movements). In India, for instance, traditional dance takes different forms: pure dance (*nritta*), dramatic dance (*natya*), and gesticulation performed with musical accompaniment, also assisted by sung words (*nritya*).

In pure dance, the priority function is the metalinguistic one, possibly accompanied by the poetic function. In theatrical dance, the referential function predominates. In romantic ballets, the referential, poetic and emotional functions are intertwined. In postmodern dance, based on innovation and the interactive dimension, three functions stand out: the expressive, the phatic (regarding the solidarity of the audience and performers) and the conative (especially in the interactive genres inspired by happening, which seek to transform the spectator into dance(act)or). The conative function underlies the history of dance from the French political ballet of the sixteenth century to *Thingspiel* and the postmodern performative genres, partially influenced by *agit-prop* (Popa Blanariu 2008, 2016). Today, as always, the aesthetic value of dance and theatre competes with the social one.

Speech acts theory in (theatrical) performance and ritual drama

We can comparatively analyse ritual drama and theatrical performance by using a unifying pragma-semiotics approach, especially Speech Acts Theory (Popa Blanariu 2019a). Speech Acts Theory is part of a theory of action (Austin 1962), confirmed not only in the very linguistic act of utterance but also in the multimodal expression (movement, gesture, word, incantation, costumes, accessories) of the ritual performances. Through ritual dance, illocutionary acts of different types can be performed: directives (to invite, to ask, to pray); commissives (to promise, to refuse, to threaten); expressives (to thank, to congratulate, to greet). Like words, ritual gestures and movement may have real and immediate efficacy, meaning that it may produce a real-world change, from the participant's viewpoint. Without a ritual context, the choreo-dramatic expression loses its pragmatic function – that of 'modification' of the real. However, it can manifest a different one, essentially 'aesthetic' (Lévi-Strauss [1964] 1995: 410). The illocutionary ritual act is thus replaced by a 'fictional act', a category which was previously described by both John R. Searle ([1979] 1982) and Gérard Genette (1991).

Regarding the process of 'aestheticization', Claude Lévi-Strauss ([1964] 1995: 410) points out: 'Where the domination of magical thinking tends to weaken and when rites acquire the character of vestige, the second function survives the former.' In Austin's terms, it means that the 'constative' function replaces the 'performative' one. The illocutionary acts performed on the stage (*ludus aestheticus*) are 'real' acts manifested in a fictional universe, assumed as such by the actors (Searle [1979] 1982, Genette 1991). However, the illocutionary ritual acts are perceived by the ritual participants as real acts in the real world. The rite for them is not fiction, but real action (Eliade 1964, Turner 1982). In contrast to this, the specific of the 'aesthetic' – 'fictional' – speech act resides in its nature of 'simulacrum' (Searle [1979] 1982: 111–13). In this case, the performer (the protagonist of *ludus aestheticus*) assumes the fictionality of his/ her discourse. This is the rule of the theatrical art. If (s)he accepts it, the spectator participates in the fictional game of illusion. Implicitly or explicitly, fiction informs the spectator that (s)he enters a universe other than the 'real' world. The author of fiction (in particular, the actor or dancer on the stage) pretends to perform some illocutionary acts but does not accomplish them in reality (Searle [1979] 1982). Based on this structure of simulacra, (s)he performs a specific illocutionary act: the fictional act which is distinct from any other. In a work of fiction, the illocutionary act is simulated, but the act of enunciation is real (Searle [1979] 1982). Fictionality is neither truth nor a mere 'lie' but something much more sophisticated than lying (Searle [1979] 1982: 111).

Briefly, *simulacrum* is a key term for how Searle defines the 'fictional act'. In our view, this is also an essential difference between ritual drama, on the one hand, and the classical tradition of theatre and dance in Europe, Japan, China or India, to name but a few, on the other hand. From the viewpoint of the observing audience, the illocutionary acts performed on stage, in a traditional theatrical performance, are real acts within a fictional universe. This is quite different in the ritual drama, where, from the participants' viewpoint, real acts are being performed within the real world. The ritual drama has such a performative power, it is a means of effectively acting on the real and transforming it. In this regard, it has much in common with contemporary performance: both seek to position themselves outside the field of fiction. In extreme forms of performance art, the performer (who no longer depicts otherness, the character, but exposes him/herself) undergoes an irreversible 'self-transformation' in front of the public: 'physical self-manipulation' often 'violent, painful' (Lehmann 2002: 221, De Marinis 2011: 60–1). In various forms, the contemporary performance draws attention to the problematic nature of theatrical simulacrum and the 'limit of the spectacular', which separates reality and fiction, actor and role (Schechner 2011; Helbo 2018; Gennep [1909] 2019). The show can be created by 'intentional semiotization' of *ad hoc* events, by transforming the real fact into a spectacular act (De Toro 2011; Helbo 2018). This relativizes the boundary between real assertions and pseudo-fictional assertions. More than once, the theme of such a performance is the self-referentiality of the fiction that produces its referent by the very fact that it refers to it. Fiction creates it through its simulated acts (Eco 1996).

Depending on the criterion of 'collective intentionality', we can therefore distinguish (at least theoretically) two categories of 'social' or 'institutional' facts (Searle 1998: 121–34; 113–15): ritual drama and (classic) theatrical performance. The latter has an essentially aesthetic stake and is constituted as a fictional alternative to the real, while the former is a pragmatic scenario, meant to act directly on the world, to take control of it, to transform it or to keep it as such.[4] Contemporary performance has a hybrid, intermediate nature, which requires a reconsideration of the relationship between the first two, the ritual and the classical drama.[5] Finally, the opposition between theatrical performance and other performative actions – all kinds of ceremonies, rites, and plays – raises the question of separating 'aesthetical' and 'anthropological' views (Pavis 2007: 17), which is not quite as simple as it appears.

Acting as polyphonic enunciation

The theatre is, in Barthes's opinion ([1964] 1991), the product of an 'informational polyphony'. The three modes of theatrical interpretation identified by Gadamer ([1960] 2013) can be seen as three types of polyphonic acting: 'transformation', 'disguise' and 'alteration' (Popa Blanariu 2010). 'Alteration *(alloiosis)*' is an 'accident of substance' 'but transformation means that something is suddenly and as a whole something else […] in comparison with which its earlier being is nil' Gadamer ([1960] 2013: 115–18). According to Stanislavsky, theatre involves a psycho-emotional transformation of the performer. The Brechtian actor, a follower of the *Verfremdungseffekt*, endures an 'alteration' *(alloiōsis)*. The ritual dance(act)or that imitates the god is, during the ceremony, the sacred character that he embodies (Cassirer [1923] 1972: 61). His interpretation is a 'transformation', a 'transubstantiation'. 'Sacred dance' and ritual drama involve such a 'transformation of expressed content' (Greimas [1970] 1975: 94). That is why the cultic act is, for its followers, an 'authentic representation' (Gadamer ([1960] 2013): the ritual image 'does not manifest the thing, it *is* that thing' (Cassirer [1923] 1972: 60). Such a representation is, par excellence, performative, according to Austin.

However, 'all good staging' involves an 'alienation effect', *Verfremdungseffekt* (Ubersfeld 1977, Ubersfeld 1981). From an anthropological perspective inspired by Van Gennep ([1909] 2019) and developed by his follower, Turner (1982), this could also be expressed in terms of 'liminality': in the tradition of psychological theatre, 'there is a liminality of the actor who is no longer entirely himself, without having become yet another person' (Pavis 2014: 143). Identification and distancing are therefore fuzzy categories. Alternative to these two, the concept of polyphony can highlight the theatrical mechanism of liminal representation and expresses it from the perspective of language sciences (Popa Blanariu 2010). In the polyphonic utterance, as in the ironic one, the speaker makes heard the enunciator's 'voice' and point of view (Bakhtine 1929; Ducrot 1989: 165–91). Brecht himself brings the *Verfremdungseffekt* closer to irony. Both involve an act of imitation, but not an illusion effect. The Stanislavskyan actor embodies his role, seeks to reduce (histrionic) duality to an identification. On the contrary, the Brechtian actor emphasizes the dichotomy; he lets both the voice of the character and that of the actor be heard polyphonically on stage. Brechtian polyphony comes from the methodical doubt with which the actor treats his character. Briefly, the actor can completely assume the character's point of view, as in Stanislavsky's 'method' and ritual drama – 'mimetic rites' (Durkheim ([1912] 2003); or he may distance himself as in Brecht's poetics and ironic statement.

On the other hand, polyphonic acting refers to the (inevitable) 'double coding' (De Toro 2011: 81) of the actor's presence on stage. In other words, the doubled way in which the actor is perceived by the spectator: as a 'mixture' between the 'living and unpredictable being' in front of us (Pavis 1982: 17) and the 'artificial signs' it creates to 'transmit the fictitious character' (Passow qtd. Pavis 1982: 17). Such a mode of reception avoids 'hypersemiotization', recognizing that there are always elements of 'scenic reality that are no sign of anything but themselves' (Ubersfeld 1978; Pavis 1982: 16; Petrilli 2019). In this case, polyphonic acting is the result of two ways of perceiving the scene and the actor's play: the fictional world of an 'illusion fabricated by sign systems' and the real world in which the spectators are situated (Pavis 1982: 16). At the other extreme, it can be considered that the spectator 'semiotizes even what, in itself, is devoid of symbolic status' (De Marinis 2011: 55). From this point of view, everything is a sign on stage: a 'sign of a sign or sign of an object' (Bogatyrev [1938] 1971: 518).

Overstepping the norm: Interaction ritual and 'dedoxification' in contemporary performance

'Duality' is inherent in the semiotic condition: the phrases that language provides us with constitute a collection of 'masks' or a 'wardrobe' (Bally qtd. Ducrot 1989). The relationship between 'representation and represented' is 'one of the most dramatic antinomies of the sign' (Jakobson qtd. Eco 1990: 290). Such a view is particularly confirmed by an element of social performance that Goffman (1959) describes by analogy with theatrical performance: the social mask, *persona* – 'the front' which 'becomes a collective representation' (Goffman 1959: 22–7). Thus theatricality 'transcends' theatre and is inserted in everyday life (Féral 1988: 352, De Toro 2011: 67–8).

Up to a point, this could explain the frequency of a particular strategy in contemporary performance. This is integrated into the new 'paradigm of the spectacular', especially through 'the pragmatic use of showing and of performativity' (Helbo 2016: 342). The premeditated confusion between the real and the fictional, between the stage and the audience, between the role of actor and that of spectator, aims to reveal the ambivalence of theatricality and, moreover, to emphasize our condition as social, (and thus) 'theatrical' beings: doubly coded beings on the everyday scene, divided between the exigency of authenticity and the standards of respectability embodied by the *persona*. The latter is the idealized figure of a 'front stage' behaviour that we adopt when we know that others are watching us (Goffman 1959). About this, contemporary performance sometimes experiences a premeditated deviation from the interaction norms. For example, the principle of the 'sacredness' of the person may be deliberately violated (Goffman 1967: 66). It manifests itself in everyday secular 'rituals' through symbolic acts and attributes, such as 'demeanor' and 'deference': 'the individual himself stubbornly remains as a deity of considerable importance. He walks with some dignity and is the recipient of many little offerings. He is jealous of the worship due him, yet, approached in the right spirit, he is ready to forgive those who may have offended him' (Goffman 1967: 66).

There can be a fragile balance between 'offense' and 'reparation' (Goffman 1959) in contemporary performance. The reception habits of the public are often broken down. The intimate dimension and the voyeuristic convention cancel out the 'contemplative distance' between stage and audience (Suquet [2006] 2009: 454–83). The perception shifts from visual to proprioceptive. The show ignores the classic *bienséances*. In fact, 'postmodern theatre does not need "classical norms", because its topic is completely different' (De Toro 2011: 97). Revealing the intimacy of performers makes the viewer just as vulnerable as those who expose themselves in this way. Spectators are asked to engage directly in a here-and-now interaction. Performing, they no longer represent a predetermined role but present themselves, reveal themselves, betray themselves, reacting in real time to the concrete situation in the performance space. The performance thus erodes the secure and dignified social mask ('front', in Goffman's terms). The weakening of the social mask is closely related to spectator's 'liminality': (s)he hesitates between remaining 'outside' the event and letting her/himself be 'absorbed' by it, intervening, for example, if (s)he considers the performer to be in danger. Postmodern performance often 'plays' with the 'uncertainty' of the audience that is hesitant between fiction and reality (Pavis 2014: 143).

The violation of the interactional norm is integrated here in a logic of 'dedoxification' (Hutcheon [1989] 2002). Such a performance aims to denounce – to 'de-doxify', to 'denaturalize' – a series of implications accepted as *doxa*, 'self-understood' truths. They converge with those 'simulations and models' which 'constitute the world' so that the distinction between real and appearance becomes problematic (Bourdieu ([1972] 1977). This kind of performance brings to attention a recurring theme in performing arts: to what extent is the show a re(-)presentation? Can it be something else? A presentation, for example, elaborated in real time, without role-play and without imitating someone else.

As a performative strategy, the premeditated transgression of the interactional norm underlies, I believe, a defining phenomenon for contemporary performing arts: 'a crisis in representation which reveals itself through profound changes in the processes and instances at work in the performance' (Helbo 2016: 342). Contemporary performance evades Aristotelian *mimesis*, refusing to accept that representation is a duplication of 'the real' and even that there is a 'real' to represent. As Hutcheon ([1989] 2002: 30) puts it, 'postmodernism challenges our mimetic assumptions about representation'. In short, the deviation from the interactional norm can serve to fulfil the 'three central functions' of a postmodern theatrical performance: 'the aesthetic function, aiming at demystifying the creative act', 'the critical/reflective function', which relates the present to tradition and, finally, 'the political function, focused on the dedoxification of representations' (De Toro 2011: 83). All these involve a reconsideration of the relationship between *mimesis* and *semiosis*, in the context of the 'schism between *Theatre Studies* and *Performance Studies*' (Pavis 2014: 184) that has marked, in the last forty years, the performing arts.

Performing arts in the age of the brain: Between the cognitive and 'corporeal' turns

Going beyond the first models of analysis inspired by the functioning of language, the semiotics of performance and dance is now open to what has become a priority for contemporary arts, cognitive science and neuroscience: exploring the mechanisms of the brain, perception and emotion. In the performing arts, a topical issue is that of (overcoming) the dualism between physical and mental, between biology and consciousness: 'How exactly do neurobiological processes in the brain cause consciousness?' (Searle 1997: 3–5). The cognitive model of Lakoff and Johnson (1999) is built around the idea of the 'embodied mind'. It reconciles the sensible and the intelligible, the perception and the concept: 'our bodies, brains, and interactions with our environment provide the mostly unconscious basis' for 'our sense of what is real'. From here derives 'who we are, how we experience our world'. Judith Lynne Hanna (2015) explores the connections between 'the brain's cognition, emotion, and movement' that dance makes possible. However, Maxine Sheets-Johnstone (2012: 39) believes that 'present-day cognitive science is unable to provide insights into dance, notably because being largely tethered to happenings in the brain, it lacks foundational grounding' in the corporeal experience of movement, particularly the kinaesthetic experience. We 'ground our understandings of the aesthetic realities of dance in the real-life kinesthetic realities' (Sheets-Johnstone 2012: 54–5). In fact, the 'ground floor of being' is not cognition. It is the 'dynamics' which seems to be 'the basic defining feature of life.' The 'tactile-kinaesthetic body' is closely related to cognition and affectivity and anchored in ontogeny and phylogeny (Sheets-Johnstone 2011: 145). The body 'understands' its world without passing through representations, without subordinating itself to a 'symbolic' or 'objectifying function' (Merleau-Ponty 1945: 164). Motricity can confer meaning in an unmediated way. There is an important distinction between 'intellectual' and 'motor' signification (Merleau-Ponty 1945: 128), or equivalently, between 'thinking through words' and 'thinking in terms of movement' (Laban [1960] 1994): 124). Thinking 'through words' serves the orientation in the external world, while 'motor thinking' is more appropriate for 'orientation in the inner world' (Laban [1960] 1994): 39–40). The latter consists of an 'accumulation of impressions of events' (Laban [1960] 1994): 39–40); it is a kind of 'physiological judgment' (Leroi-Gourhan [1964–5] 1983). The body is an 'expressive space'. Moreover, it is the source of the 'other' spatialities. The body is a 'means' of 'having a world' (Merleau-Ponty 1945: 171). This is why Sheets-Johnstone (2019: 33–4) outlines a 'movement-anchored corporeal semiotics' supposed to 'describe what is existentially meaningful in the lives of animate organisms'. This 'kinetic silence of movement' is what 'informs a cognitive semiotics'.

Some of these key ideas are implemented in contemporary dance (Popa Blanariu 2008, 2016, 2021). (Post)modern choreographers are concerned with the connections between external manifestation and the kinaesthetic sense. In classical ballet, the movement recovers a motor symptom of emotion, which the academic convention has reified. The (post)modern choreographer no longer tries to fill a conventional movement with his/her own emotion. (S)he seeks bodily expression in the motor echo of inner states, as long as every perception causes, often unconsciously, motor reactions. The silence and stillness of the body lying on the dance mat often respond to the need for reaching the (pre-intentional) source of movement. The outer movement is born from an unconscious inner 'rumor' (Suquet [2006] 2009). (Post)modern performance thus reveals 'foundations of meaning in a movement-anchored corporeal semiotics […] a semiotics that encompasses bodily felt realities of affectivity' (Sheets-Johnstone 2019: 40–8).[6]

Smith (2017) finds a close relationship between 'Nineteenth-Century Neuroscience and the Birth of Modern Theatre'. He reveals 'a dialogue between theatre artists and neurological scientists' which could be the premise of 'a new form of aesthetics' (Smith 2017: 13–14). Taking into account that the subject is 'primarily and essentially a nervous system', Smith traces a theatrical 'history of the neural subject'. Through the relationship between the psyche and (semiotics of) gesture, Smith questions the Cartesian thesis of body-mind separation. In the neuroscientific approach, stage gestures are of particular concern to a semiotic model of the mind.

In turn, contemporary theatre-makers and choreographers drew on both the idea of 'the neural subject' (Smith 2017) and that of the centrality of the body. They often work at the intersection of performance and the sciences of sensation and perception. The semiotization processes for which the spectator is responsible are questioned through a double 'immersion', both cognitive and physical. The first concerns the 'mechanisms of adhesion' to the performance, while the second involves the penetration of the spectator 'in a technological environment that interrogates his perceptions' (Marranca 2008; Helbo, Bouko and Verlinden 2011: 94–6). Breaking down the sensory and perceptual habits of the audience is enacted in different ways. Instead of the frontal positioning of the theatre *à l'italienne*, the actors are placed among the audience, so that the sound comes towards the spectator from all directions, surrounding him. The use of a large screen near the audience can amplify the visual immersion effect, the viewer having the impression that he is absorbed by the projected image. The contemporary performance also uses 'sensory deprivation' of the spectator to draw attention to the relationship between bodily perception and a 'coherent representation' of the world (Helbo, Bouko and Verlinden 2011: 98–100). Under normal circumstances, we create a unitary representation based on the sensory stimuli we receive. But by using digital technology, perceptions can become contradictory (visual perceptions no longer correspond, for example, to kinaesthetic sensations), the sense of balance is disturbed, and the spectator finds it difficult to form a coherent image of the world. The public thus experiences 'an intensified awareness of its bodily perceptions' (Helbo, Bouko and Verlinden 2011: 94, 98–100). Such a (re)presentation is an 'experiential' process. Its finality is the 'production of the Self' (Helbo, Bouko and Verlinden 2011: 101), by detaching itself from some habits inoculated by historical and cultural tradition. Contemporary performance is therefore the meeting place between a 'relational aesthetic' and a non-representational theory. The former is interested in the analysis of works 'according to the interpersonal relationships' that they portray or produce (Bourriaud 1998: 117). The latter values the processes that precede conscious, reflective thought. From this point of view, human behaviour is the result of interactions (which facilitate knowledge here and now) rather than of already assimilated, rationally controlled codes and representations. Thus, the audience discovers an alternative to the Western classical theatre, based on the principle of *mimesis* and the reality effect.

Also from the perspective of neuroscience, Paul Bouissac (2011: 103–14) formulates the premises of a semiotics of reception. What determines us to go to the show, what are the 'neurological bases of motivation' in this case? Bouissac hypothesizes that the well-being created by the show (whether successful or not) is 'closely related to the level of dopamine produced by the spectator's brain' in these circumstances. The study of primates showed that dopamine production is stimulated when something is gained, some material or symbolic good (112). Or, the show is a particular kind of game, after which the audience gets a cognitive and emotional reward. 'The pleasure of drama' – comedy or tragedy – is 'the same in both cases: it is the joy of knowledge' (Gadamer [1960] 2013: 116).

THE SHOW MUST GO ON: OPEN THEMES

The concerns of semioticians converge today on a problematic subject: is a 'general theory of performance' (De Toro 2011: 75), a 'unified theoretical vision' (Bouissac 2011: 113), a 'unified semiotics' possible (Helbo 2021)? The difficulty of such a task comes, first of all, from the complexity and heterogeneity of the object of analysis. Or, in a semiotic approach, it is a priority to delimit the 'epistemological object to transform it into an ontological object' (De Toro 2011: 76). Today, the performing arts encompass a variety of 'spectacular' events: theatre, dance, dance-theatre, opera, circus, street arts, happening, ritual, folklore, etc. The accumulation (and thus the pulverization of the specific) of the analysed phenomena makes it difficult to constitute the object. Against the background of the vast transformation of the performing arts, beginning with the second half of the twentieth century (and even earlier, with Dada and the historical avant-garde), the question of André Helbo (2021) is entirely justified: 'Does the spectacle exist as an object'? An attempt to define and systematize such diverse 'spectacular' forms, based on 'deep or convergent structures' (De Toro 2011: 80–1), is a significant challenge. The mission is complicated by the weakening of the boundaries between the different contemporary performative genres (dance-theatre, post-dramatic theatre, performance, postmodern dance, non-dance) and also between the stage professions (actor/dancer) (Barba and Savarese [2008] 2012: 10–11). Practices transcend genre differences. However, in the opinion of Helbo (2021), 'despite the convergent use of hybrid techniques' in today's theatre, it would be preferable for methodologies to approach it such that each of them retains its individuality. This observation is itself one possible answer to the above question: is a 'unified semiotics' of performing arts possible? De Toro (2011: 75) formulates the same problem, of a 'general theory of performance', in terms of an 'integrative' approach, able to adequately constitute its object (dance, theatre, etc.). Similarly, Pavis (2014: 240) opts for the study of 'art' theatre (Western 'aesthetic' theatre, 'misanscene theatre'), from an inclusive perspective, by placing it in 'an expanded corpus of cultural performances and performativity'.

Interdisciplinary openness – to the contribution of (inter)cultural studies, phenomenology, performance studies and theories of performativity, psychoanalysis and neuroscience – could revive the semiotics of performance. The relationship with phenomenology would legitimize a semiotics of the sensible, which integrates the spectator's experience, central in postmodern performance: presence, corporeality, proprioception, beyond visual perception (dominant in the Western classical theatre, but not in other cultures). Complementarity with reception theory would be useful as long as 'presence and corporeity unite production and reception' (Helbo 2016: 349). Some aspects related to the central position of the spectator could be described by the collaboration of semiotics with psychoanalysis ('identification/denial') or with neuroscience ('emotional contagion') (Helbo 2016: 349). The performative perspective would allow a different vision of 'art' theatre than that provided by the 'structuralist-semio-analytical' approach (Pavis 2014: 240). On the other hand, it remains to be seen to what extent the performative turn will succeed in contributing to a general theory of theatre, dance and show, more widely speaking: one in which both 'aesthetic theatre' and 'all other cultural performances' may finally co-exist and find their place (Pavis 2014: 240).

CODA

Initially aiming to describe the specifics of Western classical theatre – based on dramatic text, *mimesis* and the reality effect – semiotics today faces an important mutation in the performing arts. The crisis it is going through is the echo of an identity crisis that the performing arts themselves – theatre and dance in particular – are going through. Hence a series of 'epistemological obstacles' (Helbo, Bouko and Verlinden 2011: 87): the variability of spectacular forms and cultural tradition, the intention to recover both text and staging, and to integrate them into the object of the new semiotics, along with a wide range of forms that take contemporary performing arts. However, the symptoms of the crisis cannot override some fundamental principles and working methods in semiotics. They still prove their validity in the theory and practice of analysing a show, be it classical or postmodern: 'identification of signs', 'interdependence of signifier and signified', 'reading of signifiers and signifieds' (Pavis 2014: 237–8). In the face of the polymorphism of its object, it remains to be seen whether, by playing the card of maximum adaptability, semiotics would be able to truly maintain its 'universalizing vocation' (Helbo 2016).

ACKNOWLEDGEMENTS

This chapter îs written in memory of two unforgettable mentors: Maria Carpov (1930–2017) and Solomon Marcus (1925–2016).

NOTES

1 Four centuries ago, this process was anticipated by Don Quixote, who stepped out of his role as a spectator and intervened in the conflict on stage, in the world of Don Pedro's puppets. Cervantes thus capitalized on the Baroque theme of the uncertain relationship between the illusion of life and the (in)consistency of fiction.
2 For Saussure, semiosis is given by the system and offered as such to the user. But in Peirce, the role of interpretive consciousness is crucial for generating meanings.
3 Hamlet knew this before the Palo Alto School, and he successfully used the fact in to expose Claudius' secret.
4 Artaud's ([1938] 1964) conception of theatre, convergent with performance art, is greatly influenced by the function of ritual drama and its specific ways of representation.
5 On the concept of performance, from an interdisciplinary perspective, De Toro (2011), De Marinis (2011), Bouissac (2011), Pavis (2007), Féral (2008).
6 On the relevance of the semio-phenomenological model for understanding dance, see Popa Blanariu (2014, 2008: 191–222); also Pelkey (2017), on the relationship between bodily experience and verbal conceptualization.

REFERENCES

Arnheim, R. (1954), *Art and Visual Perception: A Psychology of the Creative Eye*, Berkeley: University of California Press.
Artaud, Antonin ([1938] 1964), *Le théâtre et son double*, suivi de *Le théâtre de Séraphin*, Paris: Gallimard.
Augustine of Hippo ([426 CE] 2002), *De doctrina christiana*, bilingual edn, trans. Marian Ciucă, introduction, notes and bibliography Lucia Wald, Bucureşti: Humanitas.
Austin, J. L. (1962), *How to Do Things with Words*, Oxford: Oxford University Press.
Bakhtine, Mikhaïl (1929), *Problèmes de la poétique de Dostoïevki*, Paris: Seuil.
Barba, Eugenio and Nicola Savarese (2008), *L'énergie qui danse. Dictionnaire d'anthropologie théâtrale*, Paris: L'Entretemps.
Barba, Eugenio and Nicola Savarese ([2008] 2012), *Arta secretă a actorului. Dicţionar de antropologie teatrală*, trans. Vlad Russo, Sibiu: Teatrul Naţional 'Radu Stanca'.
Barthes, Roland ([1964] 1991), *Essais critiques*, Paris: Seuil.
Bateson, Gregory and Jurgen Ruesch ([1951] 1988), *Communication et société*, Paris: Seuil.

Birdwhistell, Ray L. (1970), *Kinesics and Context: Essays on Body Motion Communication*, Philadelphia: University of Pennsylvania Press.
Bogatyrev, Petr ([1938] 1971), 'Les signes du théâtre', *Poétique*, 8: 517–30.
Bogatyrev, Petr ([1938] 1976) 'Semiotics in the Folk Theatre', in Ladislav Matejka and Erwin R. Titunik (eds), *Semiotics of Art. Prague School Contributions*, 33–49, Cambridge, Massachusetts & London: The MIT Press.
Bouissac, Paul (2011), 'L'Invisible et l'impensable du spectacle vivant', in André Helbo (ed.), *Performance et savoirs*, 103–14, Brussels: De Boeck.
Bouissac, Paul (2015), *The Semiotics of Clowns and Clowning: Rituals of Transgression and the Theory of Laughter*, London: Bloomsbury.
Bourdieu, Pierre ([1972] 1977), *Outline of a Theory of Practice*, trans. Richard Nice, Cambridge: Cambridge University Press.
Bourriaud, Nicolas (1998), *Esthétique relationnelle*, Dijon: Presses du réel.
Bouvet, Danielle (1997), *Le Corps et la métaphore dans les langues gestuelles*, Paris: L'Harmattan.
Brušák, Karel ([1938] 1976), 'Signs in the Chinese Theater', in Ladislav Matejka and Erwin R. Titunik (eds), *Semiotics of Art. Prague School Contributions*, 59–73, Cambridge, Massachusetts & London: The MIT Press.
Cassirer, Ernst ([1923]1972), *La Philosophie des formes symboliques*, II, trans. J. Lacoste, Paris: Minuit.
Coşeriu, Eugen ([1952] 1967), 'Sistema, norma y habla', in E. Coşeriu (ed.), *Teoría del lenguaje y lingüística general. Cinco estudios*, 11–113, Madrid: Gredos.
De Marinis, Marco (1993), *The Semiotics of Performance*, Bloomington: Indiana University Press.
De Marinis, Marco ([2008] 2012), 'Travaliul asupra acţiunilor fizice: dubla articulare', in Eugenio Barba and Nicola Savarese (eds), *Arta secretă a actorului. Dicţionar de antropologie teatrală*, trans. Vlad Russo, 182–5, Sibiu: Teatrul Naţional 'Radu Stanca'.
De Marinis, Marco (2011), 'Représentation, présence, performance: pour un dialogue entre nouvelle théâtralogie et *Performance Studies*', in André Helbo (ed.), *Performance et Savoirs*, 53–63, Brussels: De Boeck.
De Toro, Fernando (1995), *Theatre Semiotics: Text and Staging in Modern Theatre (Toronto Studies in Semiotics and Communication)*, Toronto: University of Toronto Press.
De Toro, Fernando (2011), 'Performance: quelle performance?' in André Helbo (ed.), *Performance et Savoirs*, 65–102, Brussels: De Boeck.
Ducrot, Oswald (1989), *Logique, structure, énonciation. Lectures sur le langage*, Paris: Minuit.
Durand, Régis (1975), 'Problèmes de l'analyse structurale et sémiotique de la forme théâtrale', in André Helbo (ed.), *Sémiologie de la représentation*, 112–19, Bruxelles: Complexe.
Durand, Gilbert (1979), *Figures mythiques et visages de l'oeuvre. De la mythocritique à la mythanalyse*, Paris: Berg International.
Durkheim, Émile ([1912] 2003), *Les formes élémentaires de la vie religieuse*, Paris: PUF.
Eco, Umberto ([1975] 1982), *Tratat de semiotică generală*, trans. A. Giurescu and C. Radu, Bucureşti: Editura Stiinţifică şi Enciclopedică.
Eco, Umberto (1977), 'Semiotics of Theatrical Performance', *The Drama Review: TDR*, 21 (1): 107–17.
Eco, Umberto (1990), 'Il Contributo di Jakobson alla Semiotica', in P. Montani and M. Prampolini (eds), *Roman Jakobson*, 287–302, Roma: Editori Riuniti.
Eco, Umberto ([1994] 1996), *Six promenades dans les bois du roman et ailleurs*, Paris: Bernard Grasset.

Elam, Keir (1980), *The Semiotics of Theatre and Drama*, London: Methuen.
Eliade, Mircea (1964), *Cosmos and History: The Myth of the Eternal Return*, trans. W. R.Trask, New York: Harper Torchbooks.
Féral, Josette (1988), 'La théâtralité: la spécificité du langage théâtral', *Poétique*, 75: 347–61.
Féral, Josette (2008), 'Entre performance et théâtralité: le théâtre performatif', *Théâtre/Public*, 190: 28–35.
Féral, Josette (2011), 'De l'événement au réel extrême: L'esthétique du choc', in André Helbo (ed.), *Performance et savoirs*, 37–52, Brussels: De Boeck.
Fischer-Lichte, Erika (1992), *The Semiotics of Theatre*, Bloomington: Indiana University Press.
Fischer-Lichte, Erika (2008), *The Transformative Power of Performance: A New Aesthetics*, trans. Saskya Jain, London: Routledge.
Gadamer, Hans-Georg ([1960] 2013), *Truth and Method*, London and New York: Bloomsbury.
Genette, Gérard (1991), *Fiction et diction*, Paris: Seuil.
Gennep, Arnold Van ([1909] 2019), *The Rites of Passage*, trans. Monika B. Vizedom and Gabrielle L. Caffee, introduction by David I. Kertzer, Chicago: University of Chicago Press.
Goffman, Erving (1959), *The Presentation of Self in Everyday Life*, New York: Doubleday.
Goffman, Erving (1967), *Interaction Ritual: Essays in face-to-face Behavior*, Chicago: Aldine Publishing Company.
Goffman, Erving ([1967]1974), *Les rites d'interaction*, trans. A. Kihm, Paris: Minuit.
Goodman, Nelson ([1968] 1976), *Languages of Art: An Approach to a Theory of Symbols*, Indianapolis/ Cambridge: Hackett Publishing Company.
Greimas, Algirdas Julien ([1970] 1975), *Despre sens. Eseuri semiotice*, trans. Maria Carpov, București: Univers.
Greimas, Algirdas Julien ([1970] 1987), *On Meaning*, trans. Frank Collins and Paul Perron, Minneapolis: Minnesota University Press.
Greimas, Algirdas Julien, Joseph Courtès (1979), *Sémiotique. Dictionnaire raisonné de la théorie du langage*, Paris: Hachette.
Hall, Edward T. ([1966] 1971), *La dimension cachée*, Paris: Seuil.
Hamon, Philippe (1972), 'Pour un statut sémiologique du personnage', *Littérature*, 6 (6): 86–110.
Hanna, Judith Lynne ([1979] 1987), *Dance Is Human: A Theory of Nonverbal Communication*, Chicago: University of Chicago Press.
Hanna, Judith Lynne (2015), *Dancing to Learn: The Brain's Cognition, Emotion and Movement*, Lanham: Rowman and Littlefield.
Helbo, André, Catherine Bouko, Elodie Verlinden (2011), 'Théâtre et spectacle vivant: Mutations contemporaines', in André Helbo (ed.), *Performance et Savoirs*, 85–101, Brussels: De Boeck.
Helbo, André (2016), 'Semiotics and Performing Arts: Contemporary Issues', *Social Semiotics*, 26 (4): 341–50.
Helbo, André (2018), 'Sémiotique et arts du spectacle', in Amir Biglari (ed.), *La Sémiotique en interface*, 451–70, Paris: Kimé.
Helbo, André (2021), 'Sémiotique(s) et propédeutique. Introduction', *Degrés: Sémiotique(s) et propédeutique I*, 184–185: 1–6.
Hutcheon, Linda ([1989] 2002), *The Politics of Postmodernism*, New York: Routledge.
Jakobson, Roman (1963), *Essais de linguistique générale*, Paris: Minuit.
Kaeppler, Adrienne (2001), 'Dance and the Concept of Style', *Yearbook for Traditional Music*, 33: 49–63.

Kaprow, Allan ([1976] 2020), 'Nontheatrical Performance', in Jeff Kelley (ed.), *Essays on the Blurring of Art and Life*, 163–80, Berkeley: University of California Press.
Kirby, Michael (1982), 'Nonsemiotic Performance', *Modern Drama*, 25 (1): 105–11.
Kowzan, Tadeusz (1968), 'The Sign in Theatre: An Introduction to the Semiology of the Art of the Spectacle', *Diogenes*, 16 (61): 52–80.
Kowzan, Tadeusz (1992), *Sémiologie du théâtre*, Paris: Nathan.
Laban, Rudolf ([1960] 1994), *La Maîtrise du mouvement*, trans. Jacqueline Challet-Haas and Marion Hansen, Arles: Actes Sud.
Lakoff, George and Mark Johnson (1999), *Philosophy in the Flesh: The Embodied Mind and its Challenge to Western Thought*, New York: Basic Books.
Lehmann, Hans-Thies ([1999] 2002), *Le théâtre postdramatique*, Paris: L'Arche.
Leroi-Gourhan, André ([1964–5] 1983), *Gestul și cuvântul*, I-II, trans. M. Berza, București: Meridiane.
Lévi-Strauss, Claude ([1964] 1995), *Mitologice*, I, trans. Ioan Pânzaru, București: Babel.
Lucian, o. S. ([2nd century CE] 1983), *Scrieri alese*, trans. R. Hîncu, București: Univers.
Lucian, o. S. ([2nd century CE] 2009), 'Of Pantomime', in *Works of Lucian of Samosata*, trans. H. W. Fowler and F. G. Fowler. Online: http://ebooks.adelaide.edu.au/l/lucian/works/chapter31.html
Marcus, Solomon (1975), 'Stratégie des personnages dramatiques', in André Helbo (ed.), *Sémiologie de la représentation*, 73–89, Bruxelles: Complexe.
Marranca, Bonnie (2008), 'Mediaturgy: A Conversation with Marianne Weems', in B. Marranca (ed.), *Performance Histories*, 189–206, New York: PAJ.
Matejka, Ladislav and Erwin R. Titunik (eds) (1976), *Semiotics of Art: Prague School Contributions*, Cambridge, MA and London: The MIT Press.
Merleau-Ponty, Maurice (1945), *Phénoménologie de la perception*, Paris: Gallimard.
Metz, Christian (1991), *L'énonciation impersonnelle ou le site du film*, Paris: Méridiens-Klincksieck.
Mukařovský, Jan ([1934] 1976), 'Art as Semiotic Fact', in Ladislav Matejka and Erwin R. Titunik (eds), *Semiotics of Art. Prague School Contributions*, 3–10, Cambridge, MA and London: The MIT Press.
Pavis, Patrice ([1980] 1996), *Dictionnaire du théâtre*, Paris: Dunod.
Pavis, Patrice (1982), *Voix et images de la scène: essai de sémiologie théâtrale*, Lille: Presses Universitaires de Lille.
Pavis, Patrice (2007), *La mise en scène contemporaine: origines, tendances, perspectives*, Paris: Armand Colin.
Pavis, Patrice (2014), *Dictionnaire de la performance et du théâtre contemporain*, Paris: Armand Colin.
Peirce, Charles Sanders ([1931–58] 1978), *Écrits sur le signe*, rassemblés, traduits et commentés par Gérard Deledalle, Paris: Seuil.
Pelkey, Jamin (2017), *The Semiotics of X: Chiasmus, Cognition, and Extreme Body Memory*, London: Bloomsbury Academic.
Petrilli, Susan (2019), 'Visualizing Theatrical and Novelistic Discourse with Bakhtin', *Southern Semiotic Review*, 11: 97–117.
Popa Blanariu, Nicoleta (2008), *Când gestul rupe tăcerea. Dansul și paradigmele comunicării* [When a gesture breaks the silence: dance and the paradigms of communication], Iași: Fides.
Popa Blanariu, Nicoleta (2010), 'Le je(u) polyphonique. Un modèle pragma-linguistique à rendre compte de la représentation théâtrale', *Philologica Jassyensia*, 2: 161–70.

Popa Blanariu, Nicoleta (2013), 'Towards a Framework of a Semiotics of Dance', *CLCweb: Comparative Literature and Culture*, 15 (1): 1–11.
Popa Blanariu, Nicoleta (2014), 'Semiotic and Rhetorical Patterns in Dance and Gestural Languages', *Southern Semiotic Review*, 4 (2): 56–76.
Popa Blanariu, Nicoleta (2015), 'Paradigms of Communication in Performance and Dance Studies', *CLCweb: Comparative Literature and Culture*, 17 (2): 1–9.
Popa Blanariu, Nicoleta (2016), *Când literatura comparată pretinde că se destramă*, II: (Inter)text [i (meta)spectacol], București: Eikon.
Popa Blanariu, Nicoleta (2017), 'Le signe agissant. D'une sémiologie de la mimesis vers une pragmatique de la performance', *SIGNA: Revista de la Asociación Española de Semiótica*, 26: 493–509.
Popa Blanariu, Nicoleta (2019a), 'Towards a Pragma-Semiotics of Ritual(ized) Gesture and Performance', *Arte, Individuo y Sociedad*, 31 (1): 41–54.
Popa Blanariu, Nicoleta (2019b), 'Theatricalization of the Ritualistic Gesture and Dancing. A Semiotic Approach', *Southern Semiotic Review*, 10 (6): 123–36.
Popa Blanariu, Nicoleta (2021), 'Prolegomena to a Semiotic Approach to Dancing', in Amir Biglari (ed.), *Open Semiotics*, Paris: L'Harmattan (forthcoming, 2023).
Robinson, Jacqueline (1981), *Éléments du langage chorégraphique*, Paris: Vigot.
Sapir, Edward (1927), 'The Unconscious Patterning of Behavior in Society', in D. G. Mandelbaum (ed.), *Selected Writings of Edward Sapir*, 544–59, Berkeley: University of California Press.
Schechner, Richard (2002), *Performance Studies*, London: Routledge.
Schechner, Richard (2011), 'L'avant-garde, la niche-garde et la Performance Theory', in André Helbo (ed.), *Performance et Savoirs*, 13–35, Brussels: De Boeck.
Searle, John R. ([1969] 1972), *Les Actes de langage. Essai de philosophie linguistique*, trans. H. Pauchard, Paris: Hermann.
Searle, John R. ([1979] 1982), *Sens et expression: études de théorie des actes de langage*, trans. J. Proust, Paris: Minuit.
Searle, John R. (1997), *The Mystery of Consciousness*, New York: The New York Review Books.
Searle, John R. (1998), *Mind, Language and Society: Philosophy in the Real World*, New York: Basic Book.
Sheets-Johnstone, Maxine (2011), 'The Corporeal Turn: Reflections on Awareness and Gnostic Tactility and Kinaesthesia', *Journal of Consciousness Studies*, 18 (7–8): 145–68.
Sheets-Johnstone, Maxine (2012), 'From Movement to Dance', *Phenomenology and the Cognitive Sciences*, 11 (1): 39–57.
Sheets-Johnstone, Maxine ([1966] 2015), *The Phenomenology of Dance*, foreword by Merce Cunningham, Philadelphia, Pennsylvania: Temple University Press.
Sheets-Johnstone, Maxine (2019), 'The Silence of Movement: A Beginning Empirical-Phenomenological Exposition of the Powers of a Corporeal Semiotics', *The American Journal of Semiotics*, 35 (1–2): 33–54.
Smith, Matthew Wilson (2017), *The Nervous Stage: Nineteenth-Century Neuroscience and the Birth of Modern Theatre*, Oxford: Oxford University Press.
Suquet, Annie ([2006] 2009), 'Scene. Corpul dansând: un laborator al percepției', in Alain Corbin, Jean- Jacques Courtine and Georges Vigarello (eds), *Istoria corpului*, III, trans. Simona Manolache, Mihaela Arnat, Muguraș Constantinescu and Giuliano Sfichi, 454–83, București: Art.

Turner, Victor (1982), *From Ritual to Theatre: The Human Seriousness of Play*, New York: Performing Arts Journal.
Turner, Victor (1988), *The Anthropology of Performance*, preface by Richard Schechner, New York: Performing Arts Journal.
Ubersfeld, Anne (1977), *Lire le théâtre*, 1, Paris: Éditions Sociales.
Ubersfeld, Anne ([1977] 1999), *Reading Theatre*, Toronto: The University of Toronto Press.
Ubersfeld, Anne (1978), 'Sur le signe théâtral et son référent', *Travail théâtral*, 31: 121–23.
Ubersfeld, Anne (1981), *L'École du spectateur: Lire le théâtre*, 2, Paris: Éditions Sociales.
Veltruský, Jiří ([1940] 1964), 'Man and Object in the Theater', in Paul Garvin L. (ed.), *A Prague School Reader on Esthetics, Literary Structure and Style*, 83–91, Washington: Georgetown University Press.
Veltruský, Jiří (1981), 'The Prague School Theory of Theatre', *Poetics Today*, 2 (3): 225–35.
Veltruský, Jiří (1995), 'Semiotics and Avant-Garde Theatre', *Theatre Survey*, 36 (1): 87–95.
Winkin, Yves, ed. (2001), *La Nouvelle Communication*, Paris: Seuil.
Zelinger, Jacob (1979), 'Semiotics and Theatre Dance', in Diana Theodores Taplin (ed.), *New Directions in Dance*, 39–50, Willowdale: Pergamon of Canada.

CHAPTER TWELVE

Semiotics in Rhetoric and Poetics

PER AAGE BRANDT AND TODD OAKLEY

INTRODUCTION

Semiotics as the study of meaning in mind, signs, language and society may be relevant to poetics as the study of artful language, or language-based art, because the fundamental modes of meaning in art depend on the signs by which they are determined. Therefore, we first have to specify the fundamental relations of sign types to meaning modes, relations that are rooted in the constitutive structure of social formations. Second, we show how poetic texts may be understood in terms of such meaning modes, and how they affect the forms of imagery, or imagistic elaborations in poetry. Imagery can be theorized as *mental signs* that account for the variable display of its meaning: standard *metaphor, simile, catachresis*. We further discuss the basic components of narrative text structure: *enunciation* and *diegesis*, and again show how the modes of meaning pervade and determine story structure. We proceed to discuss the recursive semiotic cascades that constitute theatrical practice and which link drama to music, as in opera and singing in general, a possibly elementary, theatrical practice of language, close to poetry as such. Finally, we show how the same sign types and relations operate in the sister art of rhetoric, where the requirement to distinguish between semiotic modes are constitutive of civil persuasion.

Meaning and semiosis

Meaning is, in semiotics, a notion as important as those of semiosis and sign types. Meaning modes are in fact a function of sign types. The semantic classification of signs that follows from the study of social functions of semiosis not only distinguishes symbolic and iconic signs, but has to contain a third basic type, diagrams. In social life, *symbols* are typically used as *instructions*, and *icons* are strong *affective* markers. Symbols are conventional and bound to specific contexts of practice of literacy and numeracy (music, mathematics, textual writing, traffic signalling, etc.), whereas icons exploit our mind's capacity to produce, understand, and memorize imagery as description of sensory and social experience. Both semiotic function types are emotionally based, but whereas the symbolic semiosis is performative and deontic, thereby creating or expressing feelings of obligatory binding between people, instead the iconic semiosis creates or expresses feelings of belonging, desire, repulsion or other affective values linked to its motifs.

The only non-emotional and non-deontic sign function is the *diagrammatic* semiosis, by which we imagine abstract or technical networks of categories whose interrelations we seek and need to comprehend through argumentation. Informative (diagrammatic) meaning, as opposed to performative (symbolic) and affective (iconic) meaning, is pre-deontic and pre-affective, it is essentially intellective and therefore crucial to all social practices of planning, collective development and sharing of knowledge, political debate, legislation and theorizing. Diagrams may indeed be the 'language of thought' (J. Fodor's expression).[1]

Society, language and semiosis

Social structure is, extremely roughly speaking, semiotically stratified and comprises three layers: In nation states, *sovereignty*, or the organized transcendent form of authority and sacredness, is necessarily symbolic; governance *institutions* in general are diagrammatically organized; and the organic base is predominantly iconic, to the extent that its communication mainly consists in showing and telling.

Language, any language, contains structure for performative (symbolic) functions, informative (diagrammatic, argumentative) functions and formative (iconic, descriptive, narrative) functions. These functions match social stratification directly, probably because social and linguistic structure have co-evolved, along a civilizational evolution also giving rise to the development of the non-linguistic sign types.

THE SPECIFICITY OF LANGUAGE AS ART

While discourse forms and practice forms tend to specialize on distinct strata, so that the techniques of rhetoric tend to be differentiated accordingly, the mental and communicative activities involved in art take us back to an undifferentiated, or pre-differentiated, semiotic state, where symbolicity, iconicity and diagrammaticity exist side by side or tend to be indistinguishable. Art works compel (create respect), resemble (create affective representations) and make us think (create diagrams of the world), ideally at the same time. The specificity of art is its semiotic non-specificity.[2]

A semiotics of literature, a *semio-poetics*, may be grounded on the same synthetic assumption. Language-based art forms in fact present meaning in all three modes, and critical aesthetic evaluation implicitly presupposes this to be expected.

Let us show this by an example. Here is the contemporary American poet David Young's translation of Charles Baudelaire's famous poem *Les chats* (from *Les fleurs du mal*, 1857):[3]

BAUDELAIRE, THE CATS
Both steamy lovers and ascetic scholars
Are equally attached, as they grow old,
To cats – soft, cruel, the household's rulers,
Lazy and idle, sensitive to cold.
Friends both to science and to sensual pleasure,
They seek out silence and Horror's darkness;
The Devil might have made them pull his treasure
If they could be persuaded into harness.

They often doze assuming noble poses
Resembling the great sphinxes, old and wise,
Dreaming an endless dream, so one supposes.
Their fertile loins are full of sparks, it seems,
And particles of gold, sand grains of dreams,
Add mystic galaxies within their eyes.
Les chats
Les amoureux fervents et les savants austères
Aiment également, dans leur mûre saison,
Les chats puissants et doux, orgueil de la maison,
Qui comme eux sont frileux et comme eux sédentaires.
Amis de la science et de la volupté,
Ils cherchent le silence et l'horreur des ténèbres;
L'Erèbe les eût pris pour ses coursiers funèbres,
S'ils pouvaient au servage incliner leur fierté.
Ils prennent en songeant les nobles attitudes
Des grands sphinx allongés au fond des solitudes,
Qui semblent s'endormir dans un rêve sans fin;
Leurs reins féconds sont pleins d'étincelles magiques,
Et des parcelles d'or, ainsi qu'un sable fin,
Etoilent vaguement leurs prunelles mystiques.

This is just a description of cats,[4] underscoring their particularities and expressing a certain fascination, one might say. Their properties contain contrasts: they are strong and yet soft, they like company and solitude, cosiness and horror (cruelty, the translator suggests), they seem to slide between life and death, to be in a dreamy state between being awake and delving into an eternal sleep. A rather appropriate, affective picture: iconicity.

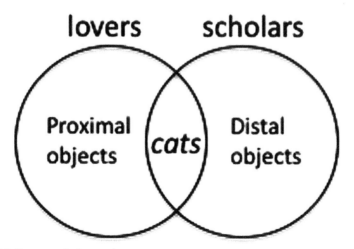

FIGURE 12.1 Lovers, scholars and cats.

Then the poem also foregrounds the contrasting pattern of their affinity to lovers and scholars, two attitudes to the world, one proximal and warm, the other distal and cold, that meet in the cats' attraction to both life and death, light and darkness. These human agents share a passion for which the cats seem to be the metaphoric emblem or signifier.

This diagrammatic idea may in turn invite a logical supplement: is there a qualification corresponding to the product of the two intersecting sets? Well, that would indeed be the generic properties of the *poet* (absent from the poem), in as far as this agent may integrate love and scholarship, as well as the feline ambivalence and the *non-serviam* attitude of resistance to other authorities than that of poetry.

Finally, the (proximal) *magic* sparks of the fur when caressed, and the (distal) *mystical* stars in cats' eyes, would be the two symbolic sources of poetry itself: the magic of the signifier and the interpretive mystery of the infinite signified. Instruction for the reader.

We will stay with poetry a little longer to make some important semiotic points. As opposed to narrative prose, which typically establishes and maintains a single literal level of spatiotemporal meaning reserved for the unfolding of the story it is 'about', poetry will most often present a multiplicity of superimposed meaning levels, and its 'story' can be reduced to a very short list of situations. This multiplicity is what is meant by poetic imagery.[5]

IMAGERY

Human minds can hold representations that are unrelated to present situations and that are in this sense 'un-pragmatic'; this is done spontaneously or in a controlled way by the use of signs whose *signifiers* in present situations have *signified contents* that activate these unrelated representations. These signifieds *recall* our representations, which in general exceed the 'literal' sign contents themselves, which is why the recalled representations can be termed *mental spaces* (as in Fauconnier and Turner 2002). Thus, when Shakespeare writes (in Sonnet 147):

My love is as a fever, longing still/For that which longer nurseth the disease.

He builds through *my love* first a link to an emotional state of passion that exceeds the present of the first person and fills a corresponding mental space. This first connection is literal (since love is indeed a passion). Second, he builds through *a fever* a mental space of illness, of which the fever is a part and a symptom, so this connection is *metonymic*. It turns out that the disease in question is psychiatric: madness. Love is to the singular state of passion as fever to a madness described as an addiction (longing for what increases the state of suffering). This relation between two mental spaces both built from signifieds of words in the sentence of the poem is *metaphoric*. The trope does not mention the addictive passion (obsession?) but lets the *disease* be its preliminary name. The entire medical semantic space 'stands for' the erotic semantic space, and the result is an inter-semantic or *mental sign relation*. In this text, the medical space is the mental signifier of a mental sign whose signified is the erotic space. Metaphors are signs in the mind, in this specific sense.[6]

Strictly speaking, the connector *as* in the first sonnet line makes the metaphor a simile, or comparison. This specification is relevant if we are interested in the socio-semiotic status of imagery. The simile markers – *as*, *like*, and may others – prepare us to expect an explicit explanation: *A is like B in respect to* C, whereas ordinary metaphors do not use markers but instead presuppose culturally shared conventional knowledge: *A is (like) B, you know what I mean* ... This explicative C, often explicit in simile, is however structurally present in all forms of metaphor, as a semiotic regulator of meaning. If we consider the A/B space-to-space relation of projection from B to A as a metaphoric *protasis*, the C, expressed or not, is their *apodosis* determining the final meaning mode of this mental sign relation. The comparison is less conventional, since its apodosis is there to 'justify' or pedagogically explain the similitude of the simile. In the example, C is indeed expressed, namely by the allegorical story of the subject's *reason*, the physician trying in vain to treat the disease, and giving up, which causes aggravated madness.[7] This iconic unfolding keeps the meaning mode in the *affective* register – *miserere mei* (have pity), there is no deontic effect to detect.

By contrast, metaphors of the much discussed[8] *butcher* kind – *this surgeon is a butcher; Arafat is a butcher* ... – are evaluative, and their hidden C involves an ethical schema: how should you treat other people, as dead meat? *Jensen is a snake in the grass*, so C: be aware, he hides and then suddenly bites you. Evaluative metaphors carry symbolic meanings, most often instructions. They do not work by similarity, are not descriptive, but rather present a conventional emblem of their *deontic* message.

The French poet Lautréamont's famous surrealistic comparison

[...] *beau comme la rencontre fortuite sur une table de dissection d'un parapluie et d'une machine à coudre* [...][9] – is a perfect affective simile, if the umbrella and the sewing machine are metonymies for a man and a woman, and the table is a love nest.[10]

So, here again the fundamental semiotic meaning classes determine the effect. There is, accordingly, a third metaphor type, namely *catachresis*, which is purely diagrammatic. Speaking of table *legs*, *head*quarters, the long *arm* of the law, is using the human body as a diagram for representing dynamic relations between entities (supporting, controlling, catching, etc.), without any affective or deontic implications, but through neutral, purely *diagrammatic*, intellective representations. The body parts in catachresis offer a standard schematic morphology for basic spatial and temporal notions, including *backwards, forwards, back and forth*, and satellite adverbs such as *up, down, in, out* can be seen as bodily based orientational metaphors in expressions like *prices go up* and *light goes out* (where the verb *go* metaphorically suggests body movement and dynamics). Catachreses are inevitable metaphors, in so far as their imagery does not replace a literal expression in ordinary language[11]; they function rather as informative relational morphemes.

To summarize, metaphors come in three varieties: creative iconic (affective) *similes*, ordinary symbolic (deontic-instructional) *standard metaphors* and grammaticalized diagrammatic (orientational) *catachreses*. So even mental signs follow the semiotic distribution of meaning types. In poetry and other literary genres of art, we find the distribution of sign values across textual performances. In theatre, as in film, iconicity is of course predominantly present in the visual display, whereas a narrative sequencing of events unfolds the basic poetic utterance, embedding it in dialogues, circumstances and actions. Narrative prose is a form of written theatre, adding overarching narrator voices. Narrative literature, whether in prose or in verse, therefore, offers an essential tension between narrat*ing* and narrat*ed* voices and subjectivities, separated by the *story* that contains the characters' voices, whereas the storytell*ing* voice inversely contains the stories. Between the voices on distinct levels, truth and evaluations may vary and form dramatic contrasts, reflecting the polyphony of our life world.

Semiotically, narrative literature gives rise to two fundamental problems: how to understand its enunciation and how to read its diegesis. We will discuss both in turn.

Enunciation

Personhood in language is ubiquitous but directly expressed by personal pronouns (*I, you, she* ...) and deictic morphemes (*this, here, now* ...). From Saussure's *parole* to Benveniste's *énonciation*, the idea of a paralinguistic structure determining speech and writing grows; we will see that it carries the weight of the linguistic sign itself (Saussure 1962; Benveniste 1966; Cervoni 1987; Kerbrat-Orecchioni 1999).

We will present the semiotic version of a model of énunciation. In this model, the elementary enunciation formula *I say this to you* presents the second person in the dative, because the *saying* is a sort of *giving*, so the first person is a *giver*. What is being given is the *signifier* of the utterance sign, and the signifier will in turn 'give' the second person the *signified*, that is, the content of the utterance-sign. The signified may further, if the utterance is a narrative text, contain an instance of enunciation with new, situated first persons and new, situated second persons. The situatedness of the embedded and embodied enunciation is of course constituted by the story, which thus separates the two levels of enunciation.

Furthermore, the narrating first person of a story that is presented as a *fiction* is a fictive person, a conventionally constructed narrator voice addressing the real reader as a *lector in fabula* (Umberto Eco 1979). This means that the narrator as a voice has been created and dubbed by the genre convention of fiction, as a constituting authority, and authorized to speak as if being a real human being. Therefore, fictions can be more or less, or even entirely, historical or biographical without losing their status as fictions. What counts is the fictivity of the narrating voice, not the story. Figure 12.2 shows this structure.

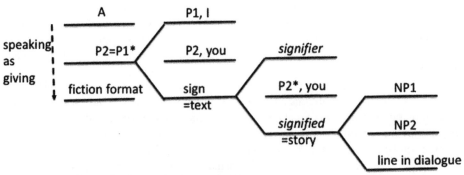

FIGURE 12.2 Elementary narrative enunciation.

In dialogue (real or written, as in the diagrammed relation NP1/NP2), the third-person line is elaborated from utterance to utterance, whereas first and second persons shift. As the model shows, the constitutive sign relation between signifier and signified can be understood as an enunciative relation, in so far as the narrative meaning is *signified-to* the implied reader (P2*) by the signifier. Semiosis and intersubjective enunciation coincide. Here, the narrating voice (P1) addresses the real reader for whom 'fiction' is a special imaginary condition of cognition – a special sort of reality; by contrast, the implied reader, an avatar of the real reader, is already *in* the story world as in a 'normal' and experienceable reality in its own right, however fantastic or absurd it may be.[12]

This intimate connection between sign and enunciation may help us understand the intersubjective force of semiotic communication. *Performative* utterances let the speaker's inherited force, stemming from A in the model, flow directly into the signifier and modify the hearer's world, whereas the speaker (P1) becomes transparent, reduced to the role of a dynamic transmitter (ordering or declaring in the name of A). In strongly *affective* appeals, or in irony, the voice of P1 inversely gets theatrical, opaque, dense, iconic, as if A were the speaker's own body. In ordinary *informative* speech, A is simply a principle of evidential truth – speaking is taken to mean showing what the speaker for some reason thinks may be true. The latter speech mode is the one that an 'Olympian narrator' simulates. The voice in poetry is basically an unstable sliding between all three modes (performative, informative, formative-affective). The status and the transformations of A thus determine the quality of enunciation and the 'meaning of meaning' in communication.

Diegesis

Narratives contain stories, as mentioned. Story structure, or *diegesis*, is not an easy affair to model.[13] One may argue that modelling diegetic structure is a problem for semiotics rather than for poetics, since storytelling is not necessarily an artful endeavour; it is cultivated in commercial communication as well as in religious pedagogy. But since narrative fiction constitutes the quantitatively predominant part of world literature, diegetic structures underlie most of these texts, especially the prose, and our understanding of the artistic phrasing of these stories presupposes our expectation of the characteristic sequencing of situations and events that makes them coherent. Let's consider a well-known example, the legend of Saint George:[14]

[I. A critical situation.]

[I.1] The town of Silene had a pond, as large as a lake, where a plague-bearing dragon dwelled that envenomed all the countryside. To appease the dragon, the people of Silene used to feed it two sheep every day, and when the sheep failed, they fed it their children, chosen by lottery.

[I.2] *It happened* that the lot fell on the king's daughter, Sadra. The king, distraught with grief, told the people they could have all his gold and silver and half of his kingdom if his daughter were spared; but the people refused. The daughter was sent out to the lake, dressed as a bride, to be fed to the dragon. (Brackets and italics added, here and in the following story text)

[II. Salvation in sight.]

[II.1] A Christian officer of the Roman army, George of Lydda, *by chance* rode past the lake. The princess, trembling, sought to send him away, but George vowed to remain. The dragon reared out of the lake while they were conversing. George fortified himself with the Sign of the Cross, charged it on horseback with his lance, and gave it a grievous wound.

[II.2] He then called to the princess to throw him her girdle, and he put it around the dragon's neck. When she did so, the dragon followed the girl like a meek beast on a leash.

[III. The new deal.]

[III.1] The princess and George led the dragon back to the city of Silene, where it terrified the people at its approach. But Saint George called out to them, saying that if they consented to become Christians and be baptized, he would slay the dragon before them. The king and the people of Silene converted to Christianity, George slew the dragon, and the body was carted out of the city on four ox-carts. Fifteen thousand men were baptized, without women and children. [III.2] On the site where the dragon died, the king built a church to the Blessed Virgin Mary and Saint George, and from its altar a spring arose whose waters cured all disease.

The simplest account would use a so-called folktale-actantial semiotic square, of the kind that A.J. Greimas' followers taught their students:

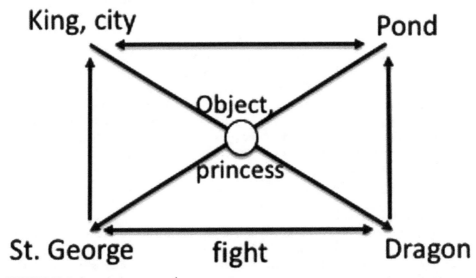

FIGURE 12.3 A semiotic square of story structure.

In this loop, there are two opposed *places*, the city and the pond, and a *value-object*, (*objet de valeur*), the princess, which is moved from the first place to the second by the Dragon, and then brought back by Saint George after the fight between him and the Dragon. The object is first in the right place, then, due to the action of the villain, transferred to a wrong place, and finally restored to the right place. There might be such a 'deep structure', as Greimas suggested, in certain simple stories, but what happens in our legend is clearly not well reflected by this model.

There is initially a problematic *contract* between the people of Silene and the dragon, who is fed by its sheep or children, through a lottery (!). Since there is also a contract between the people and its king, he must respect the lottery and offer his daughter to the dragon – a clear destabilization of the regime. There is further a contract of collaboration between Sadra and George, who together manage to wound and submit the dragon, using girdle and cross, respectively.[15] George forces a new contract upon the king by suggesting his ultimatum: Christen your people or live with the dragon! Since the king accepts the condition, a last contract is set up between the christened people and God, marked by the building of the church, where the divinity lets a healing spring remind everybody of the plague-bearing dragon.

The first contract (C1: people – dragon) already has an element of *chance* built into it (sheep or children); the second contract (C2: people – king) has the lottery choosing the victims; the third contract (C3: Sadra – George) has the chance of their fortuitous encounter as a condition. By the fourth contract (C4: George – king), the king just has to take the chance, not knowing what he is committing his people to; and it turns out, in the fifth contract (C5: people – God), celebrated by the church building, that he had luck: the miraculously curative spring seals the bond and manifests the divine gratitude for (the future saint of plague hospitals) George's act.

As we see, contracts have an inherent affinity to chance. They are symbolic acts, so they come into being by performative acts whose arbitrariness expresses transcendent authorities (and chance is its marker, as in fights and games). In the present case, we have summarized the network of contracts that is necessary in order to make sense of the fight between the hero and the villain (Figure 12.4):

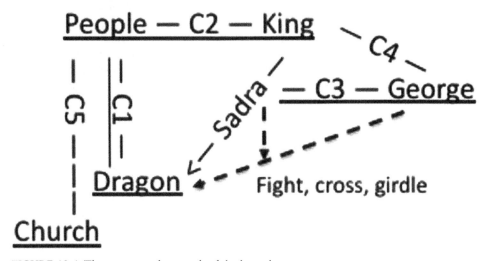

FIGURE 12.4 The contractual network of the legend.

The princess indeed plays a central role in the legend; without her, there would have been neither conflict nor solution. But she is not a 'value-object'; she is a partner of contract and a co-agent.

There is, as always in narratives, a spatio-temporal unfolding of the structure; it falls into a mould, which may be a default or generic format, of four basic stages and a corresponding temporal sequence of places, thus, an elementary display of diegesis (Figure 12.5):

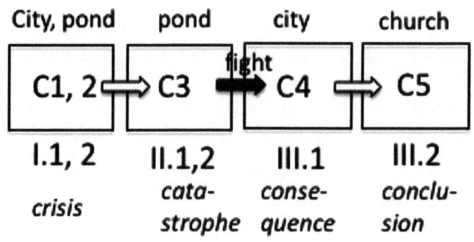

FIGURE 12.5 Diegesis of the legend.

The four scenes account for the iconic coherence of the story, whereas the scenically framed contents account for its symbolic and modal meaning. The diagrammatic lesson for the philosophical reader could be the somewhat Darwinian view that a society can overcome its existential problems by using alien support and thereby letting its own existential or spiritual substance be changed, for the better or the worse (anyway, everything has a price). The final *change* does not have to relate to the initial *problem* – in our example, religion is not really a response to the plague, unless you add a miraculously healing spring, *a posteriori*.

In narrative literature, as we have seen, the story concerns the social and individual life world[16] with its spectacular, *iconic*, affective episodes and outcomes and its *symbolic*, dynamic networks, contracts and fights. The third semiotic aspect of narratives is thus their temporal unfolding of causal and intentional causalities, the diagram of their 'logic', which literary or philosophical criticism finds relevant to the interpretation of texts. Textual interpretation thus adds a meta-semantic layer of meaning to the literal and the imagistic layer that plain reading activates. On this point, semiotics clearly offers a perspective that addresses an important problem of poetics: how to theorize the relation holding between literal reading and literary interpretation, between literal meaning and final meaning. One being semantic and iconico-symbolic, the other being meta-semantic and diagrammatic.

Theatre

The analysis of the inherent imbrication of enunciation and narrative semiosis proposed here finally allows us to offer a semiotic perspective on the poetics of the theatrical genre. There is again a basic format, which is subject to modification by recursion or collapsing of levels but has a stable triadic stratification. Theatre is *writing, staging* and *acting*. So, at least, it implies three categories of agents: writers, directors and actors. Obviously, these

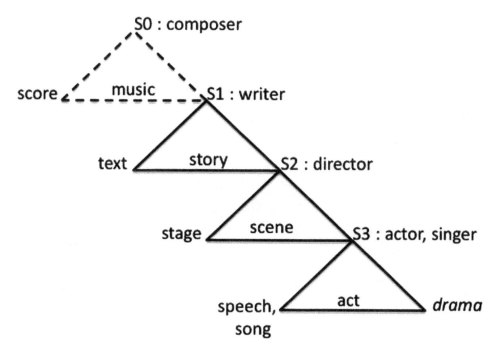

FIGURE 12.6 The semiotic cascade of theatre, opera and song.

instances form a structure, since the acting depends on the staging, which depends on the writing. This structure can be described as a cascade of semioses: the superordinate one being the diegetic semiosis containing (the embedded iconic idea of) the scenic semiosis, which again contains (the embedded symbolic idea of) the actual performative semiosis. However, if we include *opera* in the theatrical genre, we must add a musical semiosis which signifies and contains (the idea of) the text (as a libretto), whereas the rest of the structure remains as before, except that speaking is now singing. The complete cascade (Figure 12.6) therefore also accounts for something as simple as a *song*; songs are staged, even in everyday life, to the extent that their performance requires specified circumstances (such as 'singing in the rain'). Singing is basically a theatrical behaviour. It is also the simplest literary, poetic act we know of.

Music is often strongly symbolic, because sound strings are used as signals and commands of all kinds; when overdetermining staged speech, as in films, it very heavily influences the meaning of a drama. Theatre, that is, iconically staged storytelling, is probably one of the oldest art forms in human civilization. Dance should be added to the acting in the model, alongside of speech and song, since it is a strong mode of staged bodily presence 'under' music and often 'under' a ritual or poetic text (from the dancing stick figures of the bronze age rock paintings to the current 'hip-hop' version).

SPECIFICITY OF RHETORIC AS ART

Having fleshed out the semiotics of poetics and singled out the poetic arts as an undifferentiated, or pre-differentiated, semiotic state that trades on the affective (iconic), performative (symbolic) and informative (diagrammatic) semiosis within a broad social landscape of nation states (sovereignty) and governance (institutions) and their organic

FIGURE 12.7 A prehistorical rock engraving of collective dancing.

formations (communication), we shift to the companion art of rhetoric for which a metasemantic conception thereof thrives in large part by the specialization of these distinct strata. As formulated most famously and influentially in the West by Aristotle ([330 BCE] 2007), as 'the faculty of observing, in any given case, the available means of persuasion' concerning matters that are fundamentally uncertain and open to disagreement. The art of rhetoric applies the techniques of imagery, enunciation, diegesis and theatricality, techniques that redound on the reputation of the speaker (ethos), affections of the audience (pathos) and practical reasoning capacities of both (logos) as practised against a semiotically stratified background of deliberation (future action), adjudication (past acts), and demonstration (present sentiment).[17] As with poetics, the sign types icons, symbols and diagrams pervade rhetoric, such that both arts share considerable metasemantic terminology, but that the goal of rhetoric, as classically understood, is to *tame* multiplicity in favour of social order. In general, western rhetoric may be regarded as diagrammatic in the sense that these practices are part and parcel of governance within institutions. With that in mind, consider two pieces of rhetoric from American common law jurisprudence.

LAW I: THE 'RIGHT TO PRIVACY'

Much like Baudelaire's Cats, common law seeks to embody lovers and scholars, meaning that good jurisprudence seeks above all to filter proximal passions through distal reason, allowing for a maximum of desire to operate within limiting boundaries.[18] What is a coequal semiotic state (passion) in poetry is subordinated in jurisprudence: juridical cats are far more 'ascetic' than 'steamy'. Case in point, consider the article 'The Right to Privacy' by Samuel Warrant and Louis Brandeis[19] from the *Harvard Law Review* (1890), one of the most influential pieces of academic writing on twentieth-century common law jurisprudence, whose reasoning is felt in such landmark cases as *Skinner v. Oklahoma* (1942, discussed below), *Griswald v. Connecticut* (1965) and *Roe v. Wade* (1973). The central argument made is that the right of privacy has been expanding as civilization expands, and thus, should be regarded as a fundamental right in common law, and, specifically for American jurisprudence, should be counted as one of the 'unenumerated' rights implied by the Constitution.

Imagery

The opening salvo presents readers with mental imagery of development and growth:

> That the individual shall have full protection in property is a principle as old as the common law; but it has been found necessary from time to time to define anew the exact nature and extent to such protection. Political, social, and economic entail the recognition of new rights, and the common law, *in its eternal youth*, grows to meet the demands of society.
>
> (1890: 193, emphasis added)

The authors elicit the mental space of *individual development* to suggest that common law is always in adolescence, growing bigger and stronger with time. The inventive metaphor (*catachresis*) is commonly used to describe institutional abstractions, such as common law. Another common metaphor for law is as a *defensive weaponry* and *fortifications*, as exemplified in the closing comment.

> Still, the protection of society must come mainly through a recognition of the rights of the individual ... Has he then such a *weapon*? It is believed that the common law provides him with one, *forged in the slow fire* of the centuries, and to-day *fitly tempered to his hand*. The common law has always recognized a man's house as his *castle, impregnable*, often even to its own officers engaged in the execution of its commands. Shall the courts thus *close the front entrance* to constituted authority, and *open wide the back door* to idle or prurient curiosity?
>
> (1890: 220, emphasis added)

A not-so-subtle means of persuasion is for readers to apprehend two critical facets of common law: it is at once a growing adolescent who must change over time; and it is a means of protection for individuals against external forces, to help render the castle impregnable against the encroachment of the state as well as the 'prying eyes' of the press.

Enunciation

A semiotic version of enunciation described above applies in subtly different measures to the realm of rhetoric. In this instance, a law review article by two practising lawyers forms the constitutional authority of speaking on matters of jurisprudence. In this instance, the deontic power of the authors and the venue is demonstrative, an encomium for the right of privacy, to establish or intensify the present sentiment among the legal community that common law includes the 'right to be left alone'. The speech act is felicitous but not performative, as neither the authors nor the publication carries the power of decree. It is rather an institutional 'handmaid' for *doxa* (settled opinion).

Diegesis

One would be hard-pressed to identify a conspicuous story structure in 'The Right to Privacy', yet the underlying and animating affective pulse behind the right to be left alone, are the innumerable instances of 'violation' to persons' privacy, and by implication, reputation. Tabloid gossip is the exemplary stalking horse for common law protection, made vivid with this claim:

> Gossip is no longer the resource of the idle and of the vicious, but has become a trade, which is pursued with industry as well as effrontery. [...] To occupy the indolent, column upon column is filled with idle gossip, which can only be procured by intrusion upon the domestic circle.
>
> (1990: 196)

Imagery of bringing before your mind's eye (see Oakley and Brandt 2009) such intrusions into your domestic tranquillity, becomes the animating story of the conflict between private thoughts, deeds, and sentiments and public display: the 'Yellow journalism' of the tabloid press is violating the right to privacy of the individual.

Theatre

Every rhetorical performance, whether written or spoken, trades on theatricality: the performer is always an object of attention in specific rational proportions within a scene, in relation to an act, under the auspices of agency, and in pursuit of some purpose, according to Burke's 'grammar of motives' (1969). What is more, a rhetorical situation (Bitzer 1968) is theatrical in the sense that it comprises of an *exigency* (a dramatic situation 'calling for' a response), an *audience* (recipients of the communication), and operates within specific constraints (the suite of semiotic resources, including available time and space). The rhetorical theatrics of 'The Right to Privacy' are appropriately soporific for anyone but 'ascetic cats'.

LAW II: *SKINNER V. OKLAHOMA* (1942)

Majority opinions delivered by the Supreme Court of the United States (SCOTUS), often soporific in tone, are, nonetheless, quite dramatic in their effects. One such occasion is the delivery in 1942 by Justice William O. Douglas of the majority opinion in *Skinner v. Oklahoma*. The petitioner (Skinner), having been convicted multiple times for felony robbery in Oklahoma, was subject to the Habitual Criminal Sterilization Act of 1935, which stipulates that subjects having been convicted of 'two or more times for crimes amounting to felonies involving moral turpitude' (U.S. 316.535) are subject to sterilization. Enacted during the height of the eugenics era, such statutes are designed to reduce the 'criminal element' in society by denying a certain class of felons the ability to procreate.

Douglas, writing for the majority, reversed the statute on the grounds that it:

1. infringes the right of privacy in matters of reproductive autonomy, and
2. violates the equal protections clause of the Fourteenth Amendment to the Constitution.

In other words, the 'soft' cats of jurisprudence wish to temper the discriminatory passions of those 'cruel' cats of the Oklahoma State Legislature. The feline *diagrammatic* logic worked nicely.

Diegetic imagery

The mental representations underlying the affective markers of this opinion appear as storylines of inequity, a violation of the social contract between the individual and the state.

Skinner, having been convicted of stealing chickens in 1926 and of armed robbery in 1929 and 1934, respectively, was sentenced to the penitentiary. In 1936, the Oklahoma Attorney General initiated forced sterilization proceedings against him. Skinner's actions are classified according to Oklahoma stature as grand larceny because the stolen property in each case exceeds the threshold amount of $20.00.

If, however, Skinner had not been a destitute robber, but a clerk who embezzles $20.00 or more from his employer, and was similarly caught and convicted twice more for the same offense, he would not be subject to sterilization, even though larceny and embezzlement are statutorily equivalent felonious crimes of grand larceny under Oklahoma state law. One just happens to be a 'white collar' crime, not amounting to moral turpitude. The juxtaposition of the case facts (i.e. the story of the 'blue collar' crimes themselves) with the counterfactual case of embezzlement throw in bas relief the arbitrary and prejudicial application of the statute to different individuals convicted of a statutorily equivalent crime of supposed equivalent menace to society. Different stories, different collars, different affective evaluations: *iconicity* counts.

The theatrical enunciation of a SCOTUS Opinion

In contradistinction to a law review article, SCOTUS opinions have a uniquely complex enunciation structure. Oakley (2020: 243–6) identifies a cascade of six distinct discourse layers of a Supreme Court Opinion, from the narrative of the case, from the decision (layer 1) all the way to the facts of the case (layer 6): layer 6 represents the basis or 'standing' of the case: the crime or tort that brings the two aggrieved parties together in the socially sanctioned roles as plaintiff and defendant; layer 1 represents the decision of the Court, finalized in a speech act that, in this case, reverses the decisions of the lower-courts and rules the Oklahoma Habitual Criminal Sterilization Act unconstitutional. Between these two layers is a cascade of semiotic structures governing the highly procedural nature of proceedings, including: the order of questions to be addressed and adjudicated (layer 5); the reasons any particular justice gives for deciding a question (layer 4); the manner in which justices address one another, as represented in the majority opinion, as well as any concurring or dissenting opinions (layer 3); and statements outlining the rationale for the decision itself (layer 2), ideally to represent the final decision as the deliberate application of disinterested principles of constitutional law.[20] The SCOTUS opinion is final, but the long-term institutional reputation of the Court depends on the polity's apprehension of them as being guided more by principle than naked partisan advantage, a presumption that has waxed and waned considerably since the Court's founding. *Symbolicity* created, the (fragile) authoritative impersonality of judiciary enunciation occurs on various levels: the 'unembodied' voice of constitutional justice is supposed to be heard through human utterances and theatrical costumes.

In the less formalized genres of modern celebrative and political rhetoric, diagrammatic accuracy is mostly weakened, whereas affective imagery and symbolic posturing tend to merge into media-formulated amalgams. These genres may be considered as serious threats to projects of rational social discourse (Habermas 2018) and as problematic contributions to postmodern entertainment, in which the public sphere becomes the frame of rhetorical reality shows. The rhetorical profile of populism may thus be due to its weakened diagrammatic meaning and consequential indifference to juridical thinking.

CONCLUSION

In a sense, poetics and rhetoric are already semiotics, even if they do not think of themselves this way. The advantage of explicitly studying the semiotics of language-based art forms is that it allows us to insert poetics and rhetoric into a larger framework of human meaning-making in the social world. It is important to understand what art, including literature, is *doing* in and across the human sociosphere: it takes us 'back' to stages of civilization where the otherwise distinct meaning modes of historically specified cultural pragmatics are still to be found in the same expressive behaviour forms, as if our 'origins' were present – a historically impossible but semiotically possible stage of restarting, so to speak, that places our mind and body in states of experienced 'indistinction' and allows us to rediscover meaning in its primordial state, as beauty or horror. It is likewise important to understand that rhetorical practices stem from these same semiotic systems of the human sociosphere, but with its origins in the 'distinction' among civilizing domains of meaning making.

NOTES

1. Jerry Fodor (1975). Cronquist and Brandt, in Brandt (2019).
2. In pictorial art, Paul Klee's art work illustrates this point particularly well: diagrammatic graphics, imagery, performative colours, as in his beautiful *Senecio* (1922). By performative colours, we mean colours that become signals when they are not natural to their support.
3. This poem is reproduced with kind permission from David Young.
4. See Brandt (2004), chapter 8, 'Poetry, Cognitive Semiotics, and Baudelaire's Cats'. And also Brandt (1997), 'Cats in Space. Baudelaire' '"Les chats" Read by Jakobson and Lévi-Strauss'.
5. See the chapter 'Three Imagistic Operators' in Brandt (2004). Brandt and Brandt (2005a) introduces the dynamic semiotic blending model for poetic imagery, which has a particular tendency to 'spin' and let conventional imagery be expanded, transformed, and inversed as to its sense.
6. In terms of classical conceptual metaphor theory (Lakoff and Johnson 1980), the disease here is a *source* item and love is a *target*. These two theoretical terms are again metaphoric, and also awkward, since sources do not have targets.
7. My reason, the physician to my love, / Angry that his prescriptions are not kept, / Hath left me, and I desperate now approve / Desire is death, which physic did except. // Past cure I am, now reason is past care, / And frantic mad with evermore unrest...
8. See Brandt and Brandt (2005b).
9. Isidore Ducasse, *Les Chants de Maldoror*, VI,1, 1869. [...]beautiful like the fortuitous encounter between an umbrella and a sewing machine on a dissection table[...].
10. Metonymies are always celebrations of the target item, positive or negative; with their displacement of focus, they express the speaker community's respect shown for the target. Surprisingly, this meaning effect seems to escape the attention of cognitive semantics. For a rich display of other semantic effects of this trope, see Littlemore (2015). 'Proust is on my book shelf' (respect). 'Message from the White House' (respect, or its negative version, disrespect).

SEMIOTICS IN RHETORIC AND POETICS 243

11 Tables *do* have legs. In French, they just have feet (*les pieds de la table*).
12 The enunciative embedding can of course continue by recursion and create stories in stories (*mise en abîme*) as in Boccaccio's *Decameron*. As to the classification of story worlds, see 'Forces and Spaces', Brandt (2020).
13 Zvétan Todorov suggested a formalization in his *Grammaire du Décaméron* (1969) and A. J. Greimas published a different model, '*Éléments d'une grammaire narrative*', the same year.
14 From *Legenda Aurea*, by Jacobus de Voragine (approx. 1260). We use a summary of the English translation. The Greek soldier George of Lydda was a martyr from the fourth century, beheaded by Diocletian as punishment for his defence of the Christians.
15 Both symbolic weapons ostensibly work by magic. The girdle may carry sexual force, a welcome complement to the religious force of the cross.
16 Story worlds are versions of our phenomenological life world, even if they are rendered fantastic or fairy-tale like, grotesque or absurd – those variations correspond to the narrator's editing style, one could say. The narrator (voice construction) has psycho-semiotic properties, and can carry personality traits (cruelty, tenderness, generosity, etc.), emotional temperature (cold and ironic or warm and enthusiastic), and mood (excited or depressed). Even the Olympian narrator does not have to be neutral and transparent. The narrator's edited and editing style determines the coordination of the two temporalities in narratives, diegetic time versus narration time. Telling a story backwards may produce an ironic effect, for example.
17 Contemporary rhetorical theory commonly regards this classical *trivium* as a means of underestimating the reach of rhetoric, especially since rhetorical practices have migrated to the written word, and then to multimedia platforms. We regard this classical distinction to be heuristically useful and broadly correct, and follow Perelman and Olbrechts-Tyteca (1969) in classifying the exponential increase of text types as greatly enlarging the third strata of demonstrative or ceremonial rhetoric (epideictic). Such rhetorical forms encompass chapters such as this one.
18 Institutions of civil law likewise share the same goal, but place much more power in the hands of lawyers, academics and legislators than judges. In modern civil law systems, inspired by ancient Roman law, the governing documents are written statutes (enactments of law or policy); judges merely establish the facts of the case. In common law, the governing documents are prior decisions that form precedents (*stare decisis*); judges actively shape the law. In the United States, the *Constitution* is the supreme governing document, with past decisions reflecting interpretations of that sovereign document, but these judicial opinions set the law of the land at any given time, at least until they are overturned.
19 Louis Brandeis served as Associate Justice of the Supreme Court from 1916 to 1939 and is widely regarded as having a one of the most distinguished careers among associate justices. Brandeis is thought to be responsible for the central argument of this article.
20 Justice Anthony Kennedy, in his concurring opinion in *Texas v Johnson* (1989), which affirms the Texas Court of Criminal Appeals holding that the Texas Penal Code §42.09(a)(3), banning the practice of flag burning, violates the First Amendment right to free speech, epitomizes the sentiment of principled reason: 'The hard fact is that sometimes we must make decisions we do not like. We make them because they are right, right in the sense that the law and the Constitution, as we see them, compel the result. And so great is our commitment to the process that, except in the rare case, we do not pause to express distaste for the result, perhaps for fear of undermining a valued principle that dictates the decision. This is one of those rare cases' (491 U.S. 397).

REFERENCES

Aristotle. ([c330BCE] 2007), *On Rhetoric: A Theory of Civic Discourse*, trans. G. A. Kennedy, Oxford: Oxford University Press.
Benveniste, É. (1966), *Problèmes de Linguistique Générale (I)*, Paris: Gallimard.
Bitzer, L. (1968), 'The Rhetorical Situation', *Philosophy and Rhetoric*, 1 (1): 1–14.
Brandt, PAa, ed. (1997), *The Roman Jakobson Centennial Conference* (Acta Lingüística Hafniensia 29), Copenhagen: Le Cercle linguistique de Copenhague.
Brandt, PAa. (2004), *Spaces, Domains, and Meaning: Essays in Cognitive Semiotics* (European Semiotics 4), Berne: Peter Lang.
Brandt, PAa. (2019), *The Music of Meaning. Essays in Cognitive Semiotics*, Newcastle upon Tyne: Cambridge Scholars.
Brandt, PAa. (2020), *Cognitive Semiotics: Signs, Mind and Meaning*, London: Bloomsbury.
Brandt, L. and PAa. Brandt (2005a), 'Cognitive Poetics and Metaphor', *European Journal of English Studies*, 9 (2): 117–30.
Brandt, L. and PAa. Brandt (2005b), 'Making Sense of a Blend: A Cognitive-Semiotic Approach to Metaphor', *Annual Review of Cognitive Linguistics*, 3 (1): 216–49.
Burke, K. ([1945] 1969), *A Grammar of Motives*, Berkeley: University of California Press.
Cervoni, J. (1987), *L'énonciation*, Paris: Presses Universitaires de France.
Eco, U. (1979), *Lector in Fabula*, Milan: Bompiani.
Fodor, J. (1975), *The Language of Thought*, Cambridge: Harvard University Press.
Fauconnier, G. and M. Turner (2002), *The Way We Think*, Conceptual Blending and the Mind's Hidden Complexities, New York: Basic Books.
Greimas, A. J. (1969), 'Éléments d'une Grammaire Narrative', *L'Homme*, 9 (3): 71–92.
Habermas, J. (2018), *Parcours 2 (1990–2017), Théorie de la rationalité – Théorie du langage*, Paris: Editions Gallimard.
Kerbrat-Orecchioni, C. (1999), *L'énonciation: De la Subjectivité dans le Langage*, Paris: Armand Colin.
Lakoff, G. and M. Johnson ([1980] 2003), *Metaphors We Live By*, Chicago: Chicago University Press.
Littlemore, J. (2015), *Metonymy: Hidden Shortcuts in Language, Thought and Communication*, Cambridge: Cambridge University Press.
Oakley, T. (2020), *Rhetorical Minds, Meditations on the Cognitive Science of Persuasion*, Oxford: Berghahn Books.
Oakley, T. and P. A. Brandt (2009), 'Hypotyposis and the Cinematic Model of Fictive Meaning: A Collector's Conceit', in W. Wildgen and B. V. Heusden (eds), *Metarepresentation, Self-Organization and Art*, 115–36, Bern: Peter Lang.
Perelman, C. and L. Olbrechts-Tyteca (1969), *The New Rhetoric: A Treatise on Argumentation*, trans. J. Wilkinson and P. Weaver, South Bend: Notre Dame University Press.
Saussure, F. (1962), *Cours de Linguistique Générale*, Paris: Payot.
Skinner v. Oklahoma (1942), 316 U.S. 535. https://supreme.justia.com/cases/federal/us/316/535/ (accessed 22 December 2020).
Texas v. Johnson (1989), 491. U.S. 397. https://supreme.justia.com/cases/federal/us/491/397/ (accessed 26 December 2020).
Todorov, Z. (1969), *Grammaire du Décaméron*, The Hague: Mouton.
Warren, S. and L. Brandeis (1890), 'The Right to Privacy', *Harvard Law Review*, 4 (5): 193–220.

CHAPTER THIRTEEN

Semiotics in Literature and Narratology

STÉPHANIE WALSH MATTHEWS AND PAUL PERRON

INTRODUCTION

The purpose of this chapter is to give an account of a number of major figures and basic theoretical principles that have shaped the field of literary semiotics from the beginning of the twentieth century to the present from both a historical and a notional perspective. In the first part of this introduction, we will focus on the ambivalence of the phrase 'literary semiotics' that became very popular in the 1960s and remains problematic today as two very different concepts and practices that are wedded together in a strained, even contradictory relationship. We shall then turn to the Swiss linguist Ferdinand de Saussure (1857–1913) and his American contemporary Charles Sanders Peirce (1839–1914), the original founders of semiotics whose seminal works gave rise not only to general semiotic theory but also influenced literary semiotics and narratology over the last century. We will raise the issue of the two different schools of thought regarding both the philosophical underpinnings of semiotic theory and its applications (1990: vi–viii),[1] notably regarding the literary sign. This will be followed by an historical overview of the state of the art. The next two sections will concentrate on contemporary semiotic literary theory inspired by the Russian Formalists, the Prague School, along with French Structuralism, all influenced directly by Saussure's *Cours de Linguistique Générale* (1916), edited and published posthumously by his former students Charles Bally and Albert Sechehaye.[2] Our penultimate section will deal with post structuralism and the Paris School; our final one with Peirce and contemporary pragmatics.

The ambiguity noted in attempting to describe what is or is not *literary* is compounded by the *Oxford English Dictionary*'s tautological definition of the term: 'Of or relating to writing, study or content of literature, esp. of the kind valued for quality of form; of the nature of literature.'[3] Here the definition of the object of study, or the content and the nature of literature, is listed in the gnomic aorist present tense (neither time nor place being presented as a universal and general truth) – in counter-distinction to Jean-Paul Sartre who in *Being and Nothingness* (1943), when discussing Marcel Proust's literary works, evokes their 'potency' that can be developed in a series of real or possible appearances: 'The genius of Proust, even when reduced to works produced, is no less equivalent to the infinity of possible points of view which one can take on that work and which we will call the "inexhaustibility" of Proust's work.' Some five years before publishing *What Is Literature* (1948), Sartre posits that literature is an ongoing socio-historic construct that can be articulated through an infinity of points of view or methodologies that readers can take on it. In brief, the essence or 'nature' of literature is radically detached form the individual appearance, since it 'must be able to be manifested by an infinite series of individual manifestations' (Sartre 1966: lvi).

The second term *semiotics* also creates terminological conundrums that have not yet been satisfactorily resolved. The Swiss linguist F. de Saussure (1916) coined the term *semiology* and defined it as 'a science that studies the life of signs within society; it would be part of social psychology and consequently of general psychology: I shall call it semiology (from Greek *semeîon* "sign")' (1916: 16). Jonathan Culler (1980: 18–43) notes that the American philosopher C. S. Peirce, Saussure's contemporary, throughout his lifetime devoted himself to '*semiotic*', which he conceived as 'the science of sciences' (Culler 1980: 25), 'since the entire universe is perfused with signs, if it is not composed entirely of signs' (Peirce 1905: CP 5.448). Culler lucidly underscores the deficiencies and complementarity of these radically different approaches that gave rise to two dominant semiotic theories of literary analyses over the last hundred years: Saussure's founded on the model of structural linguistics and Peirce's on a vast complex anatomy of signs. Yet, even though the two researchers claim to found their theories on 'science' they each designate very dissimilar areas of study and methodologies.

THE LITERARY SIGN

Peirce and Saussure begin with dissimilar definitions of what constitutes a 'sign'; for Saussure the linguistic sign consists of a signifier (an acoustical image) and a signified (a concept) which he later compared to the front and the back of a sheet of paper that constitute linguistic form. For him 'the bond between the signifier and the signified is arbitrary', which is not the case for the symbol where the bond is never arbitrary (Saussure 1916: 66–7). On the other hand, Peirce 'begins with a distinction between arbitrary signs, which he calls "symbols," and two types of motivated signs, indices and icons'; however, he reaches a conclusion similar to Saussure's (Culler 1980: 24).

As Ronald Scheiffer and Gabrial Rupp (2005: 889–90) perceptively note Ferdinand de Saussure's (1857–1913) seminal work on twentieth-century linguistics and literary studies was first labelled '*structuralism*' by Roman Jakobson (1896–1982), one of the key founders of the Russian Formalist School (1916–29). They highlight the fact that for Jakobson Saussure's theory of language was based upon four assumptions: (a) the *systematic* nature of language, where the whole is greater than the sum of its parts; (b) the *relational* nature of the elements of language where all entities are defined in terms of their combination; (c) their *arbitrary* nature where elements are defined in terms of their function and purpose; (d) and the *social* nature of language which provides the larger context for analysis. For Jakobson the first three assumptions were the cornerstones of *structural* theory and method (Schleifer and Rupp 2005: 889–95). A half-century later, Algirdas Julien Greimas (1917–92) and Joseph Courtés (1982) note that the boundaries of the fields of literary semiotics or – if one considers it as a semiotic *process* – literary discourse, have still not yet been clearly defined and seem to have been established more by tradition than by formal criteria. Contrary to other semiotic systems, for example, legal or religious discourse it cannot be distinguished by its own specific content (Greimas and Courtés 1982: 179). The issue of genres (such as what distinguishes the fantastic from the surreal), and the instability of the categories defining the specificity of literary texts in relation to other texts as Jørgen Dines Johansen in his seminal work *Literary*

Discourse (Dines 2002: 3–21) argues for a semiotic-pragmatic approach to literature as well as his innovative and lucid essay 'Structuralism and/or the Semiotic-Pragmatic Approach to Literature' (2009) accentuate and mark a crucial change in the plurality of semiotic approaches today that continue to redefine the study of literary texts (Dines 2009: 12–32).

A BRIEF OVERVIEW AND STATE OF THE ART[4]

Literary semiotics seeks to uncover the production of meaning of texts by establishing paradigmatic and syntagmatic models that can explore the ways in which literary texts generate signification. It is beyond the scope of this chapter to review all the major contributions to literary semiotics during the twentieth century and the first two decades of the twenty-first century.[5] The 'Russian Formalists' (Margolin 2005: 814–20), whose aim was to lay the foundations for an autonomous science of the study of literature, had a seminal influence on twentieth-century literary semiotic theory. The Formalists identified their object of study of what Roman Jakobson (1896–1982) called *literaturnost*, 'literariness' or what constitutes the pertinent features of literature that distinguish it from other discourse. Their goal was to define 'the devices' by which literary texts – especially poems – foreground their own language, in meter, rhyme, and other patterns of sound and repetition (Baldick 2008). Victor Shklovsky contributed to the expansion of fundamental structural principles discovered in poetry in the short story and the novel, thereby extending the theory to account for the notion of literary text (Shklovsky [1925] 1990). In *O Teorie Prozy* (1925) – *Theory of Prose* (1993) – by examining a large number of texts from different genres, Shklovsky demonstrated how processes of composition were linked to stylistic processes. His review of the Formalists' research endeavours insisted on the necessity of theory in order to locate, delimit and understand the systematic nature of literary facts (Eikenbaum [1927] 1965: 31–75). These literary theoreticians identified techniques that were mainly concerned with plot construction that 'led them to formulate the distinction between elements in the construction of a work (*subject*) and those that make up its materials (*fable*) ... which laid the groundwork for Vladimir Propp's *Morphologija Skazki* (1928), *Morphology of the Folktale* (1958) seminal discovery of function in the plot analysis of folk tales, one of the crowning achievements of Formalist investigation' (Perron 1986: 597). Mikhail Bakhtin and Yuri Lotman also made lasting contributions to literary criticism, semiotics and the philosophy of language. The former (Bakhtin 1981, 1984, 1986) wrote major works on the carnival, Rabelais and Renaissance popular culture, the theory of the novel, configurations of how space and time are represented in the language and discourse of the novel, and, of course, on dialogism which sets the stage for post-structuralist considerations. The latter, Lotman (1976), born in St. Petersburg, Russia, a prolific and original literary scholar and semiotician who wrote on the limits of the structural description of a text, the analysis of the poetic text, the semiotics of cinema, the structure of the artistic text, the theatre and theatricality, myth, cinema, the dynamic model of a semiotic system, also founded the Tartu-Moscow School of Semiotics and the discipline of cultural semiotics. Lotman's contributions also underscore the inherent relationship between culture and sign systems, coining the term *semiosphere*.

The Russian Formalists, notably Jakobson and Nikolai Trubetskoy, also played critical roles in 'The Prague Linguistic School' (1926–48) that greatly influenced this group's theoretical investigations and contributions to literary studies from a European structuralist perspective. Jan Mukarovsky (1934) proposed linguistic categories inherited from Saussure, for example, between (langue) the existing norm, or language, and (parole) individual speech that could also be applied to literature (Mukarovsky 1934: 1065–72). He subsequently incorporated his semiotic theories on narrative structures into the general framework of communication theory that provided the basis for Hans Robert Jauss's reception theory (Jauss 1982). Other members of the Prague School whose works originally appeared in Czech during the first half of the twentieth century that investigated the vast domain of art as semiotic fact were not translated into English until the end of the 1970s. Petr Bogatyrev published original studies on the costume as a sign, folk songs, semiotics in the folk theatre, forms and functions of folk theatre. Researchers examined the dynamics of signs in the theatre; Veltrusky the dramatic text as a component of theatre, basic features of dramatic dialogue, the construction of semantic contexts and aspects of the pictorial sign; Jakobson on cinema, poetry and Hussite literature; Ladislav Matejka on Prague School Semiotics, whereas Lubomir Dolezel proposed a theoretical scheme of narrative time. In a series of numerous important works, he would later explore narrative worlds that had a decided impact on literary semiotics by integrating possible world semantics into a more empirical theory of literature (Dolezel 1979, 1990, 1998, 2010). Anglo-American literary critics were also concerned with the technical aspects of the art of fiction but were, in the main, very much unaware of the theoretical advances made by the Russian Formalists or the Prague School. The first generation did not consider their object of study from a systematic point of view or as a system of signs governed by definable rules.[6] Yet, a second generation of critics such as Northrop Frye (1957) and Norman Friedman (1975) who attempted to clarify literary works by means of taxonomies and non-formalized typologies were also unaware of the major advances made by Formalists and Prague School researchers.

French literary semiotics integrated and developed major theoretical concepts and theories articulated by the Russian Formalists and Prague School Semioticians. The structural Saussurean semiotic turn of the early 1960s in Europe, particularly in Paris, saw the emergence of an unprecedented radical rethinking in the social sciences and humanities, above all in literary semiotics. This movement owed much to Jakobson and Claude Lévi-Strauss both exiled in New York during the Second World War. Lévi-Strauss saw a clear relationship between anthropology and linguistics and noted that the social sciences could benefit from more rigorous structural linguistic concepts and methods. First of all, because it shifts from the study of *conscious* linguistic phenomenon to the study of their unconscious infrastructure; second, it considers *terms* not as singular entities but as taking on their meaning in relationship to other terms, thereby introducing the concept of *system*; and finally it aims at discovering *general laws* by induction or logical deduction (Lévi-Strauss 1963: 33, 63, 71).

In a seminal issue of *Communications,* entitled 'Introduction à l'analyse structurale des récits' Roland Barthes (1966, 1975: 237–72) also influenced by Saussure, highlights the importance of Jakobson and Lévi-Strauss's research on current semiotic theory that focused mainly on deducted procedures based on structural linguistics particularly level of description each level has a hierarchical relationship to other levels and narrative elements that have both distributional and integrative relationships with each other (cf. Perron 2005: 852–9). Notwithstanding, Tzvetan Todorov (1939–2017), who was born in Sophia, Bulgaria, and who immigrated to Paris in 1963 was instrumental in introducing the Russian Formalists in France through his publications on literary semiotics and poetics (Todorov 1965, 1967, 1969, 1970, 1971, 1978). Todorov (1969) elaborated his *Grammaire du Décaméron* on the principle that there exists a universal grammar that can formally account for all narratives, which adheres to the propositions laid out in the very first page of Barthes's chapter 'An Introduction to the Structural Analysis of Narrative' (1966: 1): 'There are countless forms of narrative in the world. First of all, there is a prodigious variety of genres, each of which branches out into a variety of media, as if all substances could be relied upon to accommodate man's stories.' He further states that narratives appear in oral or written language, pictures, cinema, gestures and a combination of each. It is also present in myths, legends, fables, tales, epics, short stories, history, tragedy, drama, comedy, pantomime, paintings, stained-glass windows, movies, local news, conversations; it is present at all times, in all places, in all societies and is unconcerned with good or bad literature. 'Like life itself, it is there, international, transhistorical, transcultural' (Barthes 1975: 237). Ways in which literature can be organized and understood by genre as well as belonging to a larger universal field is still a common belief widely held by many working in literary circles. Furthermore, with Gérard Genette (1966–72, 1980),[7] Torodov launched the avant-garde journal *Poétique* in 1970 that continues to play a fundamental role in literary semiotics and literary theory in general founded on narratology, semiotics and linguistics. Following Todorov, Genette (1972) worked out a stratificational structural model of textual analysis based on Sausurrian-Hjelmslevian[8] definitions of sign where he studied the relations between the story, the narrative content or signified (*histoire*), the narrative or signifier (*récit*) and narration (*narration*); narration and signified, narration and signifier.[9] He analysed Time and Mood in terms of the relationship between narration and signified and narration and signifier. Under Time he introduced the categories of order, duration and frequency and under Mood those of point of view and distance, whereas under Voice the status of the narrator and problems of the time of narration. Theoretically innovative and widely commented, Genette's contribution to literary semiotics would have had a longer impact were it not for terminological fluctuations. However, as Poiana states, the problem of ambiguous and fluctuating terminology is not singular to Genette. Rhetorical, narratological and stylistic studies have long been using layered language, with polysemic uses. Genette merely inherited this ineffective tradition (Poiana 1994: 23–36).

TOWARDS A CONTEMPORARY SEMIOTIC LITERARY THEORY

Current semiotic literary theory owes much to Barthes's programmatic 'An Introduction to the Structural Analysis of Narrative' where he underscores the notion of level of description where each level bears a hierarchical relationship to other levels, and where narrative elements have both a distributional relationship and an integrative one. Barthes three levels of description, 'functions', 'actions' and 'narration' are linked together; thus a function takes on meaning only in the domain of an actant's (sender, receiver, opponent, adjuvant, etc.) action; and action is meaningful only at the level of narration. The two main tendencies that evolved in France were grounded, on the one hand, in Saussurean and Hjelmslevean structural and post-structural semiotics, represented by Greimas (1987) and Fontanille (Greimas and Fontanille 1992), the 'Paris School', François Rastier (1972, 1997), Denis Bertrand (2000), Jacques Fontanille (1999), along with Barthes (1964; see also Todorov 1969; Bakhtin 1981), Todorov and Genette who in the 1960s and early 1970s espoused structural analysis. These theoreticians initially worked out a semio-narrative actional and cognitive theory of literary texts as interactional discursive communication and those who concentrated on the syntactic and semantic domains of literary semiotics were criticized for espousing an immanentist perspective in their textual analyses (cf. Derrida 1967: 83).

In his response to the critics who reduced most structural analyses to an imminent point of view cut off from daily life, the linguist and philosopher Herman Parret (1989, 1994, 2018) clarifies and lays to rest the criticism of post-structuralist semiotic researchers of the mid-1980s. He noted how Greimas and the Paris school progressively introduced pragmatic (J. L. Austin 1962), phenomenological (Maurice Merleau Ponty) hermeneutic (Greimas and Ricoeur (1989: 551–62) dimensions when *developing their theories and methodologies in progress. In an extensive discussion* with Greimas that took place in 1974 quoted in Parret's 'Introduction' to *Paris School Semiotics I* (1989: vii–xxvi) who raised the issue of reductionism in his semio-narrative theory:

> It has been said that Greimas, like other 'orthodox' structuralists, believe meaning to be an *immanent universe* which has nothing to do with real life, with observable and experienced practices of real human beings [...] This is a total misunderstanding. Semiotics is about (daily) life, about real beings and situations, about the natural and cultural worlds [...] However, it should be said that semiotics *assumes* its proper reductionism: it 'reconstructs' reality, i.e. it projects a so-called 'deep grammar' which exists only at the level of *understanding* (explanation) of the observable phenomena, [...] every scientific approach is reductionist by definition – and it cannot be otherwise. Has botany ever been considered to be the description of all plants, and zoology, of all animals, taken one by one? Every scientific approach supposes the choice of a definite level of generality and a treatment of individuals *inside classes.* Scientific research is first of all a research for *invariants.*

The deconstructionist philosopher Jacques Derrida's provocative statements that incited numerous heated reactions and debates, in particular with John Searle, philosopher of language in the 1980s with his 'Il n'y a pas de hors texte' (*'There is no outside-text'*, translation ours) who ended their public dispute with a perfunctory dismissive remark on the lack of rigour and value of the former's research (cf. Wheeler 2020). Moreover, those who retain close ties with the Paris School are attempting to rethink semio-narrative theory in general by integrating a semiotic dimension of passions. On the other hand, critics from the second tendency, including Julia Kristeva (Kristeva 1969, 1980) and Roland Barthes (1974),[10] subsequently radically questioned their post-structuralist founding semio-narrative principles.

POST-STRUCTURALISM AND THE PARIS SCHOOL

What characterizes especially The Paris School is that semiotics – and in our case literary semiotics – is an ongoing process that began in the early 1960s and even today considers linguistics as a way of thinking philosophically by using a number of philosophical concepts and to think of philosophy in terms of linguistics by integrating a number of linguistic notions. Paul Perron and Paolo Fabbri in their 'Foreword' to Algirdas Julien Greimas and Jacques Fontanille, *The Semiotics of Passion* (op. cit., 1993: vii–xvi) remark that for Greimas and the Paris School, a dual thrust exists in the general field of semiotics with respect to the application of semiotic theory and its philosophical foundations. The originality of semiotics is that it maintains an articulation between the epistemological level and the level of application. Greimas and the Paris School's semiotic project are characterized by both their speculative and empirical intent insofar as for them 'methodology constituted the meeting ground for the theory of signs and the human sciences insofar as its function is to establish the missing link between epistemological and textual knowledge' (1993, vii).

In order to find a pertinent way of speaking about philosophical problems from a semiotic perspective they made use of linguistic terms such as 'agent', 'object', 'modalization' and 'aspectualization' that implied certain philosophical assumptions. They then elaborated a semio-narrative actional and cognitive grammar. When confronted with the inadequacies of this grammar to account for the specificity of a literary text, they integrated a theory of passions into their grammar which increased the descriptive potential of the model and established a coherent methodology that used text descriptions to enrich and to reconfigure the theoretical level. Here, methodology does not only provide categories but is essential to disengage concepts from texts and to reconfigure the texts in the theory itself (cf. Ricœur 1989). The critical importance of a semio-narrative methodology as a mediating instance between theory and text, as well as numerous studies of the passional dimension of literary texts, was accompanied by a disengagement with Peirce's semiotic (which we will soon discuss) and phenomenology and an engagement with Maurice Merleau Ponty's phenomenology and René Thom's catastrophe theory (Petitot 1986: 991–1022), which both originate from very different contexts and traditions (Perron and Fabbri 1993: xv–xvi).

Feminist criticism by Teresa De Lauretis (1987), Mieke Bal (1988) and Kaja Silverman (1984) extend semiotic theory into other domains of literary inquiry including gender theory. Other studies were written to focus and refocus semio-narrative literary theory and its apprehension through the reading process, David Herman Brian McHale and James Phelan (Herman, McHale and Phelan 2010); Bertrand Gervais (1990, 2007, 2012) focuses on the activity of reading and studies the structural features of a conceptual network of actions from the theoretical perspectives of semiotics, artificial intelligence and cognitive sciences. In a much more radical departure from structuralist and post-stucturalist literary semiotics, Ricœur, like Greimas, for whom signification cannot live without narrativity, also situates narrative at the very core of human existence where it has a social or institutional existence: 'narratives already have their social functions, and they are understood in a certain way in social intercourse among writers, readers and speakers' (Ricoeur 1989: 551; cf. Blamey and Pellauer 1988).

Numerous volumes have been published over the last half-century since Greimas, A. J. and Courtés's, *Sémiotique. Dictionnaire raisonné de la théorie du langage* (1979), translated into English (1982), which highlighted the development of the theory and the methodology that provided the *Paris School* 'truly international in scope, given its numerous correspondents and research affiliates in Italy and Switzerland, in Belgium, in the Netherlands and Scandinavia, in Spain and Portugal as well as in the Americas (Canada, U.S.A., Mexico, South America) and in other parts of the world (Japan, North Africa)'.[11] A number of collective works, notably the 1,076 page two volume *Essays in honor of Algirdas Julien Greimas* edited by Parret and Rupretch (1985) by ninety-two scholars representing twenty-three different countries and *Greimassian Semiotics* that appeared in *New Literary History* (eds) Perron and Collins (1989) also included contributions by fifteen international Scholars who dialogued with and commented on the innovation and importance of the ground breaking theoretical and methodological work by the Paris School. Amir Biglari *Entretiens Sémiotiques* (2014) who interviewed twenty-two renowned European and American semioticians, ongoing members and contributors to the Paris School, on Greimas's theory and practice on their own work and on post-structural literary semiotics in general. The ongoing impact of Greimas and the Paris School is confirmed today in the recently published two-volume, one-thousand-page compendium, *A. J. Greimas – Life and Semiotics* and *Semiotics Post-Greimas* (Broden and Walsh Matthews 2017), in two special issues of *Semiotica*, the Journal of the International Association for Semiotic Studies (vols. 214 and 219, respectively), with sixty contributors worldwide, covering the development of this ongoing research project. Moreover, the evolution of this lifelong work that began with Greimas (1917–92) in the mid-1960s, when elected Professor at the École des Hautes Études en Sciences Sociales and Director of his seminar on general semantics, was taken up by his former graduate students, who continue to organize the research seminar today that began some fifty years ago.

In addition, Louis Hébert and his international team who pioneered the website *Signo*, which has had more than 3,000,000 visits since 2004, makes available in French and English general applied semiotic theories from the above mentioned scholars. The website includes, in more detail, a number of major semioticians such as Umberto Eco (1979, 1994, 2000); Jean-Marie Klinkenberg (1990, 1991); Michael Riffaterre (1978, 1983, 1990) in addition to other theorists who have made significant contributions to the semiotic analysis of literary texts, besides providing tools for their analysis (Eco 1979a, 1979b, 1994; Klinkenberg 1990, 1991). Moreover, Louis Hébert has just published a major volume on theoretical and applied semiotic analysis for text and image analysis with Classics Garnier (2020), an abridged version of which was translated into English and appeared almost simultaneously at the end of December 2019 under the title *An Introduction to Applied Semiotics: Tools for Text and Image Analysis*.

PEIRCE AND THE PRAGMATICS OF TEXT

As introduced in Winfried Nöth's chapter on 'Pragmatist Semiotics' (this collection, Volume 1, Chapter 4), Peirce's contributions to sign and sign theory, come through a practical approach of sign and sign relations. As Peircean semiotics venerates the triadic sign instead of Saussure's dyadic one, some key articulation of engagement is via phenomenological theory. More importantly, rooted in understanding 'meaning' and the way in which it is generated, Peircean approaches to texts differ from the more specialized Greimassian ones. One key difference is how the sign is defined and, from there, what role semiotics plays more generally. As semiotics has offered a number of potential definitions of the sign, many of the bifurcations can be easily resolved, as demonstrated by Louis Hébert (2020). The sign and its different approaches can be unified through a reframing of concepts, rendering the operational function of meaning and meaning making central once again.

In *Redefining Literary Semiotics*, H. Veivo's introduction states that: 'If literature is communication, it is about different life-worlds and experiences and about the thoughts, desires and emotions animating them' (2009: 4). He goes on to add that 'literature is also to a very high degree [of] signification, a dynamic process in which meaning is developed by the complex features and structures of the text and their insertion into varying contexts of production and reception' (Veivo 2009: 4). As such, literature can transcend context and can extend beyond. The sentiment of outspreading past established (albeit disputed) approaches carries the tone of the collection where one can see literary semiotics move from structuralism/post-structuralism into a pragmatic approach.

More critically, in 'Structuralism and/or the Semiotic-Pragmatic Approach to Literature' (Johansen 2009: 12–32), Dines Johansen determines the possible move from structuralism to pragmatism. Avoiding a rejection of structuralism, a pragmatic approach can instead fold Shklovsky, Jakobson, Bühler, and others' dialogic sign conception into Peirce's and Morris's sign action, or 'sign in use'. This approach allows for the text to be analysed through the triadicity of signs (icon, index, symbol), but also linguistically, as utterance. This approach has given rise to new models, such as the Semiotic Pyramid (2009: 17–22) or a presentation of Fauconnier and Turner's metaphorical model 'Generic Spaces' (2002: 222, 274, 288), which position the text as part of semiosis without limiting it as such:

> In essence, moving away from the structural approach and considering both the interpretative and representational functions means that: In literature, it is the dynamic process of semiosis which makes representation and communication possible although without being reduced to these functions and with the potential for undermining them.
> (Veivo 2009: 4)

Other key features that help to bridge what may otherwise seem as a divide between the Greimassian legacy and the potential for pragmatic approaches to literary analysis, may be viewed through Peirce's correspondence with Lady Welby (Winner 1989: 277–300). Parallels may even be found between Jakobson's approach and that of Peirce's with regard to the phonic-semantic knot-both finding themselves intrigued at the level of universals in poetic texts. As such, Peirce's approach was at once syntactic and semantic, refusing to be satisfied with the Formalists or the hermeneuts, as they both sought to 'repudiate the existence of meaning' (Winner 1989: 284).

Hypotheses abound as to what Peirce would have considered structural-semiotics with respect to the treatment of literary texts; and, as stated above, much of that would be gleaned through his correspondence with Lady Welby. In her own rights, Victoria Lady Welby's (1837–1912) Significs project accounts for an important support of context with respect to the literary sign, an approach that is concerned with both the signifying and the interpretative quality of literary texts (Welby 1883).

As explored more closely in S. Petrilli's seminal work on Welby (Petrilli 2009), useful schemes such as modelling systems (as developed by Sebeok and Danesi 2000) can also support the signific project. With respect to Welby, and beyond (as suggested by both Nuessel 2011 and Wang 2013), literary analysis circles back to the dialogical, as considered by Bakhtin. What the diaological, the text in context, and the signific project have in common, is that literary signs emanate from a space that is intrinsically linked to it: both by production and interpretation.

The movements to and from text and context, production and reproduction, presentation and representation underline literary semiotics aim, which is to understand narratives. This further highlights the potential for a multi-perspective with regard to approaches, but critically focused on the tangible necessity for providing not only textual analytical tools but also methodologies and semio-narrative principles. These tie back, via pragmatism, linguistics and cognition, to a critical engagement with the text aided by tools that, together, are part and parcel (symbolic) of literary semiotics' heritage and founding figures. The works of P.A. Brandt (2004), H. Parret (1979), P. Zima (1978), P. Stockwell (2002), U. Eco (2000), and J. Lotman (2004) are exemplary of this need to rigorously analyse the text in context, via the sign and its interpretation.

CONCLUSION

Contemporary cognitive semiotics seek to uncover the relationship between narratives and mental schemas just as cognitive approaches to language and human behaviour underscore the irreducible recurring structural elements of narrative. Literary semiotics and narratology provide the early theories that define the literary sign in order to understand what is, broadly speaking, literature and, in so doing, shaped semiotic theory broadly.

Literary semiotics, like the rest of the semiotic disciplines, has been shaped by the two competing sign theories: that of Peirce and that of Saussure. Approaches to the literary sign still differ broadly, however literary semiotics offers a space of reconciliation between the main ones. This chapter sought to provide the relevant methodologies including the evolutionary pathways and intersections of various theories and schools of thought which offer a comprehensive genealogy and future direction of the discipline.

In the early days of literary semiotics, the Russian Formalists' pursued the question of what constitutes *literariness* and explored defining devices, in so doing they insisted on the systematic nature of literary facts. Their approach to plot analysis and functions of the text are still used today. Bakhtin's theories as well as Lotman's have provided key notions and approaches that remain relevant in semiotic theory today and even outside of the literary realm.

By the early to mid-twentieth century, structuralism had become the widely adopted basis from which the literary sign came to be theorized. Even without reference to the work of the Russian Formalists, Frye and Friedman started organizing literary texts taxonomically. Russian Formalism began dissipating as a major approach around this time. But it was revived by the French critics who, contrary to their Anglo-American counterparts, continued to develop Prague School structuralism, recovering its main elements and fostering, in consequence, a major turn in scientific inquiry influencing the humanities and social sciences broadly. Both Jakobson and Lévi-Strauss were primary figures in igniting this shift, exploring how different structures cohere into systems of meaning that define a particular culture. System thinking is interested in the discovery of general laws by way of a combination of logical and inferential analysis.

Barthes's and Todorov's structural approaches and analysis to narrative elements exemplify the accessibility of the approach. Methods for understanding the 'universal grammar that can formally account for all narratives' becoming virtually *de rigueur* in the 1970s, as illustrated by Genette's structural and stratificational analysis, which provided a new method, based on Saussurean and Hjemeslevian sign theories that showed how the structural approach can take various forms. In France, these theories were given new adaptations (including those by Greimas, Fontanille, Bertrand, Barthes, Todorov, and Genette), leading to the emergence of semio-narrative actional and cognitive theory of literary texts, which were initially opposed and criticized by those who considered structuralism itself reductive, stating that semiotics' aim should be that of representing the variability of daily life, not some ideological structural system.

Post-structural approaches, including that of Derrida, broke away from structuralism, examining works not in an abstract way, but in terms of the feelings and emotions that they impelled. Post-structuralism led to a re-examination of the philosophical-structural foundations of semiotics paving the way towards a new speculative approach to the semiotics of literary texts.

However, in retrospect it can be claimed that literary semiotics is not preclusive, and can adapt elements of the two approaches. The literary text can be studied empirically and historically and, as such, can be mapped against the emotions, whereby a theory of passions can be developed from the analysis itself. This has led to new semio-narrative methodologies that have allowed for a new understanding of the relation between theory and text.

Critical to this turn of emphasis were Greimas's contributions to the study of the literary text which have provided notions and analytical tools with which the text can be taken apart and understood better. Fundamentally, Greimas and Fontanille's work address the bridge between theory and practice by using a relation approach. The sign's definition as an emotive structure is what separates Greimas's approach from classic structuralist semiotic theories, bringing it in line with Peircean pragmaticism, whereby the dialogical sign is an agent in how narratives come about, allowing for a multi-level approach to text analysis. In effect, the structure of the text can be analysed along with its interpretative variables, its representation with its telic ability, without being reductive.

As meaning is fundamental in all definitions of the sign, the practical way in which the literary sign can be evaluated should therefore employ as many methods and approaches as possible to uncover where the 'meaning' lies, however it is conceptualized. This would continue to feed our curiosity with regard to not only 'how the literary text works' but 'why it works'. Currently, and moving forward, cognitive and interdisciplinary approaches' work on explaining the role of the brain and narrative are intimately linked to these very questions. New, interesting approaches into game design and narrative schemas are paving the way to future storytelling and its affect.

NOTES

1 Cf. 'Foreword', P. Fabbri and P. Perron (1990), *A. J. Greimas, The Social Sciences: A Semiotic View*, trans. P. Perron and F. Collins, Minneapolis: University of Minnesota Press, pp. vi–viii.
2 Saussure, F. de (1916), *Cours de Linguistique Générale*, Paris: Payot.
3 www.oed.com.
4 For a more detailed overview, cf. Walsh Matthews (2012, 2017), Perron (2005), Cobley (2001).
5 In this entry we will focus on schools of thought that have had a lasting impact on the theoretical and methodological transformations of the discipline, or individuals who have made a significant contribution over the last five or six decades.
6 Cf. Henry James (1934) prefaces that dealt with 'dramatic scenes', 'scenes', 'form' and 'character', from a non-formal perspective, as well as Percy Lubbock (1921) and E. M. Forster (1927), along with Northrup Frye (1957) and Norman. Friedman (1955) made contributions to the study of narrative prose, but were more empirical than systematic in their theoretical presentations. However, during this period, Anglo-American contribution to narrative theory was crowned by Wayne Booth's monumental *The Rhetoric of Fiction* (1961).

7   Genette provides a practical language and systematic approach to understanding narrative, the role of various textual functions, including time, the reader, etc.
8   Louis Hjelmslev (1899–1965) was a Danish linguist who made a major contribution to Saussure's theory of sign, defined as a union of signifier and signified. Greimas, A. J. and Courtés, J. underscore that by defining the sign as the result of semiosis for Hjelmslev the size of the linguistic units is not pertinent for the definition of the sign that can refer to single 'words' or to 'discourse-signs' and that: 'The use of language produces, then, semiotic manifestations in the forms of strings of signs. The analysis of signs, produced by the articulation of the form of expression and that of content, is possible only if the two planes of language are first dissociated the one from the other in order to be studied and described, each one separately.' Op.cit., pp. 296–8.
9   For a critique of Genette's use of this terminology, see M. Bal, *Narratologie*, Paris, Klincksieck, 1977. M. Bal, *Narratology: Introduction to the Theory of Narrative*. Toronto: University of Toronto Press, 1988.
10 When he begins his analysis of Balzac's *Sarrazine*, by questioning the very possibility of structural semiotic theory to account for the specificity of any literary text, and substitutes a narratology of addessers and addressees, of codes and interpreters for signs.
11 Cf. Parret (1989, vii–viii).

REFERENCES

Austin, J. L. (1962), *How to Do Things with Words*, Oxford: Oxford University Press.
Bakhtin, M. M. ([1965] 1984), *Rabelais and His World*, trans. H. Izwolsky, Cambridge: MIT Press.
Bakhtin, M. M. (1981), *The Dialogic Imagination: Four Essays*, trans. C. Emerson and M. Holquist, ed. M. Holquist, Austin: University of Texas Press.
Bakhtin, M. M. ([1986] 2010), *Speech Genres and Other Late Essays*, trans. V. McGee, C. Emerson and M. Holquist (eds), Austin: University of Texas Press.
Bal, M. (1977), *Narratologie*, Paris: Klincksieck.
Bal, M. (1988), *Narratology: Introduction to the Theory of Narrative*, Toronto: University of Toronto Press.
Baldick, C. (2008), *The Oxford Dictionary of Literary Terms*, Oxford: Oxford University Press.
Barthes, R. (1964), *Éléments de Sémiologie*, Paris: Éditions du Seuil.
Barthes, R. (1966), 'Introduction à l'analyse structural des récits', *Communications*, 8: 1–27.
Barthes, R. (1974), *S/Z: An Essay*, trans. R. Miller, New York: Hill and Wang.
Barthes, R. (1975), 'An Introduction to the Structural Analysis of Narrative', *New Literary History*, 6 (2): 237–72.
Bertrand, D. (1985), *l'Espace et le Sens. Germinal, d'Émile Zola*, Paris: Hadès-Benjamins.
Bertrand, D. (2000), *Précis de Sémiotique Littéraire*, Paris: Nathan Université.
Biglari, A. (2014), *Entretiens sémiotiques*, Limoges: Éditions Lambert-Lucas.
Booth, W. C. ([1961] 1983), *The Rhetoric of Fiction*, Chicago: University of Chicago Press.
Brandt, P. A. (2004), *Spaces, Domains, and Meanings: Essays in Cognitive Semiotics*, Frankfurt am Main: Peter Lang.
Broden, T. F. and S. Walsh Mathews, eds (2017), 'A. J. Greimas – Life and Semiotics/La vie et la sémiotique d'A.J Greimas; Semiotics Post-Greimas/La sémiotique post-Greimassienne', *Semiotica*, 214.
Cobley, P. (2001), *Narrative*, London: Routledge.

Culler, J. (1980), *The Pursuit of Signs*, Ithaca: Cornell University Press.
De Lauretis, T. (1987), *Technologies of Gender: Essays on Theory, Film, Fiction*, Bloomington: Indiana University Press.
Derrida, J. (1967), *De la grammatologie*, Paris: Éditions Minuit.
Dines, J. J. (2002), *Literary Discourse: A Semiotic-Pragmatic Approach to Literature*, Toronto: University of Toronto Press.
Dines, J. J. (2009), 'Structuralism and/or the Semiotic-Pragmatic Approach to Literature', in H. Veivo, C. Ljungberg and J. Dines Johansen (eds), *Redefining Literary Semiotics*, 12–32, Newcastle upon Tyne: Cambridge Scholars Publishing.
Doležel, L. (1979), *Essays in Structural Poetics and Narrative Semantics*, Toronto: Toronto Semiotic Circle.
Doležel, L. (1990), *Occidental Poetics: Tradition and Progress*, Lincoln: University of Nebraska Press.
Doležel, L. (1998), *Heterocosmica: Fiction and Possible Worlds*, Baltimore: Johns Hopkins University Press.
Doležel, L. (2010), *Possible Worlds of Fiction and History: The Postmodern Stage*, Baltimore: Johns Hopkins Press.
Eco, U. (1979a), *A Theory of Semiotics*, Bloomington: Indiana University Press.
Eco, U. (1979b), *The Role of the Reader: Explorations in the Semiotic of Texts*, Bloomington: Indiana University Press.
Eco, U. (1994), *Six Walks in the Fictional Woods*, Cambridge: Harvard University Press.
Eco, U. (2000), *Kant and the Platypus: Essays on Language and Cognition*, San Diego: Harcourt.
Eikenbaum, B. ([1927] 1965), 'La Théorie de la « méthode formelle', in T. Todorov (ed.), *Théorie de la Littérature*, 31–75, Paris: Presses Universitaires du Mirail.
Fabbri, P. and P. Perron (1990), 'Foreword', in P. Perron (trans.) and F. Collins (eds), *A.J. Greimas. The Social Sciences: A Semiotic View*, vi–xii, Minneapolis: University of Minnesota Press.
Fauconnier, G. and M. Turner (2002), *The Way We Think: Conceptual Blending and the Mind's Hidden Complexities*, New York: Basic Books.
Fontanille, J. (1999), *Sémiotique et Littérature*, Paris: Presses universitaires de France.
Forster, E. M. (1927), *Aspects of the Novel*, Cambridge: Cambridge University Press.
Friedman, N. (1975), *Form and Meaning in Fiction*, Athens: University of Georgia Press.
Frye, N. (1957), *Anatomy of Criticism*, Princeton: Princeton University Press.
Genette, G. (1966–72), *Figures I–III*, Paris: Éditions du Seuil.
Genette, G. (1980), *Narrative Discourse: An Essay in Method*, trans. J. E. Lewin, Ithaca: Cornell University Press.
Gervais, B. (1990), *Récits et actions: pour une théorie de la lecture*, Longueil: Le Préambule.
Gervais, B. (2007), *Théories et pratiques de la lecture littéraire*, Québec: Presses de l'Université du Québec.
Gervais, B. (2012), *Idiots: figures et personnages dans la littérature et les arts* in an extensive discussion *littérature et les arts*, Nancy: PUN-Éditions universitaires de Lorraine.
Greimas, A. J. (1987), *Maupassant: The Semiotics of Text. A Demonstration*, trans. P. Perron, Amsterdam: John Benjamins.
Greimas, A. J. and J. Courtés (1982), *Semiotics and Language: An Analytical Dictionary*, trans. L. Christ, D. Patte, L. James, E. McMahonII, G. Phillips and M. Rengstorf, Bloomington: Indiana University Press.

Greimas, A. J. and J. Fontanille (1992), *The Semiotic of Passions: From States of Affairs to States of Feelings*, trans. P. Perron and F. Collins, Minneapolis: University of Minnesota Press.

Greimas, A. J. and P. Ricoeur (1989), 'On Narrativity', P. Perron and F. Collins (eds), *Greimassian Semiotics, New Literary History*, 20 (3): 551–62.

Hébert, L. (2020), *Cours de sémiotique: Pour une sémiotique Applicable*, Paris: Classiques Garnier.

Herman, D., B. McHale and D. Phelan (2010), *Teaching Narrative Theory*, New York: Modern Language Association.

James, H. (1934), *The Art of the Novel*, New York: Sribners.

Jauss, H. R. ([1977] 1982), *Aesthetic Experience and Literary Hermeneutics*, trans. M. Shaw, Minneapolis: University of Minnesota Press.

Johansen, J. D. (2009), 'Structuralism and/or the Semiotic-pragmatic Approach to Literature', in H. Veivo, C. Ljungberg and J. Dines Johansen (eds), *Redefining Literary Semiotics*, 12–32, Newcastle upon Tyne: Cambridge Scholars Publishing.

Klinkenberg, J. M. (1990), *Le Sens Rhétorique: Essais de sémantique littéraire*, Brussels: Les Éperonnniers.

Klinkenberg, J. M. (1991), *Sept Leçons de Sémiotique et de Rhétorique*, Toronto: Groupe de recherches en études francophones.

Kristeva, J. ([1969] 1980), *Desire in Language: A Semiotic Approach to Literature and Art*, trans. T. Gora, A. Jardine, A. L. S. Roudiez, Oxford: Blackwell.

Kristeva, J. (1970), *Le Langage, Cet Inconnu*, Paris: S.G.P.P.

Kristeva, J. (1970), *Le texte du roman: approche sémiologique d'une structure discursive transformationnelle*, The Hague: Mouton.

Lévi-Strauss, C. (1963), *Structural Anthropology*, New York: Basic Books.

Lotman, J. M. (1975), 'Notes on the Structure of the Literary Text', *Semiotica*, 15 (3): 199–205.

Lotman, J. M. (1976), *Analysis of the Poetic Text*, trans. D. B. Johnson, Ann Arbor: Ardis.

Lotman, J. M. (1976), *Semiotics of Cinema*, trans. M. E. Suino, Ann Arbor: University of Michigan Press.

Lotman, Y. (2004), *Culture and Explosion*, trans. W. Clark, ed. M. Grishakova, Berlin: De Gruyter Mouton.

Lubbock, P. (1921), *The Craft of Fiction*, London: Cape.

Margolin, U. (2005), 'Russian Formalism', in M. Grodon, M. Kreiswirth and I. Szeman (eds), *The John Hopkins Guide to Literary Theory and Criticism*, 814–20, Baltimore: The John Hopkins University Press.

Mukarovsky, J. (1934), 'L'art comme fait sémiologique', in Editorial Committee (eds), *Actes du Huitième Congrès International de Philosophie à Prague*, 2–7 September, 1065–72, Prague: Orbis.

Nuessel, F. (2011), 'Victoria Welby and the Signific Movement', *Semiotica*, 184 (1–4): 279–99.

Parret, H. (1979), 'Significance and Understanding', *Dialectica*, 33 (3–4): 297–317.

Parret, H. (1989), 'Introduction', in trans. P. Perron and F. Collins (eds), *Paris School Semiotics 1 Theory*, vii–xxvi, Amsterdam: John Benjamins Publishing Company.

Parret, H. (2018), *Structurer: Progrès sémiotiques en épistémologie et en esthétique*, Paris: Academia.

Parret, H. and H.-G. Ruprecht, eds (1985) *Aims and Prospects of Semiotics. Essays in honour of Algirdas Greimas*, T. 1. *The Theoretical Paradigm*, pp. 1–549, T. 2. *Domains of Application*, 553–1065, Amsterdam: John Benjamins Publishing Company.

Peirce, Charles Sanders ([1866–1913] 1931–58) *The Collected Papers of Charles Sanders Peirce*, vols. 1–6, ed. C. Hartshorne and P. Weiss, vols. 7–8, ed. A. Burks, Cambridge: Harvard University Press. Cited as CP.

Perron, P. (1986), 'Narratology', in T. Sebeok (ed.), *Encyclopedic Dictionary of Semiotics*, 596–601, Berlin: Mouton de Gruyter.

Perron, P. (1994), 'Narratology', in T. A. Sebeok (ed.), *Encyclopedic Dictionary of Semiotics, Supplement to T. 2*, 26–9, Berlin: Mouton de Gruyter: Berlin, New York, Amsterdam.

Perron, P. (2005), 'Semiotics', in M. Groden, M. Kreiswirth and I. Szeman (eds), *The John Hopkins Guide to Literary Theory & Criticism*, 852–9, Baltimore: The John Hopkins University Press.

Perron, P. and F. Collins (1989), *Paris School Semiotics, I. Theory*, Perron, P. and F. Collins (eds), Amsterdam and Philadelphia: John Benjamins Publishing Company.

Perron, P. and P. Fabbri (1993), 'Foreword', in F. Collins and P. Perron (eds), *Algirdas Greimas and Jacques Fontanille: The Semiotics of Passions. From States of Affairs to States of Feeling*, vii–xvi, Minneapolis: University of Minnesota Press.

Petitot, J. (1986), 'Structure', in T. Sebeok (ed.) and P. Perron (trans.), *Encyclopedic Dictionary of Semiotics*, T. 2, 991–1021, Berlin: Mouton de Gruyter: Berlin, New York, Amsterdam.

Petrilli, S. (2009), *Signifying and Understanding*, Berlin: De Gruyter Mouton.

Poiana, P. (1994), « Figure et style: Concepts esthétiques dans la théorie du discours de Gérard Genette », *Persée*, 95: 23–36.

Rastier, F. (1972), *Idéologie et Théorie des Signes. Analyse Structurale des Éléments de l'Idéologie d'Antoine -Louis – Claude Destutt de Tracy*, The Hague: Mouton.

Rastier, F. (1997), *Meaning and Textuality*, trans. F. Collins and P. Perron, Toronto: University of Toronto Press.

Ricœur, P. (1984–85), *Time and Narrative*, vols. 1–2, trans. K. McLaughlin and D. Pellauer, Chicago: The University of Chicago Press.

Ricœur, P. ([1985] 1988), *Time and Narrative*, vol. 3, trans. K. Blamey and D. Pellauer, Chicago: The University of Chicago Press.

Ricœur, P. (1989), 'On Narrativity', *Greimassian Semiotics, Op. cit.*, 1989, 551–62.

Riffaterre, M. (1978), *Semiotics of Poetry*, Bloomington: Indiana University Press.

Riffaterre, M. (1983), *Text Production*, trans. T. Lyons, New York: Columbia University Press.

Riffaterre, M. (1990), *Fictional Truth*, Baltimore: The Johns Hopkins Press.

Sartre, J. P. (1966), *Being and Nothingness*, trans. H. Barnes, New York: Washington Square Press.

Saussure, F. de. ([1916] 1959), *Course in General Linguistics*, ed. C. Bally, A. Sechehaye and A. Riedlinger, trans. W. Baskin, New York: McGraw-Hill.

Schleifer, R. and G. Rupp (2005), 'Structuralism', in M. Grodon, M. Kreiswirth and I. Szeman (eds), *The John Hopkins Guide to Literary Theory and Criticism*, 889–95, Baltimore: The John Hopkins University Press.

Sebeok, T. and M. Danesi (2000), *The Forms of Meaning: Modeling Systems and Semiotic Analysis*, Berlin: De Gruyter Mouton.

Shklovsky, V. (1925), *Theory of Prose*, trans. B. Sher, London: Dalkey Archive Press.

Silverman, K. (1984), *The Subject of Semiotics*, Oxford: Oxford University Press.

Stockwell, P. (2002), *Cognitive Poetics: An Introduction*, London: Routledge.

Todorov, T. (1965), *Théorie de la littérature, textes des formalistes russes*, Paris: Éditions du Seuil.

Todorov, T. (1967), *Littérature et Signification*, Paris: Larousse.

Todorov, T. (1968), *Qu'est-ce que le structuralsime? Poétique*, Paris: Éditions du Seuil.
Todorov, T. (1969), *Grammaire du 'Décaméron'*, Paris: Mouton.
Todorov, T. (1970), *Introduction à la littérature fantastique*, Paris: Éditions du Seuil.
Todorov, T. (1971), *Poétique de la prose*, Paris: Éditions du Seuil.
Todorov, T. (1978), *Les genres du discours*, Paris: Le Seuil, 1978.
Todorov, T. (1981), *Mikhaïl Bakhtine – Le principe dialogique suivi de Ecrits du Cercle de Bakhtine*, Paris: Éditions du Seuil.
Veivo, H. (2009), 'Introduction', in H. Veivo, C. Ljungberg and J. Dines Johansen (eds), *Redefining Literary Semiotics*, 1–9, Newcastle upon Tyne: Cambridge Scholars Publishing.
Walsh Mathews, S. (2017), 'Semiotics', *Oxford Bibliographies: Literary and Critical Theory*, online: doi: 10.1093/obo/9780190221911-0024.
Walsh Matthews, S. (2012), « Le plaisir du texte: comment décoder sans dévoiler », in K. Haworth, L. G. Sbrocchi and A. Johnson (eds), *Semiotics 2012: Semiotics and the New Media*, 275–83, Ottawa: Legas
Wang, Y. (2013), 'The "Dialogue" between Victoria Lady Welby and Mikhael Bakthine: Reading Susan Petrilli's Signifying and Understanding', *Semiotica*, 196: 125–37.
Welby, V. ([1883] 2016), *Links and Clues*, New York: Palala Press.
Wheeler, S. C. (2020), Review of Raoul Moati's *Derrida/Searle: Deconstruction and Ordinary Language*, Notre Dame Philosophical Review.
Winner, T. (1989), 'Peirce and Literary Studies with Special Emphasis on the Theories of the Prague Linguistic Circle', in H. Parret (ed.), *Peirce and Value Theory: On Peircian Ethics and Aesthetics*, 277–300, Amsterdam: John Benjamin's Publishing Company.
Zima, P. (1978), *Pour une sociologie du texte littéraire*, Paris: L'Harmattan.

CHAPTER FOURTEEN

Semiotics in Structural Linguistics

ANNE-GAËLLE TOUTAIN AND EKATERINA VELMEZOVA

INTRODUCTION

Structural linguistics was formed in the late 1920s in Europe, Russia and the United States. In Europe, structuralism is seen as an implementation of the thinking of Ferdinand de Saussure (1857–1913) as it is presented in his *Cours de linguistique générale* [*Course in general linguistics*], published in 1916 by Albert Sechehaye and Charles Bally, and to which, although with varying degrees of critique, all European structuralists refer. In the United States, the situation is more complex insofar as, while the *Cours de linguistique générale* has also nourished the work of the protagonists of American structuralism, the latter have also, and above all, developed upon the works of linguists Leonard Bloomfield (1887–1949) and Edward Sapir (1884–1939). Whereas the Saussurean theorization of *langue*[1] implies a semiological horizon, the formalism stemming from Bloomfield's linguistics, excludes the semantics of linguistics, making the question of the sign marginal to American structuralism. In this contribution we will therefore focus on European structuralism.

After a brief presentation of Saussure's semiology, we will consider, in the following order, functional semiology, the place of semiology in Benveniste's elaborations, Hjelmslevian semiotics, Jakobson's work and, finally, the work of several Russian linguists. We will thus proceed, to a certain extent, in reverse chronological order, as the founding of the Prague Linguistic Circle on 6 October 1926, followed by that of the Copenhagen Linguistic Circle in 1931, marked the beginning of European structuralism. This order of presentation allows us to show the importance that structural semiotics bears for contemporary semiotics. Indeed, it is, along with Peircean theory, Hjelmslevian semiotics that has had the most significant influence on the development of semiotic studies. Moreover, the work of Jakobson, a Russian who emigrated first to Prague and then to the United States, where he lived from 1942 onwards, establishes a bridge between European and American structuralisms on the one hand, and Western and Soviet structuralisms on the other. Contemporary semiotics is also heir to Soviet structuralism, on which American structuralism had a great deal of influence. It is with this Soviet structuralism that we will conclude our presentation.

SAUSSUREAN LINGUISTICS AND SEMIOLOGY

Ferdinand de Saussure is generally regarded as the father of European structuralism. One of us has tried to show[2] that while such a conception corresponds to a historical reality, it nevertheless constitutes a theoretical and epistemological error, insofar as the Saussurean and the structuralist problematics are in fact radically different from each other. Indeed, the structuralists misunderstood the content and the stakes of the Saussurean theorization of *langue*. In setting themselves the task of implementing and developing Saussure's theory, they paradoxically blocked access to it by disseminating an erroneous representation of it. Though it is what we have called 'historical reality' that interests us in this contribution, which has no other purpose than to present structuralist semiotics, it is important to mention this misunderstanding, as the question of semiotics – in Saussure's case, *semiology* – is one of those that was most likely to foster it. This question is in fact endowed, in Saussure's texts themselves, with a complex and problematic character.

Saussure's fundamental contribution to linguistics is the theorization of the sound/meaning relationship within the framework of a definition of the sign that breaks radically with the traditional, plurisecular definition. He substitutes an opposition between sound and meaning (however they might be referred to – form and idea, signifier and signified, expression and content, etc.) with an opposition between sound and sign. The sign is no longer decomposed into its two constituent elements – in accordance with the traditional definition of it as a combination of signifier and signified – but is defined as the constitutive point of view of an entity whose empirical manifestation then appears as an effect of *langue*. We read in particular in *De l'essence double du langage* [*On the Double Essence of Language*] (1891):

> The deep dualism that splits language does not lie in the dualism of sound and idea, of vocal phenomenon and mental phenomenon; that is the easy and pernicious way to conceive it. This dualism resides in the duality of the vocal phenomenon as such, and of the vocal phenomenon as sign – of the physical fact, (objective) and of the physical-mental fact (subjective), in no way of the 'physical' fact of sound as opposed to the 'mental' fact of meaning. There is a first domain, internal, psychic, where the sign exists as much as the signification, one indissolubly linked to the other; there is a second, external, where only the "sign" exists; but at this moment the sign reduced to a succession of sound waves deserves for us only the name of vocal figure. (Saussure 2002: 20–1)[3]

In this early text, sign has the meaning of 'signifier', as evidenced by the opposition between *sign* and *meaning*. This terminological ambiguity, however, is facilitated by the fact that sign, in the sense of general linguistics courses (i.e. in the sense of a double entity, and not in the sense of signifier), is here defined as the 'indissoluble link' between 'sign' and 'signification', which makes the 'vocal phenomenon' a sign (a signifier), a 'vocal phenomenon AS SIGN', as opposed to the 'vocal phenomenon AS SUCH'.[4] This opposition between the two 'vocal phenomena' is formulated, in Saussure's manuscripts, in radical terms: the non-existence, in linguistics, of any given object, and the absolute relativity of linguistic objects to constitutive points of view. For example, let us take this statement from 'Notes pour un livre sur la linguistique générale, 2' [Notes for a book on general linguistics, 2] (1893–4): 'Elsewhere there are *things*, given objects that we are free to consider next from different points of view. Here there are first points of view, right or wrong, but only points of view with the help of which we secondarily CREATE things' (Saussure 2002: 200). The primacy of this point of view in linguistics is the strict correlate of the absence of any given object, and confers to linguistic objects a particular mode of existence, which is that of value, for the sign, and of semiological life, for *la langue*.

The concept of value institutes an equivalence between the vertical relationship constituting signs and the horizontal relationship between signifiers and signifieds: this horizontal relationship consists of reciprocal delimitation, which in turn is determined by the combination constituting the sign, a combination in turn inseparable from this delimitation. Values are thus purely differential and negative, a mode of existence which is correlative of the Saussurean definition of signs as *articuli*, 'small members in which thought becomes self-aware <takes on value? B.)>[5] by a sound' (Saussure 1997: 22), according to which *la langue* appears not as an entity, but as a 'functioning', that of the articulation of thought in phonic matter, a functioning of which sound, meaning and sign, as linguistics, are the effects. Saussure thus asserts in his third course that the '"<linguistic> fact" will give rise to values that, as for them, will be determined <for the first time>, but that will nevertheless remain values, with the meaning that can be attached to this word' (Saussure and Constantin 2005: 285). This linguistic fact is defined in the second course as 'the <in some sense> mysterious fact that the thought-sound implies divisions that are the final units of linguistics' (Saussure 1997: 21).[6]

This definition of *la langue* as a 'functioning' breaks with the representation of language as an entity, endowed with an objectal consistency.[7] Saussure substitutes it with what could be called a 'constitutive exteriority', conferred on *la langue* by its social character. This social character is not the result of a 'primitive contract' (Saussure 1997: 13) or of an 'initial convention' (Saussure 1997: 13), as in the arbitrary of the sign of philosophical reflection since Plato. It is defining a non-objectal mode of existence, that of a *langue* transmitted from one generation to the next, and 'launched into circulation' (Saussure 1986: 30). Language's existence thus consists of this circulation,[8] what Saussure calls, in his second course, 'semiological life' (Saussure 1997: 12). To the concept of value, which defines the sign, and thus allows for the theorization of the sound/sense relationship that constitutes *la langue*, responds the social character, defining a non-objectal mode of existence, the existence of a *langue* defined as a functioning, instead of the entity of traditional representation.

It is within the framework of this radically new definition of the sign and of language that Saussure's adoption of a semiological point of view comes into play, as shown in particular by the development of his second course. Saussure affirms, first of all, that:

Anything that sets the language apart from another semiological system, even though it may seem at first sight important, must be set aside as the least essential <for studying its nature> (thus the play of the vocal apparatus: there are semiological systems which do not use it, which are based entirely on something else). Secondly, the primitive contract, the initial convention, is what is least important; this is not the heart of the facts relative to a semiological system.

(Saussure 1997: 13)

The adoption of a semiological point of view appears here to be correlative to a rejection of the traditional conception of language as a set of vocal signs (which elsewhere takes the form of an opposition between form and substance, correlative to the concept of value) as well as of the convention of the philosophical tradition. Semiological systems are then defined as social products and systems of values:

> We <therefore> recognize as semiological only that part of the phenomena which characteristically appears as a social product, <and we refuse to consider as semiological what is properly individual.> When we have defined it we will have defined the semiological product, and <through this> the language itself; <that is to say that the language is a semiological product and that the semiological product is a social product.> But what is it more specifically? Any given semiological system is comprised of a quantity of units (more or less complex units, <suffixes, etc.,> of different orders) and the true nature of these units < – what will prevent them from being confused with something else – > is that they are values. This system of units which is a system of signs is a system of values. Everything that can be defined with respect to value can also be applied <in a general way> to those units which are signs.
> (Saussure 1997: 14)

However, for Saussure, semiological systems are also the object of a science yet to be constituted: semiology, whose ambivalent relationship with linguistics has been widely noted.[9] This ambivalence seems to be linked to the contradiction inherent in this Saussurean projection of a semiological horizon: while the adoption of a semiological point of view is inseparable from a redefinition of the sign and of language, the inclusion of *la langue* in a larger set, that of sign systems, simultaneously brings with it a taxonomic perspective, which leads us back to the traditional definition of the sign. This is how the arbitrary, redefined by Saussure (who instituted it at the basis of the concept of value and designated by this principle the absence of any sound/sense relationship prior to *la langue*) becomes, when it comes to semiology, susceptible to degrees whose recognition will allow the classification of the different sign systems.[10] It is this taxonomic perspective, which, after Fehr,[11] can be characterized as *semiotic*, as opposed to *semiological*, that the structuralists will adopt. They will then, in their misunderstanding of Saussure's theory, assume the traditional definition of the sign.

FUNCTIONAL LINGUISTICS AND SEMIOLOGY

Functional linguistics, founded by André Martinet (1908–99), belongs to a double filiation: Saussurean, like all European structuralism, and Praguese or, more precisely, Trubetzkoyan. The central notion is that of *function*, conceived as a correlative of that of *structure*: the structure of language is uncovered in the framework of the functional analysis of speech, which consists of a sequential application of the principle of relevance. This application leads to the selection of elements relevant to the exercise of communication, at different levels which are those of language conceived of as a structure of structures (phonology/phonetics, syntax/morphology, axiology/semantic), and to the establishment of a functional hierarchy, taking into account the existence of different functions. This notion of function is related to a definition of language as a doubly articulated instrument of communication – in significant units, signs, and in distinctive units, phonemes – which can be found, for example, in the glossary of *Mémoires d'un linguiste* [*Memoirs of a linguist*]: '**Language**. We stipulate here that we reserve this term for instruments of communication which are doubly articulated and of a vocal character' (A. Martinet 1993: 376). This definition – which is that of common knowledge – takes us back to the traditional definition of the sign as *aliquid quod stat pro aliquo* [something that stands for something else] and the combination, as such, of a signifier and a signified, whose nature and relationships must be studied. Thus, we read in particular in 'Substance phonique et traits distinctifs' [Phonic substance and distinctive features]: 'We must not forget that language is a means to communicate, using something that is manifest, something that is not. That something that is manifest is phonic substance' (A. Martinet 1965: 133). It is about language. In 'Le point de vue fonctionnel en grammaire' [The functional point of view in grammar], Martinet says the same thing about the sign: 'It is therefore appropriate to move away from the conception of the sign according to which the signifier and the signified are placed on the same level and to recall an obvious fact: that the signifier is there to manifest the signified, that the signified is an end and the signifier a means' (A. Martinet 1989: 54).

André Martinet himself did not contribute to the field of semiotics. Nevertheless, in the wake of functional linguistics, a 'functional semiology' has been developed, principally by Jeanne Martinet (1920–2018), Georges Mounin (1910–93) and Luis Prieto (1926–96).[12] For these three authors, as for André Martinet, the central notion is that of communication. In 'Linguistique et sémiologie fonctionnelle' [Linguistics and functional semiology], Jeanne Martinet thus defines semiology as follows: '**Semiology**, initially at least, is the scientific study of the sign systems by means of which humans communicate, but limiting it, first of all, to systems other than languages. Obviously, humans also communicate with languages' (A. Martinet and J. Martinet 1981: 31). In 'Sémiologie' [Semiology], Luis Prieto contrasts two 'tendencies between which current semiological research seems to be distributed' (Prieto 1968: 93), represented by Éric Buyssens (1910–2000) and Roland Barthes (1915–80). Prieto distinguishes the two based on their way of defining the object of semiology: 'For Buyssens, it would be communication, and for Barthes, signification, which would constitute the object of semiology' (Prieto 1968: 94).[13] He adopts the first definition. From this perspective, the central notion is that of the *semic act*, the semiological counterpart of the act of speech, which is purely linguistic. Any semic act mobilizes semes, that is, sets, comparable to the sign – which is a minimal seme – associating a *signal*, one of the defining criteria of which is the intention to communicate, with the *message* it conveys.[14] We can clearly identify, here, the traditional definition of the sign.

This centrality granted to communication – which we will find, in another way, in Jakobson's work – is one specificity of functional semiology. Another is an approach that extends the conceptual apparatus of linguistics to semiology, which Jeanne Martinet very clearly explains in 'Linguistique et sémiologie fonctionnelle' when she states that she prefers an approach that

> consists of focusing on a complex object, but on which we have been working for a long time, a limited object for which we have a proven method of analysis and a proven method of observation for us, those of linguistics, then from there to widen its field and to verify the adequacy of this methodology and this conceptual apparatus to the study of semiological systems other than languages.
>
> (A. Martinet and J. Martinet 1981: 32)

Such an approach seemed to her to make it possible to 'develop an original semiological theory and then, in a third phase' (1981: 32), to 'take another look at languages and at linguistic communication, this time from a semiological point of view that may be slightly different from the initial linguistic point of view' (1981: 32). This to-and-fro between linguistics and semiology resolves the question of the relationship between the two disciplines, which Jeanne Martinet had rejected from the outset, and also makes the double articulation the framework of functional semiology.[15] Indeed, as Jeanne Martinet continues:

> I therefore start from functional linguistics and from what is central in functional linguistics, namely the theory of double articulation. [...] even if the theory of the double articulation is developed for the study of languages, in the true sense of the term, this theory does provide the framework in reference to which a functional semiology can fruitfully develop.
>
> (A. Martinet and J. Martinet 1981: 32)

The double articulation is not amongst the defining criteria of semiological systems, but it does allow for a typology of the latter.[16] This taxonomic character is another characteristic feature of functional semiology, which, as indicated above, is in fact shared by European structuralist semiotics. Note that for Prieto typology is part of the definition of semiology: 'Semiology is the science that studies the general principles governing the functioning of sign systems or codes and establishes their typology' (Prieto 1968: 93).

Functional semiology thus appears to be determined by the notion of communication. The taxonomic dimension is fundamental to it, and it is specified by its construction in the wake of linguistics, and as a discipline distinct from it. If we find a taxonomic dimension in Benveniste's work, the two elaborations are opposed on three points: Benveniste's semiology emphasizes the notion of signification; it develops within the framework of linguistic theorization, within which it emerges, not as an enlargement of the field of application of the linguistic method, but by virtue of an internal necessity, and of the recognition of a semiotic problematics common to the human sciences; finally, it is specified by a structural construction of the fundamental character of language among semiological systems.

LINGUISTICS, SEMANTICS AND SEMIOTICS

The departure point for the semiotics of Émile Benveniste (1902–76) is the Saussurean principle of the sign, which makes language a semiotic system. Thus, we read in 'Saussure après un demi-siècle' [Saussure after half a century]:

> But what we want to emphasize here is the significance of this principle of the sign as a unity of *la langue*. As a result, *la langue* becomes a semiotic system: 'the task of the linguist', says Saussure, 'is to define what makes *la langue* a special system within the set of semiological facts ... For us, the linguistic problem is above all a semiological one'.[17]
>
> (Benveniste 1966: 43)

This principle is understood within the framework of the traditional definition of the sign, which appears, for example, at the beginning of the second part of 'Sémiologie de la langue' [Semiology of language]: 'The role of the sign is to represent, to take the place of something else by evoking it as a substitute' (Benveniste 1974: 51). Benveniste continues, writing that, 'Any more precise of a definition, which would in particular distinguish several varieties of signs, supposes a reflection on the principle of a science of signs, a semiology, and an effort to elaborate it' (Benveniste 1974: 51). From the traditional definition of the sign, a taxonomic vocation of semiology thus follows from the outset, a taxonomy in which the attempt to 'define what makes *la langue* a special system within the set of semiological facts' will be inscribed. This principle also determines a problematics common to the human sciences. In 'Saussure après un demi-siècle', Benveniste went on to say that we 'now see this principle spreading beyond the linguistic disciplines and penetrating the human sciences, which are becoming aware of their own semiotics', (Benveniste 1966: 43), giving rise to 'innovative investigations' (Benveniste 1966: 43) that 'suggest that the fundamental character of *la langue*, that of being composed of signs, could be common to all the social phenomena that constitute *culture*' (Benveniste 1966: 43–4). This type of assertion is repeated throughout Benveniste's texts,[18] and the central notion is then not, as in Martinet's work, communication, but rather meaning. Let us quote in particular 'Structuralisme et linguistique' [Structuralism and linguistics]:

> And, in fact, the whole mechanism of culture is a mechanism of symbolic character. We give a sense to some gestures, we give no sense to others, within our culture. It's like that, but why? It will be a question of identifying, breaking down and then classifying the significant elements of our culture, it is a work that has not yet been done. It requires a capacity for objectivation that is quite rare. We would then see that there is a kind of semantics that passes through all these elements of culture and organizes them – organizes them at several levels.
>
> (Benveniste 1974: 25)

The recognition of a problematics common to the human sciences is another point of divergence between Benveniste's and Martinet's elaborations. Indeed, Martinet has always kept his distance from what has been called 'generalized structuralism', in which, on the other hand, Benveniste's assertions are inscribed, and which we will find in Jakobson and, in a slightly different form, in Hjelmslev.

The taxonomic and comparative approach, correlative of a highlighting of the specificity of the linguistic sign, is implemented in 'Structure de la langue et structure de la société' [Structure of language and structure of society][19] and once again in 'Sémiologie de la langue'. In 'Sémiologie de la langue', Benveniste questions the 'place of language among systems of signs' (Benveniste 1974: 43), asserting that 'the central problem of semiology' (Benveniste 1974: 50) is 'the status of language among systems of signs' (Benveniste 1974: 50). He first defines criteria for analysing and comparing the different semiotic systems – mode of operation, domain of validity, nature and number of signs, type of functioning[20] – and the various possible relationships between systems of signs – generation, homology and interpretation.[21] According to Benveniste, the latter, 'from the point of view of language' (Benveniste 1974: 61), is 'the fundamental relationship, the one that divides systems into systems that articulate, because they manifest their own semiotics, and systems that are articulated and whose semiotics appear only through the grid of another mode of expression' (Benveniste 1974: 61). In this context, 'language occupies a special position in the universe of systems of signs' (Benveniste 1974: 54), insofar as it 'is the interpretant of all semiotic systems' (Benveniste 1974: 61): 'No other system has a "language" in which it can categorize and interpret itself according to its semiotic distinctions, whereas language can, in principle, categorize and interpret everything, including itself' (Benveniste 1974: 61–2). The taxonomic perspective is thus coupled with the recognition of the fundamental character of language among semiotic systems, a fundamental character also recognized by Saussure, but without the latter having specified 'in what respect' (Benveniste 1974: 49). In Benveniste's work, this recognition constitutes the axis of an ordering of the universe of signs. Indeed, the relationship of interpretation, with the 'fundamental dissymmetry' (Benveniste 1974: 54) implied by the universal metalinguistic role of language towards other semiotic systems, provides 'a general principle of hierarchy, which can be introduced into the classification of semiotic systems and which will be used to construct a semiological theory' (Benveniste 1974: 54). The fundamental character of language is also the subject of a structural construction, based on the Benvenistian distinction between semiotics and semantics,[22] which opposes two significances and two modes of existence of language. The semiotic domain is that of the significance of signs, and the semantic domain is that of 'language in use and in action' (Benveniste 1974: 224) – in other words, the significance of enunciation. The two systems are superimposed 'in language as we use it' (Benveniste 1974: 229):

> At the foundation, there is the semiotic system, an organization of signs, following the criterion of meaning, each of these signs having a conceptual denotation and including in a subunit the set of its paradigmatic substitutes. On this semiotic foundation, speech-language builds its own semantics, a meaning of intent produced by word syntagmation in which each word retains only a small part of its value as a sign.
> (Benveniste 1974: 229)

It is this 'double significance' (Benveniste 1974: 63) that gives language its special position within semiotic systems:

> Language is the only system whose significance is thus articulated along two dimensions. The other systems have a one-dimensional significance: either semiotic (courtesy gestures; mudrās) without semantics; or semantic (artistic expressions) without semiotics. The privilege of language is to contain both the significance of signs and the significance of enunciation. This is where its major power comes from, that of creating a second level of enunciation, where it becomes possible to make significant statements about significance. It is in this metalinguistic faculty that we find the origin of the relationship of interpretation by which language encompasses other systems.
> (Benveniste 1974: 65)

The Benvenistian elaboration is thus distinguished by the emergence, within the framework of linguistics, of a semiotic problematics, which simultaneously inscribes linguistics in an approach common to the human sciences, and determines a structural ordering of the universe of signs and a structural construction of the fundamental character of language. In Martinet's elaboration, on the other hand, linguistics and semiology remain independent of one another, their relations being reduced to the recognition of a characteristic common to their objects: the sign (the seme) and communication. It should be noted, however, that the extension of the linguistic method led to the use of double articulation, a structural characteristic of language, as a taxonomic criterion, just as double significance makes it possible here to account for the fundamental character of language and to compare semiotic systems. This point of departure in linguistic theorization, correlative to the framework of the traditional definition of the sign and guiding the taxonomic approach, is therefore a characteristic common to both elaborations, which are distinguished only by the type of articulation between the two sciences adopted by them. As we will see in what follows, the Hjelmslevian elaboration promotes yet another type of articulation between linguistics and semiology, which is a literal implementation of the Saussurean adoption of a semiological point of view on language: the redefinition of linguistics as semiotics.

HJELMSLEVIAN SEMIOTICS

Louis Hjelmslev (1899–1965) is known as the founder of glossematics, a linguistic theory based on the postulate of the purely formal character of language, which can then be manifested in different substances, whether it be on the plane of expression or on that of content. Hjelmslev refers to the Saussurean statement that language is form, not substance.[23] His theorization is also based on the traditional definition of the sign, which he assumes while proposing a particular elaboration of it, within the framework of the distinction between form and substance. One reads in particular in the *Prolegomena to a theory of language*:

> It seems to be true that a sign is a sign for something, and that this something in a certain sense lies outside the sign itself. [...] That a sign is a sign for something means that the content-form of a sign can subsume that something as content-substance. [...] in the interest of clarity, despite the time-honored concepts whose shortcomings now become increasingly evident, we feel a desire to invert the sign-orientation: actually we should be able to say with precisely the same right that a sign is a sign for an expression-substance. [...] The sign is, then – paradoxical as it may seem – a sign for a content-substance and a sign for an expression-substance. It is in this sense that the sign can be said to be a sign for something.
>
> (Hjelmslev 1961: 57–8)

We see here, indeed, the traditional definition of the sign as *aliquid quod stat pro aliquo*, followed by a reinterpretation in terms of relations between form and substance. If functional semiology takes the notion of communication as its framework, and if Benvenistian semiology emphasizes that of meaning, Hjelmslevian semiology or semiotics is set apart by its formal character, which defines glossematics.

It is thus the formal definition of glossematic language that determines the Hjelmslevian interpretation of Saussurean semiology. As we can see in the *Prolegomena to a theory of language*:

> It is true, in Saussure's Cours this general discipline [semiology] is thought of as erected on an essentially sociological and psychological basis. At the same time, Saussure sketches something that can only be understood as a science of pure form, a conception of language as an abstract transformation structure, which he elucidates from a consideration of analogous structures.
>
> (Hjelmslev 1961: 108)

According to this interpretation, linguistics is redefined as semiotics, a redefinition presented as a consequence of the formal definition of language. Hjelmslev thus states in 'La structure morphologique' [The morphological structure]:

> The glossematic method is not only for linguistics. It is usable and necessary for any semiology, and it is on this broad basis that it must be established. The deductive method requires that we start from the most general terms possible. Immanent

linguistics cannot be established in the narrow sense of this term. It is immanent semiology that must be said, and it is only with this proviso that one can demand the immanent method.

(Hjelmslev 1971: 142)

He then specifies, in the *Prolegomena to a theory of language*, that it is 'Precisely because the theory is so constructed that linguistic form is viewed without regard for "the substance" (purport), [that] it will be possible to apply our apparatus to any structure whose form is analogous to that of a "natural" language' (Hjelmslev 1961: 102). We find, in this framework, the taxonomic and comparative approach common to European structuralism. This approach nevertheless takes the particular form of a reconstruction of the linguistic structure, within the framework of semiotic analysis. As Hjelmslev posits in '[Linguistique structurale]' ([Structural linguistics]), 'it is through the study of non-linguistic languages, and by comparing them with linguistic languages, that the *differentia specifica* of the linguistic language will be discovered' (Hjelmslev 1971: 33). This approach is implemented, in particular, in the London and Edinburgh conferences, published under the title 'The Basic Structure of language',[24] where Hjelmslev endeavours first to study the simplest possible structures, in order to uncover the fundamental structure of language, and, within this framework, to define the structure of languages. As he explains in 'Structural Analysis of Language':

> I have developed these examples [of simple structures] in a series of lectures I have been giving recently in the University of London [...] in order to gain a deeper insight in the basic structure of language and of systems similar to language; in comparing them with ordinary language in the conventional sense, I have used them to throw light upon the five fundamental features which, according to my definition, are involved in the basic structure of any language in the conventional sense, namely the following:
>
> 1. A language consists of a content and an expression.
> 2. A language consists of a succession, or a text, and a system.
> 3. Content and expression are bound up with each other through commutation.
> 4. There are certain definite relations within the succession and within the system.
>
> There is not a one-to-one correspondence between content and expression, but the signs are decomposable in minor components. Such sign components are e.g. the so-called phonemes, which I should prefer to call taxemes of expression, and which in themselves have no content, but which can build up units provided with a content, e.g. words.
>
> (Hjelmslev 1948: 77–8)

We are close, here, to the definition given by Martinet, for whom the fundamental characteristic of human language is double articulation. However, the approach is fundamentally different: Martinet defines a type of communication, Hjelmslev a type of structure, which is inseparably a type of analysis,[25] and which is not necessarily specific to natural languages. The question of the specificity of languages is posed in particular in the *Prolegomena to a theory of language*,[26] and this time with a response that is – again *mutatis mutandis* – analogous to that given by Benveniste:

> A language may be defined as a paradigmatic whose paradigms are manifested by all purports, and a text, correspondingly, as a syntagmatic whose chains, if expanded

indefinitely, are manifested by all purports. By a purport we understand a class of variables which manifest more than one chain under more than one syntagmatic, and/or more than one paradigm under more than one paradigmatic. In practice, a language is a semiotic into which all other semiotics may be translated – both all other languages, and all other conceivable semiotic structures. This translatability rests on the fact that languages, and they alone, are in a position to form any purport whatsoever; in a language, and only in a language, we can 'work over the inexpressible until it is expressed'. It is this quality that makes a language usable as a language, capable of giving satisfaction in any situation.

(Hjelmslev 1963: 109)

Whereas Benveniste proposes a structural construction of this metalinguistic faculty specific to languages, Hjelmslev, for his part, oscillates between usage fact – *usage* opposing, in Hjelmslevian terminology, the *schema*, which defines language as pure form – and 'structural particularity',[27] a hesitation that is correlative to the redefinition of linguistics as semiotics. This redefinition has an epistemological dimension, as it appears in particular in the last chapter of the *Prolegomena to a Theory of Language*. As Hjelmslev writes, 'In a higher sense than in linguistics till now, language has again become a key-position in knowledge. Instead of hindering transcendence, immanence has given it a new and better basis; immanence and transcendence are joined in a higher unity on the basis of immanence' (Hjelmslev 1963: 127). This conjugation of immanence and transcendence refers in particular to the Hjelmslevian hierarchy of semiotics,[28] which was adopted and developed by Algirdas Julien Greimas (1917–92), but also by Barthes – despite a less properly Hjelmslevian and more ecumenical perspective that synthesizes Saussure, Martinet, Jakobson and Hjelmslev.[29]

Hjelmslevian semiotics is thus characterized by its important posterity. This is a point in common with Jakobsonian semiotics, which implements a last type of articulation between linguistics and semiology, determined in particular by the double reference to Saussure and Charles Sanders Peirce (1839–1914): the dissolution of linguistics in semiotic analysis, by applying semiotic analysis to language. The primacy of the sign thus takes the place of that of form in the Hjelmslevian elaboration, bringing the Jakobsonian elaboration closer to that of Martinet, on the one hand, because of the central character of communication, and to that of Benveniste, on the other, with the recognition of a problematics and an object common to the human sciences, and the structural construction of the specificity of language.

JAKOBSONIAN SEMIOTICS

Jakobsonian semiotics is based on the traditional definition of the sign as *aliquid quot stat pro aliquo*. Thus, we read in 'The Phonemic and Grammatical Aspects of Language in their Interrelations':

As modern structural thinking has clearly established, language is a system of signs, and linguistics is part of the science of signs, or semiotic (Saussure's sémiologie). The ancient definition of the sign – 'aliquid stat pro aliquo' – has been resurrected and proposed as still valid and productive.

(Jakobson 1971b: 103)

In this framework, the linguistic sign appears as a type of sign; and linguistics is conceived as '"the main tributary of semiotics"'[30] (Jakobson 1973: 28), inasmuch as it allows us to uncover the specific features of linguistic signs. As Jakobson states in 'Linguistics in Relation to Other Sciences', 'any confrontation of language with the structure of different sign patterns is of vital significance for linguistics, since it shows what properties are shared by verbal signs with some or all other semiotic systems and what the specific features of language are' (Jakobson 1971b: 658). Besides Saussure, Jakobson mentions Peirce,[31] to whom we owe the well-known triad of icons, indices and symbols. Benveniste criticized Peirce for constructing a semiotic edifice that abolishes the distinction between different systems of signs,[32] asserting that on this point, 'Saussure presents himself, from the outset, in methodology as well as in practice, as the exact opposite of Peirce' (Benveniste 1974: 45). For his part, Jakobson promotes a semiotic analysis of linguistic signs, dissolving linguistics into semiotics. In the first development he devotes to the comparison and classification of signs – according to the comparative and taxonomic perspective of European structuralist semiotics – in 'Zur Struktur des Phonems' [On phoneme structure],[33] semiotic analysis is thus applied to language itself, whose different types of signs must be highlighted by successively adopting the three points of view of the *signifying* (*des Bezeichnens*), the *signified* (*des Bezeichneten*) and the *signifier* (*des Bezeichnenden*). Subsequent texts[34] refer to the Peircean tripartition, which allows Jakobson, by the same method, to account for the diversity of signs in language. In 'A Glance at the Development of Semiotics' Jakobson significantly states that, '[f]rom the distinctive feature to the whole of the discourse, the linguistic entities, despite their differences in structure, function and size, all remain subject to a common and unique science, that of signs' (Jakobson 1975: 15). The object of linguistics – the linguistic entities – is thus defined as a set of objects belonging to semiotics, which testifies to the specificity of the Jakobsonian articulation between linguistics and semiology: Jakobsonian linguistics is a semiotics, a semiotics from which it is only distinguished by its object: language, a particular system of signs. Unlike in Hjelmslev's work, linguistics is not redefined as semiotics, but linguistic analysis dissolves into semiotic analysis, because of the framework of analysis privileged[35]: that of the relations between *signans* and *signatum*. In 'Language in Relation to Other Communication Systems', Jakobson states in particular:

> Stoic doctrine viewed the essence of signs, and especially of verbal signs, in their necessarily twofold structure, namely, an indissoluble unity of an immediately perceptible signans and an inferable, apprehensible signatum, according to the ancient Latin translation of the corresponding Greek terms. In spite of the early and recent attempts to revise the traditional conception or at least to alter one of the three notions involved – signum, signans, signatum – this more than bimillenary model remains the soundest and safest base for the newly developing and expanding semiotic research. The multifarious relations between the signans and the signatum still offer an indispensable criterion for any classification of semiotic structures.
> (Jakobson 1971b: 699)

Jakobson also insists, however, as do Benveniste and Hjelmslev, on the fundamental character of language. Let us quote, for example,[36] 'Results of a Joint Conference of Anthropologists and Linguists':

> [T]here is no equality between systems of signs, and […] the basic, the primary, the most important semiotic system is language: language really is the foundation of culture. In

relation to language, other systems of symbols are concomitant or derivative. Language is the principal means of informative communication.

(Jakobson 1971b: 556)

In addition, like Benveniste, Jakobson offers a structural explanation of this fundamental character of language. In 'Language in Relation to Other Communication Systems' he thus states that '[t]he uniqueness of natural language among all other semiotic systems is manifest in its fundamentals' (Jakobson 1971b: 707), before enumerating a series of structural particularities. These consist of the generic nature of meanings, which are particularized according to the context, the double articulation, which notably makes it possible to greatly extend the repertoire of significant units, and the existence of three types of coding: the lexical and idiomatic units are entirely coded, whereas the syntactic structure consists only of coded matrices allowing a relatively free lexical choice, and finally the combination of phrasal units into higher units of discourse allows even greater freedom. The difference between this and the Benvenistian elaboration, however, is very clear: it is not a structural construction, but a result of comparison and classification. And Jakobson insists above all on the interdisciplinarity implied by any semiotic study, as he states in 'Linguistics in Relation to Other Sciences':

> The comparative study of formalized and natural languages is of great interest for the elicitation of their convergent and divergent characters and requires a close cooperation of linguists with logicians as experts in formalized languages. According to Bloomfield's reminder, which is still opportune, logic 'is a branch of science closely related to linguistics' [...]. Such mutual assistance helps linguists to determine the specificity of natural languages with ever greater precision and explicitness. On the other hand, the logician's analysis of formalized superstructures requires a systematic collation with their natural fundament, subject to a strictly linguistic interpretation.
>
> (Jakobson 1971b: 659)

Finally, like Benveniste, Jakobson acknowledges the existence of a problematics and an object common to the human sciences. The fundamental character of language is in fact echoed by that of linguistics, which allows the ordering of the human sciences. Jakobson states the following in 'Linguistics in its Relation to Others Sciences':

> Some doubts arose as to whether the 'admirable interdisciplinary collaboration' which ties together the natural sciences could actually be matched by the sciences of man, in view of the fact that a firm logical filiation and a hierarchical order of underlying concepts in respect to relative generality and complexity are manifestly present in the interconnection of natural sciences but seem to be missing among the sciences of man [...]. Apparently, this uncertainty goes back to those early classificatory attempts which did not take into account the science of language. If, however, precisely linguistics is chosen and used as the point of departure for a tentative ordering of the sciences of man, such a system based 'on the principal affinities of the objects classified' proves to find its solid theoretical grounds.
>
> The internal logic inherent in the sciences of man, in turn, demands their serial arrangement paralleling the linkage and concatenation of the natural sciences.
>
> (Jakobson 1971b: 657)

This ordering is a series of three concentric circles. The smallest and innermost is that of linguistics, the science of the communication of verbal messages, which is surrounded by that of semiotics, the science of communication of messages, itself surrounded by that of an 'integrated science of communication which embraces social anthropology, sociology, and economics' (Jakobson 1971b: 698), based on the generality of the notion of communication, with regard to which, according to Levi-Strauss' 'triadic conception', 'in any society communication operates on three different levels: exchange of messages, exchange of utilities (namely goods and services), and exchange of women (or, perhaps, in a more generalizing formulation, exchange of mates)' (Jakobson 1971b: 663). It is thus the notion of communication that is central to Jakobsonian semiotics, as it is to functional semiotics. From 'Language in Relation to Other Communication Systems' (1968), semiotics is also no longer defined as the science or theory of signs, but as that of the communication of messages – and linguistics, likewise, as that of the communication of verbal messages.

It thus appears that while semiology is both constitutive of the Saussurean theorization of language and problematic within this very theorization, European structuralism implements different types of articulation between linguistics and semiotics.

THE PRAGUE LINGUISTIC CIRCLE AND SOVIET SEMIOTICS

Such is how Jakobson's semiotics looked in connection with structural linguistics beginning in the 1970s, when he lived and worked in the United States.[37] He would however, before arriving in the United States, pass through an important stage in his intellectual life in Prague, where his work with the Prague linguistic circle would give us another type of relationship between structuralism and what we could call today semiotics, at least in one of the senses of the word. As we will see in this part of the article, as we 'move' from Western to Central and Eastern Europe, the role of external (in relation to scientific) factors influencing the development of science evidently increases.

The pilot branch of linguistic structuralism in the twentieth century was phonology. The work on phonology that would come to be often considered as a founding work of the discipline, a kind of apotheosis of Prague structuralism, was written within the framework of the Prague linguistic circle. This is Nikolai S. Trubetzkoy's posthumously published *Grundzüge der Phonologie* [*Principles of Phonology*] (1939).[38]

However, the elaboration of a phonological theory as such was not Trubetzkoy's main purpose, in the sense that the entire system of his scientific views obeyed some more general principles referring to what could be called 'synthetic science' (Sériot 1999). It was rather the Eurasian conception that was of great interest to Trubetzkoy – as well as to some other Russian members of the Prague linguistic circle, Jakobson and the geographer Petr N. Savitsky (1895–1968) in particular. In this approach, the attempts to 'show', or even to 'prove' the ontological existence of a particular world – Eurasia – based on a number of criteria (geographical, ethnographic, historical, economic, linguistic), caught the attention of these scientists. As P. Sériot writes:

> [T]heir reflection (at the same time social, political and scientific) put forward the geographical, historical, cultural and scientific affinities between the regions and the peoples of Russia and those of adjacent territories, supposed to form a natural

unit. [...] therefore Eurasia was for them a natural geographical unit, whose geographical (geophysical), cultural, historical, ethnic, anthropological characteristics coincide.

(Sériot 1996: 13)

This desire to 'prove' the existence of Eurasia as a particular (real) space that did not coincide with the existing (conventional) political boundaries[39] is comparable to the desire of the Prague structuralists to discover (real) important entities – phonemes – behind a variety of less important units – sounds.

In their attempts to present an ontological basis for the existence of Eurasia, the Prague researchers 'used [...] to try to make isoglosses *coincide* with isotherms and other cultural and natural isolines' (Sériot 1999: 175) (see Trubetzkoy 1925; Jakobson 1931). Thus the 'linkage' [*uvjazka*] method (Sériot 1999: 182) was elaborated, supposing the 'linkage' of different kinds of phenomena. The 'destruction' or 'disappearance' of boundaries between the different fields of knowledge within the framework of this method supposed the development of a 'holistic' approach to the object of the Eurasianists' research. And even if the word *semiotics* was not used by Eurasianists in this context, it was precisely this 'holistic' and interdisciplinary character that largely distinguished the semiotics formed in the Soviet Union from 'Western' semiotics. Trubetzkoy's theories came to Russia after Stalin's death – a lateness, if you will, largely explained by political and ideological reasons. Nevertheless, even during the first half of the twentieth century the 'holistic' approach to the object of study also characterized the studies of other scholars, even those who were not structuralists or who were considered adversaries of Trubetzkoy – among others, the school of Nikolai Ja. Marr (1864/65–1934), etc. (see Velmezova 2007: Part III).[40]

Linguistics (and phonology in particular) turned out to be a part of this pre-semiotic (in the sense of semiotics as it will be later understood by one of the leading semiotic schools in the USSR, see below), holistic method of the Eurasianists. In particular, in his well-known *K xarakteristike evrazijskogo jazykovogo sojuza* [*For a characterization of the Eurasian language union*] (1931), Jakobson writes: 'Eurasia is characterized by a set of specific features [...]. The task of science is to grasp the interdependence of diverse phenomena, to reveal a regular structure in this connection of phenomena of various nature. Let's call this way of research the linkage method' (Jakobson 1931: 5). It was the linguists' turn to study their objects in this particular way. As Jakobson writes, '[a]nd again [...] the basic question is: is there any unity in this multilingualism which confuses the Europeans? What is it – a random gathering, a chaotic set – or a regular combination, a harmonious union?' (Jakobson 1931: 5).

Jakobson wrote about the phonological features of territorially adjacent Eurasian languages, noting the monotony of the Eurasian languages along with the presence of a phonological correlation of consonants in terms of softness/hardness (Jakobson 1931: 38). However, as Jakobson believed, the search for distinctive morphological and syntactic features of Eurasian languages was a matter for the future (Jakobson 1931: 51), and if the characteristic features of the Eurasian languages had so far only been formulated at the phonological level, this could be explained by the fact that 'of all linguistic plans by now the sound system is the most covered by science' (Jakobson 1931: 8–9).

Trubetzkoy also wrote about the linguistic features of the Eurasian union. He mostly reflected on declination, but in a number of works also turned to the phonology of the Eurasian languages (Trubetzkoy 1931; see Sériot 1999: 125). It was by developing their 'Eurasian', pre-semiotic/holistic reflections that the Eurasianists also developed phonology, presented as a complete conception in Trubetzkoy's posthumous book.

Thus, Trubetzkoy's 'holistic' – somehow pre-semiotic – approach did not 'follow' from his structuralism, but was developed in parallel and was, from an ideological point of view, even more important for the Russian scientists from the Prague linguistic circle than was their 'purely academic', structuralist project of phonology.

Moreover, regarding Trubetzkoy's 'phonology', this Prague structuralism – which seemingly was the most 'ontological' of all currents of structuralism in general – can in many ways be considered a part of studies of a more general nature, of 'holistic' or 'Eurasian' studies, which led to the 'ontological' character of this structuralism.

Structuralism came to the homeland of the 'Russian Prague' researchers – to Russia (or, more precisely, to the Soviet Union) – at the moment when it was beginning to fade in 'Western linguistics', giving way to new trends, Chomsky's generative linguistics in particular. The reasons for this delay were primarily political and ideological. Until 1950, Marr's doctrine was actually dominant in Soviet linguistics – although even before the famous 'Stalin linguistic discussion' of 1950, which would put an end to this domination, structuralism was commented upon in the USSR – but in a negative context, as it was opposed to the 'advanced Soviet linguistics'. In the 1950s–60s, different things might be written about structuralism in the USSR: the current was either blasphemed or extolled to heaven. The situation changed dramatically in 1956 when, at the 20th Congress of the communist party of the Soviet Union, automatic translation was declared a priority line of research in connection with the 'general program of technical progress' (Nikolaeva 1958: 150), which required work with structural methods. In this regard, from that time on, even the recent seemingly irreconcilable opponents of structuralism began to speak about this trend more cautiously. The years that followed would become, to some extent, the years of the triumphant march of structuralism in the USSR: works on structuralism were published (in 1960, twenty-one years after its original publication in German, Trubetzkoy's book *Principles of Phonology* was translated into Russian; F. de Saussure also seemed rehabilitated), conferences were organized, and new university departments and academic institutions were created (Velmezova 2014: Chapter 6). One such department was created in 1960 at the Institute of Slavic Studies of the USSR Academy of Sciences, and employed linguists who would later became co-founders of the so-called Moscow-Tartu (or Tartu-Moscow) semiotic school, the most famous Soviet semiotic current, which we will address here. In 1962, they organized a Symposium in Moscow on the structural study of sign systems. The very name of the event testifies to the connection between semiotics and structuralism for Soviet researchers at the time: the structural methods developed in linguistics were transferred to other sign systems in the studies presented at the symposium. In the preface to the volume of abstracts from the symposium, V. V. Ivanov (1929–2017) gives the following definition of semiotics: it is a new science, the object of which is any system of signs used in human society (Ivanov 1962: 3). In the same text Ivanov substantiates the connection between structural, semiotic and mathematical methods in the humanities: in his opinion, the role of semiotic methods for all related humanities is comparable to the importance of mathematics for the natural sciences (Ivanov 1962: 8). According to Ivanov, as Saussure was one of the founders of semiotics, the methodological orientation of European semiotics towards Saussurian (structural) linguistics is made clear (Ivanov 1962: 8).

Subsequently, this symposium was criticized primarily for ideological reasons: its participants were accused of emasculating the content of the objects of their study by reducing research to the study of formal techniques. In light of such criticism, it became impossible for them to publish in Moscow, and the proposal of the historian of literature Juri M. Lotman (1922–93) from Tartu to conduct further meetings and publish in Estonia, on the periphery of the Soviet world where the atmosphere was less ideologically loaded, was welcome (Nikolaeva 1997).

The first summer school 'on secondary modelling systems'[41] was held in 1964; the meetings of the Moscow-Tartu school participants took place primarily in the 1960s–80s; they mainly brought together scientists from Moscow and Tartu. It was at the University of Tartu that the organizer of meetings in Estonia, Lotman, who had previously studied in Leningrad and who inherited the academic traditions of the school of Russian formalists, worked at that time. In the 1960s, Lotman himself was very interested in structuralism in connection with semiotics (see the recently published collection Lotman 2018) – in particular, thinking about signs in the framework of reasoning about the possibility of transferring structural methods from linguistics to the study of literature (Lotman 1963). In 1964, Lotman's *Lekcii po struktural'noj poètike* [*Lectures on Structural Poetics*] were published, opening the series of *Trudy po znakovym sistemam* [*Proceedings on Sign Systems*].[42] As early as in the book's introduction, Lotman once again wrote about the transfer of structuralist methods from linguistics to literary criticism:

> The modern stage of scientific thinking is more and more characterized by the desire to consider not separate, isolated phenomena of life, but vast unities, to see that each seemingly simple phenomenon of reality, upon closer examination, turns out to be a structure consisting of simpler elements, and it itself, in turn, enters as a part in a more complex unity. […] This desire to move from observing individual phenomena and describing them to analysing systems, which has long been established in the so-called 'exact' sciences, is increasingly penetrating the natural and human sciences […]. The peculiarity of structural study is that it does not imply the consideration of individual elements in their isolation or mechanical connection, but the determination of the correlation of elements in their relationship to each other and to the structural whole.
> (Lotman [1964] 1994: 17)

However, '[i]f nowadays there are rarely voices questioning the advisability of such an approach to the natural and exact sciences, and in the humanities – to the phenomena of language, the perspectives of the structural study of literature are still more than vague', writes Lotman ([1964] 1994: 18–19). As to the structural methods of studying literature in his other works, in the introduction to his 1964 book Lotman put 'semiotics' and 'structuralism' together in the same sentence, writing of the 'mathematical and structural, semiotic study of literature' ([1964] 1994: 21).

Therefore, the question of structuralism and semiotics for Soviet scientists presupposed, first of all, the question of general methods that could (or could not) be applied to the study of both languages and texts; discussions on this topic were conducted by the Moscow-Tartu semiotic school (Lotman 1995: 48). This can be seen in particular with the structural approach to literature that Lotman, following Saussure (more precisely, the *Course in General Linguistics*), identified with the semiological (semiotic) take (Lotman [1967] 2018).

At the same time, the very definition of language was expanded. In *The Structure of the Artistic Text*, Lotman writes that all sign systems 'are built like language' (Lotman [1970] 1998: 19), but language was henceforth understood as 'any system serving the purposes of communication between two or many individuals' (Lotman [1998] 1970: 19). Elaborating this definition, Lotman speaks of the languages of 'theater, cinema, painting, music', as well as of 'customs, rituals, trade, religious beliefs' as languages (Lotman [1970] 1998: 20).

On the whole, there was much less reasoning about signs as such (their types, structure, etc.) in the reflections of the Moscow-Tartu semioticians; methodologically, their discussions and works developed the idea of semiotics rather as a meta-science, as an interdisciplinary umbrella.[43] In particular, in an interview with Ivanov, one of the co-founders of the Moscow-Tartu semiotic school, a couple of definitions of *semiotics* are mentioned: 'Semiotics is usually defined as a science of signs and their systems. However, another interpretation of semiotics is also possible – as a 'holistic science', a dialog or even a synthesis of sciences' (Velmezova and Kull 2012: 299). The researcher answers the question about the specificity of Moscow-Tartu semiotics as follows:

> Q. As to the 'Moscow semiotic school', was it (and maybe still is) 'semiotic' precisely in the sense of 'aspirations for a holistic science'? Whereas the range of subjects in the researches of Moscow semioticians is so strikingly large, reflections on signs and their systems are often absent [...]. V.V.I. For me, one of the essential distinctive features of the Moscow and Tartu (Lotman's) groups consists in their attention not only to signs, but also to their complexes and sequences, among other things, to various texts (including myths, films and canvases as systems of organised signs). This way, the limits of semiotics were considerably broadened. We tried to include in semiotics fields such as history and the study of religion which, at that time, suffered particularly from the dominance of official pseudoscientists.
>
> (Velmezova and Kull 2012: 299)

The contemporary semiotician Mihhail Lotman (Ju. Lotman's son) describes this tendency in the following manner: 'A distinctive feature of the Tartu *structural-semiotic* school [our italics. – E.V.] is its pronounced text-centricity: not a language, not a sign, not a structure, not binary oppositions, not grammatical rules, but the text is the center of its conceptual system' (Lotman 1995: 214).

Ju. Lotman's work on structuralism sparked debate in the USSR. He was reproached for returning to formalism – a rebuke that was addressed, of course, not only to him but also to some other Moscow-Tartu semioticians. Above, a kind of triumph of structuralism in the USSR after the communist party congress in 1956 was mentioned; however, one can only partly speak of a triumph, since along with Soviet scientists who were convinced by structuralism, there were also 'traditional' researchers who did not accept structuralist views and continued to be hostile to structuralism. 'Big history' once again interfered with the 'small' history of linguistics. It turns out that among the enemies of structuralism there were many scientists who were loyal to the Soviet regime. In contrast, there were many more covert or overt dissidents among the structuralists. Thus, the semiotics that was associated with structuralism in the USSR has been transformed, since the mid-1960s, into a sort of measure of the dissidence of those scientists who dealt with it.[44] Rejection of the Soviet power has proven to be a powerful factor uniting the Moscow-Tartu semioticians. This is perhaps why their meetings actually stopped with the onset of perestroika.

On the whole, in the works of the majority of both Moscow and Tartu semioticians written later, the influence of structuralism can be discerned to a much lesser extent, partly recalling Umberto Eco's 'parting with structuralism'.[45]

CONCLUSION

It thus appears that the connection between the notions of structuralism and semiotics is highly complex and problematic. First of all, although the foundation of structuralism and, partly, semiotics is traditionally attributed to Ferdinand de Saussure, the Saussurean and structuralist problematics are in fact radically different. Furthermore, European structuralism is itself characterized by the diversity of its elaborations of semiotics, which constitute so many articulations between linguistics and semiotics. Moreover, this diversity itself was fostered by the ambiguity of Saussurean semiotic thinking. Finally, although Jakobson and, to a lesser extent, Trubetzkoy constitute a bridge between East and West, Soviet structuralism and semiotics seemingly remained on the fringes of (Western) European structuralism. This complexity poses a challenge for current semiotic research. On the one hand, the consequences of the epistemological break constituted by Saussurean linguistics have not yet been fully assessed. On the other hand, the influence of (Western) European and Soviet structuralism on current semiotics is both considerable and dynamic, so that historical insight and epistemological reflection are more essential than ever for the fruitful development of semiotic studies.

NOTES

1 To avoid misunderstanding, we decided, here and afterwards, not to translate the term for Saussure's concept of *langue*, because the English term *language* is ambiguous. Roy Harris, in Saussure 1997 (see note 3), renders the term as 'the language'.
2 See in particular Toutain (2012), Toutain (2014), Toutain (2015a) and Toutain (2016) and, with regard to the question of semiotics, Toutain (2015b).
3 Except for the Danish texts of Hjelmslev, for Saussure 1997 (which is a bilingual edition) and for the texts Sériot (1999) and Velmezova, Kull (2012), for which we chose to quote the published English translations, we give references to the original text, which we translate when the original language is not English.
4 According to Saussure, this terminological ambiguity is thus unavoidable. See Saussure and Constantin (2005: 238).
5 Here and in the other quotations of Saussure's and his students' notes, broken brackets indicate a marginal insertion.
6 See more broadly Saussure (1997: 21–2) and Saussure and Constantin (2005: 285–6), as well as the correspondent of these passages from students' notes in the *Cours de linguistique générale*: the paragraph 'Language (*la langue*) as thought organized into phonic matter', i.e. Saussure (1916 [1972]: 155–7).
7 This break constitutes one of the stakes in the affirmation of the non-existence in linguistics of any given object, as discussed above. This non-existence is asserted relentlessly in Saussure's early texts. See, for example, in the single manuscript « De l'essence double du langage », Saussure (2002: 19–20, 26–7, 33, 65 et 84).
8 Indeed, Saussure states in this text on Germanic legends that 'any symbol exists only because it is thrown into circulation' (Saussure 1986: 30).

9 See in particular Benveniste (1974: 49), Arrivé (2007: 88–100), Chiss and Puech (1992: 8–11), Bouquet (1997: 190–9) and Fehr (2000: 108–13), as well as Toutain (2015b).
10 See Saussure (1997: 10) and Saussure and Constantin (2005: 222).
11 See Fehr (1992: 80, note 25) and Fehr (2000: 122). In the remainder of this contribution, unless otherwise specified, the terms *semiotic* and *semiological* will not be used in the context of this opposition, but in accordance with the uses made of them by the various authors presented.
12 See in particular J. Martinet (1973), A. Martinet and J. Martinet (1981), Mounin (1970), Prieto (1966) and Prieto (1968).
13 See too Mounin (1970: 11–15) and J. Martinet (1973: 9–11). Jeanne Martinet then contrasts *semiology* (functional) and *semiotics* (Greimassian). See A. Martinet and J. Martinet (1981: 73). Nevertheless, she refuses to limit herself, as Prieto does, to the 'semiology of communication'. Functional semiology seems to her to be able to include the study of indices, which are distinguished from signals by the absence of communicative intention (1981: 73).
14 The definition is somewhat different according to Prieto, who distinguishes between the *signal*, which is concrete, and the *signifier*, which is abstract (see Prieto 1968: 122), and consequently defines the seme as a combination of a signifier and a signified (see Prieto 1968: 125).
15 See A. Martinet and J. Martinet (1981: 31).
16 See A. Martinet and J. Martinet (1981: 34–7). See too Prieto (1968: 136–7). However, other criteria are also used. See Prieto (1968: 133–6 and then 137–44).
17 Benveniste here quotes the *Cours de linguistique générale*. See Saussure (1916 [1972]: 34–5). The reference is given by Benveniste. See Benveniste (1966: 43, note 2).
18 See thus, in addition to the passages quoted in the preceding and following, Benveniste (1966: 13, 15 and 30) and Benveniste (1974: 38–9 – it is about epistemology, a dimension whose central character we shall see in the Hjelmslevian elaboration – and 223).
19 In Benveniste (1974).
20 See Benveniste (1974: 51–2).
21 See Benveniste (1974: 60–2).
22 For this distinction, see in particular 'La forme et le sens dans le langage' [Form and meaning in language], *in* Benveniste (1974), an article to which Benveniste refers in 'Sémiologie de la langue' (see Benveniste 1974: 63, note 1). It should be noted that it introduces additional confusion into terminology, even within Benveniste's texts, where *semiotic(s)* sometimes has the restricted meaning conferred by this distinction, and sometimes the meaning of a relation adjective ('of signs') or that of a synonym of 'semiology' or 'semiological'. This polysemy accounts for the paradox of the existence of semiotic systems devoid of signs. See Benveniste (1974: 57–60).
23 See Saussure (1916 [1972]: 157, 169).
24 In Hjelmslev (1973: 119–53).
25 This point is particularly clear in the *Résumé of a Theory of Language* (Hjelmslev 1975).
26 See too Hjelmslev (1985: 85), Hjelmslev (1970: 104), Hjelmslev (1973: 122) and Hjelmslev (1971: 70).
27 See, respectively, Hjelmslev (1963: 107, 109).
28 See Hjelmslev (1963: 114–25).
29 See Greimas (1970), Greimas (1986) and Barthes (1964).
30 Jakobson quotes here a text by Bloomfield, *Linguistic Aspect of Science*. See Jakobson (1973: 28).
31 See in particular Jakobson (1973: 27), Jakobson (1971b: 346, 555 and 657), and Jakobson (1975: 9–10).

32 See Benveniste (1974: 45).
33 See Jakobson (1971a: 295–8).
34 See Jakobson (1971b: 335, 346–7 and 699–701) and Jakobson (1975: 8–9).
35 However, Jakobson considers other parameters of sign classification. See Toutain (2015b: 118–19, note 6).
36 Then see in particular Jakobson (1971b: 658, 662, 663, 666 and 698–9).
37 At the same time, even after the 1970s Jakobson remained in contact with Soviet semioticians, in particular with the researchers of the Moscow-Tartu semiotic school, which will be analyzed below.
38 Particular articles on phonology were, of course, written in Russian much earlier. Among those scientists somehow connected with the 'Russian academic tradition', Jan Niecisław Ignacy Baudouin de Courtenay (1845–1929) is usually mentioned as the forerunner of modern phonology. As for the contemporaries of scientists – members of the Prague linguistic circle or, in the 1920s, their colleagues from the Soviet Union – whose works were published in collections edited by Prague linguists (Yevgeny D. Polivanov [1891–1938], Nikolai F. Jakovlev [1892–1974]), many came to phonology trying to solve practical problems such as the creation of alphabets for those people of the USSR whose languages still had no written form; or teaching the phonetics, for example, of Russian as a foreign language to representatives of the same groups of people (see, for instance, Velmezova 2014: 148–65).
39 The search for Eurasia was, for Eurasianists, partly associated with their desire to find a new homeland that was, in a sense, more important and significant than their beloved Russia that had been lost forever with the 1917 revolution (Velmezova 2010).
40 It did not exclude other common points in their theories – for example, reflections on linguistic convergence (the Eurasianists wrote about the acquired common properties of the Eurasian languages, while Marr's school insisted on the convergence of languages in general, etc.).
41 This term belongs to Vladimir A. Uspensky (1930–2018). The 'primary modelling systems' meant natural languages, and the 'secondary ones' – systems built over the primary ones.
42 Today *Sign Systems Studies* is the oldest semiotic journal in the world.
43 In this respect, Marrism, with its aspirations for holism and interdisciplinarity, seems to have been another forerunner of the Moscow-Tartu semiotics, though much less explicitly so (Velmezova 2007: Part III).
44 Here we are speaking about Moscow-Tartu semiotics. In the USSR there were, of course, semioticians who worked outside of this school – for example, Juri S. Stepanov (1930–2012), whose relationships with the Soviet regime developed differently, amongst others.
45 At the same time, for instance, the work of the late Lotman supposed a certain return to structuralism (in a sense that Lotman built some important semiotic concepts – such as *semiosphere* – arguing with the *Course in General Linguistics*), while realizing the impossibility to apply its notions for semiotic studies beyond the 'primary modelling systems' (see Velmezova 2022).
46 The date 1916 is the first edition of this book. The date 1972 is the first edition accompanied by the critical apparatus of Tullio de Mauro.

REFERENCES

Arrivé, M. (2007), *À la recherche de Ferdinand de Saussure*, Paris: PUF.
Barthes, R. ([1964] 1965), 'Éléments de sémiologie', in R. Barthes (ed.), *Le Degré zéro de l'écriture* suivi de *Éléments de sémiologie*, 77–176, Paris: Gonthier.

Benveniste, É. ([1966] 2002), *Problèmes de linguistique générale*, no. 1, Paris: Gallimard.
Benveniste, É. ([1974] 2004), *Problèmes de linguistique générale*, no. 2, Paris: Gallimard.
Bouquet, S. (1997), *Introduction à la lecture de Saussure*, Paris: Payot.
Chiss, J.-L. and Puech, C. (1992), 'Signe et langue: idée, projet, point de vue sémiologiques', *Langages*, 7: 6–27.
Fehr, J. (1992), 'La vie sémiologique de la langue: esquisse d'une lecture des Notes Manuscrites de Saussure', *Langages*, 107: 73–83.
Fehr, J. (2000), *Saussure entre linguistique et sémiologie*, Paris: PUF.
Greimas, A. J. ([1970] 2012), *Du sens I. Essais sémiotiques*, Paris: Seuil.
Greimas, A. J. ([1986] 2002), *Sémantique structurale*, Paris: PUF.
Hjelmslev, L. (1948), 'Structural Analysis of Language', *Studia Linguistica*, 1 (1–3): 69–78.
Hjelmslev, L. ([1961] 1963), *Prolegomena to a Theory of Language*, revised English edn, Madison: The University of Wisconsin Press.
Hjelmslev, L. (1970), *Language: An Introduction*, Madison: The University of Wisconsin Press.
Hjelmslev, L. ([1971] 1997), *Essais linguistiques*, Paris: Les Éditions de Minuit.
Hjelmslev, L. (1973), *Essais linguistiques II*, Copenhague: Nordisk Sprog- og Kulturforlag.
Hjelmslev, L. (1975), *Résumé of a Theory of Language*, Madison: The University of Wisconsin Press.
Hjelmslev, L. (1985), *Nouveaux essais*, Paris: PUF.
Ivanov, V. V. (1962) – Иванов, В. В. (1962), 'Предисловие', *Симпозиум по структурному изучению знаковых систем: Тезисы докладов*, 3–9, Москва: Издательство Академии наук СССР.
Jakobson, R. O. (1931) – Якобсон, Р. О. (1931), *К характеристике евразийского языкового союза*, Париж: Издание евразийцев.
Jakobson, R. (1971a), *Selected Writings, I*, Paris: Mouton Publishers.
Jakobson, R. (1971b), *Selected Writings, II*, Paris: Mouton Publishers.
Jakobson, R. ([1973] 1979), *Essais de linguistique générale*, vol. 2, Paris: Les Éditions de Minuit.
Jakobson, R. (1975), *Coup d'œil sur le développement de la sémiotique*, Bloomington: Indiana University.
Lotman, Ju. M. (1963) – Лотман, Ю. М. (1963). 'О разграничении лингвистического и литературоведческого понятия структуры', *Вопросы языкознания*, 3: 44–52.
Lotman, Ju. M. (1964) – Лотман, Ю. М. ([1964] 1994), 'Лекции по структуральной поэтике', А.Д. Кошелев (сост.), Ю. М. *Лотман и тартуско-московская семиотическая школа*, 17–245, Москва: Гнозис.
Lotman, Ju. M. (1967) – Лотман, Ю. М. ([1967] 2018), 'Семиотика и литературоведение', in Лотман 2018, 143–51.
Lotman, Ju. M. (1970) – Лотман, Ю. М. ([1970] 1998), 'Структура художественного текста', in Ю.М. Лотман, *Об искусстве*, 14–285, Санкт-Петербург: «Искусство – СПБ».
Lotman, M. Ju. (1995) – Лотман, М. Ю. (1995), 'За текстом: Заметки о философском фоне тартуской семиотики: (Статья первая)', in Е.В. Пермяков (ред.-сост.), *Лотмановский сборник*, 214–22, Москва: ИЦ-Гарант, [вып.] 1.
Lotman, Ju. M. (2018) – Лотман, Ю. М. *О структурализме. Работы 1965–1970 годов* (под ред. И.А. Пильщикова), Таллинн: Издательство ТЛУ.
Martinet, A. ([1965] 1970), *La linguistique synchronique*, Paris: PUF.
Martinet, A. (1989), *Fonction et dynamique des langues*, Paris: Armand Colin.
Martinet, A. (1993), *Mémoires d'un linguiste: Vivre les langues*, Paris: Quai Voltaire.

Martinet, A. and J. Martinet (1981), *Linguistique et sémiologie fonctionnelles*, Istanbul: Publications de l'école supérieure des langues étrangères de l'Université d'Istanbul.
Martinet, J. ([1973] 1975), *Clefs pour la sémiologie*, Paris: Seghers.
Mounin, G. (1970), *Introduction à la sémiologie*, Paris: Les Éditions de Minuit.
Nikolaeva, T. M. (1958) – Николаева, Т. М. (1958), 'Конференция по машинному переводу', *Вопросы языкознания*, 5: 149–50.
Nikolaeva, T. M. (1997) – Николаева, Т. М. (1997), 'Введение', in Т. М. Николаева (сост.), *Из работ Московского семиотического круга*, VII–XLIX, Москва: Языки русской культуры.
Prieto, L. J. (1966), *Messages et signaux*, Paris: PUF.
Prieto, L. J. (1968), 'La sémiologie', in A. Martinet (ed.), *Le Langage*, 93–144, Paris: Gallimard.
Saussure, F. de (1916 [1972^{46}(1995)]), *Cours de linguistique générale*, Paris: Payot.
Saussure, F. de (1986), *Le Leggende germaniche*, Este: Éditions Zielo.
Saussure, F. de (1997), *Deuxième Cours de linguistique générale, d'après les cahiers d'Albert Riedlinger et Charles Patois*, Oxford and New York and Tokyo: Pergamon.
Saussure, F. de (2002), *Écrits de linguistique générale*, Paris: Gallimard.
Saussure, F. de and É. Constantin (2005), 'Ferdinand de Saussure: Notes préparatoires pour le cours de linguistique générale 1910–1911, Émile Constantin: Linguistique générale. Cours de M. le professeur de Saussure 1910–1911', *Cahiers Ferdinand de Saussure*, 58: 83–289.
Sériot, P. (1996), 'N. S. Troubetzkoy, linguiste ou historiosophe des totalités organiques?', in N. S. Troubetzkoy, *L'Europe et l'humanité*, 5–35, Liège: Mardaga.
Sériot, P. ([1999] 2014), *Structure and the Whole*, trans. Amy Jacobs-Colas, Berlin: De Gruyter Mouton.
Toutain, A.-G. (2012), '*Montrer au linguiste* ce qu'il fait': *Une analyse épistémologique du structuralisme européen (Hjelmslev, Jakobson, Martinet, Benveniste) dans sa filiation saussurienne* [online], Paris IV-Sorbonne, PhD. http://www.e-sorbonne.fr/sites/www.e-sorbonne.fr/files/theses/TOUTAIN_Anne-Gaelle_2012_Montrer-au-linguiste-ce-qu-il-fait.pdf and http://tel.archives-ouvertes.fr/tel-00788676.
Toutain, A.-G. (2014), *La rupture saussurienne. L'espace du langage*, Louvain-la-Neuve: Academia-Bruylant.
Toutain, A.-G. (2015a), *La problématique phonologique. Du structuralisme linguistique comme idéologie scientifique*, Paris: Classiques Garnier.
Toutain, A.-G. (2015b), 'De la circularité des rapports entre linguistique et sémiologie ou sémiotique: pour une sémiotique saussurienne?', *Bulletin de la Société de linguistique de Paris*, 110 (1): 115–48.
Toutain, A.-G. (2016), *Entre langues et logos. Une analyse épistémologique de la linguistique benvenistienne*, Berlin: De Gruyter.
Trubetzkoy, N. S. (1925) – Трубецкой, Н. С. (1925), 'О туранском элементе в русской культуре', *Евразийский временник* 4: 351–77.
Trubetzkoy, N. (1931), 'Phonologie und Sprachgeographie', *Travaux du Cercle linguistique de Prague*, 4: 228–34.
Trubetzkoy, N. (1939), *Grundzüge der Phonologie* (Travaux du Cercle Linguistique de Prague 7), Prague.
Velmezova, E. (2007), *Les lois du sens: la sémantique marriste*, Berne et al.: Peter Lang.
Velmezova, E. (2010), 'Les linguistes russes à l'épreuve de l'émigration: quelques pistes pour une future recherche sur les contacts russo-tchèques dans le domaine de la linguistique', in I. Foletti (ed.), *La Russie et l'Occident: Relations intellectuelles et artistiques au temps des révolutions russes*, 53–63, Roma: Viella.

Velmezova, E. (2014) – Вельмезова, Е. В. (2014), *История лингвистики в истории литературы*, Москва: Индрик.

Velmezova, E. (2022), 'Lotman and Saussure', in M. Tamm and P. Torop (eds), *The Companion to Juri Lotman. A Semiotic Theory of Culture*, 33–46, London et al.: Bloomsbury Academic.

Velmezova, E. and K. Kull (2012), 'Interview with Vyacheslav V. Ivanov about semiotics, the languages of the brain and history of ideas', *Sign Systems Studies*, 39 (2–4): 290–313.

INDEX

actants 197
aestheticization 214
Agawu, K. 193–4
Alasuutari, P. 117
Alcoff, L. M. 23–6
Allanbrook, J. 192
Almén, B. 198
Alston, W. 26
alterity 1, 3, 5, 13, 84–5, 89–90, 93, 95, 97, 101, 103
Althusser, L. 58, 98
Altman, R. 172
A-nalyse Struc-turale (ASTRUC) 74
anglophone 17, 20–1, 26–7, 31–2, 179
anthropocentrism 45, 99, 131, 137
anthropology 45 n.2
    biosemiotic 43–5
    empire of Grammar 36–7
    linguistic 38–9
    pragmatic 60–2
    semiotic 6, 35–7, 39–45, 72, 76
    socio-cultural 6, 35–6, 38–40, 42–3, 45, 45 n.2
    symbolic 40–2
Appiah, K. A. 23
archaeology 49, 57. *See also* anthropology
    pragmatic 60–2
    and structuralism 57–9
architectonics 88
Aristotle 2, 86, 115, 238
Artaud, A. 221 n.4
Asafiev, B. 191
audiovisual 11, 169–70, 172, 174–9, 181–3
Augustine of Hippo 8, 69, 131, 208–9, 213
Austin, J. L. 214–15

Bakhtin, M. 4, 12–13, 83–6, 88–90, 94–6, 100, 131, 247, 254
Bally, C. 261
Bal, M. 251
Bar-Hillel, Y. 28–9
Baron, J. 61
Barthes, R. 110–11, 114, 152–3, 161, 169, 171–2, 215, 248–50, 254, 265, 271

Bateson, G. 43
Baudelaire, C. 228
Bauer, A. 62
Beaudry, M. 59
Beethoven, L. v. 192, 195, 198–9
Being and Nothingness (Sartre) 245
Benveniste, É. 69, 171, 266, 270–1, 280 n.22
Berger, P. L. 114
Bernstein, R. J. 22, 29
Bettetini, G. 172
Biglari, A. 252
Bildwissenschaft 149
biosemiotics 2, 35, 82, 89, 91, 96, 103, 132, 135–7, 141
    and anthropology 2, 35, 43–5, 82, 89
Birdwhistell, Ray L. 211
Blair, A. 151
Bloomfield, L. 261, 273
Bogatyrev, P. 209, 248
Boklund-Lagopolous, K. 52
Bolter, J. D. 176, 182
Booth, W. C. 255 n.6
Bouissac, P. 95–6, 99, 219
Bourdieu, P. 112, 123
Brandeis, L. 243 n.19
Brooks, V. 155–6
Buckland, W. 179
Burke, K. 240
Burn, N. 156
Butler, J. 43
Buyssens, E. 265

Cage, J. 213
Call, J. 157
Carani, M. 153
care 9, 61, 82–3, 86–7, 90–3, 98, 103–4, 199
Carrère, E. 69–70
Cartesian legacy 135, 141
Cary, S. 156
Casetti, F. 170, 172, 179
catachresis 231, 239
Cavell, S. 18
Centre for the analysis of the religious discourse (CADIR) 75

Certeau, M. de 60, 74
Champagne, M. 151
Charred Lullabies: Chapters in an Anthropography of Violence (Daniel) 42–3
Children, G. 60
Christianity 69–70, 131, 234
cinema 170–2, 175–9, 182
circulation categories 160
civil war 26–8
Cobley, P. 129–30, 136
cognitive semiotics 10–11, 81, 84, 87, 90, 99, 137, 155, 157, 242 n.10, 254
Coker, W. 191
Colapietro, V. 6
collective intentionality 215
Collins, F. 251
Conkey, M. W. 58
connotation 152
Conquest of America, The (Todorov) 51
constitutive exteriority 263
construction categories 160
contractual network 235
convergence 178
Coquet, J.-C. 8, 69, 72
Courtés, J. 138, 152, 246, 251, 256 n.8
Covid-19 pandemic 87, 97, 104–5, 164
Cox, A. 196–7
critical
 common sense 137
 rationalism 18
 rationality 18, 24–6
 theory 6, 18
cryptosemioticians 81, 91, 101
Culler, J. 246
cultural 38
 performance 41–3, 61, 210, 220
 theory 117
Cumming, N. 196
Curry, B. 199

Dahl, R. 116
dance 11, 208–10, 237. *See also* performance
 anthropological approach 211
 basic 212
 classical theatre and 213
 pure 213
 ritual 214–15
 sacred 215
 theatrical 213
Daniel, E. V. 42–3
Davidson, I. 164

Deacon, T. 44–5
De Doctrina Christiana (Augustine) 131
dedoxification 211, 217
Deely, J. 4, 27
Deetz, J. 57–9
De Lauretis, T. 251
Deledalle, G. 154
DeLoache, J. 156
Delorme, J. 72, 75
democracy 115–19
denotation 152
Derrida, J. 25, 112, 250, 254
De Toro, F. 220
detotalizing method 1–4, 9, 13, 86–8, 90–2, 99–100
Dewey, J. 21, 31, 39, 135, 140–2
dialogism 1, 4–6, 85, 88–91, 96–7, 100, 247
Dickens, C. 177
diegesis 233–6, 238, 240
digital media 177–8
discourse-theoretical approach 118
Doležel, L. 173, 248
Donald, M. 164
double significance 268
Douglas, M. 117
Douglas, W. O. 240
duality 215–16, 262
Dubois, P. 161
Dummett, M. 17
Durkheim, É. 110, 112–13

Echard, W. 195
ecological
 civilization 91
 crisis 87, 94–9
Eco, U. 4, 28, 30–1, 71, 73, 89, 103, 187
 on television 174–6, 182
Edeline, F. 153
education 129–30
 accountability in 139
 formal 139–40
 on Greimas 138–9
 Peircean approach to 136–8
 philosophy of 132, 134–7
 policy and practice 139–40
 to practices of gifting 92
edusemiotics 10, 129, 133–6, 138–9, 141, 143
Elam, K. 213
Elementary Forms of Religious Life, The (Durkheim) 110
Elements of Semiology (Barthes) 110, 169

embodiment. *See also* music/musical, gesture
    and embodiment
  embodied mind 217–18
  'Mind and Body in Music' (Lidov) 195–6
  mind-body dualism 129, 140–1, 143
  tactile-kinaesthetic body 218
empiricism 135
Entretiens Sémiotiques (Biglari) 252
enunciation 69, 75, 171–2, 175–6, 179–80,
    182–3, 214–16, 227, 232–3, 236, 239,
    241–2, 268
epistemic governance 117
epistemology industry 27
Esclapez, C. 199
Essex School 118, 122–3
esthesic *(esthésique)* 188
ethics 9, 81–103
ethnography 42–4
etic/emic distinction 37, 45 n.5
Existential Graphs 137
Existential Semiotics (Tarasti) 199

Fabbrichesi, R. 141
Fabbri, P. 250
fictional act 214
Fischer, F. 117
Fischer-Lichte, E. 207
Floch, J. -M. 152, 158–9
Fluid Signs: Being a Person the Tamil Way
    (Daniel) 42–3
Fondements d'une sémiologie de la musique
    (Nattiez) 188, 201 n.2
Fontanille, J. 153, 179, 255
Foucault, M. 111, 117
Four Ages of Understanding (Deely) 4
Frazer, J. 36
Friedman, N. 248, 254, 255 n.6
Frye, N. 248, 254, 255 n.6

Gadamer, H. -G. 215
Gallie, W. B. 19
Gal, S. 39
Garfinkel, H. 114
Geertz, C. 42
Geisslerliede (Ruwet) 189
Genette, G. 178, 249, 256 n.7
Gennep, A. V. 215
Geoltrain, P. 72, 75
George, St. 233, 235
Gibson, J. 133
gift economy 92–3
Gift in the Heart of Language, The (Vaughan) 92

Ginzburg, C. 75
'Glance at the Development of Semiotics, A'
    (Jakobson) 272
global communication 9, 82, 86–8, 96, 100–1
globalization 7, 9, 82–3, 87–8, 93, 97, 100–1
Gluckman, A. 157
Goffman, E. 114, 210, 216
Goldberg, G. 91
Goodman, N. 151
Gottweis, H. 117
governance 115–19, 122
Grabócz, M. 191, 194, 197–8
Green, T. M. 52–3
Greimas, A. J. 7–8, 12, 51, 69, 71, 111,
    119–20, 173, 256 n.8
  aesthetic apprehension 179
  educational theory 138–9
  isotopies 191
  school 152–4, 158, 250–1
Grusin, R. 176, 182
Güttgemans, E. 75

Habermas, J. 118
Haidu, P. 51
Halliday, M. 154
Hamon, P. 207
Hanna, J. L. 218
Hatten, R. 192, 194, 196, 198–9
Hébert, L. 252
Hegel, G. W. F. 22–3, 94
hegemony 119, 122
Heiskala, R. 120–2
Helbo, A. 210, 220
Hendon, J. 62
hermeneutic approach 194
heteroglossia 131
Hintikka, J. 173
Hippocrates 2–3, 81–2
historical reality 262
Hjelmslev, L. 156 n.8, 159, 249, 256 n.8,
    261, 267–72
Hobbes, T. 94, 97, 102, 115
Hochberg, J. 155–6
Hodder, I. 59–60
Hoffmeyer, J. 141
Holmes, O. W. Jr. 20
hope 17, 28, 31, 53, 96–9
*How Forests Think: Toward an Anthropology
    beyond the Human* (Kohn) 44
Hribar, A. 157
human
  properly human 95

responsibility 83, 86, 96, 98–101
rights 92–4
survival 91, 94–9, 104
Husserl, E. 151–2, 154
Hutcheon, L. 217

identity 93–5, 99, 101
imagery, poetic 230–7, 239
Innis, R. E. 135
Interpreting Musical Gestures, Topics, and Tropes (Hatten) 196
intonatsia 191, 197
Introducing Relational Political Analysis (Selg and Ventsel) 121–2
Irvine, J. T. 39
Ivanov, V. V. 276

Jakobson, R. 38–9, 71, 81, 110, 123, 178, 193, 213, 246–8, 253–4, 261, 265, 267, 271–5, 279
James, H. 255 n.6
James, W. 19–20, 23, 31
Jappy, A. 154
Jauss, H. R. 248
Jenkins, H. 178
Johansen, J. D. 246–7, 253
Johnson, M. 217
Joyce, R. 62

Kaeppler, A. 211
Kanaev, I. I. 89
Kandinsky, W. 211
Kennedy, A. 243 n.20
Klinkenberg, J. -M. 153
Knappett, C. 61
Kohn, E. 44–5
Krampen, M. 155
Kress, G. 152, 154
Kristeva, J. 250
Kuhn, T. 17, 23, 28
Kull, K. 135

Lack, R. 71
Laclau, E. 119
Lagopoulos, A. -P. 52
Lähteenmäki, M. 131
Lakoff, G. 217
Landowski, E. 172, 176, 180
Langer, S. K. 21
language 4–8, 13, 21–2, 37–9, 50, 54–5, 72–4, 85, 88–9, 101–3, 262–78
Eurasian 275

field 37
functional model of 213
human 21, 37, 43, 85, 270
and pictures 151
plastic 158–9
relation and 73
semiotics and philosophy 3–5
sign and 101
specificity of 228–30
television 174–5, 182
verbal 3, 73, 102, 132, 150, 170, 182, 207
written 131–2
'Language in Relation to Other Communication Systems' (Jakobson) 272–4
Lautréamont, C. de. 231–2
learning 134, 140, 143. *See also* education
cognitive 135
nature of 141–2
Peircean approach to 136–8
Pikkarainen approach to 138
Lecourt, D. 98
Legg, C. W. 136–7
Lenninger, S. 156
Leone, M. 58
Leroi-Gourhan, A. 57
Les chats (Baudelaire) 228–30
Levinas, E. 69, 86, 90, 92–5, 97, 100–3
Lévi-Strauss, C. 38, 40–1, 57, 71, 110, 171, 199, 214, 248, 254, 274
Lidov, D. 195–6, 201 n.3
life 9, 28, 37–8, 42, 81–7, 90–3, 95–101, 104, 210
liminality 215, 217
Lindekens, R. 155, 158
linguistics
anthropology 38–9, 41, 44
functional 264–6
Linguistics and Semiotics in Music (Monelle) 195
'Linguistics in Relation to Other Sciences' (Jakobson) 272–3
listening 1, 4, 6–8, 86, 88–92, 97–8, 101, 103–4
Liszka, J. J. 198
literacy 130–3, 142–3
Literary Discourse (Johansen) 246–7
literary semiotics 11–12, 245, 247–55
literary sign 246–7, 253–5
Li, Y. 53
Locke, J. 12, 22, 81
Lopiparo, J. 62

INDEX

Lotman, J. 49–50, 53–7
Lotman, Ju. M. 277–8, 281 n.45
Lotman, M. 50
Lotman, Y. 247
Luckmann, T. 114
Lyotard, J. F. 139

McKay, N. 195
Mahon, A. 18
Malinowski, B. 6–7, 36–7
Marin, L. 152, 176
Marrone, G. 174
Martinet, A. 264–5, 267–8, 270
Martinet, J. 265–6, 280 n.13
maternal 92–3
Mauss, M. 110
Mead, G. H. 40, 113
Mead, M. 35
meaning and semiosis 227–8
Meaning of Meaning, The (Ogden and Richards) 6–7, 36–7
media 9, 61, 113, 130, 149, 157, 169, 172–4, 176–80, 182
Medlin, B. 96–8
Merleau-Ponty, M. 179
metaphor 12, 88, 101, 119, 123, 173, 195–7, 230–1, 239
metasemiosis 2, 85–7
metonymies 101, 119, 123, 230–1, 242 n.10
Metz, C. 170–1, 182
Meyer, L. B. 190, 194
Milbank, J. 73–4
Miller, D. 59
Milliken, R. 22
mirror neurons 180–1
Mitchell, W. J. T. 149
modalities 12, 92, 103, 133, 158–9, 169–71, 174, 197–8
Molino, J. 188
Monelle, R. 195
monolingualism 131
Morgan, L. H. 36
Morris, C. 1, 3, 12, 84, 90, 191, 253
Moscow-Tartu (Tartu-Moscow). *See* Tartu-Moscow School of Semiotics
Mouffe, C. 119
Mounin, G. 265
Mozart 192–3, 200
Mukarovsky, J. 248
μ-group 152–3, 158
Musical Meaning in Beethoven (Hatten) 192, 194

Musical Topic, The (Monelle) 195
Music and Embodied Cognition (Cox) 196–7
Music as Discourse (Agawu) 194
music/musical 187–8, 191, 195, 201, 237
    gesture and embodiment 195–7
    narrativity 197–9
    philosophy 199–201
    topic 192–5
    units 188–92
Myth and Music (Tarasti) 191
Mythologies (Barthes) 110

narrative literature 231–2, 236
narrative prose 230–1
Nash, G. 60
Nattiez, J. -J. 188
Neo-TV 175
neurosciences 180–3, 219–20
neutral level *(niveau neutre)* 188–90
New Communication 212–13
Noble, W. 164

Odin, R. 172
Ogden, C. K. 36–7
Ojala, J. 199
Olbrechts-Tyteca, L. 243 n.17
Olteanu, A. 141, 165 n.4
orchestral model 212–13
Orlov, H. 187
Osmond-Smith, D. 191
otherness 1–2, 12, 85–8, 91–4, 96–9, 102, 104, 211
O'Toole, M. 154
out of place 95

Paca, W. 58
Panier, L. 8, 74–5
Paris School 12, 51, 245, 249–52
Parret, H. 250–1
Parsons, T. 113–14
Pasolini, P. P. 7
Passerini, L. 53
passions 179–80
Passmore, J. 17–18
Patte, D. 72
Pavis, P. 210, 220
peacemakers 101–3
Peirce, C. S. 3, 5–7, 11–13, 24, 26–8, 31–2, 37–44, 49–51, 60–3, 70, 72–3, 83–5, 89–90, 96–7, 103–4, 120–1, 130, 272
    history and semiotics 51–7
    interpretation semiotics 94

learning and education 136–8
and pragmatic approach 252–4
system approach 154
Pelkey, J. 161
Pencak, W. 7, 50, 52
Perelman, C. 243 n.17
performance 210–11. *See also* dance
contemporary 208, 211, 213–17, 219–21
general theory of 219–20
mimesis vs. 211, 213, 217, 219–20
nontheatrical 208
postmodern 210–13, 217–18, 220
theatrical 209, 213–17
Perron, P. 250–1
Phenomenology of the Social World (Schütz) 112
philosophical vocation 103
philosophy. *See also* education, philosophy of; music/musical, philosophy
contemporary 19, 21–3, 27, 29, 31, 137
professional 19, 23–4, 26–30
Philosophy in a New Key (Langer) 21
Pickwick Papers (Dickens) 177
pictorial semiotics 149–53, 157–60, 164
densification of 162–3
depictions 158–9
experimental approach 155–7
history 163–4
kinds of 160–1
photography, study of 161–2
plastic and pictorial layers 158
systems/types 154–5
texts/tokens 152–4
and visual signs 159
Pietarinen, A.-V. 151
Pikkarainen, E. 138–9
Playing with Signs (Agawu) 193
poetic/poetry 213, 227, 230–1, 233, 236–8, 242, 247–8
Poiana, P. 249
poietic *(poiétique)* 188
political science 109, 115–19, 123–4
polyphonic acting 215–16
Ponzio, A. 81
Popper, K. 18, 23–4
post-humanism 43–4
post-structuralism 250–5
power 115–19
pragmatic archaeology 60–2
Pragmatism (James) 19
Pragmatist's Progress (Rorty) 28
Prague Linguistic Circle 192, 261, 274–9

Prague School 207, 209, 245, 248, 254
Preissler, M. 156
pre-reflexive semiotics 180–2
Preziosi, D. 159
Prieto, L. 265, 280 n.14
Principles of Phonology (Trubetzkoy) 274, 276
print literacy 130–3, 142–3
'Problem of Meaning in Primitive Languages, The' (Malinowski) 36–7
Prolegomena to a theory of language (Hjelmslev) 269–71
Przeworski, A. 115–16
Putnam, H. 18, 23

Qadir, A. 117
Quebec school 152
Quixote, D. 221 n.1

Ramírez, J. 162
Rappaport, R. A. 41
rationalism 135
Ratner, L. 192
Redefining Literary Semiotics (Veivo) 252
Reflex Arc Concept in Psychology, The (Dewey) 142
religions 69–72, 76–7
ante litteram 5, 72
approaches to 72–5
benefits of 75–6
resurgence 22, 43–5
Reybrouck, M. 199
Reyes, E. 155
rhetoric 92
classical 119, 153
contemporary 243 n.17
specificity of 237–8
Richards, I. A. 36–7
Right to Privacy 238–40
ritual drama 213–16
Rorty, R. 21, 23, 28–9
Rosen, C. 194
Rossi-Landi, F. 1, 85
Rupp, G. 246
Russian Formalists 11, 171, 209, 245–8, 254, 277
Ruwet, N. 189

Sachs-Hombach, K. 149
Saint-Martin, F. 153, 158–9
Sapir, E. 261
Sartre, J.-P. 111, 245–6

Saussure, F. 12, 37–9, 49–50, 53, 57, 70–2, 81–2, 85, 102–3, 109–10, 120–2, 221 n.2
   Cours de Linguistique Générale 245
   la langue 110, 263–4, 266–7, 279 n.6
   linguistics and semiology 262–4
   Tartu-Moscow school 53–7
Savitsky, P. N. 274
Schaeffer, J.-M. 161
Schechner, R. 210
Scheiffer, R. 246
Schirra, J. 149
Schmidt, P. 58
Schütz, A. 112–14, 120
SCOTUS opinion 241–2
Scruton, R. 26
Searle, J. R. 214, 250
Sebeok, T. 1–2, 9, 12, 51, 70, 72, 81, 88–90, 95–6, 98, 100, 103, 130, 132, 136–7
Sechehaye, A. 261
Selg, P. 119, 121–3
Semetsky, I., ed. 134
semioethics 9, 81–4, 86, 88–96, 98–100, 102–3
semiology, functional 261, 265–6, 269
semioses, cascade of 237
semiosis 81–90, 92–3, 95–6, 99–100, 103–4, 129, 134–7, 140, 142, 154, 195, 227–8, 236–7
semiosphere 3, 9, 82, 88, 99, 123–4, 247, 281 n.45
semiosy 142
semiotics 81–3. *See also* biosemiotics; cognitive semiotics
   in archaeology 57–62
   and decodification 2, 5
   and ethics 86
   global 2–3, 9, 13, 81–3, 86–7, 90, 95–6, 99–100, 103–4
   and history 50–7, 83–5
   and interpretation 2, 94
   and literary theory 249–50
   of materiality 5, 7, 91
   and mediation 8, 61
   of music 91, 187, 193
   neostructuralist 121
   of religions (*See* religions)
   semeiotics 70, 82–3, 90–1, 98
   semiotic animal 2, 4, 85–7, 95–6, 98–9
   semiotic anthropology 6, 35–7, 39–45, 57–62, 72, 76
   semiotic practices 117–18
   semiotic square 234

Semiotics of Theatre (Fischer-Lichte) 207
Semiotic Theory of Learning (Stables) 142
Sense of Music, The (Monelle) 195
seriality 177, 182
Sériot, P. 274–5
Shakespeare, W. 230
Shapiro, M. 192
Sheets-Johnstone, M. 218
Shklovsky, V. 247
sign
   and enunciation 233
   and language 101
signification 3, 5, 8, 83–4, 89
Signification and Significance (Morris) 84
sign masters 81, 101–3
Signs of the Past: Semiotics and History (Boklund-Lagopolous and Lagopoulos) 52
Silverman, K. 251
simulacrum 214
Singer, M. 40–2, 44
Skinner v. Oklahoma 240–2
Smith, J. E. 24, 29
Smith, M. W. 218
Snow, C. P. 12
Social Construction of Reality, The (Berger and Luckmann) 114
social contract 132, 241
social purpose categories 160
social structure 228
Society as Semiosis (Heiskala) 120
socio-cultural anthropology 6, 35–6, 38–40, 42–3, 45, 45 n.2
sociology, interpretation of meaning 110–14
Sonesson, G. 152, 154–5, 157–8, 163
Sonic Self, The (Cumming) 196
sound symbolism 158
Speech Acts Theory 213–15
Stables, A. 133
Stanislavski, K. 215
Starobinski, J. 71
Star Trek 173
Stjernfelt, F. 151
Stoichita, V. 176
Strand, T. 136–7
'Structural Analysis of Language' (Hjelmslev) 270
structuralism 12, 38, 54, 57–9, 71–2, 76, 109, 188, 207, 253–4, 261–2, 274, 276–9
structuralist approach 194

structural linguistics 57–9, 211, 246, 248, 261, 274
Structure of Social Action, The (Parsons) 113
Studies in Ethnomethodology (Garfinkel) 114
symbolicity 241
symbols 227
symptom 82, 87, 212, 218, 230
symptomatology 2, 81–3
synthetic science 274

Tarasti, E. 191–2, 197–200, 201 n.4
Tartu-Moscow School of Semiotics 7, 51, 53–7, 81, 122, 247, 276–9, 281 n.44
Taylor, C. 22
television 172–5, 177, 182
   and enunciation 175–6
Texas v Johnson 243 n.20
theatre 236–7, 240
theatrical semiology 208–9
Theory of Musical Semiotics, A (Tarasti) 197–8
Theory of Prose (Shklovsky) 247
Theory of Semiotics (Eco) 71
Thompson, R. J. 177
Thürlemann, F. 153
Tilley, C. 60
Todorov, T. 51, 248–9, 254
Tomasello, M. 157
transmediality 178–9
transvaluation 198
Trubetskoy, N. 247
Trubetzkoy, N. S. 274–6
Tull, J. R. 191
Turner, V. 215
Tylor, E. B. 36, 45 n.3

Uexküll, J. v. 3, 82, 89, 95, 136
Umwelt 82, 95, 135
unit act 113
United States 51–7
Unpredictable Workings of Culture, The (Lotman) 54
Uspenskij, B. 50–1, 53–5, 63
Uspensky, V. A. 281 n.41

Van Leeuwen, T. 152, 154
Van Lier, H. 161
Vaughan, G. 92
Veivo, H. 252
Veltrusky, J. 248
Ventsel, A. 119, 121–3
Verfremdungseffekt 215
Volney, G. 72
Vološinov, V. 85

Warner, L. 42
Weber, M. 112–14, 116, 120
Wedeen, L. 117–18
Welby, V. 3, 5–8, 37, 41, 83–4, 90, 92, 94, 96, 99, 253
Whitehead, A. N. 29
Wildavsky, A. 117
Wildgen, W. 159
Williams, B. 51–2
Wollheim, R. 151, 154
Word Made Strange, The: Theology, Language, Culture (Milbank) 73–4

Yentsch, A. 59
Young, D. 228

Zemic model (Tarasti) 199–200